# CERTIFICATE

# *BANKING:*
# *THE LEGAL ENVIRONMENT*

First edition 1988
Fifth edition October 1992

ISBN 0 86277 583 3 (previous edition 0 86277 592 2)

**British Library Cataloguing-in-Publication Data**

A catalogue record for this book
is available from the British Library

Published by

BPP Publishing Limited
Aldine House, Aldine Place
London W12 8AW

Printed in England by
DACOSTA PRINT
35/37 Queensland Road
London N7 7AH
(071) 700 1000

We are grateful to the Chartered Institute of Bankers, the Chartered
Institute of Management Accountants and the Association of Accounting
Technicians for permission to reproduce past examination questions.
The suggested solutions have been prepared by BPP Publishing Ltd.

# CONTENTS

|  |  | Page |
|---|---|---:|
| **PREFACE** | | (v) |

**INTRODUCTION** ... (vii)
Syllabus – analysis of past papers – the structure of this study text –
how to study law – the examination – study checklist

**PART A: SOURCES OF LAW AND RESOLVING CONFLICT**

| 1 | Sources of English law | 3 |
| 2 | Resolving conflict | 23 |

**PART B: BASIC CONTRACT LAW**

| 3 | The basics of contract law | 47 |
| 4 | Capacity to make contracts | 76 |
| 5 | Misrepresentation, duress and undue influence | 84 |
| 6 | Statutory intervention in contracts | 98 |
| 7 | Breach of contract | 106 |

**PART C: THE BANK'S CONTRACTS**

| 8 | Essentials of the banker-customer contract | 115 |
| 9 | Other features of the banker-customer relationship | 134 |
| 10 | Operating a bank account | 145 |
| 11 | Special types of bank account | 165 |
| 12 | Company accounts | 176 |

**PART D: PROPERTY AND SECURITY**

| 13 | Land | 195 |
| 14 | Land as security | 211 |
| 15 | Other forms of security | 238 |

**PART E: CHEQUES AND OTHER MEANS OF PAYMENT**

| 16 | Cheques | 269 |
| 17 | The protection of banks | 300 |
| 18 | Electronic banking | 320 |

**APPENDIX 1: THE CODE OF BANKING PRACTICE** ... 331

**APPENDIX 2: SECTION A EXAMINATION QUESTIONS** ... 339

**ILLUSTRATIVE QUESTIONS** ... 369

**SUGGESTED SOLUTIONS** ... 382

# CONTENTS

| | Page |
|---|---|
| INDEX OF CASES | 411 |
| INDEX OF SUBJECTS | 417 |
| FURTHER READING | 421 |

## PREFACE

The examinations of the Chartered Institute of Bankers are a demanding test of students' ability to master the wide range of knowledge and skills required of the modern professional. The Institute's rapid response to the pace of change is shown both in the content of the syllabuses and in the style of examination questions set.

BPP's experience in producing study material for the Institute's examinations is unparalleled. Over the years, BPP's Study Texts and Practice and Revision Kits, now supplemented by the Password series of multiple choice (objective test) question books, have helped thousands of students to attain the examination success that is a prerequisite of career development in banking.

This Study Text is designed to prepare students for the CIB Certificate examination in *Banking: the Legal Environment*. It provides comprehensive and targeted coverage of the syllabus (reproduced on pages (vii) to (ix)) in the light of recent developments and examination questions (analysed on pages (ix) to (xi)).

BPP's Study Texts are noted for their clarity of explanation. They are reviewed and updated each year. BPP's study material, at once comprehensive and up to date, is thus the ideal investment that aspiring bankers can make for examination success.

### The October 1992 edition of this Study Text

This Study Text has been improved in the following ways.

(a) The publication and effect of the Code of Banking Practice is given full coverage. The full text of the Code is included in an Appendix.

(b) A new chapter on electronic banking has been included to reflect the addition of this topic to the syllabus.

(c) Exercises have been added to the text to enable students to test their grasp of new material as they work through it.

(d) There is coverage of new case law, including important cases on express terms in the banker-customer contract, constructive trustees, matrimonial homes as security, the bank's duty towards non-customers and the bank's duty to explain surety documents to spouses.

(e) New legislation is included, in particular the Criminal Justice Act 1991 and the Cheques Act 1992.

(f) The effect of the High Court and County Court Jurisdiction Order 1991 has been explained in more detail.

(g) The section on rights of the bank in the banker-customer contract has been revised to facilitate study of this area.

(h) There is a new section on legal aid.

*BPP Publishing*
*October 1992*

For details of other BPP titles relevant to your studies for this examination, please turn to page 421. Should you wish to send in your comments on this Study Text please turn to page 422.

# INTRODUCTION

## Syllabus

*Aim*

To enable students:

(a) to demonstrate knowledge and understanding of the principles of law relating to the business of banking;

(b) to apply those principles to practical banking situations and problems;

(c) effectively to communicate their responses to such problems to colleagues and customers.

*Chapter(s) in this Text*

### 1 *Sources of law*

NB. Students are only required to have an *outline* knowledge of topics in this section.

| | |
|---|---|
| (a) Custom (including mercantile custom, eg negotiable instruments); case law (eg *Devaynes v Noble (1816)*); legislation relevant to banking (eg Bills of Exchange Act 1882), including delegated legislation (with relevant examples); EC legislation of relevance to banking. | 1 |
| (b) Common law and equity. | 1 |
| (c) Role of legislation with particular reference to banking. | 1 |
| (d) Statutory interpretation - rules in outline only. | 1 |

After studying this topic block, students should:

(a) know the sources of law;
(b) understand the relevance of these sources to the business of banking; and
(c) be able to apply the law appropriately to given situations.

### 2 *Conflict resolving*

| | |
|---|---|
| (a) Judicial and quasi-judicial processes. | 2 |
| (b) Court system - an *outline* knowledge of the role and jurisdiction of the major civil and criminal courts. | 2 |
| (c) Quasi-judicial bodies - an *outline* knowledge of the role and jurisdiction of tribunals and arbitration processes. | 2 |
| (d) Banking Ombudsman. | 2 |

After studying this topic block, students should:

(a) be aware of the different processes and institutions for resolving legal and quasi-legal conflicts;
(b) be aware of the wider factors to take into account before starting legal proceedings, eg cost, publicity, need for a legal ruling.

# INTRODUCTION

*Chapter(s) in
this Text*

### 3  *Contract law*

(a) Role of contract law in business transactions, eg as a regulating and
enabling framework of rules.  3
(b) Essentials of a contract: the agreement and bargain.  3
(c) Capacity to make contracts (with special reference to banking, eg borrowing);
the use of standard forms by banks.  4, 11, 12
(d) Banker-customer contract: opening and closing an account; types of customers
(companies, partnerships, minors, personal representatives, trustees,
unincorporated clubs and societies); effect of death and mental incapacity;
express and implied terms; rights and duties; undue influence and
misrepresentation; termination of relationship.  5, 7-10
(e) Statutory intervention in voluntary agreements with special reference to banking,
eg Consumer Credit Act 1974 (in outline), Unfair Contract Terms Act 1977.  7

After studying this topic block, students should:

(a) understand the role of contract law in banking;
(b) be able to explain the nature and essential elements of a contract;
(c) be aware of use and implications of 'standard form' contracts; and
(d) be able to relate and apply legal principles to the banker/customer contract and other typical
workplace situations.

### 4  *Property and its use as security*

(a) Real and personal property; estates and interests/ownership and possession;
methods of transferring title; documents of title.  13
(b) Security: functions and types; types of security arrangement, eg whole ownership,
documents of title. The nature of a mortgage, charge, pledge, lien. Legal and
equitable charges.  14, 15
(c) How charges are taken over different types of property (in outline).  14
(d) A bank's rights and duties as a mortgagee (in outline).  14
(e) Attributes of different types of security.  14, 15

After studying this topic block, students should:

(a) be able to explain the legal classification of property;
(b) be able to explain how title to different types of property is proved and transferred;
(c) understand the function and attributes of different securities used in banking;
(d) appreciate a bank's position as holder of security; and
(e) be able to relate and apply legal principles to routine bank procedures and workplace
situations.

### 5  *Cheques and other means of payment*

(a) Cheques: definition, types and effects of crossings; statutory protection
of bankers.  16, 17
(b) Concepts of negotiability and assignment compared; development and
contemporary use of negotiable instruments.  16
(c) Issue of a bill; parties to a bill; negotiation; endorsement; discharge;
types of holder - in particular, as they relate to cheques.  16
(d) Cheque cards and credit cards.  16
(e) Electronic banking  18

## INTRODUCTION

After studying this topic block, students should:

(a)  understand the nature and functions of cheques and other bills of exchange, cheque cards and credit cards;

(b)  be able to explain a bank's position with regard to their use and misuse; and

(c)  be able to relate and apply legal principles to routine bank procedures and typical workplace situations.

### Format of the examination paper

Section A contains 20 multi-choice or short-answer questions, all of which should be answered. *Four* other questions should be answered, at least *one* from Section B and *two* from Section C which contain two and five questions respectively; these questions carry 20 marks each.

### Analysis of past papers

Below is an analysis of the topics examined in the last six sittings of the *Banking: the Legal Environment* examination.

*May 1992*

*Section A*
1    20 short answers

*Section B*
2    Cheques - crossings
3    Security - attributes of good security

*Section C*
4    Opening an account - partnership and limited companies
5    The Banking Ombudsman
6    Contract law - essential features of a contract
7    The banker-customer contract - relevance of case law
8    Cheques - passing of legal rights, negotiability


*October 1991*

*Section A*
1    10 short answers; 10 multiple choice answers

*Section B*
2    Cheques - returning a cheque unpaid
3    Cheques - negotiability

*Section C*
4    The banker-customer contract - rights and duties of the bank
5    Judicial process - the High Court
6    Legislation - the Consumer Credit Act 1974
7    Security - legal and equitable mortgages
8    Security - different types of property

**INTRODUCTION**

*May 1991*

*Section A*
1    10 short answers; 10 multiple choice answers

*Section B*
2    Cheques - legal position on returning cheques unpaid
3    Cheques - endorsements

*Section C*
4    The bank's contracts - safe custody
5    Sources of law - judicial and quasi-judicial processes; superior and inferior courts; original and appellate jurisdiction
6    Security - good security; life policies; mortgages
7    Basic contract law - the banker/customer contract
8    Security - guarantees

*October 1990*

*Section A*
1    10 short answers; 10 multiple choice answers

*Section B*
2    Cheques - forgery of amount and endorsement, theft
3    Cheques - endorsement

*Section C*
4    Opening an account - information required by banks
5    Important banking statutes - aims and effects
6    The Bank Ombudsman
7    Basic contract law and banks
8    Security offered by companies

*May 1990*

*Section A*
1    12 short answers; 8 multiple choice answers

*Section B*
2    Types of cheque and cheque crossing
3    Collection of third party cheques

*Section C*
4    *Ratio decidendi* and *obiter dicta;* binding and persuasive precedents
5    Legal steps in taking a first mortgage over freehold registered land
6    Contract law - offer and acceptance
7    Confidentiality - disclosure of information on customers' account
8    Credit card contracts

# INTRODUCTION

*October 1989*

*Section A*
1    12 short answers; 8 multiple choice answers

*Section B*
2    Collection of cheques
3    Payment of cheques - forged amounts

*Section C*
4    Case law in banking
5    Contract - payment and promissory estoppel
6    Joint and several liability on joint accounts
7    Life policies as security
8    Bank's error leading to dishonour of cheque

## The structure of this Study Text

The starting point for this study text is the syllabus laid down by the CIB. All of the topics suggested in the syllabus are covered by the text, as far as possible in the same order as set out by the syllabus.

The text is divided into five parts as follows:

A    Sources of law and resolving conflict
B    Basic contract law
C    The bank's contracts
D    Property and security
E    Cheques and other means of payment

Within each part of the text are a number of chapters which take you logically through the topics to be covered. Each chapter ends with a summary, including treatments and definitions of matters covered in the text, and a 'Test your knowledge' quiz. You should satisfy yourself that you understand the chapter summary before attempting these short questions - in your head if you wish. They are all cross-referenced to the text so that you may check your accuracy. You are then referred to relevant illustrative questions to try.

At the end of the text is a comprehensive bank of illustrative questions, including past examination questions taken from the *Banking: the Legal Environment* exam paper. Each of the past examination questions is commented on in the light of the examiner's remarks, and a useful summary of the points which should be included in your answer is provided in the form of an outline solution. These questions will give you an insight into the type and level of problem set for the *Banking: the Legal Environment* paper. All of the other illustrative questions are provided with full suggested solutions.

Do not be tempted to skimp in your attempts at these questions. With law, practice really does make perfect: you will learn nothing by reading through the question, glancing at the answer and telling yourself 'Yes, I would have produced that solution'. Nobody could, without practice, but with the right amount you should be successful in this paper and be well on your way to completing the Banking Certificate.

# INTRODUCTION

In an appendix before the full-length illustrative questions you will find a bank of short-answer and MCQ questions taken from exams from Autumn 1987 to Spring 1992. These are the compulsory questions set in Section A of the examination, and being able to answer them accurately and quickly will greatly enhance your chances of examination success. It is suggested that you attempt these questions - divided up into the syllabus subject areas - during the revision phase of your studies. You will find that doing so is an excellent way to consolidate your knowledge at the same time as practising examination technique.

## How to study law

As well as displaying detailed knowledge and intelligent problem-solving skills in the examination, you must also provide the style of answer required by this examination. The examiner prefers practical questions, set in the form of a memo to the student from a manager, requesting a response in the form of a memo, a letter, a newsletter, a set of notes for a lecture or meeting or a circular to staff. As well as learning, therefore, you need to brush up on your writing skills well in advance of the exam.

In order to obtain full benefit from this text in every area, you might follow the approach set out below.

(a)  *Read* the chapter you are tackling to get a flavour of the topic. This may be one to three times.

(b)  *Identify the main principles* and attempt to understand their significance and application.

(c)  *Read slowly* through the chapter again.

(d)  *Learn* the points contained in the text. As you proceed slowly through the chapter, pause at the end of each paragraph or set of paragraphs to ensure that you can remember the details.

(e)  *Make short notes* if you find this helpful, but try to avoid the temptation to write out the text in full!

(f)  *Move on* to another topic once you have learnt a point - but try to recall it again later to see if the knowledge is really there.

(g)  *Tackle the test your knowledge questions.* These are partly to test you learning, and partly to help you in the first, short-answer section of the exam.

(h)  *Study the specimen examination questions and attempt the illustrative questions* at the end of your work on an entire part, or alternatively on the completion of your study of the text. You are referred to relevant questions at the end of each chapter. Writing full answers in examination conditions is an excellent way to learn - you are putting all your knowledge and skills to the test at one time, as you will be in the final exam. Compare your answers with the comments and suggested solutions. If you are not satisfied that your answer is correct or full enough, refer back to the text to identify those points you have forgotten or failed to understand.

(i)  *Attempt the compulsory Section A questions* when you feel satisfied that you have fully studied and understood the areas specified in the syllabus.

# INTRODUCTION

## The examination

*Writing bookwork-style examination answers*

If the questions requires, say, a discussion of legislation and case law affecting banking, it is best to state the main distinctions (legislation is passed by Parliament, case law is decided in response to particular facts by the courts) and then carry on to provide examples.

Structuring your answer in this way helps you to write a coherent essay and shows that your understanding is such that you can distinguish principles.

Examples, preferably drawn from case law which itself comes from real-life situations, are a very good idea in this type of question.

*Answering problem-type questions*

It is a useful practice when answering this kind of question to set out first of all the principle of law which is at stake (for instance, whether there has been agreement in contract), and then to outline the rules which must be applied to the facts in order to reach a conclusion. Only then should you proceed to a consideration of the facts.

Again this approach helps both you and the marker in the same way as the approach to bookwork questions, discussed above. It shows your basic understanding of the principles and also allows you to demonstrate that you can apply rules in a way which does not sink into abstraction at the first hurdle. An incorrect final conclusion is not a disaster in the way an answer which shows little or no reasoning is a disaster.

Remember to produce your answer in the format required - a letter, a memo, a briefing note etc. It is important to ensure that any such example of written communication:

(a) is dated

(b) is addressed *to* the person/people in receipt of it

(c) is identified as being from a particular person (that is, *you* in the guise of a student, a supervisor, a manager etc)

(d) is headed up in some way: '**Briefing note: guarantee procedures**'

(e) is concluded and signed.

*Examiner's comments*

Although the percentage pass-rate has improved in this examination, it is still below 50%. The examiner consistently laments one particular factor in exam scripts: 'too much emphasis on "common sense" practical points - "what my bank does" - at the expense of legal principles'.

You must concentrate on what the law says, not what your bank does, particularly in light of the fact that in many areas banking practice and legal principle actually diverge (for instance, in procedures for opening accounts).

# INTRODUCTION

*Practical points in the examination*

(a) Read the question through carefully, jotting down points.

(b) Write legibly and space your answers clearly.

(c) Write short paragraphs and sentences.

(d) Underline case-names (not in red, as this may confuse the marker).

(e) If you cannot remember the exact name, try to point out in some other way that you know there is a decided case on the topic.

(f) Answer every part of each question attempted.

(g) Answer the question in the style requested.

It may seem premature at the beginning of your studies on law to be thinking about how to write examination answers. However, your approach to both the text and the answers should be the same:

> - identify the principle
> - state the rules
> - apply them to the facts

# INTRODUCTION

## Study checklist

This checklist is designed to help you chart your progress through this Study Text and thus through the Institute's syllabus. You can record the dates on which you complete your study of each chapter, and attempt the corresponding illustrative questions. You will thus ensure that you are on track to complete your study in good time to allow for revision before the exam.

| | *Text chapters* Ch Nos/Date Comp | *Illustrative questions* Ques Nos/Date Comp |
|---|---|---|
| **Sources of law and resolving conflict** | | |
| Sources of English law | 1 | 1-3 |
| Resolving conflict | 2 | 4-6 |
| **Basic contract law** | | |
| The basics of contract law | 3,4 | 7,8 |
| Misrepresentation, duress and undue influence | 5 | 9 |
| Statutory intervention in contracts | 6 | 10 |
| Breach of contract | 7 | 11 |
| **The bank's contracts** | | |
| The banker-customer contract | 8-10 | 12-17 |
| Types of bank account | 11,12 | 18-20 |
| **Property and security** | | |
| Land | 13 | 21 |
| Security | 14,15 | 22-27 |
| **Cheques and other means of payment** | | |
| Cheques | 16 | 28-30 |
| The protection of banks | 17 | 31-35 |
| Electronic banking | 18 | 36 |

# PART A
## SOURCES OF LAW AND
## RESOLVING CONFLICT

*Chapter 1*

# SOURCES OF ENGLISH LAW

---

**This chapter covers the following topics.**

1. The nature of law
2. Sources of English law
3. Historical sources of law
4. Case law
5. Legislation
6. Other sources of law

---

## 1. THE NATURE OF LAW

1.1 The laws of any country are those rules which the nation through its law-enforcing machinery makes compulsory by the imposition of penalties and other sanctions against law-breaking. The body of law is not static but changes and develops. In this process it reflects the values and institutions of each era. Until Parliament was reformed in the nineteenth century, the main purpose and effect of English law was to define and safeguard rights of property and to uphold public order. Since that time there has been an increasing flow of new laws designed to deal with social problems and to develop the national economy. Many old laws have been repealed; for instance, a broken promise of marriage was formerly actionable by the jilted woman as a breach of contract, but this is no longer so. Any study of English law as it now is requires a brief explanation of the process of historical development which has made it what it is.

1.2 As we shall see, English law, like most other legal systems, makes a fundamental distinction between civil and criminal law.

1.3 Although English law has many features which are common to other national legal systems, it also has some distinctive features of its own. It differs from the law of many Western European countries (and also Scotland) in having absorbed only a small amount of Roman law, which is a major heritage of Western civilisation. Secondly, English law is case law made by decisions of the courts to a much greater extent than the law of many other countries. The countries of the Commonwealth and also the United States of America have absorbed much of the English legal tradition into their own law.

## 2. SOURCES OF ENGLISH LAW

2.1 The term 'sources of law' is used in several different senses.

(a) *Historical* sources of law are generally regarded as *common law* and *equity*.

(b) *Legal* sources are those means by which the law is currently brought into existence. There are four legal sources:

    (i) case law;
    (ii) legislation;
    (iii) EC law; and
    (iv) custom.

(c) *Subsidiary* sources are not currently responsible for the direct creation of law. They include, for example, merchant law, Roman law and canon (or ecclesiastical) law.

2.2 The important elements of each will now be explained in greater detail.

## 3. HISTORICAL SOURCES OF LAW

3.1 English law's historical sources are those procedures, rules and ways of thinking which have given rise to today's current sources of law. Hence a legal problem today may be decided on the rules of the legal sources, but these in themselves (particularly judicial precedent) have been derived from the historical sources of common law and equity.

### Common law

3.2 At the time of the Norman Conquest in 1066 there was no system of law common to the whole country. Rules of local custom were applied by local manorial courts. To improve the system, the King sent royal commissioners on tour (circuit) of different parts of the realm to deal with crimes and civil disputes. These commissioners, who often heard their cases with the assistance of a local jury, at first applied the local customary law of the neighbourhood. On their return from circuit the commissioners sat in the royal courts at Westminster to try cases there. In time the commissioners in their judicial capacity developed rules of law, selected from the differing local customs which they had encountered, as a *common law (ius commune)* which they applied uniformly in all trials (before the King's courts) throughout the kingdom.

3.3 To commence an action before any of these courts, the plaintiff obtained from the main royal office, the Chancery, an order (writ) issued under the King's authority and addressed to the Sheriff of the county in which the defendant resided, by which the Sheriff was required to ensure that the defendant appeared for the trial. The writs specified the ground of complaint and gave a brief summary of the facts on which the plaintiff required judgement. After some earlier uncertainty it was established that writs might only be issued in one of the established forms, or grounds of action. If there was no appropriate writ it was not possible to have a new one in order to bring a grievance before the royal courts. This principle was slightly relaxed in 1285 to permit the issue of new writs, if they were similar to established forms. But the common law system, based on the availability of standard writs, was still very rigid and hence an inadequate means of providing justice.

3.4 The procedure of common law courts was also unsatisfactory. A plaintiff might lose his case owing to a minor technicality of wording or be frustrated by specious defences, deliberate delay or corruption, or find himself unable to enforce a judgement given in his favour because there was no suitable common law remedy.

## Equity

3.5 Citizens who would not obtain redress for grievances in the King's common law courts petitioned the King to obtain relief by direct royal intervention. These petitions came before the King in Council and by custom were referred to the principal civil minister - the Chancellor, who was usually a cleric. In dealing with each petition his concern was to establish the truth of the matter and then to impose a just solution without undue regard for technicalities or procedural points. The Chancellor enforced his authority by summoning the parties to attend for interrogation; the penalty for failure to comply could be imprisonment or confiscation of property. Thus royal power was made available to make the law more effective.

3.6 Because the principles on which the Chancellor decided points were based on fair dealing between two individuals as equals, it became known as *equity*.

3.7 The system of equity, developed and administered by the Court of Chancery, was not a complete alternative to the common law. It was a method of adding to and improving on the common law; it provided a gloss on the law. This interaction of equity and common law produced three major changes.

(a) *New rights:* equity recognised and protected rights for which the common law gave no safeguards. If, for example, A transferred property to the legal ownership of B to pay the income of the property to C (in modern law B is a trustee for C) the common law simply recognised that B was the owner of the property at common law and gave no recognition to B's obligations to C. Equity recognised that B was the owner of the property at common law but insisted, as a matter of justice and good conscience, that B must comply with the terms of the trust imposed by A (the settlor) and pay the income to C (the beneficiary).

(b) *Better procedure:* as explained above, equity could be more effective than common law in bringing a disputed matter to a decision.

(c) *Better remedies:* the standard common law remedy for the successful plaintiff was the award of monetary compensation - damages - for his loss. This is said to be an action *in rem* - against property (the resources of the defendant). Equity brings an action *in personam*, that is against the person in question. It can therefore order different remedies. Equity is able to order the defendant to do what he has agreed to do *(decree of specific performance)*, to abstain from wrongdoing *(injunction)*, to alter a document so that it reflects the parties' true intentions *(rectification)*, to restore the pre-contract *status quo (rescission)* or to pay the plaintiff as much as he deserves *(quantum meruit)*.

3.8 The development of equity was based on a number of 'equitable maxims', or principles. These are still applied today if an equitable remedy is sought. The following are examples.

(a) *He who comes to equity must come with clean hands.* To be fairly treated, the plaintiff must have acted fairly himself.

(b) *Equality is equity.* The law attempts to play fair and redress the balance; hence what is available to one person must be available to another. As an example, this principle can be observed in relation to contracts of minors. Equity does not allow the remedy of specific performance to be granted against a minor, and so it does not allow a minor to benefit from the remedy either.

(c) *He who seeks equity must do equity.* Similar to (a) above, this means that a person wanting equitable relief must be prepared to act fairly himself. For example, a mortgagor wishing to redeem his security under the principle of 'equity of redemption' must give reasonable notice of this to the mortgagee.

(d) *Equity looks at the intent, not the form.* However a person may try to pretend that he is doing something in the correct form, equity will look at what he is actually trying to achieve. For example, if an agreed damages clause in a contract is not a genuine pre-estimate of likely loss, equity will treat the clause as a penalty clause.

## Common law and equity: later developments

3.9 In theory, equity accepted common law rights but insisted that they should be exercised in a just fashion. The practical effect was nonetheless that a decision of the Court of Chancery often reversed or conflicted with common law rules. At one stage, the Court of Chancery went so far as to issue orders by which litigants were forbidden to bring an action at common law to enforce strict common law rights. The rivalry between Chancery and common law courts was resolved in 1615 by a decision of the King (in the *Earl of Oxford's Case*) that where common law and equity conflict, *equity must prevail.*

3.10 Equity was not in its origins a consistent code of law: it was simply disconnected intervention in legal disputes. Each Chancellor (and the Chancery judges acting under his authority) applied a personal and sometimes arbitrary standard of what he considered fair. Equity, it was said, 'varied with the length of the individual Chancellor's foot'. From the sixteenth century onwards, however, the Chancellor and his deputies were usually recruited from the legal profession trained in common law. (Sir Thomas More, appointed Chancellor by Henry VIII, was the first of these.) Under common law influence, equity become a consistent body of doctrine and at least as technical as the common law.

3.11 Thus the common law, administered in royal courts, was supplemented and sometimes overruled by principles of equity administered in the Court of Chancery. A plaintiff who began proceedings in one set of courts might, after years of expensive litigation, find that for some technical reason he could not obtain the desired result but must abandon his case and begin again in the other courts. This dual court system was ended by the Judicature Acts 1873 - 1875 which amalgamated the English courts. It is now possible to rely on any principle of common law or equity in any court of law in which the principle is relevant. *In case of conflict equity still prevails over common law.*

3.12 Although the courts have been amalgamated, common law and equity remain distinct. Where common law applies it tends to be automatic in its effect. Equity recognises the common law, as it always did; it sometimes offers an alternative solution but the court has discretion as to whether or not it will grant an equitable remedy in lieu of a common law one.

3.13 For example, if breach of contract is proved, the plaintiff will at least get common law damages as compensation for his loss automatically; in certain circumstances the court may, at its discretion, an alternative remedy of equity. It may, for instance, order the defendant to perform the contract rather than allow him to buy his way out of his contractual obligations by paying damages. The discretionary nature of equitable remedies means that a person who wins an action will not necessarily get the remedy he wants.

*Case: Miller v Jackson 1977*
The Court of Appeal held that a cricket club had committed both negligence and nuisance by allowing cricket balls to be struck out of the ground into M's adjoining premises. However, the court refused to grant the injunction that M had sought. They awarded damages instead on the grounds that the interest of the public in being able to play and watch cricket on a ground where it had been played for over 70 years should prevail over the hardship of a few individual householders who had only recently purchased their homes.

## 4. CASE LAW

4.1 The development of common law and equity has led to one of the main legal sources of law - case law - and informs much of the other main source - legislation, or the passing of statutes.

### Precedent

4.2 Both common law and equity are the products of decisions in the courts. They are judge-made law but based on a principle of consistency. Once a matter of principle has been decided (by one of the higher courts) it becomes a *precedent* enshrined in *case law*. In any later case to which that principle is relevant the same principle should (subject to certain exceptions) be applied. This doctrine of consistency, or following precedent, is expressed in the maxim *stare decisis* - 'to stand by a decision'.

4.3 Case law is based on three elements.

(a) There must be adequate and reliable *law reports* of earlier decisions.

(b) There must be rules for extracting from each earlier decision on a particular set of facts the *legal principle to be applied* in reaching a decision on a different set of facts.

(c) Precedents must be classified into those which are *binding* and those which are merely *persuasive*.

4.4 Each of these three elements is discussed below.

### Law reports

4.5 Until the mid-nineteenth century law reports - reports of decided cases - were notes made by practising lawyers. Later on, reports were published without official authorisation by professional law reporters. In modern times there are major series of law reports on general law published weekly and then bound as annual volumes. In addition there are other special series of reports, eg. of tax cases, commercial cases, industrial relations cases etc. At a hearing in court, the barrister who cites a case as a precedent upon which he relies will read aloud from the reports the passage from the reported judgement.

4.6   When a case is referred to by its name it is said to be 'cited'. Every case has a title, usually (in a civil case) in the form *Brown v Smith* – that is Brown (plaintiff) versus (against) Smith (defendant). In the event of an appeal, the plaintiff's name is still shown first, whether he or she is the appellant or the respondent. Some cases are cited (for technical reasons of procedure) by reference to the subject matter eg *Re Enterprises Limited* (company case) *Re Black's Settlement* (a trust case) ('re' means 'about'); or in  shipping cases the name of the ship, eg *The Wagon Mound*. In a full citation the title of the case is followed by abbreviated particulars of the volume of the law reports in which the case is reported, eg *Best v Samuel Fox & Co Ltd* (1952) 2 All ER 394 (The report is at p 394 of Vol. 2 of the All England Reports for 1952). The same case may be reported in more than one series of law reports and sometimes under different names.

4.7   Note the following points regarding content:

(a)   each report begins with a summary *(head note)* of the points of law established by the case and a list of the earlier cases cited as precedents at the hearing;

(b)   the verbatim text of the judgement (or judgements if more than one) follows as given in court but with any minor corrections which the judge decides to make at the proof stage.

4.8   Only decisions of the higher courts – the High Court, Court of Appeal and Judicial Committee of the House of Lords – are included in the general law reports. Only the important cases (in the effect on the law) are included in the law reports (though certain libraries hold a copy of the judgements in unreported cases also).

4.9   Students are often perplexed as to how much they are expected to memorise of cases referred to in textbooks, teaching manuals etc. The important aspect of a leading case is what it was about, –  its essential facts and the point of law which it illustrates or establishes. It is always useful to preface the mention of a case (in a written answer) by citing the name of the case. But if you cannot remember the name you can say 'In a decided case...'.

## Identifying the legal principle in an earlier decision

4.10   The doctrine of judicial precedent is designed to provide consistency in the law. It is not the function of a judge to make law, but to decide cases in accordance with existing rules. In order that this should be done in a coherent manner, the *ratio decidendi*. which may be binding, must be identified. It must be shown that the material facts are the same and that the preceding court had a superior (or in some cases, equal) status to the later court.

*Ratio decidendi* and *obiter dicta*

4.11   A judgement will start with a description of the facts of the case and probably a review of earlier precedents and possible alternative theories. The judge will then  make statements of law applicable to the legal problems raised by the material facts. Provided these statements are the basis for the decision, they are known as the *ratio decidendi* of the case. The *ratio decidendi* (which literally means 'reason for deciding') is the vital element which binds future judges.

4.12 If a judge's statements of legal principle do not form the basis of the decision (eg a dissenting (minority) judgement) or if his statements are not based on the existing material facts, but on hypothetical facts, they are known as *obiter dicta* statements – something said 'by the way'. A later court may respect such statements, but it is not bound to follow them. They are only of *persuasive* authority.

*Case: Rondel v Worsley 1969*
The House of Lords stated an opinion that a barrister could be held liable for negligence when not acting as an advocate, and that a solicitor would be immune from action when acting as an advocate. Since the case actually concerned the liability of a barrister when acting as an advocate these opinions were *obiter dicta*.

4.13 It is not always easy to identify the *ratio decidendi*. The same judgement may appear to contain contradictory views of the law in different passages. In decisions of appeal courts, where there are three or even five separate judgements, the members of the court may reach the same conclusion but give different reasons. Most of all, the *ratio* will often be intermingled with *obiter* statements. To assist the process of legal reasoning, many judges indicate in their speeches which comments are *ratio* and which *obiter*.

*Distinguishing the facts*

4.14 Although there may arguably be a finite number of legal principles to consider when deciding a case, there are necessarily an infinite variety of facts which may be presented. Apart from identifying the *ratio decidendi* of an earlier case, it is also necessary to consider how far the facts of the previous and the latest case are similar. Facts are never identical. If the differences appear significant the court may 'distinguish' the earlier case on the facts and thereby avoid following it as a precedent.

*Status of the court*

4.15 Not every decision made in every court is binding as a judicial precedent. The court's status has a significant effect on whether its decisions are binding, persuasive or disregarded.

(a) The Judicial Committee of the House of Lords stands at the apex of the judicial system. Its decisions are binding on all other English courts. The House of Lords generally regards itself as bound by its own earlier decisions but since a Practice Statement in 1966 it reserves the right to depart from its own precedents in exceptional cases.

(b) The Court of Appeal's decisions are binding on all English courts (except the House of Lords). It is bound by its own previous majority and unanimous decisions, by those of its predecessors and by those of the House of Lords: *Young v Bristol Aeroplane Co 1944*.

(c) A single High Court judge (hearing a case at first instance) is bound by decisions of higher courts but not by a decision of another High Court judge sitting alone (though he would treat it as strong persuasive authority). When two or more High Court judges sit together as a Divisional Court (an appeal court), their decisions are binding on any other Divisional Court (and on a single High Court judge sitting alone).

(d) Lower courts (Crown Courts, county courts, magistrates' courts) do not make precedents (their decisions are not usually reported) and they are bound by decisions of the higher courts.

You should refer to the next chapter for a description of the way in which the court system is structured as a whole.

## Binding and persuasive precedents

4.16 Apart from binding precedents as described above, reported decisions of any court (even if lower in status) may be treated as *persuasive* precedents - they may be, but need not be followed in a later case. Reported decisions of the Judicial Committee of the Privy Council (which is technically a court of appeal from certain Commonwealth countries), of higher courts of Commonwealth countries which have a common law legal tradition and of courts of the United States of America may be cited as persuasive precedents. With persuasive precedents much depends on the personal reputation of the judge whose earlier decision is cited.

4.17 A court of higher status is not only free to disregard the decision of a court of lower status. It may also deprive it of authority and expressly overrule it. This does not reverse the previous decision; overruling a decision does not affect its outcome as regards the defendant and plaintiff in that earlier decision.

4.18 If, in a case before the House of Lords, there is a dispute about a point of European Community law it must be referred to the European Court for a ruling. English courts are also required to take account of principles laid down by the European Court in so far as these are relevant. The European court does not, however, create or follow precedents as such, and the provisions of EC directives should not be used to interpret UK legislation.

4.19 A case in the High Court may be taken on appeal to the Court of Appeal. If the latter reverses the former decision, that first decision cannot be a precedent, and the reversed decision becomes a precedent. However, if the original decision had been reached by following precedent, then reversing that decision overrules the precedent which formed the *ratio*. Overruling a precedent does not affect the parties in that original precedent's case, but the parties in the reversed decision are affected by the new decision.

### *Avoidance of a binding precedent*

4.20 Even if a precedent appears to be binding, there are a number of grounds on which a court may decline to follow it:

(a) by distinguishing the facts;

(b) by declaring the *ratio decidendi* obscure, particularly when an Appeal Court decision by three or five judges gives a number of different *rationes decidendi;*

(c) by declaring the previous decision made *per incuriam* -without taking account of some essential point of law, such as an important precedent;

(d) by declaring it to be in conflict with a fundamental principle of law, for example where a court has failed to apply the doctrine of privity of contract: *Beswick v Beswick 1968*;

(e) by declaring an earlier precedent to be too wide - for example, the duty of care to the parties found in *Donoghue v Stevenson 1932.* has since been considerably refined; or

(f) because the earlier decision has been subsequently overruled by another court or by statute.

## The advantages and disadvantages of case law

4.21 Many of the strengths of case law as the cornerstone of English law also indicate some of its weaknesses. Generally the arguments revolve around the principles of consistency, clarity, flexibility and detail.

(a) *Consistency* - the whole point of following binding precedent is that the law is decided fairly and predictably. In theory therefore it should be possible to avoid litigation because the result is a foregone conclusion. However, judges are often forced to make illogical distinctions to avoid an unfair result, which combined with the wealth of reported cases serves to complicate the law.

(b) *Clarity* - following only the reasoning in *ratio* statements should lead to statements of principle for general application. In practice, however, the same judgement may be found to contain propositions which appear inconsistent with each other or with the precedent which the court purports to follow.

(c) *Flexibility* - the real strength of the system lies in its ability to change with changing circumstances in society since it arises directly out of the actions of society. The counter-argument is that the doctrine limits judges' discretion and they may be unable to avoid deciding in line with a precedent which produces an unfair result. Often this may only be resolved by passing a statute to correct the law's failings.

(d) *Detail* - precedents state how the law applies to facts, and it should be flexible enough to allow for details to be different, so that the law is all-encompassing. As has been noted above, however, judges often distinguish on facts to avoid a precedent. The wealth of detail is also a drawback in that it produces a vast body of reports which must be taken into account; again, though, statute can help by codifying rules developed in case-law - this, for instance, was the source of the Sale of Goods Act 1979.

## 5. LEGISLATION

### Statute law

5.1 Statute law is made by Parliament (or in exercise of law-making powers delegated by Parliament). Until the United Kingdom entered the European Community in 1973 the UK Parliament was completely sovereign - its law-making powers were unfettered. In that respect there was a marked contrast with the position in some other countries, eg the USA, where there is a written constitution and it is possible to challenge in the courts (as unconstitutional) legislation made by the statutory law-making body.

5.2 Parliamentary sovereignty means that:

(a) Parliament is able to make the law as it sees fit. It may repeal earlier statutes, overrule case law developed in the courts or make new law on subjects which have not been regulated by law before.

(b)   No Parliament can legislate so as to prevent a future Parliament changing the law:

*Case: Vauxhall Estates v Liverpool Corporation 1932*
If compensation for compulsory purchase were assessed under an Act of 1919 the plaintiffs would receive £2,370, whereas if it were assessed under an Act of 1925 they would only receive £1,133. The Act of 1919 provided that any Act inconsistent with it would have no effect.

*Held:* this provision did not apply to subsequent Acts because Parliament cannot bind its successors. In addition the 1925 Act by implication repealed the 1919 Act so far as it was inconsistent with it. The plaintiffs therefore received £1,133.

(c)   The courts are bound to apply the relevant statute law however distasteful to them it may be. But the judges have to *interpret* statute law (as we shall see later) and they may find a meaning in a statutory rule which those members of parliament who promoted the statute did not intend.

5.3   In practice, Parliament usually follows certain conventions which limit its freedom. It does not usually enact statutes which alter the law with retrospective effect or deprive citizens of their property without compensation. In addition to making new law and altering existing law, Parliament may make the law clearer by passing a codifying statute (such as the Sale of Goods Act 1979) to put case law on a statutory basis, or a consolidating statute to incorporate an original statute and its successive amendments into a single statute (such as the Companies Act 1985).

*Parliamentary procedure*

5.4   A proposal for legislation is originally aired in public in a Government Green Paper. After comments are received a White Paper is produced which sets out the intended aims of the legislation. It is then put forward in draft form as a Bill, and may be introduced into either the House of Commons or the House of Lords. When the Bill has passed through one House it must then go through the same stages in the other House (see paragraph 5.7). When it has passed through both Houses it is submitted for the Royal Assent, which in practice is given on the Queen's behalf by a committee of the Lord Chancellor and two other peers. It then becomes an Act of Parliament (or statute) but it does not (unless the Act itself so provides) come into operation until a commencement date is notified by statutory instrument (see paragraph 5.24).

5.5   Most Bills are Public Bills of general application, whether introduced by the government or by a private member. A Private Bill has a restricted application: for example, a local authority may promote a Private Bill to give it special powers within its own area. Private Bills undergo a different form of examination at the committee stage.

5.6   If the House of Commons and the House of Lords disagree over the same Bill, the House of Lords may delay its passing for a maximum of one year (only one month if it is a financial measure, such as the annual Finance Act).

5.7   In each House the successive stages of dealing with the Bill are as follows.

(a)   *First reading* - publication and introduction into the agenda: no debate.

(b)   *Second reading* - debate on the general merits of the Bill: no amendments at this stage.

(c)   *Committee stage* - the Bill is examined by a Standing Committee of about 20 members, representing the main parties and including some members at least who specialise in the relevant subject. The Bill is examined section by section and may be amended. If the Bill is very important all or part of the Committee Stage may be taken by the House as a whole sitting as a committee.

(d)   *Report stage* - the Bill as amended in committee is reported to the full House for approval. If the government has undertaken in committee to reconsider various points, it often puts forward its final amendments at this stage.

(e)   *Third reading* - this is the final approval stage at which only verbal amendments may be made.

## Legislation affecting banking

5.8   Banking operations have been considerably shaped by legislation, and this is a very wide area. However, we will only consider in chronological order a few examples of legislation that affect the main business of everyday banking. These examples are not exhaustive, and many are also discussed elsewhere in this text.

5.9   *Bills of Exchange Act 1882* - This Act was passed to codify commercial law, as bills of exchange were frequently used by merchants and traders in the late 19th century. It gave the banks protection and, even though the use of bills as such has declined, the Act still gives limited protection to the paying banker in respect of cheques which are also bills of exchange. A number of definitions were established relating to both bills and cheques which will be discussed further in Part E of this text.

5.10  *Cheques Act 1957* - This Act was introduced to amend certain provisions of the Bills of Exchange Act 1882 in relation to cheques. The two Acts together are still highly relevant to us as bankers and will be dealt with in depth in Part E of this text.

5.11  *Consumer Credit Act 1974* - The purpose of this Act was to bring under one statute all credit regulations in respect of facilities up to £15,000 to private individuals, sole traders, partnerships and all other unincorporated bodies. This affects not only banks but all firms involved in the provision of credit, such as hire purchase companies and money-lenders. This Act is discussed in more detail in Part B of this text.

5.12  *Sex Discrimination Act 1975* - This Act relates both to employment (it is relevant to the bank as an employer of a large number of staff) and to everyday banking operations. In the past certain case law dictated that it was necessary for banks to ask married women questions regarding their husbands, such as details of his employers: *Lloyds Bank Ltd v Savory & Co 1933*. However, it would now contravene the Act if these practices were continued.

5.13 *Unfair Contract Terms Act 1977* - The consumer is protected by this Act since it restricts how far liability for breach of contract and negligence can be excluded. The purpose of the Act is to allow only legitimate disclaimers and exclusion clauses. If liability for financial loss arises due to the bank's own negligence, loss can be restricted or excluded under the Act only as long as the disclaimer or exclusion clause satisfies conditions of reasonableness. An example of this is the production of status enquiries by the banks. They can be subject to a disclaimer which was successfully relied upon in the case of *Hedley Byrne & Co Ltd v Heller & Partners 1963*. However, such a disclaimer would now have to be subject to the test of 'reasonableness', which is discussed further in the chapter on statutory intervention in contracts. It is unlikely that any bank contract would include terms that were considered 'unreasonable' by a court of law.

5.14 *Supply of Goods and Services Act 1982* - Under this Act it is implied that a supplier of services (such as a bank) will show proper skill and care and complete the service within a reasonable time. He is entitled to make reasonable charges. This Act does not significantly alter the common law rules applicable to banks in the past in respect of charges for the services they provide.

5.15 *Data Protection Act 1984* - All information about individuals which is stored on computer is regulated by this Act. The data must be accurate and up to date and must not be disclosed to any outside parties. It obviously affects banks since a wealth of information regarding customers' accounts is stored on bank computers. Therefore the banks are regulated under this Act as are many of their customers who store information in this way. It is covered in more detail in the chapter on essentials of the banker-customer contract.

5.16 *Companies Acts 1985 and 1989* - The 1985 Act consolidates all previous law on companies, whilst the 1989 Act makes certain major amendments. They are discussed further in the chapter on company bank accounts.

5.17 *Insolvency Act 1986* - This Act relates to insolvency of both individuals and companies. Insolvency means the inability to pay debts as and when they fall due. It is very important to the banks, who make available overdrafts, loans etc to their customers. The Act provides a clear framework for dealing with both personal and corporate insolvency; it was passed in order to codify rules which had developed through case law.

5.18 *Drug Trafficking Offences Act 1986* and *Prevention of Terrorism Act 1989* - The disclosure of information which comes into the bank's hands during the normal course of business is required by these Acts, if it is likely that the customer is dealing in drugs or terrorism or the bank holds money obtained from the sale of drugs. These Acts are discussed in more detail in the chapter on essentials of the banker-customer contract.

5.19 *Financial Services Act 1986* - This very important Act established a system of regulations for the conduct of investment business. The Act relies upon self-regulation which is controlled by the Securities and Investment Board (SIB). Any institution or company providing investment services has to be authorised. This includes banks who provide services to enable customers to purchase stocks and shares, life assurance etc.

5.20 *Banking Act 1987* – This Act was brought to the statute book as a result of the rescue of Johnson Matthey Bankers by the Bank of England in 1984. It replaced the Banking Act 1979, and its main purpose is prudential supervision of banking on a statutory basis by the Bank of England, in addition to regulation of the use of the words 'bank' and 'deposit taking'.

5.21 *Cheques Act 1992* – This Act was passed following recommendations for reform of banking law made by the Jack Committee. It deals with one very specific issue: the 'account payee' crossing on cheques.

## Delegated legislation

5.22 To save time in Parliament it is usual to set out the main principles in the body of the Act as numbered sections and to relegate the details to schedules (at the end of the Act) which need not be debated though they are visible and take effect as part of the Act. But even with this device there is a great deal which cannot conveniently be included in the Act. It may for example be necessary, after the Act has been passed, for the government to consult interested parties and then produce regulations, having the force of the law, to implement the Act or to fix commencement dates to bring the Act into operation or to prescribe printed forms for use in connection with it. To provide for these and other matters, a modern Act usually contains a section by which power is given to a minister, or public body such as a local authority, to make subordinate or delegated legislation for specified purposes only.

5.23 This procedure is unavoidable and essential for various reasons.

(a) Parliament has not time to examine these matters of detail.

(b) Much of the content of delegated legislation is technical and is better worked out in consultation with professional, commercial or industrial groups outside Parliament.

(c) If new or altered regulations are required later, they can be issued without referring back to Parliament, and in much shorter time than is needed to pass an amending Act.

5.24 The disadvantages of delegated legislation are that Parliament loses control of the law-making process and a huge mass of detailed law appears piecemeal each year. It is difficult for persons who may be affected by it to keep abreast of the changes. Yet ignorance of the law is not accepted as an excuse for infringing it.

5.25 Delegated legislation appears in various forms. Ministerial powers are exercised by *statutory instrument* (including emergency powers of the Crown exercised by Order in Council). Two such enabling acts of direct relevance to banking are the Consumer Credit Act 1974 and the Insolvency Act 1986. The latter Act in particular has spawned a vast amount of statutory instruments, including the Insolvency Rules (SI 1986 No 1925) and the Insolvency Regulations (SI 1986 No 1994). Local authorities are given statutory powers to make *bye-laws*, which apply within a specific locality.

5.26 Parliament does exercise some control over delegated legislation by restricting and defining the power to make rules and by keeping the making of new delegated legislation under review as follows:

(a) some statutory instruments do not take effect until approved by affirmative resolution of parliament;

(b) most other statutory instruments must be laid before Parliament for 40 days before they take effect. During that period members may propose a negative resolution to veto a statutory instrument to which they object.

5.27 There are standing Scrutiny Committees of both Houses whose duty it is to examine statutory instruments with a view to raising objections if necessary, usually on the grounds that the instrument is obscure, expensive or retrospective. The power to make delegated legislation is defined by the Act which confers the power. A statutory instrument may be challenged in the courts on the grounds that it is *ultra vires* - that is, it exceeds the prescribed limits or has been made without due compliance with the correct procedure. If the objection is valid the court declares the statutory instrument to be void.

5.28 Statutes, including delegated legislation, are expressed in general terms. For example, a Finance Act may impose a new tax on transactions described as a category; it does not expressly impose a tax of a specified amount on the particular transaction of a particular person. If a dispute arises as to whether or how a statute applies to particular acts or events, the courts must *interpret* the statute, determine what it means and decide whether or not it applies to the given case.

**Interpretation of statutes**

5.29 In the interpretation of a statute the court is concerned with what the statute itself provides. It is never required to take account of what may have been said in parliamentary discussion, even by a government spokesman explaining the intended effect of the Bill. No opinion of an individual member is to be accepted as the collective intention of Parliament. For the same reason the report of a committee or commission recommending legislation is not to be used as a guide to the interpretation of a statute.

5.30 Unless the statute contains express words to the contrary it is presumed that the following 'canons of statutory interpretation' apply:

(a) a statute does not alter the existing law nor repeal other statutes;

(b) if a statute deprives a person of his property, say by nationalisation, he is to be compensated for its value;

(c) a statute does not have retrospective effect to a date earlier than its becoming law;

(d) a statute does not bind the Crown;

(e) any point on which the statute leaves a gap or omission is outside the scope of the statute; and

(f) a statute cannot impose criminal liability without proof of fault (though many modern statutes rebut this presumption).

In practice a statute usually deals expressly with these matters (other than (e)) to remove any possible doubt.

5.31 Since judges are called upon to interpret statutes, a system has been developed to guide them. This consists of statutory assistance and a set of general principles, or 'canons', of statutory interpretation.

5.32 Statutory assistance consists of:

(a) the Interpretation Act 1978, which defines certain terms frequently found in legislation;

(b) interpretation sections to Acts - particularly long, complicated and wide-ranging Acts often contain self-explanations; for instance, s 207 of the Financial Services Act 1986 defines 'authorised persons' and 'recognised investment exchanges' for its purposes;

(c) preambles or long titles to Acts often direct the judge as to its intentions and objects; private Acts must have a preamble, public ones recently have just contained long titles. But preambles may only be used to resolve an ambiguity - they may not be used when the enacted words are already clear;

(d) sidenotes - statutes often have summary notes in the margin which may be used to give a general interpretation of the clauses to which they are attached.

5.33 In interpreting the words of a statute the courts have developed the following well-established general principles.

(a) *The literal rule:* words should be given their ordinary grammatical sense. Normally a word should be construed in the same literal sense wherever it appears throughout the statute.

(b) *The golden rule:* a statute should be construed to avoid a manifest absurdity or contradiction within itself.

*Case: Re Sigsworth 1935*
The golden rule was applied to prevent a murderer from inheriting on the intestacy of his victim although he was, as her son, her only heir on a literal interpretation of the Administration of Estates Act 1925.

(c) *The contextual rule:* a word should be construed in its context - it is permissible to look at the statute as a whole to discover the meaning of a word in it.

(d) *The mischief rule:* if the words used are ambiguous and the statute discloses (say, in its preamble as explained above) the purpose of the statute, the court will adopt the meaning which is likely to give effect to the purpose or reform which the statute is intended to achieve (this is to take account of the mischief or weakness which the statute is explicitly intended to remedy).

*Case: Gardiner v Sevenoaks RDC 1950*
The purpose of an Act was to provide for the safe storage of inflammable cinematograph film wherever it might be stored on 'premises'. A notice was served on G who stored film in a cave, requiring him to comply with the safety rules. G argued that 'premises' did not include a cave and so the Act had no application to his case.

*Held:* the purpose of the Act was to protect the safety of persons working in all places where film was stored. Insofar as film was stored in a cave, the word 'premises' included the cave.

(e) The *eiusdem generis* rule: statutes often list a number of specific things and end the list with more general words. In that case the general words are to be limited in their meaning to other things of the same kind (Latin: *eiusdem generis*) as the specific items which precede them.

*Case: Evans v Cross 1938*
E was charged with driving his car in such a way as to 'ignore a traffic sign'. He had undoubtedly crossed to the wrong side of a white line painted down the middle of the road. 'Traffic sign' was defined in the Act as 'all signals, warning signposts, direction posts, signs or other devices'. Unless, therefore, a white line was an 'other device', E had not ignored a 'traffic sign' and had not committed the offence charged.

*Held:* 'other device' must be limited in its meaning to a category of signs in the list which preceded it. Thus restricted it did not include a painted line which was quite different from that category.

(f) *Expressio unius est exclusio alterius:* to express one thing is by implication to exclude anything else. For example, a statutory rule on 'sheep' does not include goats.

(g) *In pari materia:* if the statute forms part of a series which deals with similar subject matter, the court may look to the interpretation of previous statutes on the assumption that Parliament intended the same thing.

5.34 The courts have been paying more attention to what Parliament intended in recent times. This is partly an extension of the mischief rule. In October 1988, for example, the Attorney-General issued a statement interpreting the word 'obtain' in the Company Securities (Insider Dealing) Act 1985. This was in order that the courts should apply the law for the purpose for which it was enacted by Parliament. A more purposive approach is also being taken because so many international and EC regulations come to be interpreted by the courts.

*Case: Re Attorney-General's reference (No 1) 1988*
The accused had received unsolicited information from a merchant banker telling him of a forthcoming merger. He knew that this was price-sensitive information and instructed his broker to buy shares in one of the companies, later netting a profit of £3,000. The Act sets out the offence of 'knowingly obtaining' such information. His defence was that he had obtained it passively, not actively.

*Held:* both the Court of Appeal and the House of Lords rejected this interpretation on the grounds that the effect of the legislation would be lessened if it was followed.

# Exercise 1

Many Bills are introduced into the House of Commons by a government minister. What stages does such a Bill go through before reaching the House of Lords?

## Solution

(a) Formal first reading.
(b) Debate and vote on second reading.
(c) Reference to a Standing Committee for line by line examination.
(d) Report stage to the House.
(e) Third reading.

---

### Exercise 2

List ten statutes of particular reference to the business of banking.

**Solution**

You should refer back to paragraphs 5.9 to 5.21 above for a description of key pieces of relevant legislation.

---

## 6. OTHER SOURCES OF LAW

**European Community law**

6.1 On becoming a member of the European Community (EC) in 1973, the United Kingdom adhered to the Treaty of Rome (and the related treaties on coal, steel and atomic energy) and agreed to conform to EC law which is concerned with free trade in manufactured goods, agricultural support price policies, transport, company law and many other economic matters.

6.2 New EC law is created in the following ways:

(a) *Regulations* may be issued. These are 'self-executing' - they have the force of law in every EC state without need of national legislation. In this sense regulations are described as 'directly applicable'. If they confer rights and impose obligations on individuals, regulations are also said to have 'direct effect'. Their object is to obtain uniformity of law throughout the EC.

(b) *Decisions* of an administrative nature are made by the EC Commission in Brussels mainly to implement the common agricultural policy (CAP). Such decisions are immediately binding on the persons to whom they are addressed.

(c) *Directives* are issued to the governments of the EC member states requiring them within a specified period (usually two years) to alter the national laws of the state so that they conform to the directive. Thus the Financial Services Act 1986 embodies certain directives on company securities and the Companies Act 1989 gives force to the Eighth Directive on company law. However, most directives are incorporated into UK law by statutory instrument.

6.3 Until a directive is given effect by a UK statute it does not usually affect the legal rights and obligations of individuals. In exceptional situations the wording of a directive may be cited in legal proceedings, but generally statutory interpretation is a matter for the UK courts.

*Case: Van Duyn v Home Office 1974*
Article 48 of the Treaty of Rome requires that nationals of EC member states should be free to take up employment anywhere in the EC area, subject to any restrictions imposed on grounds of public policy. An EC directive required that any such restriction of 'public policy' should be limited to matters arising from personal conduct of the individual. The plaintiff challenged the decision of the Home Office to deny her entry to the UK entirely on the grounds of her membership of an organisation (the Church of Scientology).

*Held:* a directive, like a regulation, could be 'directly applicable' (if its wording was appropriate). But the plaintiff's membership of an organisation was 'personal conduct' and so the decision to exclude her was consistent with the directive.

6.4 Directives are the most significant and important means of importing continental law into the UK legal system since the EC has a wide-ranging programme of assimilating the laws of member states to a common EC model. Recommendations and opinions may also be issued but these are merely persuasive and not binding.

6.5 It is true that membership of the EC restricts the sovereignty of the UK Parliament (and other EC national legislatures). But the directives to which Parliament must ultimately conform are issued as a result of negotiation and often agreement between the UK government and the other governments of the EC. The UK government in turn is dependent on the support of a majority of Members of Parliament to retain office. To that extent, Parliament has indirect influence on the EC law-making process. It is certainly true to say, however, that since 1973 the EC has had considerable impact on the law, and this is set to increase.

6.6 The House of Lords acknowledged the supremacy of EC law in the *Factortame* litigation, which appears to affect not only areas of actual conflict between UK and EC law, but also areas of *potential* conflict.

*Case: Factortame Ltd v Secretary of State for Transport (No 2) 1991*
Article 52 of the Treaty of Rome prohibits discrimination against the nationals of another EC member state. The Merchant Shipping Act 1988 requires 75% of directors and shareholders in companies operating British-registered fishing vessels to be British. Certain UK companies controlled by Spanish nationals and fishing in British waters were unable to meet these conditions. They brought a claim against the UK government on the grounds that the Act was incompatible with EC law.

*Held:* the House of Lords granted interim relief by suspending relevant provisions of the 1988 Act and referred the matter to the European Court of Justice (see next chapter), which laid down that EC law must be fully and uniformly applied in all member states.

6.7 The words of Hoffmann J in *Stoke-on-Trent CC v B & Q plc 1991* sum up the current position.

'The EEC Treaty is the supreme law of this country, taking precedence over Acts of Parliament. Our entry into the European Economic Community meant that (subject to our undoubted but probably theoretical right to withdraw from the Community altogether) Parliament surrendered its sovereign right to legislate contrary to the provisions of the Treaty on matters of social and economic policy which it regulated.'

## Custom

6.8 In early mediaeval times the courts created law by enforcing selected customs. Custom is now of little importance as a source of law, but it is still classified as a legal source of law.

6.9 For example, in determining what are the implied terms of a contract, the court may take account of local or trade customs which the parties intended should be part of their contract.

*Case: Hutton v Warren 1836*
The parties were landlord and tenant of a farm. The landlord gave notice to the tenant to quit. Disputes arose as to the tenant's obligation to continue to cultivate the farm until the notice expired and as to his entitlement to allowances for work done and seed supplied.

*Held*: these matters were to be resolved according to local custom which had been incorporated in the contract.

6.10 In disputes over claims to customary rights, such as to use the land of another or to remove things from it, the alleged custom may be established subject to the following conditions.

(a) It must have existed since *time immemorial*, in theory since 1189 AD. It usually suffices to show that the custom has existed without interruption from as far back as records (if any) exist.

(b) It must have been enjoyed *openly as of right*. If it has only been enjoyed secretly, by force, or with permission of the landowner, it is not a custom which amounts to a right.

(c) The custom must be reasonable, certain in its terms, consistent with other custom or law and exercised within a definite locality.

**Subsidiary sources of law**

6.11 The main sources of law as set out above are case law (derived from common law and equity) and parliamentary and EC legislation. However, a number of subsidiary sources have had some influence on the law's development, and are still recognisable today. Of these, only merchant law is relevant to your syllabus.

*Merchant law*

6.12 In mediaeval times, traders (who were often foreigners) submitted their disputes to courts which applied mercantile custom at main ports, fairs and markets. For example, the law of negotiable instruments was brought to England as a commercial practice recognised by bankers and traders in Northern Italy, Germany and elsewhere in late mediaeval times. The work of these courts was absorbed (with the merchant law) into common law in the seventeenth century.

## 7. CONCLUSION

7.1 This chapter provides an introduction and a background to the more specific material in the later chapters. It is largely historical but it has its practical relevance to the current state of the law. It is particularly important to bear in mind the distinction between legal and equitable parts of law - we will see later on (particularly in contract law) that the different principles can lead to very significantly different results. You should also pay careful attention to the individual statutes of relevance to banking set out in the chapter.

## TEST YOUR KNOWLEDGE

*The numbers in brackets refer to paragraphs of this chapter*

1  What are:

    (a)   the historical; and — *Common law + EQUITY*
    (b)   the legal sources of law? (2.1) — *Case law, legislation, EC law, Custom*

2  Explain how common law and equity developed as part of English law. (3.2-3.13)

3  How does the idea of judicial precedent work? (4.3)

4  What three things must be considered when examining and applying a precedent? (4.10)

5  Which courts are bound by decisions of the Court of Appeal? (4.15)

6  What are the effects of Parliamentary sovereignty? (5.2)

7  What is meant by delegated legislation? (5.22)

8  How does Parliament exercise control over delegated legislation? (5.26)

9  What presumptions are made about the effect of a statute? (5.30)

10  State six general principles used to interpret statutes. (5.33)

11  How are the principles of EC law incorporated into English law? (6.2)

12  How must a customary right be established? (6.10)

13  What is the present-day significance to bankers of merchant law? (6.12)

*Now try questions 1 to 3 at the end of the text*

# Chapter 2

# RESOLVING CONFLICT

---

**This chapter covers the following topics.**

1. 'Conflict' and the bank
2. Civil and criminal liability
3. Civil liability - contract and tort
4. Structure of the court system
5. The courts of law
6. The quasi-judicial process
7. The Banking Ombudsman
8. Legal aid

---

## 1. 'CONFLICT' AND THE BANK

1.1 'Conflict' means a dispute or disagreement. These happen in both our personal and business life. In our business life conflict can be measured in terms of financial loss, or loss of orders, customers, commission or opportunities. To a business, a conflict means that the business resources are not being used to their best advantage; it can result in the business making a loss and eventually closing down.

### The court process

1.2 In order to try to overcome 'conflict' a business may decide to take legal action via the courts. This is not only costly but time-consuming and banks go to great lengths to try to avoid court action even if they know that they would win the case. The publicity involved in court hearings may also be felt to be prejudicial to the bank's interests. However, due to its size a major bank will find itself involved in legal action, both as the person bringing the action ('plaintiff') and as the person defending the action being brought against it by another party ('defendant').

(a) As *plaintiff* the normal situation would be for the bank to be taking legal action through the courts for the recovery of a debt or the right to enforce an item of security.

(b) As *defendant* it would usually be defending an action brought against it by a customer who may, for example, allege that the bank has broken a contract it made with him, or that the bank had been negligent in its handling of his affairs.

1.3 A bank may let matters proceed through the courts where it considers that previous case law is not clear and/or where it is seeking clarification on the course of action that it should adopt. Such proceedings have been taken to clarify a wife's position regarding the matrimonial home: *Williams and Glyn's Bank Ltd v Boland 1980*, or to test whether a bank could be involved in undue influence in contract: *Lloyds Bank Ltd v Bundy 1975*.

1.4 The principal function of the judicial process is that an official adjudicates and makes reasoned decisions, according to the known rules of law, on the basis of evidence available to both parties and offered to the court.

(a) Each party, through his legal representative (usually a solicitor), tests the facts laid before the court. They do this by using factual and legal arguments.

(b) A reasoned decision is then made by the relevant person(s): magistrates (magistrates' court), judge (Crown Court and county court), High Court judges (High Court) or, if a jury sits with a judge (indictable offences in the Crown Court and some civil actions in the Queen's Bench Division of the High Court), the judge decides the points of law and the jury decides the points of fact.

1.5 This process assumes that there is always a legal rule which will resolve the conflict and that it can be discovered by the examination of statutes and case law.

**Quasi-judicial process**

1.6 The quasi-judicial process is similar to the court process, but it differs due to less strict rules of evidence and procedure. This system also benefits from being generally cheaper and far less formal, and it normally provides a quicker decision.

1.7 The court process uses the courts whereas the quasi-judicial process uses conflict-resolving bodies which are not part of the court structure. These are formal arbitration bodies and administrative tribunals. Their use is particularly well suited to resolving welfare and employment disputes. Since 1986 we have had the Banking Ombudsman to resolve conflict in banking. This office is voluntary and so is outside both court and quasi-judicial systems.

1.8 Later in this chapter we shall outline the practical topics of how the English legal system is structured, and whom one is likely to encounter if ever the system has to be called upon. We shall see in particular how the two types of process, namely the judicial (the court system) and the quasi-judicial (arbitration and tribunals) operate differently in practice. We shall also examine the voluntary Banking Ombudsman scheme which was set up by the banks as an alternative to both judicial and quasi-judicial process.

## 2. CIVIL AND CRIMINAL LIABILITY

2.1 In brief the difference between criminal prosecutions and disputes which concern civil liability is as follows.

(a) Criminal proceedings (prosecutions) are usually commenced by the State, via the police and the Crown Prosecution Service, although they may be brought by a private citizen. Some crimes, for example assault, have specific victims. Others, for example treason, can be committed without causing loss to any particular person. If there is a victim he will not usually have a say in whether or not a prosecution is commenced, nor will he benefit from a conviction, since fines are payable to the State. There are separate courts for civil and criminal hearings, with different rules of procedure. There is also a different standard of proof. In a criminal trial the prosecution must prove its case *beyond reasonable doubt*.

(b) Civil law exists to regulate the disputed rights and obligations of persons in their dealings with each other. The general purpose of civil proceedings is to impose the appropriate settlement of matters in dispute, sometimes by financial compensation in the award of damages. Civil proceedings are concerned with a number of different types of issue such as breach of contract, liability for infringing the general rights of another person (torts) and breach of trust. In a civil action it is sufficient that the facts be proved on the *balance of probabilities*.

2.2 This chapter describes the system of courts which decide civil and criminal cases. You will see that most courts deal only with civil or only with criminal cases. If the same court, eg a magistrates' court, does have civil and criminal jurisdiction, it keeps the two types of case distinct in its working procedure, since the principles of liability are essentially different.

2.3 At the end of a *criminal* case the accused person, if he is found guilty, is *punished*. This is usually by imposing on him a fine payable to the State or a sentence of imprisonment.

2.4 At the end of a *civil* case the defendant, if the decision of the court goes against him, usually has to pay damages, which are a form of monetary *compensation*, to the successful plaintiff and also his legal costs in bringing the case. If the plaintiff loses his case he may have to pay the defendant's legal costs.

2.5 In civil cases the court sometimes makes orders requiring the person concerned to do or to refrain from doing something. The chapter on remedies for breach of contract provides some examples of court orders. But it is important to remember that civil cases contain no element of punishment.

2.6 With regard to liability, there are two other terms which you may encounter and will need to understand.

(a) *Strict liability*. Irrespective of whether an act is done deliberately or not, the defendant in both criminal and civil cases may have strict liability: this means that the fact that a thing is done at all gives liability. In civil cases, strict liability may arise for breach of contract, conversion or supplying defective products.

(b) *Vicarious liability*. One person may be jointly liable for the acts of another. This is most often seen in employment contracts, where the employer may be vicariously liable for the acts of his employee. For example, a bank will be vicariously liable for injury inflicted on a third party by one of its employees acting in his employment capacity.

## 3. CIVIL LIABILITY – CONTRACT AND TORT

3.1 Criminal liability does not greatly concern us in this text, since (for the most part) a bank is more likely to be involved in civil law disputes, either in contract or in tort.

### Contractual disputes

3.2 Later on in this study text you will find several chapters on the law of *contract*. You will see that if a person enters into a legally binding agreement, called a contract, he must abide by it or incur liability to pay damages for breach of contract.

3.3 The basis of liability in contract is that an agreement has been made. If there is no agreement there is no liability for breach of contract.

3.4 If, for example, a person asserts that there is a contract between himself and another person for sale of goods and he fails to persuade the court that there ever was such a contract, that is the end of the matter. If, on the other hand, he succeeds in establishing that there was a contract and that the defendant has broken it then the other party is liable, because there was a contractual obligation, to pay damages as compensation.

### Disputes in tort

3.5 Tort is an old word which means 'wrong'. It denotes various kinds of wrongs done to other people by infringement of the rights which exist between people. For example:

   (a) each person has a right to exclude other people from land of which he is in possession, unless someone enters by legal authority, for example to read the gas meter. Any unauthorised entrant is a trespasser and the occupier may take legal proceedings against him;

   (b) a person of good reputation has a right to keep his reputation undamaged. If a newspaper publishes a damaging and untrue statement about him he may sue the newspaper for damages for defamation, which is injury to his reputation.

3.6 The basis of liability in tort is that a right, given by law to everyone, has been infringed. It has nothing to do with contract. If a person sues for trespass or for defamation or for any other of the numerous forms of tort he is not required to show that the defendant made a contract with him. The defendant is often a complete stranger to him. It is sufficient, to establish liability in tort, that a right enjoyed by anyone has been infringed.

3.7 Although it is necessary in dealing with disputes to distinguish between different rules of law the same events may cause legal proceedings of different kinds.

3.8 As an example, suppose that a self-employed taxi driver is involved in an accident in which both his passenger and a pedestrian are injured. The following issues may arise.

(a) *Crime:* the driver may be charged with dangerous or careless driving and be prosecuted by the State in a criminal court. He will only be convicted if it is proved beyond reasonable doubt that he is guilty of the offence with which he is charged.

(b) *Breach of contract:* it is an implied term of contract that the driver will drive with reasonable care. The passenger may sue the driver for breach of contract in a civil court. Here a different standard of proof is required and the purpose of the claim is to recover compensation, not to punish for a crime.

(c) *Negligence:* the injured pedestrian or the passenger may sue the driver on the ground that the driver was negligent (in that he owed him a duty of care and, in breaching that duty, caused him damage). This is liability in tort.

(d) *Statutory liability of insurers:* the driver should be insured against liability under (b) and (c) above. If the passenger and pedestrian obtain judgement in their favour against the driver and he fails to pay, they may recover their damages from his insurers, although the latter have no primary liability either in contract or in tort.

## 4. STRUCTURE OF THE COURT SYSTEM

4.1 For most people outside the legal profession, the legal system is something of a closed book, surrounded by the mystery created by archaic language and costumes. In fact, for the most part it consists of practical and down-to-earth sets of procedures designed to provide resolutions to ordinary problems.

4.2 Publicity tends to focus on the higher courts and, in particular, on criminal proceedings. 97% of the cases heard by the courts take place in magistrates' courts, however, and a vast number of civil cases are heard.

4.3 The courts have to be organised to accommodate the working of the legal system. There are four main functional aspects of the court system which underlie its structure.

(a) *Civil and criminal law differ* so much in substance and procedure that they are best administered in separate courts.

(b) *Local courts* allow the vast bulk of small legal proceedings to be decentralised. But important civil cases, in which large sums of money are at stake, begin in the High Court in London.

(c) Although the courts form a single system (as a result of the Judicature Acts 1873-75), there is some *specialisation* both within the High Court (split into three divisions) and in other courts with separate functions.

(d) There is a system of *review by appeals* to higher courts.

4.4 The Judicature Acts are consolidated by the Supreme Court Act 1981, which states that the Court of Appeal, the High Court and the Crown Court comprise the Supreme Court. Before launching into a description of all the courts of law, the diagram on the next page should give you an overall view of the system.

# CIVIL COURT STRUCTURE

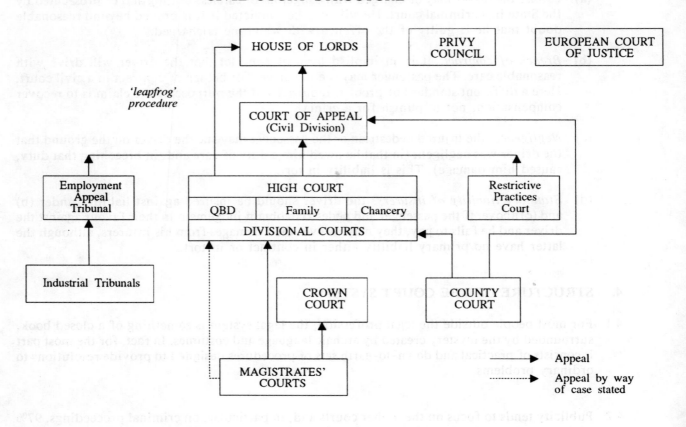

# CRIMINAL COURT STRUCTURE

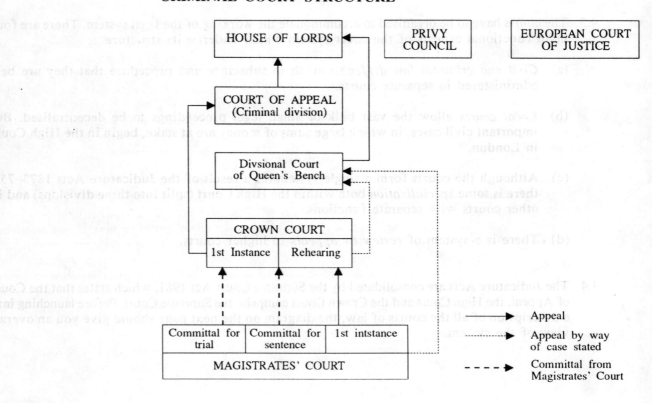

4.5 Note that in criminal cases the Crown Court is at once a court of first instance and a court of appeal.

(a) A court of first instance is where the case is originally heard in full.

(b) The appeal court is the court to which an appeal is made against the ruling or the sentence.

4.6 If the appeal court finds in favour of the appellant the original decision is reversed. This is different from 'overruling' which happens when a higher court finds a lower court's precedent to be wrong. Although the precedent is overruled and hence not followed again, the overruling has no effect on the actual outcome of the original case.

4.7 The system of appeals is very important and you should make sure that you are clear which higher courts hear which type of appeal from which lower courts.

## 5. THE COURTS OF LAW

5.1 As we have seen, some courts deal only with civil cases and some only with criminal. Most, however, can deal with both. But a court is a court by virtue of its constitution, not of its situation - the Old Bailey, for instance, is a court-room, but a judge and jury who visit the scene of an alleged crime are a court.

### Magistrates' courts

5.2 Magistrates' courts deal with *criminal* cases as follows.

(a) They try summarily (without a jury) all minor offences and may try offences which are triable summarily or on indictment with a jury, if the accused consents and the magistrates' court considers that the case is suitable for trial in that court.

(b) They conduct committal proceedings, which are preliminary investigations of the prosecution case, when the offence is triable only on indictment (by a Crown Court), or if it is an offence triable either way which (see (a) above) it is decided should not be tried summarily. If the magistrates are satisfied they commit the defendant for trial in a Crown Court.

5.3 The maximum penalties which magistrates may impose on a defendant convicted summarily of a criminal offence are six months' imprisonment or a fine of up to £5,000. The magistrates also have discretion to order the defendant to compensate his victim, up to £5,000. If in a summary trial the magistrates consider that their sentencing powers are inadequate they may convict and commit the defendant to a Crown Court for sentence. They may also make compensation, community service, restitution, supervision and probation orders. Other miscellaneous sentences include binding over to keep the peace (a fine being payable in the event of a breach), disqualification from driving and endorsement of a driving licence.

5.4 A defendant convicted on a criminal charge has a general right for a rehearing by a Crown Court. Either the defendant or the prosecution may appeal on a point of law only by way of 'case stated' to a divisional court of the Queen's Bench Division.

5.5 A 'case stated' appeal is based on the idea not that magistrates (or the Crown Court) have wrongly decided the facts but that they have wrongly interpreted the law. The magistrates produce written reasons for the way in which they decided the case. These, together with the facts, are considered by the Divisional Court to ensure that the law was correctly applied. If not then the case may be sent back to the lower court with instructions as to how it should be decided.

5.6 Magistrates' *civil* jurisdiction includes various types of licensing and enforcement of local authority charges and rates. The magistrates' courts also have an important role to play in the law relating to children; they are the first tier in what is in effect an embryo Family Court in which specially trained magistrates and judges apply uniform procedures across the magistrates', County and High Courts. Family law has always been included in the magistrates' remit, but it has been greatly changed and enlarged by the enactment in October 1991 of the Children Act 1989.

5.7 The magistrates' court is staffed by lay magistrates (the majority) who are not legally qualified and sit part-time. They are appointed on the Lord Chancellor's advice and are assisted by a salaried, legally-qualified clerk, who must be a solicitor or barrister of at least five years' standing. Stipendiary magistrates sit in large towns and are salaried. They must be solicitors or barristers of at least seven years' standing. Lay magistrates sit two or three to a court; stipendiary ones sit alone.

## County courts

5.8 County courts have *civil* jurisdiction only but deal with almost every kind of civil case arising within the local areas for which the courts are established.

The county court is involved in:

(a) contract and tort claims (see below);
(b) equitable matters concerning trusts, mortgages and partnership dissolution;
(c) disputes concerning land;
(d) family cases;
(e) probate matters (disputes as to the grant of authority to personal representatives);
(f) miscellaneous matters under various statutes, such as the Consumer Credit Act 1974;
(g) some bankruptcy, company winding-up and admiralty cases; and
(h) 'small claims'.

5.9 A circuit judge usually presides, being a barrister of at least ten years' standing. A recorder, a part-time appointment in the Crown Court, is a solicitor or barrister of at least ten years' standing, and may be appointed as a circuit judge if he has three years' experience as a recorder. A district judge, who must be a solicitor or barrister of at least seven years' standing, assists the circuit judge; the district judge may also hear small claims, or any other with the consent of the parties. The circuit judge normally sits alone, although in a limited number of civil cases there may be a jury.

5.10 To assist litigants who decide to conduct their case in person the court may, if the amount involved does not exceed £1,000 or if the parties agree, refer a case to an arbitrator to hear and decide informally in a Small Claims Court. The arbitrator is usually the district judge but may be another person chosen by the parties. The arbitrator's award is recorded as a county court judgement. This is a cheaper and quicker way of settling small claims in an informal atmosphere, and is often used in consumer cases, motor accident and personal injury claims, employment, tenancy, travel and debt disputes.

5.11 Allocation of cases between the county court and the High Court used to be made purely on the basis of monetary limits. This had the disadvantage that there was not always an appropriate match between the case and the judge presiding over it. In particular some cases which did not really require the relevant resource and expertise were being heard in the High Court.

5.12 The High Court and County Court Jurisdiction Order 1991 makes new arrangements for the distribution of proceedings between the High Court and the county courts. Criteria are laid down for determining where proceedings are to be commenced and tried and where judgements are to be enforced. In particular, actions in respect of *personal injuries* are to be commenced in a county court unless the claim is worth £50,000 or more.

5.13 Actions in contract and tort worth less than £25,000 must normally be tried in a county court and those worth £50,000 or more must normally be tried in the High Court, with those in between going either way, subject to:

(a) the 'financial substance' of the action;
(b) whether questions of public interest are raised;
(c) the complexity of the facts, the legal issues, procedures or remedies involved; and
(d) whether transfer is likely to result in a more speedy trial.

5.14 These criteria may also be used to transfer an action worth less than £25,000 to the High Court or an action worth over £50,000 to the county court.

5.15 From the county court there is a right of appeal direct to the Civil Division of the Court of Appeal.

5.16 The practical importance of the county courts is that they deal with the majority of the country's civil litigation. Over one and a half million actions are commenced each year (about one million are for debt), although only about 5% result in trials since most actions are discontinued or settled out of court before the trial stage is reached.

## Crown Court

5.17 The Crown Court is theoretically a single court forming part of the Supreme Court, but in fact it comprises local courts in large towns (and also the Central Criminal Court (the Old Bailey) in the City of London). It tries all serious criminal (indictable) offences with a jury and hears appeals and deals with committals for sentencing from magistrates' courts. It also deals with a few types of civil cases, being appeals from the magistrates' court on matters of betting, gaming and licensing. From the Crown Court there is a right of appeal on criminal matters to the Criminal Division of the Court of Appeal. An appeal by way of 'case stated' on a point of law may also be made to a Divisional Court of QBD.

5.18  A circuit judge, a recorder or a High Court judge may sit in the Crown Court. Sometimes lay magistrates also sit. Indictable offences, such as murder and treason, may only be heard by a High Court judge in the Crown Court. All indictable offences will be heard by a judge with a jury of 12 persons.

**The High Court**

5.19  The High Court is organised into three divisions – Queen's Bench, Chancery and Family. Except where other special courts have exclusive jurisdiction, the High Court can deal with any civil matter.

5.20  The High Court is staffed by no more than 85 *'puisne'* (pronounced 'puny') judges, who must be barristers of at least ten years' standing. At least two judges must sit in each divisional (appeal) court, but a single judge may hear a case at first instance.

    (a)  QBD has 54 judges and is presided over by the Lord Chief Justice.
    (b)  Chancery has 13 judges and is presided over (nominally) by the Lord Chancellor.
    (c)  Family division has 16 judges and its President presides.

5.21  In hearing a case for the first time *(at first instance)* a High Court judge sits alone. A divisional court of two or more High Court judges sits to hear appeals from magistrates (and from Crown Courts in respect of civil matters tried in those courts). It also exercises the supervisory jurisdiction of the Queen's Bench Division.

*Queen's Bench Division*

5.22  The Queen's Bench Division (QBD) deals mainly with common law matters such as actions based on contract or tort. It includes a separate Admiralty Court (as successor to the Court of Admiralty) to deal with shipping matters such as charterparties, salvage, collisions at sea etc. It is the largest of the three divisions.

5.23  There is also within the Queen's Bench Division an important Commercial Court which specialises in commercial cases, eg insurance claims. The Commercial Court offers a rather simpler trial procedure to meet business needs. Judges of the Commercial Court may also sit as arbitrators.

5.24  A Divisional Court of QBD has a supervisory role over other courts. It may issue a writ of *habeas corpus*, which is an order for the release of a person wrongfully detained, and also prerogative orders against inferior courts, tribunals and other bodies such as local authorities, insofar as they have a duty to exercise a discretion fairly. There are three types of prerogative order.

    (a)  *Mandamus* which requires the court or other body to carry out a public duty. For example, a tribunal may be ordered to hear an appeal which it has wrongly refused to do or a local authority may be ordered to produce its accounts for inspection by a ratepayer.

    (b)  *Prohibition* which prevents a court or tribunal from exceeding its jurisdiction *(before* it has done so).

(c) *Certiorari*, ordering a court or tribunal which has taken action to submit the record of its proceedings to the High Court for review. The High Court may then quash the decision but cannot substitute its own decision (as it can under ordinary appeal procedure). The exact scope of this power of review is not clearly defined. It is exercised when an inferior court has acted illegally, exceeded its jurisdiction or reached its decision contrary to the principles of natural justice - without giving the person concerned the right to know of and reply to the case against him. Essentially, it is a review of what has been done *after* it has been done.

### Chancery Division

5.25 This division deals with traditional equity matters such as:

(a) trusts and mortgages;
(b) revenue matters;
(c) bankruptcy (though outside London this is a county court subject);
(d) disputed wills and administration of estates of deceased persons;
(e) partnership and company matters.

There is a separate Companies Court within the Division which deals with liquidations and other company proceedings.

### Family Division

5.26 This division deals with the same matters of family law, under the same procedures, as the magistrates' and county courts.

## The Restrictive Practices Court

5.27 This is not part of the High Court but is co-ordinate in status with it - appeals from it go to the Court of Appeal. It investigates the merits (if any) of agreements registered under the Restrictive Trade Practices Act 1976 and agreements falling under the Resale Prices Act 1976. In these functions it is required to have regard to EC law. It is also concerned with proceedings to prohibit practices deemed prejudicial to consumers under the Fair Trading Act 1973. Usually a High Court judge and two lay assessors from a panel appointed on the Lord Chancellor's recommendation sit.

## Employment Appeal Tribunal (EAT)

5.28 In spite of its name, this is a court of equal status with the High Court. It hears appeals from industrial tribunals mainly on employment matters (claims for unfair dismissal, redundancy pay, sex discrimination etc). Again, a High Court judge and two lay assessors sit. From the EAT there is a right of appeal to the Court of Appeal.

## The Court of Appeal

5.29 The Civil Division of the Court of Appeal can hear appeals from county courts, the High Court, the Restrictive Practices Court, the Employment Appeal Tribunal and various other special tribunals such as the Lands Tribunal. It does not conduct a complete re-hearing but reviews the record of the evidence in the lower court and the legal arguments put before it. It may uphold or reverse the earlier decision or order a new trial. A majority decision is sufficient, and a judge who disagrees gives an express dissenting judgement.

5.30 The Criminal Division of the Court of Appeal hears appeals from Crown Courts. It may also be invited to review a criminal case by the Home Secretary or to consider a point of law at the request of the Attorney General. Its powers and procedures are very similar to those of the Civil Division.

5.31 There are 28 Lord Justices of Appeal, promoted from the High Court, and three judges normally sit together. In the Criminal Division, the Lord Chief Justice presides. Both he and judges of the High Court may be selected to sit along with the 18 Civil Division judges. In the Civil Division the Master of the Rolls presides, but he may also sit in the Criminal Division. A majority decision is sufficient and dissenting judgements are expressed.

## The Judicial Committee of the House of Lords

5.32 Apart from the limited jurisdiction of the European Court, the Judicial Committee of the House of Lords is the highest court of appeal of the English, Scottish and Northern Irish legal system. It hears appeals from both the civil and the criminal divisions of the Court of Appeal (and in certain circumstances direct from the High Court).

### The Judicial Committee of the Privy Council (JCPC)

5.33 Some countries of the Commonwealth (though not many) still retain a right of appeal from their national court to the Queen's Privy Council. The Judicial Committee (with a slightly different representative membership) is in effect the same body as the corresponding Committee of the House of Lords. It also deals with appeals from the English ecclesiastical courts.

5.34 Judges are usually promoted from the Appeal Court to be members of the House of Lords. They are known as Lords of Appeal in Ordinary, or Law Lords. Five judges normally sit together, though there may only be three. Majority decisions hold and dissenting judgements are made.

## The European Court of Justice

5.35 The court operates under the treaties of the European Communities (European Community, European Coal and Steel Community and European Atomic Energy Community).

5.36 The jurisdiction of the European Court falls under two main heads:

(a) legal matters arising from the acts or omissions of member states, such as failure of a member state to fulfil its treaty obligations;

(b) rulings on legal issues affecting persons which arise from EC law.

5.37 When an issue in category (b) comes before the Judicial Committee of the House of Lords, which is the final court of appeal in the UK, the Judicial Committee is obliged to refer it to the European Court for a ruling. Any lower court may also do so. Any such reference is merely to establish what is the meaning of the relevant part of EC law. Thereafter the English court (duly instructed as to the meaning) must apply the rule to the case before it. This system has already begun to affect the development of English law. Over a period of years it may make a considerable impact.

5.38 13 judges are appointed for six year periods on recommendation of member states from distinguished judges and legal experts. They are assisted by six Advocates-General who submit reasoned argument on the issues before it. The court gives a single judgement and dissenting opinions are not expressed.

**The European Court of Human Rights**

5.39 This Court does not hear cases involving national or EC *law*, however you may have wondered what its jurisdiction is. This Court was set up to ensure that the Convention for the Protection of Human Rights and Fundamental Freedoms is observed by those states which have agreed to be bound by the jurisdiction of the convention. Alleged breaches of the Convention are referred first to the European Commission on Human Rights and may then be examined by the Court, which cannot be approached directly. Breaches of the convention on which the Court has decided have included birching on the Isle of Man and caning of schoolchildren in the UK against the wishes of their parents.

---

## Exercise 1

List the court (or courts) to which an appeal may be made from each of the following:

(a) the county court; and
(b) the High Court (civil cases).

**Solution**

(a) The Court of Appeal (Civil Division) or the High Court (Chancery - for bankruptcy cases); and

(b) the Court of Appeal (Civil Division) or the House of Lords.

---

## 6. THE QUASI-JUDICIAL PROCESS

6.1 We shall now look at those quasi-judicial bodies which have been set up in order to make the law cheaper, more relevant and more accessible.

## Administrative tribunals

6.2 Administrative tribunals are specialised courts established by statute to deal with disputes between government agencies and individuals or between two individuals in a simpler and less formal way than is possible in a court of law. Some of the more important ones are listed below.

(a) *Lands Tribunal:* this tribunal deals with disputes over the value of property, such as compulsory purchase orders. It is usually composed of two members, an experienced lawyer and a qualified valuation expert.

(b) *Rent tribunals:* these assess rents of certain furnished dwellings. County courts assess rents of unfurnished dwellings.

(c) *ACAS:* the Advisory, Conciliation and Arbitration Service has various functions including conciliation in disputes between employer and employee before such disputes go to an industrial tribunal.

(d) *Industrial tribunals:* have membership similar to that of social security tribunals. They deal mainly with claims for compensation for unfair dismissal, redundancy pay, equal pay and sex discrimination. There is a right of appeal to the Employment Appeal Tribunal (EAT).

(e) *Administrative enquiries:* some statutes, eg town and country planning legislation, provides that objectors may put their case at a public enquiry conducted by an *inspector* (a professionally qualified expert) appointed by a minister. The inspector makes a report to the minister who takes the final decision.

6.3 Administrative tribunals are a quicker and less expensive method of resolving a dispute than a court action. But they may make mistakes of law or fail to convince interested parties that a fair and impartial hearing has been given to their case.

6.4 The working of this system of administrative tribunals is supervised by a Council on Tribunals. In many instances, especially industrial tribunals, there is of course a statutory right to appeal from a tribunal to a higher court on points of law. The High Court may also make prerogative orders to prevent or remedy errors and injustices. At the appeal stage (but not usually in the proceedings before the lower tribunal) the applicant may be able to obtain legal aid which is the professional services of legal advisers and advocates provided at public expense.

## Domestic tribunals

6.5 Within some professions, trade associations and trade unions, there are *domestic tribunals* which deal with charges of professional misconduct or breach of membership obligations. Some of these domestic tribunals are established by statute, eg the Solicitors' Disciplinary Tribunal and the disciplinary panel of the General Medical Council. Others are created merely by contract between the members of the relevant body who, on becoming members, agree to submit to a code of rules, including disciplinary procedures. This is the position in, for example, trade unions. If a domestic tribunal is established by law there is often a statutory right of appeal. The High Court may make prerogative orders to remedy misconduct of a domestic tribunal where there is no other relief available.

## Arbitration

6.6   A dispute may be referred to arbitration:

   (a)   by agreement out of court;
   (b)   by statute; or
   (c)   by order of a court.

6.7   It is common practice to include in commercial contracts (and also in partnership agreements) a clause providing that any dispute is to be settled by arbitration under the Arbitration Act 1950 (as amended by the 1975 and 1979 Acts and the Consumer Arbitration Agreements Act 1988). The main advantage of this procedure is privacy since the public and the press have no right to attend a hearing before an arbitrator. It is also possible to appoint as arbitrator an expert in the matter in dispute and to simplify the rules of evidence and procedure to suit the parties. Arbitration is usually quicker and less expensive than an action, say, in the Commercial Court.

6.8   If either party institutes proceedings in a court in breach of the agreement for arbitration, the other party may apply to the court to suspend the proceedings while the arbitration takes its course. The court will usually do so.

6.9   The parties may name their arbitrators or provide that some other person, eg the President of the Law Society shall appoint him. It is usual to appoint only one arbitrator; if two are appointed they jointly appoint a third as umpire. The High Court has power to appoint an arbitrator. Judges of the Commercial Court may accept appointment as arbitrators in commercial matters if their other duties permit.

6.10  Unless otherwise agreed, a hearing before an arbitrator follows the same essential procedure as in a court of law. The appeals system is different however.

   (a)   There is a restricted right of appeal to the High Court from the decision of an arbitrator: there may be an appeal (on a preliminary point of law only) if both parties consent or if the High Court gives leave to appeal (on being satisfied that the rights of the parties could be substantially affected by the result).

   (b)   There is a further restricted right of appeal from the High Court to the Court of Appeal.

   (c)   However, the parties may agree in writing to exclude all right of appeal from the arbitrator's decision so that it becomes final.

   (d)   The right to appeal against an award (that is, the remedy) made in arbitration is restricted, but the arbitrator is required in certain cases to state reasons for his awards.

6.11  The award of an arbitrator may be enforced in the same manner as a judgement of the High Court.

6.12  In addition to voluntary arbitration as described above, compulsory arbitration may be enforced in the following circumstances:

(a) certain statutes provide for arbitration in disputes arising from the provisions of the statute;

(b) the High Court may order that a case of a technical nature shall be tried (or investigated with report back to the court) by an Official Referee or other arbitrator. This procedure is used when prolonged examination of accounts or technical documents is necessary;

(c) a county court may order that a small claim (not exceeding £1,000) shall be referred to arbitration under the Small Claims Court procedure.

6.13 In recent years it has become more common for arbitration clauses to be inserted into standard form contracts between business organisations and *consumers*. This can be to the detriment of the consumer, who has very little ability to negotiate contract terms and who might be able to settle a dispute more cheaply in the small claims court. The Consumer Arbitration Agreements Act 1988 provides that, where an action falls within the jurisdiction of the county court, the arbitration agreement cannot be enforced against a consumer except in certain circumstances, for example where he has given his written consent to submission to arbitration.

---

## Exercise 2

What are the relative merits of arbitration and court proceedings as a means of settling a dispute between a bank and a customer?

**Solution**

The advances of *arbitration* are as follows.

(a) *Parties' own choice*. The parties to a contract may provide for settlement of any disputes to be judged by a third party. Thus they can have their problems solved by a person trusted by both. This person is also likely to be an expert in the issue in question, which may be invaluable in complex cases.

(b) *Privacy*. Arbitration proceedings are usually private affairs, with none of the publicity which surrounds many court proceedings.

(c) *Legal recognition*. Awards by arbitration are enforceable between both parties in the same way as an award by the High Court.

(d) *Right of appeal*. The Act of 1979 restricts the rights of appeal from arbitration; the losing party may not usually apply for reconsideration of the case by the High Court.

Generally, the *court system* is not preferred by businessmen as a forum for resolving commercial disputes for a number of reasons.

(a) *Control*. A judge is allocated to the case - the parties may not make their own choice. They therefore have less control over whether the person is an expert in the matter.

(b) *Privacy*. Court proceedings are generally held in public while arbitration proceedings are in private. Litigation therefore may have harmful effects on the reputation of the bank involved.

(c) *Time*. Whereas arbitration may proceed quickly from picking an arbitrator and venue to resolving the dispute, court proceedings often take a long time.

(d) *Atmosphere*. Because the English court system is adversarial, the atmosphere in a court may be much more hostile than in arbitration. Such an atmosphere may militate against compromises being made.

Against these disadvantages the court system does have some things in its favour. It may be cheaper than an arbitration case, where the arbitrator's remuneration must be paid and all the venue costs met. More importantly the rights to appeal from a court decision are more entrenched, the judge's interlocutory powers are greater and a judge may grant interim relief or even make a summary judgement.

---

## 7. THE BANKING OMBUDSMAN

7.1 A bank is inevitably not always going to agree with its customers. This may lead to a dispute, which can normally be resolved by the bank and the customer amicably. Disputes usually relate to either the bank or customer misplacing an item or not acting in a certain manner as the other party would have expected. If the bank and the customer cannot resolve these problems amicably then the matter can be referred to the judicial process, which is not only time-consuming but costly and may cause the bank bad publicity. To avoid the necessity of a dispute being referred to the courts, the non-statutory office of the Banking Ombudsman was set up voluntarily in January 1986, sponsored by twenty member banks which agree to be bound by his decisions.

7.2 The role of the Banking Ombudsman is as an independent neutral arbitrator. This independence is guaranteed by the fact that the office is an institution which continues despite changes in its incumbent. It has three branches.

(a) The scheme is funded by the banks, and the *Board of the Ombudsman's office* collects levies due from the banks and approves the Ombudsman's election.

(b) The *Ombudsman Council* - this is made up of three banking people and five lay assessors. Its aim is to keep the Ombudsman impartial, by acting as a buffer between the latter and the Board, and channelling his findings and his annual report to the banking and consumer worlds. It appoints the Ombudsman.

(c) The *Ombudsman* - he is a neutral arbitrator in disputes between banks and customers (strictly any person who has received banking services). He has a deputy, three senior and two junior legal officers and a seconded banking adviser.

7.3 Personal customers, that is individuals as defined within the Consumer Credit Act 1974 (individuals, sole traders, partnerships, clubs, trade unions and charities) may take to him any dispute they have with their bank, provided they have tried to resolve the matter at branch and Head Office level and the dispute involves less than £100,000. Referral to the Banking Ombudsman is thus the last resort before full-blown legal proceedings are begun. Usually he will not investigate if these have already commenced.

7.4   As a rough guide, the Ombudsman will deal with complaints about all types of banking business, including credit cards and some bank executor, trustee, insurance and taxation services. Estate and travel agency services are not within his brief.

7.5   Particularly with respect to cash card transactions, the Ombudsman can only decide a case where the terms and conditions attached to the card allow. His power is further restricted by the fact that all complaints regarding banks' investment services must now be referred to the Securities and Investment Board or other self-regulatory organisation (SRO).

7.6   By reference to what is 'fair in all the circumstances' the Ombudsman will make an award only where the bank is considered to be in breach of its duty (including maladministration) and this breach is the source of the complaint causing loss, damage or inconvenience.

7.7   The most important limitations on the Ombudsman's powers are that:

(a)   he has no jurisdiction in claims involving a bank's commercial judgement or lending policy decisions; and

(b)   company customers are excluded from the Ombudsman scheme.

7.8   But a way in which the scheme is less limited than the judicial process is that, because the Ombudsman can make awards for 'inconvenience' as well as loss or damage, his power to award compensation is more extensive than that of the courts.

7.9   The Banking Ombudsman can order the bank to take whatever action is necessary to rectify the dispute and can award up to £100,000 to the complainant. The banks have to abide by the decision of the Ombudsman and this enhances the value of their contributions to this scheme. It improves customers' confidence, as they know that if they have a valid dispute or mistake they do not have to resort to the expensive procedures of pursuing the claim via the courts.

7.10  Presently it seems as if the Banking Ombudsman is inundated with complaints - and that is just from non-corporate customers (which leaves out a lot of small businesses). Purported 'phantom' withdrawals from ATMs and bank charges about which the customer purports to know nothing are the main causes of complaint. The Code includes a section on handling customers' complaints. It is usually only after the bank's internal procedures have been exhausted that a customer will approach the office of the Banking Ombudsman. It is laid down in the Code that:

'each bank and building society will have its own internal procedures for the proper handling of customers' complaints (s 1).

Banks and building societies will tell their customers that they have a complaints procedure. Customers who wish to make a complaint will be told how to do so and what further steps are available if they believe that the complaint has not been dealt with satisfactorily either at branch or more senior level within the bank or building society (s 2)'.

7.11 The Ombudsman's healthy independence from the banks was amply demonstrated during the preparation of the Code of Banking Practice. His views were summarised in the July 1991 edition of *Banking World*, where his Ernest Sykes Memorial lecture was reported. In that lecture, he criticised the draft Code of Banking Practice produced in December 1990 as 'deficient', in particular because:

(a) it contained no overriding statement of the principle that banks should act fairly;

(b) the terms and conditions prevailing between bank and customer were not required to be fully spelled out;

(c) it made no changes to the way banks can make charges;

(d) it did not go far enough to protect customer confidentiality. He was especially critical of the way in which bankers' references are handled.

7.12 Largely as a result of this criticism, certain aspects of the Code were subjected to substantial revision before its publication.

7.13 The Code of Banking Practice in its final form contains a summary of governing principles. The governing principles of the Code are:

'(a) to set out the standards of good banking practice which banks, building societies and card issuers will follow in their dealings with their customers;

(b) that banks, building societies and card issuers will act fairly and reasonably in all their dealings with their customers;

(c) that banks, building societies and card issuers will help customers to understand how their accounts operate and will seek to give them a good understanding of banking services;

(d) to maintain confidence in the security and integrity of banking and card payment systems. Banks, building societies and card issuers recognise that their systems and technology need to be reliable to protect their customers and themselves.'

7.14 Other changes made following criticism by the Ombudsman, Laurence Shurman, included:

(a) an extension of the £50 limitation of liability, previously applicable only to credit cards, to cashcards and debit cards. This move is particularly relevant in cases of 'phantom withdrawals' from ATMs;

(b) moves towards the publication of tariffs by banks; and

(c) restrictions on the use of customer details for marketing purposes.

7.15 It should be noted that the code is a voluntary code. It is not a statement of the *law*, but a code of minimum standards of good bank *practice*. Thus for example the extension of the £50 limitation of liability is open to voluntary adoption by individual banks, although the Government is expected to make amendments to the Consumer Credit Act 1974 in due course. Even though the Code does not have statutory effect, it is expected that it will be used by the Banking Ombudsman and by the courts for guidance in reaching decisions.

7.16 The Code is examined in greater detail in Part C of this text. The full text of the Code is included in Appendix 1.

## 8. LEGAL AID

8.1 The grant of legal aid in both civil and criminal matters is governed by the Legal Aid Act 1988 and the regulations passed under it and under earlier legislation. The scheme is administered by the Legal Aid Board.

8.2 In *criminal cases*, application for aid is made to the court of trial. The applicant must submit a written statement as to his means and the court must be satisfied that it is desirable *in the interests of justice* for legal aid to be given, and that the applicant's *means* are such that he needs assistance to meet the costs of the case. When assessing the 'interests of justice' the clerk of the court will consider whether there is a serious risk that the accused will lose his liberty, job or reputation. If there is such a risk, legal aid is more likely to be granted.

Nevertheless, there is concern that these criteria are not being applied consistently. In some areas, only 4% - 5% of applications to magistrates' court are refused. In other areas nearly 40% of applications are rejected.

8.3 In *civil proceedings*, legal aid is only available to persons of very limited means. A person must satisfy a means test both on 'disposable income' and 'disposable capital'. He must also satisfy a 'merits test' - has he a good arguable case with which, if he were paying his own costs, a solicitor would advise him to proceed? Two types of help are available:

(a) *legal advice and assistance*. Under this scheme solicitors can undertake work falling short of court appearances. There is a relatively low limit on the value of this work, but it may be extended with the consent of the local area office of the Legal Aid Board;

(b) *legal aid*. This is available for nearly all civil court hearings (except defamation). It is administered by local Legal Aid Board offices. Depending upon his financial position, the applicant for legal aid may receive legal services free of charge or he may be required to make some financial contribution to the total cost.

## 9. CONCLUSION

9.1 The main differences between categories of legal issues are that:

(a) the purpose of criminal proceedings is to establish whether the defendant is guilty of the offence charged and if so, to impose on him a suitable punishment;

(b) to recover damages for breach of contract, it must be shown that there was a contract and that the defendant broke it; and

(c) to recover damages for tort, it must be shown that the defendant's act or omission infringed a legal right of the plaintiff which he possessed by general principles of law.

9.2 There is a lot of detail to be learnt about the structure of the courts: The 'functional aspects' defined at the beginning of the chapter may assist you to see the structure as a whole before grappling with the detail. The quasi-judicial processes of tribunals and arbitration and the Banking Ombudsman Scheme (which is one of many such schemes in operation) are very important and must be clearly understood.

9.3 You should grasp the following main practical aspects.

(a) What type of case each court deals with - its 'jurisdiction'.

(b) In which court a litigant with a particular cause of action would commence his proceedings to obtain a remedy. Remember that, generally speaking, the victim of a crime has no control over any subsequent legal proceedings (criminal prosecution). The State, through the police and the Crown Prosecution Service, has the duty of prosecuting persons charged with criminal offences; private prosecutions when permitted at all are relatively infrequent - partly because of the expense.

(c) If either party is dissatisfied with the decision given by the court which tries his case, he usually has a right of appeal to a higher court. Note that appeals from county and Crown Courts are usually direct to the civil or criminal side of the Court of Appeal respectively and not to the High Court.

(d) Arbitration on major disputes, where the amount at issue is large, is generally compulsory where there is an agreement to this effect in the contract. But on small matters it is much more common as an alternative to formal civil proceedings in court. One of the practical considerations in favour of arbitration is that the hearing before an arbitrator is private. This can be valuable if either party anticipates that publicity, for example in a case alleging a banker is professionally incompetent, could be damaging to him even if the case against him is dismissed.

9.4 It is important to be able to draw out the principal features of both the judicial and non-judicial processes, so that they may be compared.

9.5 The Banking Ombudsman's role is as an independent neutral arbitrator in disputes between banks and personal customers which have exhausted internal procedures for resolution. There are frequently articles in *Banking World* about the Ombudsman which you would do well to read.

**TEST YOUR KNOWLEDGE**

*The numbers in brackets refer to paragraphs of this chapter*

1   Why would a bank attempt to resolve conflicts in court? (1.2 - 1.4)

2   What is the standard of proof of:

   (a)   criminal; and
   (b)   civil proceedings? (2.1)

3   In what circumstances does a person who has behaved in an unlawful fashion:

   (a)   pay a fine; or
   (b)   pay compensation (damages)? (2.3, 2.4)

4   Explain the basis of liability in an action:

   (a)   in contract; and
   (b)   in tort. (3.3, 3.6)

5   Give examples of the kind of case tried:

   (a)   in a magistrates' court;
   (b)   in a county court; and
   (c)   in a Crown Court. (5.2, 5.8, 5.17)

6   What is the jurisdiction of the Queen's Bench Division of the High Court? (5.22)

7   Give examples of an administrative tribunal. (6.2)

8   How is the Banking Ombudsman's independence ensured? (7.2)

9   If the Ombudsman finds errors, what may he order the bank at fault to do? (7.9)

*Now try questions 4 to 6 at the end of the text*

# PART B
## BASIC CONTRACT LAW

*Chapter 3*

# THE BASICS OF CONTRACT LAW

---

**This chapter covers the following topics.**

1. Role of contract law
2. The essentials of a contract
3. Offer
4. Acceptance
5. Consideration
6. Privity of contract
7. Intention to create legal relations
8. Contract terms
9. Form of the contract

---

## 1. ROLE OF CONTRACT LAW

1.1 *A contract is an agreement which legally binds the parties.* Sometimes contracts are referred to as *enforceable agreements.* This is rather misleading since one party cannot usually *force* the other to fulfil his part of the bargain; he will usually be restricted to the remedy of damages.

1.2 The role of contract law is to provide a legal framework of rules against which individuals, companies and partnerships can conduct their businesses. The existence of such rules allow parties to a contract to deal with each other fairly informally and yet to know that what they do is legally binding. Contract law *enables* business to be conducted while *regulating* the way in which this is done.

1.3 The principle underlying contract law is that of freedom of contract: within the enabling and regulating framework of rules the parties should be allowed to reach what agreements they please. However, this principle is greatly modified in a number of ways:

   (a) Mass production and nationalisation have led to the standard form contract. The individual must usually take it or leave it - he does not really 'agree' to it. For example, a customer usually accepts the running of his account on the bank's mandate's terms - which he may well not have read or understood.

   (b) Public policy sometimes requires that freedom of contract should be modified. For example, the Consumer Credit Act 1974 and the Unfair Contract Terms Act 1977 both regulate the extent to which contracts can contain certain terms.

(c) The law will sometimes imply terms into contracts because the parties are expected to observe certain standards of behaviour. A person is bound by those terms even though he has never agreed to them, or never even thought of them; for example, sections 12-15 of the Sale of Goods Act 1979 imply terms as to title, fitness and quality of goods into all contracts for the sale of goods.

1.4 A bank, just like any other legal person, is affected by the rules of contract law in the way in which it conducts its business. We shall see just how it may be affected throughout this part of the text.

---

## Exercise 1

Think of as many examples as you can of contracts which a bank enters into.

**Solution**

A bank enters into many different types of contract. Examples might include:

(a) contract with a customer for the operation of a current account;
(b) contract to buy or sell the bank's own property;
(c) contracts with the bank's employees;
(d) contracts with customers for specific services; and
(e) contracts with suppliers.

---

## 2. THE ESSENTIALS OF A CONTRACT

2.1 The essential elements of a contract are that:

(a) it is an agreement made by *offer and acceptance;*

(b) it is a bargain by which the obligations assumed by each party are supported by *consideration* (value) given by the other. (But a gratuitous promise is binding if made by deed); and

(c) the parties *intend to create legal relations* between themselves.

2.2 The validity of a contract may also be affected by any of the following factors.

(a) *Content* - in general the parties may enter into a contract on whatever terms they choose. But it can only be enforced if it is sufficiently complete and precise in its terms. Some terms which the parties do not express may be implied and some express terms are overridden by statutory rules.

(b) *Form* - some contracts (not all) must be made in a particular form or supported by written evidence.

(c) *Genuine consent* - mistake, misrepresentation, duress or undue influence may affect the validity of a contract.

(d) *Legality* – the courts will not enforce a contract which is deemed to be illegal or contrary to public policy.

(e) *Capacity* – some persons have only restricted capacity to enter into contracts and are not bound by agreements made outside those limits.

2.3 A contract which does not satisfy the relevant tests may be either void, voidable or unenforceable.

(a) A *void* contract is not a contract at all. The parties are not bound by it and if they transfer property under it they can sometimes (unless it is also an illegal contract) recover their goods, even from a third party.

(b) A *voidable* contract is a contract which one party may avoid, that is terminate at his option. Property transferred before avoidance is usually irrecoverable from a third party.

(c) An *unenforceable* contract is a valid contract and property transferred under it cannot be recovered even from the other party to the contract. But if either party refuses to perform or to complete his part of the performance of the contract, the other party cannot compel him to do so. A contract is usually unenforceable when the required evidence of its terms, for example, written evidence of a contract relating to land, is not available.

2.4 You may find it easier to grasp these general principles after you have studied their application in particular areas of the law of contract.

## 3. OFFER

3.1 The particular significance of offer and acceptance is that they represent the agreement of the parties to the terms of the contract:

(a) new terms cannot thereafter be introduced into the contract unless both parties agree; and

(b) the terms of the contract appear from the offer and acceptance rather than from the unexpressed intentions of the parties.

3.2 An offer must be distinguished from:

(a) the mere supply of information;
(b) an invitation to make an offer (an *invitation to treat*); or
(c) an invitation to the other party to enter into negotiations.

Only an offer in the proper sense (made with the intention that it shall become binding when accepted) may be accepted so as to form a binding contract.

*Supply of information*

3.3 A statement of the price of goods or of a service in response to an enquiry is a supply of information.

*Case: Harvey v Facey 1893*
A telegraphed to B 'Will you sell us Bumper Hall Pen? Telegraph lowest cash price.' B replied 'Lowest price for Bumper Hall Pen £900.' A telegraphed to accept what he regarded as an offer; B made no further reply.

*Held*: B's telegram was merely a statement of his price if a sale were to be agreed. It was not an offer which A could accept. No contract had been made.

3.4 But if, in the course of negotiations for a sale, the vendor states the price at which he will sell, that statement may be an offer which can be accepted.

*Case: Bigg v Boyd Gibbons 1971*
X in the course of correspondence rejected an offer of £20,000 by Y and added 'for a quick sale I would accept £26,000 .... if you are not interested in this price would you please let me know immediately' (so that X might open negotiations with another potential purchaser). Y accepted the offer of £26,000 and X acknowledged his acceptance stating that he had given instructions for the sale to his solicitor.

*Held*: in this context X must be treated as making an offer (at £26,000) which Y had accepted.

*Invitation to treat*

3.5 To display goods in a shop window or on the open shelves of a self-service shop (with a price tag), or to advertise goods for sale is to invite customers to make offers to purchase, or an 'invitation to treat'. It is not an offer to sell.

*Case: Fisher v Bell 1961*
A shopkeeper was prosecuted for offering for sale an offensive weapon by exhibiting a flick knife in his shop window.

*Held*: 'the display of an article with a price on it in a shop window is merely an invitation to treat. It is in no sense an offer for sale.'

3.6 The use or absence of the word 'offer' is not conclusive. For example, a company is said to make an 'offer' of its shares when it publishes a prospectus (Companies Act 1985 s 744) but this is in fact an invitation to the public to make offers. The company has only a limited number of shares available and cannot intend to allot whatever number the public may apply for. In addition it has already been shown that an offer may be made although it is expressed as a willingness to accept (as in *Bigg v Boyd Gibbons*). It may therefore be difficult to distinguish between an offer and an invitation to treat since the distinction depends on the criterion of intention.

*Vague terms*

3.7 An offer is a definite promise to be bound on specific terms. It cannot be vague.

*Case: Gunthing v Lynn 1831*
The offeror offered to pay a further sum for a horse if it was 'lucky'.

*Held*: the offer was too vague.

However, if an apparently vague offer can be made certain by reference to the parties' previous dealing or the customs of the trade, then it will be regarded as certain. Contract terms are considered further later in this chapter.

3.8 An offer may only be accepted by a person to whom the offer has been made. But it is possible to make an offer (which may be in any form) to the members of a group or even to the public at large for acceptance by those persons who wish to do so.

*Case: Carlill v Carbolic Smokeball Co 1893*
The manufacturers of a patent medicine published an advertisement by which they undertook to pay '£100 reward .... to any person who contracts ... influenza, colds, .... after having used the smoke ball three times daily for two weeks.' The advertisement added that £1,000 had been deposited at a bank 'showing our sincerity in this matter.' C read the advertisement, bought the smoke ball at a chemist's shop, used it as directed for eight weeks and while doing so contracted influenza; she then claimed her £100 reward. In their defence the manufacturers argued that:

(a) the offer was so vague that it could not form the basis of a contract; it specified no period of immunity after use;

(b) it was mere sales promotion, or 'puff', not intended to create legal relations;

(c) it was not an offer to make a contract which could be accepted since it was offered to the whole world;

(d) C had not supplied any consideration; and

(e) C had not communicated to them her acceptance of their offer.

*Held*: it was an offer to the whole world which C could accept and had accepted. Points (b), (d) and (e) are explained in their context later. Point (a) did not succeed since the court found that the terms of the offer were sufficiently clear - they were not vague.

## Termination of offer

3.9 An offer may only be accepted (so as to make a contract) while it is still open. An offer is terminated (and can no longer be accepted) in any of the following circumstances:

(a) if it has expired by lapse of time;
(b) if the offeror has revoked it;
(c) if the offeree has rejected it;
(d) if the offeree dies or (usually) if the offeror dies.

*Lapse of time*

3.10 An offer may be expressed to last for a *specified time*. It then expires at the end of that time. If however, there is no express time limit it expires after a *reasonable time*. What is reasonable depends on the circumstances of the case, on what is usual and to be expected.

*Case: Ramsgate Victoria Hotel Co v Montefiore 1866*
M applied to the company for shares and paid a deposit to the company's bank. Five months later the company sent him an acceptance by issue of a letter of allotment. M contended that his offer had expired and could no longer be accepted.

*Held*: M's offer was for a reasonable time only and five months was much more than that. The offer had lapsed.

*Revocation*

3.11 The offeror may *revoke* his offer at any time before acceptance. If he undertakes that his offer shall remain open for acceptance for a specified time he may nonetheless revoke it within that time, unless by a separate contract (an option agreement) he has bound himself to keep it open for the whole of the specified time.

*Case: Routledge v Grant 1828*
G offered to buy R's house, requiring acceptance within six weeks. Within the six weeks G withdrew his offer.

*Held*: as there was no option agreement (for which consideration must be given), G could revoke his offer at any time.

3.12 Revocation may be an express statement to that effect or be an act of the offeror indicating that he no longer regards the offer as in force. But however he revokes it, his revocation does not take effect (and the offer continues to be available for acceptance) until the revocation is *communicated* to the offeree, either by the offeror or by any third party who is a sufficiently reliable informant.

*Case: Byrne v Van Tienhoven 1880*
The offeror was in Cardiff: the offeree in New York. The sequence of events was:

1 October      Letter of offer posted in Cardiff.

8 October      Letter of revocation posted in Cardiff.

11 October     Letter of offer received in New York and telegram of acceptance sent; this was confirmed by letter posted on 15 October.

20 October     Letter of revocation received in New York. The offeree had meanwhile re-sold the contract goods.

*Held*: the letter of revocation could not take effect until received (20 October); it could not revoke the contract made by acceptance of the offer on 11 October. Simply posting a letter does not revoke the offer until it is received.

*Case: Dickinson v Dodds 1876*
A, on 10 June, wrote to B to offer property for sale at £800, adding 'This offer to be left open until Friday 12 June, 9.00 am.' On Thursday 11 June B delivered a letter of acceptance to an address at which A was no longer residing so that A did not receive it. A later sold the property to another buyer. C, who had been an intermediary between A and B, informed B that A had sold to someone else. On Friday 12 June, before 9.00 am, C delivered to A a duplicate of B's letter of acceptance.

*Held*: A was free to revoke his offer and had done so by sale to a third party; B could not accept the offer after he had learnt from a reliable informant (C) of A's revocation of the offer to B.

*Rejection*

3.13 An offer may be *rejected* outright or by a *counter-offer* made by the offeree. Either form of rejection terminates the original offer. If a counter offer is made, the original offeror may accept it, but if he rejects it his original offer is no longer available for acceptance.

*Case: Hyde v Wrench 1840*
W offered to sell property to H for £1,000. H made a counter offer of £950 which W rejected three weeks later. H then informed W that he (H) accepted the original offer of £1,000.

*Held:* the original offer of £1,000 had been terminated by the counter offer of £950; it could not therefore be accepted.

3.14 Many banks produce leaflets which explain their services and state the price at which they are available; for instance, a bank may advertise loans to personal customers of up to £3,000 at an APR of only 20.6% etc. This is construed legally as an invitation to treat, and it is not open to any person to walk in off the street and say 'yes, I accept your offer of a loan' so as to oblige the bank to make it. To make certain of the point, however, the bank should include a notice such as 'subject to status' to make it clear that the bank is entitled to review the creditworthiness of any customer before making an offer on the terms outlined in the leaflet.

## 4. ACCEPTANCE

4.1 Acceptance may be by express words or by action (as in *Carlill's* case). It may also be implied from conduct.

*Case: Brogden v Metropolitan Railway Co 1877*
For many years B supplied coal to M. He suggested that they should enter into a written agreement and M's agent sent a draft to him for consideration. B made some alterations and additions and returned the amended draft to M's agent indicating that he (B) approved it. M's agent took no further action on it. B continued to supply coal to M and the parties applied to their dealings the special terms of the draft agreement. But they never signed a fair copy of it. B later denied that there was any agreement between him and M.

*Held*: the draft agreement became the contract between the parties as soon as M ordered and B supplied coal after the return by B of the draft to M's agent.

4.2 But there must be some act on the part of the offeree to indicate his acceptance. Mere passive inaction is not acceptance.

*Case: Felthouse v Bindley 1862*
After previous negotiations had produced an agreed price P wrote to J offering to buy a horse for £30.15s [£30.75], adding 'If I hear no more about him, I consider the horse mine at that price'. J intended to accept but did not reply and owing to a misunderstanding the horse was sold at auction to someone else. P sued the auctioneer for conversion, ie misappropriation, of P's property.

*Held:* there could be no acceptance by silence in these circumstances – the offeror cannot impose acceptance merely because the offeree does not reject the offer.

4.3 Acceptance must be unqualified agreement to the terms of the offer. Acceptance which introduces any new terms is a counter-offer, and therefore a rejection.

*Case: Neale v Merrett 1930*
A offered to sell land for £280 to B. B replied accepting the offer, enclosing £80 and undertaking to pay the balance of £200 by monthly instalments of £50.

*Held:* there had been no acceptance. The normal terms are that the entire price is payable as a single sum at completion. A proposal for deferred payment is a variation of the terms implicit in the offer.

**Acceptance 'subject to contract'**

4.4 It is possible, however, to respond to an offer without accepting or rejecting it by a request for information or by acceptance 'subject to contract'.

*Case: Stevenson v McLean 1880*
M offered to sell iron at £2 per ton. S enquired whether M would agree to a contract by which delivery would be spread over two months. M did not reply and (within the time limit fixed by M in his offer), S then accepted the offer as made originally.

*Held:* there was a contract since S had merely enquired as to a variation of terms which was not a rejection.

4.5 Acceptance 'subject to contract' is neither acceptance nor rejection by counter-offer. It means that the offeree is agreeable to the terms of the offer but proposes that the parties should negotiate a formal (usually written) contract on the basis of the offer. Neither party is bound until the formal contract is signed (hence in a house property sale the vendor is free to 'gazump' by selling to another buyer).

4.6 Acceptance 'subject to contract' must be distinguished from outright and immediate acceptance on the understanding that the parties wish to replace the preliminary contract later with another more elaborate one. Even if the immediate contract is described as 'provisional', it takes effect at once.

*Case: Branca v Cobarro 1947*
A vendor agreed to sell a mushroom farm under a contract which ended 'this is a provisional agreement until a fully legalised agreement drawn up by a solicitor and embodying all the conditions herewith stated is signed.'

*Held:* the parties were bound by their provisional contract until, by mutual agreement, they made another to replace it.

**Communication of acceptance**

4.7 The general rule is that *acceptance must be communicated to the offeror and is not effective until this has been done.* Note that the offeree's first letter of acceptance in *Dickinson v Dodds* was ineffective because the offeror did not receive it.

*Case: Entores v Miles Far Eastern Corporation 1955*
The legal issue was whether a contract had been made in London (within the jurisdiction of the English court) or abroad (outside it). The offeror sent off an offer by telex to the offeree's agent in Amsterdam and the latter sent an acceptance by telex.

*Held:* the acceptance took effect (and the contract was made) when the telex message was printed out on the offeror's terminal in London.

4.8 But the offeror may by his offer dispense with communication of acceptance. For example, the offer to Mrs Carlill merely required that she should buy and use the smokeball. This was sufficient acceptance although not reported to the manufacturer (*Carlill's* case, point (e)).

*Acceptance by specified means*

4.9 The offeror may call for acceptance by specified means. Unless he stipulates that this is the only method of acceptance which suffices, the offeree may accept by some other means (if it is equally advantageous to the offeror).

*Case: Yates Building Co v R J Pulleyn & Sons (York) 1975*
The offer called for acceptance by registered or recorded delivery letter. The offeree sent an ordinary letter which arrived without delay.

*Held:* the offeror had suffered no disadvantage and had not stipulated that acceptance must be made in this way only. The acceptance was valid.

4.10 Where no specific method of communication of acceptance is requested by the offeror, the method chosen will be judged in relation to the particular circumstances of the case. Thus an offer by telex might reasonably be deemed to imply that acceptance must similarly be indicated by telex.

*Use of the post*

4.11 The offeror may expressly or by implication indicate that he expects acceptance by letter sent through the post. The acceptance is then complete and effective as soon as a letter (if it is correctly addressed and stamped and actually put in the post) is posted, even though it may be delayed or even lost altogether in the post.

*Case: Adams v Lindsell 1818*
L made an offer by letter to A requiring an answer 'in course of post'. The letter of offer was misdirected and somewhat delayed in the post. A posted a letter of acceptance immediately. But L assumed that the absence of a reply within the expected period indicated non-acceptance and sold the goods to another buyer.

*Held:* the acceptance was made 'in course of post' (no time limit was imposed) and effective when posted.

4.12 The intention to use the post for communication of acceptance may be deduced from the circumstances – for example, if the offer is made by post – without express statement to that effect.

*Case: Household Fire and Carriage Accident Insurance Co v Grant 1879*
G handed a letter of application for shares to the company's agent in Swansea with the intention that it should be posted (as it was) to the company in London. The company posted an acceptance (letter of allotment) which was lost in the post.

*Held:* the parties intended to use the Post Office as their common agent and delivery of the letters of allotment to the Post Office was acceptance of G's offer.

4.13 The offeror may be unaware that a contract has been made by acceptance of his offer. If that possibility is clearly inconsistent with the nature of the transaction (and of course if the offeror so stipulates), the rule (complete acceptance by posting) is excluded and the letter of acceptance takes effect only when received.

*Case: Holwell Securities v Hughes 1974*
Hughes granted to HS an option to purchase land to be exercised 'by notice in writing'. A letter giving notice of the exercise of the option was lost in the post.

*Held:* the words 'notice in writing' must mean notice received by the vendor; hence notice had not been given to accept the offer (ie the option).

4.14 Unlike revocation of an offer, which can be communicated to the offeree by any reliable person (as in *Dickinson v Dodds*), acceptance of an offer may only be made by a person authorised to do so.

*Case: Powell v Lee 1908*
P applied for a job and after a series of interviews the management decided to give it to him; however, no decision was made as to how the appointment was to be communicated. Without authorisation, P was informed of the appointment. Later, it was decided to give the post to someone else. P sued for breach of contract.

*Held:* since communication of acceptance was unauthorised, there was no valid agreement and hence no contract.

---

## Exercise 2

In *Brinkibon v Stahag Stahl 1982* an offer was made by telex to Vienna. It was accepted by a telex message from London to Vienna. Where do you think the contract was made?

**Solution**

Following the decision in the *Entores* case, the contract was held to have been made in Vienna. Acceptance was only effective when communicated to the offeror.

---

---

### Exercise 3

Services available to potential customers are widely advertised by banks. Customers may approach banks to open current accounts in response to these advertisements. Identify the offer and the acceptance in the process of opening an account for a new customer.

**Solution**

The would-be customer makes an offer to the bank by completing a standard application form. The bank may then accept or reject the offer by opening an account for the customer or by rejecting the application.

---

## 5. CONSIDERATION

5.1 We saw earlier that the second essential element of a valid contract is the bargain. A promise given in a contract is only binding on the person who makes it (the promisor) if:

(a) it is supported by consideration; or
(b) the promise is in the form of a deed.

5.2 The requirement of consideration for a promise made in a simple contract (one not made by deed) has a long history which has encrusted this artificial doctrine with many technicalities.

Basically, in distinguishing the characteristics of a contract the law looks for an element of *bargain* - a contractual promise is one which is not purely gratuitous. Consideration is what the promisee must give in exchange for the promise to him (or alternatively in a contract made by deed, the promisor binds himself by a document of maximum formality).

5.3 *Dunlop v Selfridge 1915* defined consideration as 'an act or forbearance of one party, or the promise thereof, is the price for which the promise of the other is bought, and the promise thus given for value is enforceable'.

5.4 There are two broad types of valid consideration - executed and executory. If consideration is 'past' then it is *not* enforceable.

(a) *Executed* consideration is an act in return for a promise. If, for example, A offers a reward for the return of lost property, his promise becomes binding when B performs the act of returning A's property to him. A is not bound to pay anything to anyone until the prescribed act is done. C's act in *Carlill's* case in response to the smokeball company's promise of reward was thus executed consideration.

(b) *Executory* consideration is a promise given for a promise. If, for example, a customer orders goods which a shopkeeper undertakes to obtain from the manufacturer, the shopkeeper promises to supply the goods and the customer promises to accept and pay for them. Neither has yet done anything but each has given a promise to obtain the promise of the other. It would be breach of contract if either withdrew without the consent of the other.

(c) *Past* consideration is anything which has already been done *before* a promise in return is given. As a general rule it is not sufficient to make the promise binding. In such a case the promisor may by his promise recognise a moral obligation (which is not consideration), but he is not obtaining anything in exchange for his promise (as he already has it before the promise is made).

*Case: Re McArdle 1951*
Under a will the testator's children were entitled to a house at their mother's death. In the mother's lifetime one of the children and his wife lived in the house with the mother. The wife made improvements to the house. The children later agreed in writing to repay to the wife the sum of £488 which she spent on improvements. But at the mother's death they refused to do so.

*Held:* at the time of the promise the improvements were past consideration and so the promise was not binding.

5.5 In three cases past consideration for a promise does suffice to make the promise binding.

(a) A statutory exception to past consideration exists in the Bills of Exchange Act 1882 s 27. This states that in relation to bills of exchange any previous or existing liability is valuable consideration. The consideration given for a promise contained in a bill of exchange or cheque is in the past, and therefore it precedes the promise. This exception is necessary in order for cheques and bills of exchange to perform their function as a method of payment.

(b) After six (or in some cases twelve) years the right to sue for recovery of a debt becomes statute-barred by the Limitation Act 1980. If, after that period, the debtor makes written acknowledgement of the creditor's claim, it is again enforceable at law. The debt, although past consideration, suffices.

(c) When a request is made for a service this request may imply a promise to pay for it. If, after the service has been rendered, the person who made the request promises a specific reward, this is treated as fixing the amount to be paid under the previous implied promise rather than as a new promise.

*Case: Re Casey's Patents. Stewart v Casey 1892*
A and B, joint owners of patent rights, asked their employee, C, as an extra task (additional to his normal duties) to find licensees to work the patents. After C had done so A and B agreed to reward C for his past services with one third of the patent rights. A died and his executors denied that the promise made was binding.

*Held:* the promise to C was binding since it merely fixed the 'reasonable remuneration' which A and B by implication promised to pay before the service was given.

## Adequacy and sufficiency of consideration

5.6 As well as determining whether consideration is valid on the grounds of being executed or executory, the court will also seek to ensure that consideration:

(a) has some value, thought it need not be adequate; and
(b) is sufficient - it must be capable in law of being regarded as consideration.

Consideration must also be legal. A promise to pay a reward for a criminal act would be unenforceable if the crime had been committed.

5.7 Consideration is sufficient if it has some identifiable value. The value may however be nominal, eg 50p in consideration of a promise worth £1 million, or it may be very subjective. The law only requires an element of bargain, not that it shall be a *good* bargain.

*Case: Chappell & Co v Nestle Co 1959*
As a sales promotion scheme, N offered to supply a record to anyone who sent in a postal order for 1s 6d [7½p] and three wrappers from 6d [2½p] bars of chocolate made by N. C owned the copyright of the popular tune to the record. In a dispute over royalties the issue was whether the wrappers, which were thrown away when received, were part of the consideration for the promise to supply the record (which N obtained in bulk for less than 4d each from the recording company).

*Held:* N had required that wrappers be sent (for obvious commercial reasons). It was immaterial that the wrappers when received were of no economic value to N. The wrappers were adequate consideration as they had commercial value.

5.8 As stated earlier, forbearance or the promise of it may be sufficient consideration if it has some value or amounts to giving up something of value. A promise not to pursue a genuine but disputed claim may be consideration. Even forbearance without any promise to forbear may suffice.

*Case: Alliance Bank v Broom 1864*
A customer who had an overdraft at his bank promised to provide security. The bank did not enforce immediate repayment of the overdraft. The customer failed to provide the agreed security and the bank sued on the promise.

*Held:* the bank's forbearance in not enforcing its rights was consideration for the customer's promise; the promise was enforceable.

5.9 But a promise not to perform an act which the promisor had no intention of performing anyway does not suffice as consideration: *Arrale v Costain Engineering 1976*. Waiver of a claim which is known to be hopeless is not consideration since nothing of value is given up; neither is abstaining from pressing a purely moral claim.

*Case: White v Bluett 1853*
In a dispute with his father's executors W said that he had given consideration to his father for a promise of benefits under his will by promising not to complain continually that his father had disinherited him.

*Held:* no consideration had been given for the promise W said he had obtained from his father.

5.10 A person who gratuitously promises to do something does not receive consideration and so no contractual liability arises if the act is performed defectively. However, there may be a claim in tort or, if there is a contract of bailment, a claim under that. Bailment arises where one person is given temporary custody of property on the understanding that it be returned – for example, when a coat is deposited at a theatre counter. The law imposes certain duties on the bailee which may be supplemented to form a contract of bailment. Consideration in these cases may be identified merely as the trust placed in the bailee, or as the loss of benefit of possession suffered by the bailor. Contracts of bailment are discussed later in the context of safe custody arrangements.

*Insufficient consideration*

5.11 If there is already a contract between A and B, and B promises additional reward to A if he (A) will perform the contract, there is no consideration to make that promise binding; A assumes no extra obligation and B obtains no extra rights or benefits.

*Case: Stilk v Myrick 1809*
Two members of the crew of a ship deserted in a foreign port. The master was unable to recruit substitutes and promised the rest of the crew that they should share the wages of the deserters if they would complete the voyage home. The shipowners however repudiated the promise.

*Held:* in performing their existing contractual duties the crew gave no consideration for the promise of extra pay and the promise was not binding.

*Case: Hartley v Ponsonby 1857*
17 out of a crew of 36 deserted. The rest were promised an extra £40 each to complete the next voyage.

*Held:* the large number of desertions made the voyage more dangerous and the original contract was discharged, to be replaced by a new contract under which the promise to complete the voyage constituted consideration for the promise of extra pay.

5.12 But if A promises B a reward if B will perform his existing contract with C, there is consideration for A's promise since he obtains a benefit to which he previously had no right and B assumes new obligations.

*Case: Shadwell v Shadwell 1860*
B, a barrister, was engaged to marry C (an engagement to marry was at this time a binding contract). B's uncle (A) promised B that if B married C (as he did) A would during their joint lives pay to B £150 p.a. until such time as B was earning 600 guineas p.a. at the bar (which B never did). The uncle died after eighteen years owing six annual payments. B claimed the arrears from A's executors who denied that there was consideration for A's promise.

*Held:* there was sufficient consideration for the reasons given above.

5.13 Performance of an existing public duty, such as to appear as a witness when subpoenaed in a lawsuit, is no consideration for a promise of reward. But if some extra service is given, that is sufficient consideration.

*Case: Glasbrook Bros. v Glamorgan CC 1925*
At a time of industrial unrest, although the police considered provision of a flying squad to be enough, colliery owners asked for and agreed to pay for a special police guard on the mine. Later they repudiated liability saying that the police had done no more than perform their public duty of maintaining order etc.

*Held:* the police had done more than they considered necessary to perform their general duties. The *extra* services given were consideration for the promise to pay.

5.14 However, the courts appear to be taking a slightly different line recently on the payment of additional consideration. The line seems to be that the principles of consideration will not be applied if the dispute before the court can be dealt with on an alternative basis.

*Case: Williams v Roffey Bros & Nicholls (Contractors) Ltd 1990*
W agreed to refurbish a block of flats for R at a fixed price of £20,000. The work ran late and so R agreed to pay W an extra £10,300 to ensure the work was completed on time. R later refused to pay the extra amount.

*Held:* the fact that there was no apparent consideration for R's promise to pay the extra was not held to be important, and in the court's view both R and W derived benefit from the promise. The telling point was that R's promise had not been extracted by duress or fraud: it was therefore binding.

5.15 If A promises B a reward if B will perform his existing contract with C, there is consideration for A's promise since he obtains a benefit to which he previously had no right, and B assumes new obligations.

*Case: Shadwell v Shadwell 1860*
B, a barrister, was engaged to marry C (an engagement to marry was at this time a binding contract). B's uncle (A) promised B that if B married C (as he did) A would during their joint lives pay to B £150 pa until such time as B was earning 600 guineas pa at the bar (which B never did). The uncle died after eighteen years owing six annual payments. B claimed the arrears from A's executors who denied that there was consideration for A's promise.

*Held:* there was sufficient consideration for the reasons given above.

## Consideration in banking

5.16 From the commercial examples of consideration it is plain to see that it is a two-way concept. The same applies to banker-customer contracts. However it is not always easy to assess what consideration is given by the customer to the bank for providing services. Consideration in specific banking contracts like safe custody, where a fee is charged for looking after the item, or a loan, where interest is charged for the facility, is easy to identify. But what is the consideration for maintaining customers' accounts? Obviously where charges are made the bank is receiving consideration, but the banks are now all offering 'free banking' whilst customers' accounts are maintained in credit. The answer is that if there are no charges, the bank obtains, by an implied term in the contract, the right to use its customers' money for lending, subject to honouring customers' cheques when they are presented. This is adequate and sufficient consideration given by the customer.

## Part payment of a debt

5.17 Particular complications arise over sufficiency of consideration for promises to waive existing rights, especially regarding rights to common law debts.

5.18 If X owes £100 but Y agrees to accept a lesser sum, eg £80, in full settlement of Y's claim, that is a promise by Y to waive his entitlement to the balance of £20. The promise, like any other, should be supported by consideration. In other words, payment on the day that a debt is due of less than the full amount of the debt is not consideration for a promise to release the balance.

*Case: Foakes v Beer 1884*
Y obtained judgement against X for the sum of £2,091 with interest. By a written agreement Y agreed to accept payment by instalments of the sum of £2,091. Later Y claimed the interest.

*Held:* Y was entitled to the debt with interest. No consideration had been given by X for waiver of any part of Y's rights against him.

5.19 There are, however, exceptions to the rule that the debtor (X) must give consideration if the waiver is to be binding, concerning variation of the original contract terms.

(a) If X arranges with a number of creditors that they will each accept part payment in full settlement, that is a bargain between the creditors. X has given no consideration but he can hold the creditors individually to the agreed terms.

(b) If a third party (Z) offers part payment and Y agrees to release X from Y's claim to the balance, Y has received consideration from Z against whom he had no previous claim.

(c) If X offers and Y accepts anything to which Y is not already entitled (for example goods instead of cash, or payment before the date payment is due) the extra thing will be sufficient consideration for the waiver.

*Case: Pinnel's Case 1602*
Pinnel sued Cole for a debt of £8.10s [£8.50] due on 11 November 1600. Cole's defence was that he had paid, at Pinnel's request, £5 2s 6d [£5.12½] on 1 October 1600 and that the latter had accepted this in full payment.

*Held:* (had it not been for a technical flaw, the judgement would have been) in favour of Cole, on the grounds that part payment had been made before the appointed day at the creditor's request.

(d) The principle of promissory estoppel may prevent Y from retracting his promise with retrospective effect.

**Promissory estoppel**

5.20 If a creditor (Y) makes a promise (unsupported by consideration) to the debtor (X) that Y will not insist on the full discharge of the debt (or other obligation), and *the promise is made with the intention that X should act on it and he does so* (by more than just making part payment), Y is estopped (prohibited) from retracting his promise, unless X can be restored to his original position. This last point will prevent Y from retracting his waiver with retrospective effect, though it may permit him to insist on his full rights in the future.

*Case: Central London Property Trust v High Trees House 1947*
In 1939, Y let a block of flats to X at an annual rent of £2,500 pa. It was difficult to let the individual flats in wartime. Y agreed in writing to accept a reduced rent of £1,250 pa. No time limit was set on the arrangement but it was related to wartime conditions. The reduced rent was paid from 1940 to 1945 and X let flats during the period on the basis of its expected liability to pay rent under the head lease at £1,250 only. In 1945 the flats were fully let. Y made a test claim for rent at the full rate of £2,500 pa for the final two quarters of 1945.

*Held:* Y was entitled to the full rent of £2,500 pa for the period for which this was claimed; the agreement to reduce the rent was a temporary expedient only. Denning J was of the opinion that had Y sought arrears for the earlier period (1940-45), he would have failed.

5.21 Two limitations to the principle of promissory estoppel are clear.

5.22 It only applies to a promise of waiver which is entirely voluntary:

*Case: D and C Builders v Rees 1966*
X owed £482 to Y (a small firm of builders). Y, which was in acute financial difficulties, reluctantly agreed to accept £300 in full settlement (in order to obtain the money quickly). X had been aware of and had exploited Y's difficulties ('he was held to ransom' said Lord Denning). The builder later claimed the balance.

*Held:* the debt must be paid in full. Promissory estoppel only applies to a promise voluntarily given. In this important case it was also held that payment by cheque (instead of in cash) is normal and gives no extra advantage which could be treated as consideration of the waiver under the rule in *Pinnel's* case.

5.23 It applies only to a waiver of existing rights. A promise which creates new obligations is not binding unless supported by consideration in the usual way. The principle is 'a shield not a sword'.

*Case: Combe v Combe 1951*
A wife obtained a divorce decree *nisi* against her husband. He then promised her that he would make maintenance payments. The wife did not apply to the court for an order for maintenance but this forbearance was not at the husband's request. The decree was made absolute; the husband paid no maintenance; the wife sued him on his promise. In the High Court the wife obtained judgement on the basis of promissory estoppel.

*Held:* (in the Court of Appeal) that promissory estoppel 'does not create new causes of action where none existed before. It only prevents a party from insisting on his strict legal rights when it would be unjust to allow him to enforce them'. The wife's claim failed.

5.24 The main uncertainties over promissory estoppel relate to (i) what action the debtor must have taken in reliance on the waiver and (ii) how far the creditor may retract a waiver of rights to payment of a lump sum as distinct from a series of periodical payments spreading over a period of time.

## 6. PRIVITY OF CONTRACT

6.1 As consideration is the price of a promise, the price must be paid by the person who seeks to enforce the promise.

If, for example, A promises B that (for a consideration provided by B) A will confer a benefit on C, then C cannot as a general rule enforce A's promise since C has given no consideration for it.

*Case: Tweddle v Atkinson 1861*
T married the daughter of G. On the occasion of the marriage T's father and G exchanged promises that they would each pay a sum of money to T. The agreement between the two fathers expressly provided that T should have enforceable rights against them. G died without making the promised payment and T sued G's executor (A) for the specified amount.

*Held:* T had provided no consideration for G's promise. In spite of the express terms of the agreement, T had no enforceable rights under it.

6.2 It is not essential that the promisor should receive any benefit from the promisee. In *Tweddle's* case above, each father as promisee gave consideration by his promise to the other but T was to be the beneficiary of each promise. Each father could have sued the other but T could not sue. (If a trust had been set up by both parties with T as beneficiary, T would have obtained rights under it.)

6.3 The rule that consideration must move from the promisee overlaps with the rule that only a party to a contract can enforce it. Together these rules are known as the **principle of** *privity of contract:* as a general rule, *only a person who is a party to a contract has enforceable rights or obligations under it.*

*Case: Dunlop v Selfridge 1915*
D, a tyre manufacturer, supplied tyres to X, a distributor, on terms that X would not re-sell the tyres at less than the prescribed retail price. If X sold the tyres wholesale to trade customers, X must impose a similar condition on those buyers to observe minimum retail prices (such clauses were legal at the time though prohibited since 1964 by the Resale Prices Act). X resold tyres on these conditions to S, the well-known Oxford Street store. Under the terms of the contract between X and S, S was to pay to D a sum of £5 per tyre if it sold tyres to customers below the minimum retail price. S sold tyres to two customers at less than the minimum price. D sued to recover £5 per tyre.

*Held:* D could not recover damages under a contract (between X and S) to which D was not a party. This is the leading case (decided in the House of Lords) on privity of contract.

6.4 In these circumstances the party to the contract who imposes the condition or obtains a promise of a benefit for a third party can usually enforce it. Damages cannot be recovered on the third party's behalf unless the contracting party is suing an agent or trustee, since a plaintiff can only recover damages for a loss he has suffered. Thus only nominal damages can be given if the contract was only for a third party's benefit.

6.5 There is some inconsistency in the case law, but the general tenor is that a seller of goods cannot impose conditions which pass with the goods to a third party even if the latter buys with knowledge of the conditions. There are, however, special rules of the law of property which enable a person to impose restrictions on land to pass with the land from one owner to the next, as we shall see later.

6.6 There are a number of real or apparent exceptions to the general rule of privity of contract.

(a) In a contract between A and B by which B is to confer benefit on C, A may constitute himself a trustee for C. C as beneficiary may then enforce the contract against B.

(b) The benefit of a contract may be transferred by assignment or negotiation of a cheque or other bill of exchange - see below.

(c)   There are statutory exceptions which permit a person injured in a road accident to claim against the motorist's insurers, and which permit husband and wife to insure his or her own life for the benefit of the other under a trust which the beneficiary can enforce: Road Traffic Act 1972; Married Women's Property Act 1882.

(d)   An undisclosed principal may adopt a contract made for him by an agent.

## Assignment

6.7   A party to a contract can assign or transfer to another person (the assignee) the benefit of the contract (subject to the rules stated below). But he cannot (without the consent of the other party) assign the burden of his contractual obligations.

6.8   A legal assignment must be in writing with notice to the other party. The assignee has no better rights under the contract than the assignor had. It is not possible to assign:

(a)   a right of action, which is a claim for unliquidated damages for breach of contract (or tort);

(b)   rights which are so personal to the original parties to the contract that assignment to another would alter them.

*Case: Kemp v Baerselman 1906*
A supplier contracted to supply to a cake manufacturer all the eggs which the latter might require over a period of a year. During the year the manufacturer sold his business to a much larger concern (the National Bakery Company) and purported as part of the sale to assign the benefit of the egg supply agreement.

*Held:* the assignment was invalid since the assignee's requirements were much larger and the supplier's right to supply all the assignor's requirements (he would no longer have any) became valueless.

6.9   Although a party to a contract cannot escape from his contractual obligations by assignment, he may (unless the contract requires personal performance by him) delegate performance to another person. But he remains liable if his substitute's performance is a breach of contract.

6.10  A bank may agree with its customer that the bank will open a commercial credit or give a performance bond for the benefit of a third party. This is in effect a bank guarantee that its customer will perform his contract with the third party and make payments (through the bank) as required by the contract. There is no privity of contract between the bank and the third party but the arrangement would be valueless if the third party had no enforceable rights against the bank. As an exception to the general principle of privity of contract, the bank is usually bound by its undertaking in favour of the third party.

We shall see in Part E of this text how the laborious nature of assignment makes the idea of negotiability far more useful in commercial contracts.

## 7. INTENTION TO CREATE LEGAL RELATIONS

7.1 An agreement is not a binding contract unless the parties intend thereby to create legal relations. Where the parties have not expressly denied such intention, what matters is not what the parties have in their minds, but the inferences that reasonable people would draw from their words or conduct - it is an objective test. In *Carlill's* case the decision might have been different if there had been no deposit of money to show sincerity.

### Express statements of intention to create legal relations

7.2 Any express statement by the parties of their intention *not* to make a binding contract is conclusive.

*Case: Rose and Frank v J R Crompton & Bros 1923*
A commercial agreement by which A (a British manufacturer) appointed B to be its distributor in USA expressly stated that it was 'not subject to legal jurisdiction' in either country. A terminated agreement without giving notice as it required, and refused to deliver goods ordered by B although A had accepted these orders when placed.

*Held:* the general agreement was not legally binding but the orders for goods were separate and binding contracts.

7.3 There is usually no legal requirement for a contract to be either written or evidenced in writing. However, within banking it is necessary for administration purposes to record transactions with customers. In particular, since the introduction of the Consumer Credit Act 1974, written credit agreements have to be entered into by both the bank and the customer. Hence in many cases the intention of both parties to create legal relations is undisputed because it is contained in an express statement.

### Implied intention to create legal relations

7.4 Where there is no express statement, as may be said to be true of the majority of contracts, the courts apply two presumptions to a case:

(a) social, domestic and family arrangements are not usually intended to be binding;
(b) commercial agreements are usually intended by the parties involved to be legally binding.

*Domestic arrangements*

7.5 In most agreements no intention is expressly stated. If it is a domestic agreement between husband and wife, relatives or friends it is presumed that there is no intention to create legal relations unless the circumstances point to the opposite conclusion.

*Case: Balfour v Balfour 1919*
The husband was employed in Ceylon. He and his wife returned to the UK on leave but it was agreed that for health reasons she would not return to Ceylon with him. He promised to pay her £30 p.m. as maintenance. Later the marriage ended in divorce and the wife sued for the monthly allowance which the husband no longer paid.

*Held:* an informal agreement of indefinite duration made between husband and wife (whose marriage had not then broken up) was not intended to be legally binding. Similarly, use of uncertain words such as 'I'll pay you £15 as long as I can manage it' will lead the court to conclude that legal relations were not intended: *Gould v Gould 1969.*

*Case: Merritt v Merritt 1970*
The husband had left the matrimonial home, which was owned by him, to live with another woman. The spouses met and held a discussion in the husband's car in the course of which he agreed to pay her £40 p.m. out of which she agreed to keep up the mortgage payments on the house. The wife refused to leave the car until the husband signed a note of these agreed terms and an undertaking to transfer the house into her sole name when the mortgage had been paid off. The wife paid off the mortgage but the husband refused to transfer the house to her.

*Held:* in the circumstances, intention to create legal relations was to be inferred and the wife could sue for breach of contract.

7.6 Where agreements between husband and wife or other relatives relate to property matters the courts are very ready to impute an intention to create legal relations. This can affect the bank in that disputes may arise between related persons concerning property over which the bank has security. It is unlikely that the court will simply conclude that any agreement between the relatives had no legal force; the bank will have to win its case on its merits.

7.7 Domestic arrangements extend to those between people who are not related but who have a close relationship of some form. The nature of the agreement itself may lead to the conclusion that legal relations were intended.

*Commercial agreements*

7.8 When businessmen enter into commercial agreements it is presumed that there is an intention to enter into legal relations unless this is expressly disclaimed or the circumstances (eg difficulty in enforcement) displace that presumption. *Carlill's* case is yet again a useful illustration of a legal principle; the deposit of £1,000 at a bank was taken as proof that the smokeball company intended the promise to be binding.

*Case: Edwards v Skyways 1964*
In negotiations over the terms for making an employee redundant, the employer undertook to make an *ex gratia* payment to him – a payment without admission of previous liability.

*Held:* the denial of previous liability (ex gratia payment) did not suffice to rebut the presumption that the agreed terms were intended to be legally binding in their future operation.

7.9 Clearly all contracts entered into by a bank are commercial agreements and so are presumed to be legally binding. Most are expressly stated to be so.

7.10 Procedural agreements between employers and trade unions for the settlement of disputes are *not* by their nature intended to give rise to legal relations in spite of their elaborate and very legal contents: s 18 Trade Union and Labour Relations Act 1974.

7.11 The presumption that commercial agreements are legally binding needs to be expressly rebutted; however, for many years, holding companies have given 'comfort letters' to creditors of subsidiaries which purport to give some comfort as to the ability of the subsidiary to pay its debts. Such a letter has always been presumed in the past not to be legally binding and the decision in the case below gives the reasons for such a presumption.

*Case: Kleinwort Benson Ltd v Malaysian Mining Corporation Bhd 1989*
The plaintiffs lent money to the defendant's subsidiary, having received a letter from the defendant stating:

'It is our policy to ensure that the business is at all times in a position to meet its liabilities to you.'

On the collapse of the International Tin Council the subsidiary went into liquidation, and the bank claimed from its holding company, MMC.

*Held:* (a) the bank had clearly acted on the strength of the letter and so believed it to be of legal force;
(b) the defendant had failed to ensure its subsidiary's liabilities could be met;
(c) the onus was on the defendant who claimed the letter was intended to have no legal effect to prove that was so.

The Appeal Court found that the statement of policy was a representation of fact and not a promise that the policy would continue in the future. This promise could not be implied where it was not expressly stated. Because both parties were well aware that in business parlance a 'comfort letter' imposed moral and not legal responsibilities, it was held not to have been given with the intention of creating legal relations. The defendant's breach of moral responsibility was of no concern to the court.

## 8. CONTRACT TERMS

8.1 As a general principle the parties may, by their offer and acceptance, include in their contract whatever terms they prefer. But the law may modify these express terms in various ways.

(a) The terms must be sufficiently complete and precise to produce an agreement which can be binding. If they are vague there may be no contract.

(b) The terms of the contract are usually classified as *conditions* or as *warranties* according to their importance.

(c) If the parties express the terms in writing, the right to introduce oral evidence of the contract's terms is restricted.

(d) Statements made in pre-contract negotiations may become *terms* of the contract or may remain as *representations*. Different rules attach to each.

(e) In addition to the express terms of the agreement, additional terms may be implied by law.

(f) Terms which exclude or restrict liability for breach of contract *(exclusion clauses)* are restricted in their effect or overridden by common law and statutory rules.

8.2 Each of points (a) - (e) is considered in the following paragraphs. Exclusion clauses are discussed later in this Part of the text.

# 3: THE BASICS OF CONTRACT LAW

## Incomplete contracts

8.3 A legally binding agreement must be complete in its terms. Otherwise there is no contract, since the parties are still at the stage of negotiating the necessary terms.

*Case: Scammell v Ouston 1941*
An agreement for the purchase of a van provided that the unpaid balance of the price should be paid over two years 'on hire purchase terms'.

*Held:* there was no agreement since it was uncertain what terms of payment were intended. Hire purchase terms vary over intervals between payments, interest charge to be added etc.

8.4 It is always possible for the parties to leave an essential term to be settled by specified means outside the contract. For example, it may be agreed to sell at the ruling open market price (if there is a market) on the day of delivery, or to invite an arbitrator to determine a fair price. The price may even be determined by the course of dealing between the parties.

*Case: Hillas v Arcos 1932*
A contract for the supply of '22,000 standards of softwood of fair specification over the season 1930' contained an option for the purchaser to buy a quantity of timber in 1931. The 1930 contract was performed in spite of the vague specification used, but in 1931 the defendants refused to supply any wood, arguing that the agreement was too vague to bind the parties.

*Held:* the missing terms of the 1931 purchase could be deduced from the conduct of the parties in their 1930 transaction. The law is not 'a destroyer of bargains' but endeavours to make them effective.

8.5 If the parties use meaningless but non-essential words, say by use of standard printed conditions of which only some are appropriate, such phrases may be disregarded.

*Case: Nicolene v Simmonds 1953*
A contract made by correspondence provided that 'the usual conditions of acceptance apply'. The contract was complete without these words; there were no usual conditions of acceptance.

*Held:* the words should be disregarded.

8.6 If however the parties expressly agree to defer some essential term for later negotiation there is no binding agreement. This is described as 'an agreement to agree' which is void, as the parties may subsequently fail to agree.

## Conditions and warranties

8.7 The terms of the contract are usually classified by their relative importance as conditions or warranties. A *condition* is a term vital to the contract. Non-observance of a condition will affect the main purpose of the agreement. Breach of a condition entitles the party not in breach to treat the contract as discharged. A *warranty* is a less important term. It does not go to the root of the contract, *but* is subsidiary to the main purpose of the agreement.

Breach of a warranty only entitles the injured party to claim damages.

*Case: Poussard v Spiers 1876*

Madame Poussard agreed to sing in an opera throughout a series of performances. Owing to illness she was unable to appear on the opening night and the next few days. The producer engaged a substitute who insisted that she should be engaged for the whole run. When Mme Poussard had recovered the producer declined to accept her services for the remaining performances.

*Held:* failure to sing on the opening night was a breach of condition which entitled the producer to treat the contract for the remaining performances as discharged.

*Case: Bettini v Gye 1876*

An opera singer was engaged for a series of performances under a contract by which he had to be in London for rehearsals six days before the opening performance. Owing to illness he did not arrive until the third day before the opening. The defendant refused to accept his services, treating the contract as discharged.

*Held:* the rehearsal clause was subsidiary to the main purpose of the contract. Breach of the clause must be treated as breach of warranty, so the defendant had no right to treat the contract as discharged and must compensate the plaintiff. He could however claim damages (if he could prove any loss) for failure to arrive in time for six days' rehearsals.

8.8 The courts will usually construe a term in the light of the parties' intentions *at the time the contract was made* as to whether it should be a condition or a warranty: *Bunge Corporation v Tradax SA 1981*. Because of its consequences they tend to lean away from construing a term as a condition.

*Innominate terms*

8.9 Unless the parties expressly agree that a particular term shall be treated as a condition, it may prove difficult to put it into the appropriate category when the contract is made. In a complicated case on sale of goods decided in 1975 the Court of Appeal developed the theory that some terms should remain unclassified (*innominate* terms or *intermediate* terms) until the seriousness of a breach could be judged: *Cehave v Bremer, The Hansa Nord 1975*. If the breach went to the root of the contract the relevant term should then be classified as a condition; if it did not then it should be treated as a warranty.

The significance of this is that breach of a condition means that the whole contract is breached, while breach of a warranty can give rise only to damages.

8.10 Thus where a term is intermediate, the courts will make the decision on the basis of the *consequences* of the term being breached, rather than simply classifying the term as a condition or warranty.

**Oral evidence relating to contracts in writing**

8.11 The general rule is that if a contract is or includes a written document, oral evidence may not be given to 'add to, vary or contradict' the document. There are the following exceptions to the rule.

(a) Oral evidence may be given of trade practice or custom.

(b) Evidence may be given to show that the parties agreed orally that their written consent should not take effect until a *condition precedent* had been satisfied, eg a written contract to buy a house subject to a verbal agreement that it would take effect only if the purchaser's surveyor gave a satisfactory report.

(c) Oral evidence may be given as an addition to a written contract if it can be shown that the document, such as printed conditions of sale, was not intended to comprise all the agreed terms. But the presumption is that a contract document is the entire contract until the contrary is proved.

*Case: SS Ardennes 1951*
A printed bill of lading (for shipment of a cargo of oranges) provided that the ship might go 'by any route ... directly or indirectly' to London. The shipowners' agent had given a verbal undertaking that the vessel would sail direct from Spain to London.

*Held:* evidence might be given of the verbal undertaking as a term overriding the bill of lading.

(d) Oral evidence may be adduced to correct a written agreement drawn up subsequently which contains a mistake (see Chapter 5).

**Representations and contract terms**

8.12 If something said in pre-contract negotiations proves to be untrue, the party misled can only claim for breach of contract if the statement became a term of the contract. Otherwise his remedy is for misrepresentation only (explained in Chapter 6). Even if the statement is not repeated or referred to in making the contract it may be treated as a contract term. But such factors as a significant interval of time between statement and contract or the use of a written contract making no reference to the verbal statement suggest that it is not a term of the contract. If, however, the party who makes the statement speaks with special knowledge of the subject it is more likely to be treated as a contract term.

*Case: Oscar Chess v Williams 1959*
A private motorist negotiated the sale of an old car to motor dealers in part exchange for a new car. The seller stated (as the registration book showed) that his car was a 1948 model. In fact it was a 1939 model (and the registration book had been altered by a previous owner).

*Held:* the statement was a mere representation. The seller was not an expert and the buyer had better means of discovering the truth.

(NB partly to relieve the hardship of these situations, the Misrepresentation Act 1967 created a right to claim damages for negligent misrepresentation. This is discussed in Chapter 5.)

**Implied contract terms**

8.13 Additional terms of a contract may be implied by law.

(a) The parties may be considered to enter into a contract subject to a custom or practice of their trade. For example, when a farm is let to a tenant there may be an implied term that local farming custom on husbandry and tenant rights shall apply. But any express term overrides a term which might be implied by custom.

*Case: Les Affreteurs v Walford 1919*
A charter of a ship provided expressly for a payment to be made on signing the charter. There was a trade custom that it should only be paid at a later stage.

*Held:* an express term prevails over a term otherwise implied by custom.

(b) Terms may be implied by statute. In some cases the statute permits the parties to contract out of the statutory terms (eg the terms of partnership implied by the Partnership Act 1890 may be excluded). In other cases the statutory terms are obligatory. For instance, the protection given by the Consumer Credit Act 1974 to a customer who borrows money under a regulated agreement cannot be taken away from him.

(c) Terms may be implied if the court concludes that the parties intended these terms to apply and did not mention them because they were taken for granted.

8.14 The parties may take something obvious for granted. For example, if a person undertakes to do work, such as the conveyance of a property, in which he claims to be proficient, it is an implied term that he will show reasonable skill in doing the work. In such cases the 'officious bystander' test is applied; if an officious bystander had intervened to remind the parties that in formulating their contract they had failed to mention a particular point they would have replied 'of course ... we did not trouble to say that; it is too clear.'

*Case: The Moorcock 1889*
The owners of a wharf agreed that a ship should be moored alongside to unload its cargo. It was well known to both wharfingers and shipowners that at low tide the ship would ground on the mud at the bottom. At ebb tide the ship rested on a ridge concealed beneath the mud and suffered damage.

*Held:* it was an implied term, though not expressed, that the ground alongside the wharf (which did not belong to the wharfingers) was safe at low tide since both parties knew that the ship must rest on it.

*Case: Liverpool City Council v Irwin 1977*
The defendants were tenants of a maisonnette in a tower block owned by the plaintiffs. There was no formal tenancy agreement. The defendants withheld rent, alleging that the plaintiffs had breached implied terms because inter alia the lifts did not work and the stairs were unlit. The council argued that there were no implied terms.

*Held:* it was necessary to consider the obligations which 'the nature of the contract itself implicitly required'. Tenants could only occupy the building with access to stairs and/or lifts, so terms needed to be implied on these matters. A term was implied that the landlord would keep these parts reasonably safe.

8.15 The terms to be implied in this way are those necessary to complete the contract and give it 'business efficacy.' Terms will not be implied to contradict the express terms of the contract (see *Les Affreteurs* case above) nor to provide for events which the parties did not contemplate in their negotiations.

## 9. FORM OF THE CONTRACT

9.1 As a general rule a contract may be made in any form - in writing, by word of mouth or even by implication from conduct. For example, a customer in a self-service shop takes his selected goods to the cash desk, pays for them and walks out. There is a contract of sale although not a word has been spoken; the till receipt is merely evidence of payment and not essential to the contract.

9.2 To the general rule there are some exceptions.

(a) *Contracts by deed.* Some rights and obligations, eg a transfer of title to land, or a lease of land for a period of three years or more, or a promise not supported by consideration (such as a covenant to make annual payments to a charity) are generally required to be in the form of a deed and may not be binding if they are not in that form.

(b) *Contracts in writing.* Some types of contract (mainly commercial) are required to be in the form of a written document, usually signed by at least one of the parties, and are void if not in that form. This category includes bills of exchange and regulated consumer credit agreements.

(c) *Contracts which must be evidenced in writing.* Certain types of contract may be made orally but are not enforceable in a court of law unless there is written evidence of their terms. The most important type of contract under this head is that of guarantee: Statute of Frauds Act 1677.

### Contracts by deed

9.3 A deed used to be referred to as a contract under seal, but s 1 of the Law of Property (Miscellaneous Provisions) Act 1989 no longer requires an individual to seal a deed. It is a written document (on paper, parchment or other substance) which has been signed by the person executing it (and sealed if created by a corporate body with a common seal) and is expressed on its face to be a deed. The signature must be witnessed. To be validly executed by an individual, the document must be delivered to the other party by the individual or his agent. *Remember that a contract by deed is binding even though no consideration is given or received.*

### Contracts in writing

9.4 A contract for the sale or other disposition of land or of any interest in land (such as the grant of a lease) must be in writing, incorporating all the expressly agreed terms and signed by or on behalf of each party to the contract: s 2 Law of Property (Miscellaneous Provisions) Act 1989. An oral contract relating to an interest in land cannot now be enforced if it is only *evidenced* in writing - it must actually be *in* writing.

9.5 Note that s 2 does not apply to the grant of a lease for less than three years where the tenant takes possession or a contract made at public auction. These may still be enforced if they are only evidenced in writing.

9.6 These new rules mean that not only a document transferring land but also the contract of sale for land must be in writing. A contract for the sale of land must be distinguished from the actual document which transfers the title to that land, that is the conveyance (unregistered land) or transfer (registered land). The contract promises to transfer title at a future date (usually four weeks hence) and must be in writing. The conveyance or transfer must be by deed and will therefore also be in writing. A contract promising to grant a lease must be in writing but the lease itself, if it is for three years or more, must be by deed.

## 10. CONCLUSION

10.1 To be valid, a contract must be formed as an agreement (implying offer and acceptance) which was intended to create legal relations and for which consideration has been given. These are the basic tenets of contract law which underlie all commercial contracts, not least the contracts entered into by the bank as supplier, consumer and employer.

10.2 The points below are a brief summary of the key topics covered in this chapter, together with an indication of their relevance to the world of banking.

| The law of contract | Relevance to banking |
|---|---|
| A contract is an agreement which legally binds the parties to it | A bank has a contract (or more than one) with each and every one of its customers |
| The parties agree to be bound when there has been an offer which has been accepted | Banks must be careful to ensure that advertisements and information leaflets do not constitute open offers which can be accepted by anyone |
| A contract is a bargain - each party must give and receive something as consideration | Banks provide services; customers pay interest, charges or fees, or simply allow their funds to be used by the bank for lending |
| The parties to a contract must intend to be legally bound by its terms | The bank's contracts with its customers, and any amendments thereto, are commercial ones which are assumed to be legally binding |
| The contract's terms may be expressed by the parties or they may be implied by law | Most banks do not explicitly state the terms of their contracts except in standard form contracts. Increasingly they are under pressure to change this practice |
| Most contracts need not be in any particular form | Security agreements, including guarantees, and consumer credit agreements are required to be in particular forms if they are to be valid |

---

### TEST YOUR KNOWLEDGE
*The numbers in brackets refer to paragraphs of this chapter*

1   What are the three constituent features of a contract? (2.1)

2   An offer is a definite promise to be bound on specific terms. It cannot be vague – What was the case in which an 'offer' was thought to have been made to the public for a patent medicine? (3.8)

3   What are the four circumstances in which an offer may lapse? (3.9)

4   Acceptance may be by express words or action. How else may it be effective? (4.1)

5   What is the effect of acceptance 'subject to contract'? (4.5)

6   What is the effect of posting a letter accepting an offer made by letter to the offeree? (4.11)

7   Distinguish between executed and executory consideration. (5.4)

8   In what circumstances is something done before a promise is made sufficient consideration to make the promise binding? (5.5)

9   What consideration is given by a customer to his bank? (5.16)

10  Is acceptance of part payment of an existing debt binding on the person who accepts it or may he still claim the unpaid balance? (5.18, 5.19)

11  What exceptions are there to the general rule of privity of contract? (6.6)

12  In contract, what may be assigned to another person? (6.7)

13  What is the effect of a statement in a business agreement that it is not intended to create legal relations? (7.2)

14  Why are commercial agreements deemed to be binding? (7.8, 7.9)

15  What is the difference between a condition and a warranty? (8.7)

16  Which types of contract must be:

    (a)   in the form of a deed;
    (b)   in writing; and
    (c)   evidenced in writing? (8.2)

---

*Now try question 7 at the end of the text*

*Chapter 4*

# CAPACITY TO MAKE CONTRACTS

---

**This chapter covers the following topics.**

1. Contractual capacity of minors
2. Contracts made by companies
3. Mental incapacity

---

## 1. CONTRACTUAL CAPACITY OF MINORS

1.1 In general any person has legal capacity to enter into a binding contract. But a minor, a corporation and a person who is insane or drunk have only restricted capacity and contracts made by such persons may be void, voidable or unenforceable.

1.2 Broadly a contract between a minor (a person under the age of 18) and another party may be of one of three types:

(a) *valid* - binding in the usual way; or

(b) *voidable* - binding unless and until the minor repudiates (rejects) the contract; or

(c) *unenforceable* against the minor unless he ratifies (confirms) it - but the other party is bound.

1.3 The law governing minors' contracts attempts to balance two distinct competing interests. The first is the interest of the minor who should be protected from the consequences of entering into unwise binding agreements. The second is the interest of persons who form such agreements often in good faith and with no intention of profiting from the minor's inexperience. With the Minors' Contracts Act 1987 the pendulum swung towards protecting those who contract with minors and away from protecting minors themselves.

**Valid contracts of a minor**

1.4 Only two types of contract entered into by a minor are valid and binding on both parties - a contract for necessaries and a service contract for the minor's benefit.

# 4: CAPACITY TO MAKE CONTRACTS

*Contracts for necessaries*

1.5 If goods or services which are *necessaries* are delivered to a minor under a contract made by him, he is bound to pay a reasonable price (not the contract price if that is excessive) for them (s 3 Sale of Goods Act 1979).

1.6 Necessaries are defined (in the Sale of Goods Act 1979 s 3) as goods suitable to the condition in life of the minor and to his actual requirements at the time of sale and delivery. Services may also be necessaries. The goods (or services) must therefore satisfy a double test – *suitability* and *need* – if they are to be necessaries.

1.7 *Suitability* is measured by the living standards of the minor. Things which are in ordinary use may be necessaries even though they are luxurious in quality (if that is what the minor ordinarily uses). Food, clothing, professional advice and even a gold watch have been held to be necessaries. However, in some cases it is clear that a broad definition of necessaries has been adopted, not for the benefit of the minor, but to protect traders who gave credit to young men from wealthy families. It has been said that an item of 'mere luxury' cannot be a necessary, for example a racehorse, but that a luxurious item of utility such as an expensive car, may be a necessary. Expensive items bought as gifts are not usually necessaries, but an engagement ring to a fiancee can be.

1.8 The second test is whether the minor requires the goods for the personal *needs* of himself (or his wife or child if any). Goods required for use in a trade are not necessaries, nor are goods of any kind if the minor is already well supplied with them and so does not need any more.

*Case: Nash v Inman 1908*
N was a Savile Row tailor who had solicited orders from I, a Cambridge undergraduate of extravagant tastes. N sued I on bills totalling £145 for clothes, including eleven fancy waistcoats, supplied over a period of nine months. It was conceded that the clothes were suitable for I but it was shown that he was already amply supplied with clothing.

*Held:* the clothes were not necessaries since, although quite suitable for his use, the minor had no need of them. It was immaterial that N was unaware that I was already well supplied.

*Case: Mercantile Union Guarantee Corporation v Ball 1937*
A minor obtained a lorry on hire purchase terms for use in his road haulage business.

*Held:* this was not a contract for necessaries since the lorry was required for business, not personal use. Under a hire purchase contract the owner could recover the lorry as still his property, but could not enforce payment of the hire purchase instalments.

1.9 If a minor uses borrowed money to pay for necessaries the lender is subrogated in equity to the rights of the supplier who has been paid with the lender's money, and the lender may recover so much of his loan as corresponds with a reasonable price for the necessaries. 'Subrogation' means that one person 'steps into the shoes' of another – so the lender takes over the supplier's right to be paid. For a bank, or indeed any other lender, this remedy is not particularly useful, since it would involve very difficult and expensive litigation.

# 4: CAPACITY TO MAKE CONTRACTS

*Service contracts*

1.10 A *service contract for the minor's benefit* is the other type of contract which is binding on the minor.

> *Case: Doyle v White City Stadium 1935*
> D, who was a minor, obtained a licence to compete as a professional boxer. Under his licence (which was treated as a contract of apprenticeship or vocation) he agreed to be bound by rules under which the British Boxing Board of Control could withhold his prize money if he was disqualified for a foul blow (as in fact happened). He asserted that the licence was a void contract since it was not for his benefit.
>
> *Held:* the licence enabled him to pursue a lucrative occupation. Despite the penal clause, it was beneficial as a whole.

1.11 Apart from the test of benefit, the contract must relate to education or training, or relate to some occupation or vocation, such as training as a dancer or as a professional billiard player.

> *Case: Chaplin v Leslie Frewin (Publishers) Ltd 1966*
> The minor, whose father was a famous actor, contracted with a firm of publishers that they could publish a book under his name entitled *I Couldn't Smoke the Grass on my Father's Lawn*. Later he sought to avoid the contract, saying it was not for his benefit as it did not portray his real view of life.
>
> *Held:* even though the contract 'exploited his discreditable conduct' (Lord Denning) it was held to be binding as it was the sort of contract which could benefit him by helping him to 'make a start as an author'. The contract was analogous to a service contract.

1.12 But a contract to pay for trade goods or business equipment (see *Ball's* case above) does not fall within this exception even if beneficial.

> *Case: Cowern v Nield 1912*
> A minor carried on business as a dealer in hay and straw. He was paid in advance for a consignment which he failed to deliver. The purchaser sued to enforce delivery or to recover his money.
>
> *Held:* this was not a contract of service but a trading contract. It was void (under the old law) and there was no right to delivery of the hay or recovery of the money paid for it. Under the Minors' Contracts Act 1987 this contract would be described as unenforceable.

## Voidable contracts of a minor

1.13 A minor may enter into a contract by which he acquires an interest of a continuing nature and accepts obligations incidental to it. There are four categories of voidable contract which the minor may choose to repudiate but which are binding on him until repudiated:

(a) contracts concerning land – for example, leases;
(b) purchases of shares in a company;
(c) partnership agreements; and
(d) marriage settlements.

1.14 Such contracts are voidable by the minor during his minority and within a reasonable time after attaining his majority. If he avoids it before his majority, he may withdraw his repudiation within a reasonable time afterwards. If he avoids it, he is relieved of any future obligations. It is not certain whether he is also discharged from liabilities incurred before avoidance and still outstanding, such as arrears of rent due before the lease is repudiated: the decided cases and judicial *dicta* conflict.

1.15 Whatever the position at common law, s 3(1) of the Minors' Contract Act 1987 gives the Court the power to order the minor to transfer to the other party to the contract any property (or property representing it) which was acquired by the minor as a result of the contract. Were *Cowern v Nield* to be decided today, for example, the Court could order (if it felt it just and equitable to do so) that the minor return the money paid in advance to the purchaser, although it would not, presumably, order that the hay be delivered.

1.16 If the minor avoids the contract he cannot recover money or property which he has paid or transferred under the contract unless he has received no consideration whatsoever for it.

*Case: Steinberg v Scala (Leeds) 1923*
S, a minor, applied for and was allotted shares in the defendant company. She paid some instalments of the subscription monies, defaulted on the next call and rescinded the contract. She sued to recover the money which she had paid. It was proved that the shares, although they had some value, could never have been sold in the market for a price equal to what she had subscribed for them. Her right to rescind and be removed from the register of members was not disputed but the company refused to repay her subscription money.

*Held:* the claim must fail as S had been a shareholder and by reason of that, had had some consideration.

## Unenforceable contracts of a minor

1.17 All other contracts entered into by a minor (including loans) are described as unenforceable – the minor is not bound (though he may ratify it) but the other party is bound. The minor must ratify the contract within a reasonable time of his majority.

1.18 The 1987 Act expressly made two changes important to banks :

(a) a contractual promise made by a minor once he reaches the age of 18 to repay a loan made to him while he was under the age of 18 will be a valid enforceable contract;

(b) if a minor's debt is guaranteed by an adult but the minor cannot be made to pay, the guarantee is still valid against the adult. Under the previous law, the guarantee was void since the primary debt was void.

## Restitution of assets

1.19 Under ss 1 and 4 Minors' Contracts Act 1987 a contract which is ratified by the minor *after* his majority is enforceable by the other party. As with voidable contracts which are avoided, the minor cannot recover money or property under an unenforceable contract which has been performed, unless there has been total failure of consideration.

1.20 The 1987 Act also increased the protection given to persons contracting in good faith with a minor by providing under s 3(1) that the court can enforce the minor to transfer property, or the proceeds of it, back to the other party to an unenforceable or repudiated contract. The court may use its discretion; it will only make such an order if it is just and equitable to do so.

1.21 It is important to note that these rules can only enforce the minor to transfer property or its proceeds under s 3(1), or to restore property or proceeds in equity. The minor cannot be forced to pay for property out of his general assets - although a minor should not be enriched by making voidable or unenforceable contracts, his wealth should not be diminished either.

### Liability of a minor in tort

1.22 It may happen that the same transaction can involve a minor in an unenforceable contract and also expose him to liability in tort (where his age gives no general exemption). In such cases the other party is not permitted to sue in tort as a means of enforcing an unenforceable contract.

*Case: Leslie v Sheill 1914*
S, a minor, obtained a loan by lying about his age. The moneylenders sued him for damages for fraud.

*Held:* the claim for damages in tort for deceit must fail since it was only an indirect means of seeking to enforce an unenforceable contract to repay money lent.

---

### Exercise

A bank lends money to a minor who has applied for a loan. What is the nature of the contract between the bank and the minor, and what are the consequences of this?

### Solution

The contract is unenforceable. This means that the debt is not enforceable against the minor. However, under the Minors' Contracts Act 1987, a court can order the minor to repay any money lent or hand over any property purchased with it. This shows how the law has shifted in emphasis towards the protection of those who contract with minors.

---

## 2. CONTRACTS MADE BY COMPANIES

2.1 The contractual capacity of a company is governed by the statute or charter which creates it. Most companies are registered under the Companies Act 1985. Basically a company is limited by its constitution (contained in the objects clause of its Memorandum of Association or in its statute) to entering only certain types of contract. Anything done outside these limits used to be called *ultra vires* (beyond the powers) and was unenforceable. However, this area of the law has recently undergone considerable changes which limit the previously harsh effects of the *ultra vires* doctrine on third parties.

2.2 Under the Companies Act 1989, a company is still required to have an objects clause, but the clause can now be greatly simplified. A company's objects may be stated in any manner in its memorandum, and a statement that the company's object is to carry on business as a general commercial company shall mean that it may 'carry on any trade or business whatsoever'. In consequence of this, the company will be deemed to have power to do all such things as are incidental or conducive to the carrying on of any trade or business.

2.3 The 1989 Act means that the *ultra vires* rule is radically reformed and simplified, with the apparent intention of removing its influence almost entirely with regard to third parties transacting with the company in good faith.

    (a)   The validity of an act done by a company cannot be questioned on the ground that the company lacks the capacity, that is because that act is beyond a company's objects. Furthermore, the power of the directors to bind the company is deemed to be free of any limitation under its constitution, as long as the third party is acting in good faith. Although the members can bring proceedings to restrain directors from acting outside their powers, this will not affect any act to be done by them in fulfilment of a legal obligation.

    (b)   A third party is presumed to be acting in good faith unless the contrary is proved; this is reinforced by an express statement that a third party is not to be held to have acted with bad faith merely because he knew that the directors had no power to bind the company to the transaction in question. A third party is under no duty to enquire whether the act is permitted by the memorandum or is otherwise outside the scope of the directors' powers.

    (c)   A party to a transaction with a company does not have to enquire:

        (i)   as to whether it is permitted by the company's memorandum; or
        (ii)  as to any limitation on the powers of the board of directors to bind the company or authorise others to do so.

2.4 The result of these provisions is that a third party who is legally in good faith can deal with the company with absolute confidence that the transaction cannot be attacked on the grounds that the company lacks the legal ability to perform it, or that the directors lack the ability to enter into it. The limits of this are, as yet, unclear. The position of, for example, a third party who is aware that the directors are acting for an improper purpose is questionable, and the matter is likely to be resolved in the courts. We will return to the topic of a company's contractual capacity in Chapter 12.

## 3. MENTAL INCAPACITY

3.1 If a person who is temporarily insane, under the influence of drugs or drunk enters into a contract it is binding on him unless:

    (a)   he is, at the time, incapable of understanding the nature of the contract; *and*
    (b)   the other party knows or ought to know of his disability.

3.2 When necessaries are supplied (not as a gift but with the intention of obtaining payment) to a person under disability, he must pay a reasonable price for them in any event (s 3 Sale of Goods Act 1979). The rules are similar to those applicable to minors - see paragraphs 1.4-1.5 above.

3.3 In extreme cases of mental imbalance, grounds may exist for an application to the Court of Protection for the appointment of a receiver if the person is a 'patient' under the Mental Health Act 1983. The Court of Protection is not a court in the usual sense but a government department which supervises the financial affairs of mentally incapable persons. Medical and financial evidence is submitted to the court which, if it is satisfied, appoints someone, usually a close relative, to manage the affairs of the patient with the title of 'receiver'.

3.4 The effect of the court order is to transfer from the patient to his receiver legal authority to deal with the patient's income (capital transactions usually require express authorisation by the court).

3.5 Where the Court of Protection has jurisdiction to manage the affairs of a long-term mentally disordered person because of an order under the Mental Health Act 1983, that person may not form contracts which interfere with the Court's power. Thus he may be completely incapacitated from entering into contracts, depending on how bad is his state of mind.

3.6 A customer who fears that mental incapacity (usually through senility) is approaching may execute a power of attorney for a person (such as a relative) to act on his or her behalf under the Enduring Powers of Attorney Act 1985. Such a power is not revoked by mental incapacity (as powers of attorney usually are). We shall return to this point in Part C of the text.

## 4. CONCLUSION

4.1 The capacity of a person to contract is fundamental to the enforceability of contractual provisions. Contractual capacity, particularly regarding minors, is unlikely to be a major element in an examination question but a knowledge of it informs the rest of contract law and is clearly of significance to retail banks which have a great number of individuals and companies as customers.

4.2 Because banks have millions of customers from all walks of life they are probably more affected by limitations on an actual or potential customer's capacity than most other business organisations.

4.3 We shall see later in this text how a bank should protect itself with regard to limited contractual capacity. Below is a summary:

| Person | Action by bank |
|---|---|
| Minors | Do not lend to minors<br>Do not canvass credit to a minor<br>Warn guarantors of a minor's debt that the guarantee is binding<br>Cherish them – they are the customers of the future! |
| Limited companies | Maintain files of documentation relating to constitution, resolutions<br>Check capacity of directors to act<br>Ensure company's full name is on its cheques |
| Mentally ill patients | Be wary of taking on as new customers<br>Ensure receiver's acts are within the remit of the Court of Protection order, especially regarding capital transactions<br>Be aware of the terms of the Enduring Powers of Attorney Act 1985 |

---

## TEST YOUR KNOWLEDGE
*The numbers in brackets refer to paragraphs of this chapter*

1 How may a minor's different general contractual liabilities be classified? (1.2)

2 In what circumstances may a minor be bound to pay for goods? (1.5, 1.6)

3 In what circumstances may a minor be bound by a contract of apprenticeship or vocation? (1.10, 1.11)

4 Give an example of a contract which is binding on a minor unless he avoids it by repudiation. (1.13)

5 When may a person with full contractual capacity:

   (a) enforce a contract which was originally unenforceable; and
   (b) recover property under such a contract from a minor? (1.19, 1.20)

6 What is a minor's liability in tort? (1.22)

7 How has the Companies Act 1989 affected a company's capacity to contract? (2.2 - 2.4)

8 When is a person who is insane or drunk not bound by a contract entered into by him? (3.1)

---

*Now try question 8 at the end of the text*

*Chapter 5*

# MISREPRESENTATION, DURESS AND UNDUE INFLUENCE

---

**This chapter covers the following topics.**

1. Reality of consent
2. Mistake - *non est factum*
3. Misrepresentation
4. Duress
5. Undue influence

---

## 1. REALITY OF CONSENT

1.1 We saw earlier that the validity of a contract may be affected by a number of factors. These were identified as

(a) contract terms;
(b) the form of the contract;
(c) contractual capacity of the parties intending to contract with one another;
(d) genuine consent of the parties; and
(e) legality of the contract.

1.2 In this chapter we examine the issue of consent. Where a party to a contract does not (or cannot) give his consent freely to the terms of the contract, there is no reality of consent.

## 2. MISTAKE - *NON EST FACTUM*

2.1 The law recognises the problems of a blind or illiterate person who signs a document which he cannot read. If it is not what he supposes he may be able to repudiate it as not his deed *(non est factum)*. The contract will then be void. The relief is not now restricted to the blind or illiterate but will not ordinarily be given to a person who merely failed to read what it was within his capacity to read and understand.

2.2 The following conditions must be satisfied in order to treat a signed contract as void for *non est factum:*

(a)   there must be a fundamental difference between the legal effect of the document signed and that which the person who signed it believed it to have; and

(b)   the mistake must have been made without carelessness on the part of the person who signed.

*Case: Saunders v Anglia Building Society 1971* (also known as *Gallie v Lee)*
Mrs Gallie, a widow of 78, agreed to help her nephew, Parkin, to raise money on the security of her house provided that she might continue to live in it until her death. Parkin did not wish to appear in the transaction himself since he feared that his wife, from whom he was separated, would then enforce against him her claim for maintenance. Parkin therefore arranged that Lee, a solicitor's clerk, should prepare the mortgage. As a first step Lee produced a document which was in fact a transfer of the house on sale to Lee. However, Lee told Mrs Gallie that the document was a deed of gift to Parkin and she signed it at a time when her spectacles were broken and she could not read. Lee then remortgaged the house as his property to a building society. Lee paid nothing to Mrs Gallie or to Parkin. Mrs Gallie sought to repudiate the document as *non est factum.*

*Held:* Mrs Gallie knew that she was transferring her house (although not to Lee). Her act in signing the document during a temporary inability to read amounted to carelessness. The claim to repudiate the transfer failed.

*Case: Foster v Mackinnon 1869*
An elderly man of feeble sight, M, was asked to sign a guarantee. He had done so before. The document put before him to sign was in fact a bill of exchange which he signed as acceptor. The bill was later negotiated to the plaintiff who sought payment from M. M repudiated it as *non est factum.*

*Held:* the document signed was so different from what it was believed to be that a defence of *non est factum* could be available.

*Case: Lloyds Bank plc v Waterhouse 1990*
The bank obtained a guarantee from a father as security for a loan to his son to buy a farm. It also took a charge over the farm. The father did not read the guarantee because he was illiterate (which he did not tell the bank) but he did enquire of the bank about the guarantee's terms. As a result he believed that he was guaranteeing only the loan for the farm. In fact he signed a guarantee securing *all* the son's indebtedness to the bank. The son defaulted and the bank called on the father's guarantee for that amount of the son's debt which was not repaid following the farm's sale.

*Held:* the father had made adequate attempts to discover his liability by questioning the bank's employees (he was not careless). They had caused him to believe he was signing something other than he believed. This was a case of both *non est factum* and negligent misrepresentation.

2.3   In a *non est factum* case the person who signs will usually rescind the contract (for misrepresentation) between himself and the person who puts forward and misdescribes the document (as in the *Waterhouse* case above). The defence of *non est factum* need only be raised when an honest third party has acquired rights. This is because a contract is void for *non est factum* (so no rights acquired by any party) whilst it is only voidable for misrepresentation (that is, valid and binding until rescinded).

## Protection of poor and ignorant persons

2.4 The law seeks to protect poor and ignorant people who enter into property transactions without any idea of the seriousness of the possible consequences. To be protected by the rule, however, the plaintiff must be shown to be ignorant of property matters and not, for instance, merely of the English language.

*Case: Bahbra v United Bank 1990*
Mr A asked Mr B, the plaintiff, if he could borrow the deeds of Mr B's house in order to provide security for a loan to Mr A. Mr A's son took Mr B to the defendant bank's branch where the manager explained the impact of the charge to Mr B in his native language, Punjabi. He also advised him to obtain independent advice. Mr B signed the mortgage but later when the bank tried to enforce its security he sought to avoid the charge on the grounds that, as a 'poor and ignorant' person, he should be protected.

*Held:* Mr B was not ignorant of property transactions: he had already had two previous mortgages. He had not been coerced and every effort had been made to explain the consequences of his actions. The facts that he had little English and was not well-educated were irrelevant.

## 3. MISREPRESENTATION

3.1 A statement made in the course of negotiations may become a term of the contract. If it is a term of the contract and proves to be untrue, the party who has been misinformed may claim damages for breach of contract. If, however, the statement does not become a term of the contract and it is untrue, the party misled may be able to treat it as a misrepresentation and rescind (cancel) the contract, or in some cases, recover damages. *The contract is voidable for misrepresentation.*

3.2 A misrepresentation is:

   (a) a statement of fact which is untrue;

   (b) made by one party to the other before the contract is made in order to *induce* the latter to enter into the contract; and

   (c) an inducement to the party misled actually to enter into the contract – it must relate to a matter of some importance and have been relied on by the party misled.

*Case: Horsfall v Thomas 1862*
H made a gun to be sold to T and, in making it, concealed a defect in the breech by inserting a metal plug. T bought the gun without inspecting it. The gun exploded and T claimed that he had been misled into purchasing it by a misrepresentation (the metal plug) that it was sound.

*Held:* T had not inspected the gun at the time of purchase and the metal plug could not have been a misleading inducement because he was unaware of it, and therefore did not rely on it when he entered into the contract.

3.3 Since to be actionable a representation must have induced the person to enter into the contract, it follows that he must have:

(a) known of its existence;
(b) allowed it to affect his judgement; and
(c) been unaware of its untruth.

3.4 Clearly if the person never knew a representation had been made, or had ignored it, or had known it to be untrue, then he cannot be said to have been induced by an untrue statement to enter into the contract. However, the misrepresentation may still be actionable even though it was not the only reason the person entered into the contract.

**Representation**

3.5 But in order to analyse whether a statement may be a misrepresentation, it is first of all necessary to decide whether it could have been a representation at all:

(a) a statement of fact is a representation;
(b) a statement of law, intention, opinion or mere 'sales talk' is not a representation; and
(c) silence is not (usually) a representation (but see paragraph 3.7 below).

3.6 A statement of opinion or intention is a statement that the opinion or intention exists, but not that it is a correct opinion or an intention which will be realised. In deciding whether a statement is a statement of fact or opinion, the extent of the speaker's knowledge as much as the words he uses determines the category to which the statement belongs.

*Case: Smith v Land and House Property Corporation 1884*
A vendor of property described it as 'let to F (a most desirable tenant) at a rent of £400 per annum for 27½ years thus offering a first class investment'. In fact F had only paid part of the rent due in the previous six months by instalments after the due date and he had failed altogether to pay the most recent quarter's rent.

*Held:* the description of F as a 'desirable tenant' was not a mere opinion but an implied assertion that nothing had occurred which could make F an undesirable tenant. As a statement of fact this was untrue.

*Case: Bisset v Wilkinson 1927*
A vendor of land which both parties knew had not previously been grazed by sheep stated that it would support about 2,000 sheep. This proved to be untrue.

*Held:* in the circumstances this was an expression of opinion, not a statement of fact.

3.7 As a general rule neither party is under any duty to disclose what he knows. If he keeps silent that is not a representation. But there *is* a duty to disclose information in the following cases.

(a) What is said must be complete enough to avoid giving a misleading impression. A half-truth can be false.

*Case: R v Kylsant 1931*
When inviting the public to subscribe for its shares, a company stated that it had paid a regular dividend throughout the years of the depression. This clearly implied that the company had made a profit during those years. This was not the case since the dividends had been paid out of the accumulated profits of the pre-depression years.

*Held:* the silence as to the source of the dividends was a misrepresentation since it distorted the true statement that dividends had been paid.

(b)  There is a duty to correct an earlier statement which was true when made but which may become untrue before the contract is completed.

*Case: With v O'Flanagan 1936*
At the start of negotiations in January a doctor, who wished to sell his practice, stated that it was worth £2,000 per year. Shortly afterwards he fell ill and as a result the practice was almost worthless by the time the sale was completed in May.

*Held:* his illness and inability to sustain the practice's value falsified the January representation; his silence when he should have corrected the earlier impression constituted misrepresentation. The sale was set aside.

(c)  In contracts of 'extreme good faith' (*uberrimae fides*- see Section 4 of this chapter) there is a duty to disclose the material facts which one knows. Non-disclosure can lead to the contract being voidable for misrepresentation, for example where a party fails to disclose to an insurer that several insurance companies have declined proposals to insure his life: *London Assurance v Mansel 1879.*

3.8  A statement of law is not a representation and hence no remedy is available if it is untrue. However, most representations on law are statements of the speaker's opinion of what the law is; if he does not in fact hold this opinion then there is a misrepresentation of his state of mind and hence a remedy should be available. In addition, a statement of the meaning of foreign law is emphatically a representation.

**Made by one party to another**

3.9  The person to whom a representation is made is entitled to rely on it without investigation - even if he is invited to make enquiries.

*Case: Redgrave v Hurd 1881*
R told H that the income of his business was £300 per annum and produced to H papers which disclosed an income of £200 per annum. H queried the figure of £300 and R produced additional papers which R stated showed how the additional £100 per annum was obtained. H did not examine these papers which in fact showed only a very small amount of additional income. H entered into the contract but later discovered the true facts and he refused to complete the contract.

*Held:* H relied on R's statement and not on his own investigation. H had no duty to investigate the accuracy of R's statement and might rescind the contract.

3.10  Although in general a misrepresentation must have been made by the misrepresentor to the misrepresentee for it to be actionable there are two exceptions to the rule:

(a)  a misrepresentation can be made to the public in general, as where an advertisement contains a misleading representation; and

(b)  the misrepresentation need not be made directly on a one-to-one basis - it is sufficient that the misrepresentor knows that the misrepresentation would be passed on to the relevant person.

*Case: Pilmore v Hood 1873*

H fraudulently misrepresented the turnover of his pub so as to sell it to X. X had insufficient funds and so repeated the representations, with H's knowledge, to P. On the basis of this P purchased the pub.

*Held:* H was liable for fraudulent misrepresentation even though he had not himself misrepresented the facts to P.

## Types of misrepresentation

3.11 Misrepresentation is classified (for the purpose of determining what remedies are available) as:

(a) *fraudulent* - a statement made with knowledge that it is untrue, or without believing it to be true, or recklessly, careless whether it be true or false; or

(b) *negligent* - a statement made in the belief that it is true but without reasonable grounds for that belief; or

(c) *innocent* - a statement made in the belief that it is true and with reasonable grounds for that belief.

*Case: Derry v Peek 1889*

D and other directors of a company published a prospectus inviting the public to apply for shares. The prospectus stated that the company (formed under a special Act of Parliament) had statutory powers to operate trams in Plymouth, drawn by horses or driven by steam power. The Act required that the company should obtain a licence from the Board of Trade for the operation of steam trams. The directors assumed that the licence would be granted whenever they might apply for it. But it was later refused.

*Held:* the directors honestly believed that the statement made was true and so this was not a fraudulent misrepresentation. The false representation was not made knowingly, without belief in its truth or recklessly, and so the directors escaped liability.

3.12 Under the Misrepresentation Act 1967, which was not then in force, this would probably have been negligent misrepresentation since there were no *reasonable* grounds for the statement. Negligent misrepresentation may be at common law (involving breach of a duty of care owed) or under the statutory protection of the Misrepresentation Act 1967 (when the defendant must disprove his negligence). Under the Act no duty of care need be shown.

## Remedies for misrepresentation

3.13 In a case of *fraudulent* misrepresentation the party misled may rescind the contract (since it is voidable), refuse to perform his part of it and/or recover damages for any loss by a common law action for deceit (which is a tort).

3.14 In a case of *negligent* misrepresentation the party misled may, under equitable principles, rescind the contract and refuse to perform his part under it. In order to gain a remedy, the plaintiff must show that the misrepresentation was in breach of a duty of care.

*Case: Esso Petroleum Co Ltd v Mardon 1976*
E negligently told M that a filling station, the tenancy for which they were negotiating, had an annual turnover of 200,000 gallons. This induced M to take the tenancy, but in fact the turnover never rose to more than 86,000 gallons.

*Held:* E owed a special duty of care and was in breach. Damages were awarded to M. (If the Misrepresentation Act 1967 had been in force M could have claimed under that.)

3.15 He may also (under the statutory protection of the Misrepresentation Act 1967) claim damages for any loss. It is then up to the party who made the statement to prove, if he can, that he had reasonable grounds for making it and that it was not in fact negligent. In the case of negligent misrepresentation the innocent party has a right to damages if he has suffered loss. However, if the maker of the statement proves that he had reasonable grounds for believing, and in fact did believe up to the time the contract was made, that the facts represented were true then he has a defence that he was not negligent: s 2(1) Misrepresentation Act 1967.

*Case: F and H Entertainments v Leisure Enterprises 1976*
FHE purchased the lease of a club premises from LE for £23,100, having been told that the rent was £2,400 per year and that no rent review notices had been served. FHE went into occupation and spent £4,000 re-equipping the premises. The landlords then demanded a revised rent of £6,500. They were entitled to do this because valid rent review notices had in fact been served.

*Held:* damages under s 2(1) would be awarded and they would include compensation for expenditure properly incurred, being the £4,000. Rescission would also be granted.

3.16 In a case of *innocent* misrepresentation the party misled may, under equitable principles, rescind the contract and refuse to perform his part of it. But he is not entitled to claim damages for any additional loss.

3.17 Under the statutory provisions of the Misrepresentation Act 1967 s 2(2) the court may, in a case of non-fraudulent - negligent or innocent - misrepresentation, award damages *instead of* rescission. This may be a fairer solution in some cases, for example where the misrepresentation is on a minor matter. But damages may only be awarded instead of rescission if the right to rescind has not been lost. The remedy of damages is discretionary and as a rule is not awarded for innocent misrepresentation. An indemnity - different from damages - may be awarded, indemnifying the misrepresentee against any obligations necessarily created by the contract.

3.18 Damages in cases of misrepresentation are measured under the rules of tort - that is, they are intended to put the injured party in the position he would have been in if he had never entered the contract. Whatever the type of misrepresentation, unforeseeable as well as foreseeable losses are recoverable, provided the losses are not too remote.

*Case: Royscot Trust Ltd v Rogerson & Others 1991*
In a hire purchase agreement for a car the dealer agreed a price of £7,600 with the hirer and took a £1,200 deposit. The plaintiff finance company agreed to finance the transaction but, because it stipulated a 20% deposit, the dealer (innocently) misrepresented the price and deposit at £8,000 and £1,600 respectively. The agreement was executed between the plaintiff and the hirer but the latter, after paying £2,774.76, dishonestly sold the car to an innocent third party who acquired good title. The plaintiff claimed damages from the dealer of £3,624.24, being the difference between the price for which it bought the car from the dealer and the amount paid to it by the hirer.

*Held:* as in a case of fraudulent misrepresentation, the plaintiff was entitled to recover for any loss which flowed from the dealer's misrepresentation, even if this could not have been foreseen. Because hire purchase cars are often dishonestly sold by hirers, the loss was also not too remote.

### Loss of the right to rescind for misrepresentation

3.19 The principle of rescission is that the parties should be restored to their position as it was before the contract was made. The right to rescind is lost in any of the following circumstances.

(a) If the party misled *affirms the contract* after discovering the true facts he may not afterwards rescind. For this purpose it is not necessary that he should expressly affirm the contract. Intention to affirm may be implied from conduct indicating that the party is treating the contract as still in operation. In a number of cases concerned with untrue company prospectuses, subscribers have lost the right to rescind by continuing to exercise their rights as shareholders even though they did not realise that this would be the effect. Mere inaction over a period of time may also be treated as affirmation.

(b) If the parties can no longer be restored to substantially the pre-contract position, the right to rescind is lost.

*Case: Clarke v Dickson 1858*
The contract related to a business which at the time of the misrepresentation was carried on by a partnership. It was later reorganised as a company and the plaintiff's interest was, with his consent, converted into shares. He later sought to rescind the conversion.

*Held:* the conversion of the plaintiff's interest in the partnership into shares in the company was an irreversible change which precluded restoration to the original position. The right to rescind had been lost.

(c) The right to rescind is not, then, lost merely because the contract has been carried through to completion before the demand for rescission is made. Lapse of time may, however, bar rescission for innocent misrepresentation.

(d) If the rights of third parties, such as creditors of an insolvent company, would be prejudiced by rescission, it is too late to rescind.

3.20 No other barrier exists to the right to rescission thanks to s 1 Misrepresentation Act 1967; in particular, the fact that the contract has been performed (eg a conveyance of land has been completed) does not mean that it cannot be rescinded for misrepresentation. But thanks to s 2(2) the court may avoid unnecessary punishment by ordering damages instead of rescission.

3.21 Where misrepresentation is fraudulent, lapse of time does not, by itself, bar rescission because time only begins to run from the discovery of the truth.

3.22 Rescission is often an illusory remedy because it may be too late to rescind when the truth is discovered. It may be more advantageous to the party misled to sue for damages for negligent misstatement under the law of tort. Generally, though, s 2(1) Misrepresentation Act 1967 is more popular because the onus of disproving negligence shifts to the defendant, and no special relationship need be proved.

3.23 Any clause of a contract which excludes liability for misrepresentation in making the contract is void unless it satisfies the test of reasonableness imposed by the Unfair Contract Terms Act 1977 (see next chapter).

## 4. DURESS

4.1 A person who has been induced to enter into a contract by duress (or undue influence) is entitled to avoid it at common law - the contract is *voidable* at his option, because he has not given his genuine consent to its terms.

4.2 Duress is fundamentally a threat. This may be of physical violence, imprisonment, damage to goods or business, and even of breaching a contract. The threat may be translated to actual violence etc, but duress may still be implied merely from the threat.

*Case: Cumming v Ince 1847*
An elderly lady was induced to make a settlement of her property in favour of a relative by a threat of unlawful imprisonment in a mental home.

*Held:* the settlement would be set aside on account of duress. (The principle of duress and undue influence is applied to gifts, as in this case, as well as to contracts.)

4.3 In older cases it has been held that threatened seizure of goods or property is not duress as it should be limited to threats of physical harm or imprisonment. But in more recent decisions the courts have set aside contracts made under 'economic duress'.

*Case: The Atlantic Baron 1979*
The parties had reached agreement on the purchase price of a ship. There was then a currency devaluation and the vendor claimed a 10% increase in price. The purchaser refused to pay. The vendor stated that if the extra was not paid he would terminate the contract and amicable business relations would not continue. The purchaser then agreed to pay the increased price.

*Held:* the threat to terminate the contract and discontinue amicable business relations amounted to economic duress. The contract was therefore voidable.

*Case: Atlas Express Ltd v Kafco (Exporters and Distributors) Ltd 1989*
K had a big order to fulfil with W for a supply of baskets. K negotiated with A that deliveries should be made at £7.50 each. This was confirmed by telex. Later A decided that £7.50 was not enough and drew up an updated 'agreement'. A's driver arrived at K's depot with the update and said that he would not collect goods unless K signed the update. K protested but was unable to speak to someone in charge at A. Being bound to supply to W, K signed under protest and continued to pay only the original agreed amount.

*Held:* A could not enforce the higher payment since consent had been obtained by economic duress - K would have suffered dire consequences if it had been unable to supply W.

4.4 Such threats can be termed 'illegitimate pressure'. Whether it is or not depends on the circumstances, but much depends on whether the person's will has been overcome to such an extent as to invalidate his consent.

# 5: MISREPRESENTATION, DURESS AND UNDUE INFLUENCE

## 5. UNDUE INFLUENCE

5.1 A contract (or a gift) is voidable if the party who made the contract or gift did so under the undue influence of another person (usually the other party to the transaction). This is an equitable relief.

5.2 To succeed in a claim for undue influence, it must be shown that:

(a) a *relationship of trust and confidence* existed (in some cases this is assumed); and

(b) the weaker party did not exercise *free judgement* in making the contract; and

(c) the resulting contract is to the *manifest disadvantage* of the weaker party and the obvious benefit of the stronger; and

(d) the weaker party has sought to *avoid* the contract *as soon as* the undue influence ceased to affect him or her.

We shall discuss each of these points in turn.

### Relationship of trust and confidence

5.3 When the parties stand in certain relationships the law assumes that one has undue influence over the other. These relationships include the following in which the stronger party is mentioned first (this is not an exhaustive list):

(a) parent and minor child (*sometimes* even if the child is an adult);
(b) guardian and ward;
(c) trustee and beneficiary under the trust;
(d) religious adviser and disciple; and
(e) doctor and patient.

5.4 Note that the following relationships are *not* assumed to be ones in which undue influence is exerted - although this assumption may of course be rebutted:

(a) bank and customer;
(b) husband and wife; and
(c) employer and employee.

5.5 It is possible to argue that any other relationship in which one person places trust and confidence in another has given the latter the opportunity for undue influence. The courts will look at all the facts in ascertaining whether in a particular case undue influence has in fact been exercised.

*Case: Hodgson v Marks 1971*
An elderly lady transferred her house to her lodger and allowed him to manage her affairs. He later sold the house.

*Held:* undue influence was to be inferred from the relationship and the benefits obtained by the lodger.

93

# 5: MISREPRESENTATION, DURESS AND UNDUE INFLUENCE

*Case: Williams v Bayley 1866*
A bank official told an elderly man that the bank might prosecute his son for forgery and to avoid such action the father mortgaged property to the bank.

*Held:* there is no presumption of undue influence in the relation of the bank and customer but it could be proved to exist (as it did in this case) by the relevant facts.

5.6 Of course it is perfectly possible for a relationship to exist where one person places trust and confidence in another without a resulting contract being voidable for undue influence. It is only where the stronger person steps outside a fair and businesslike relationship and obtains a benefit from the abuse of trust that undue influence arises: *National Westminster Bank v Morgan 1985* (see below).

## Free judgement

5.7 If it appears that there is undue influence, the party who is deemed to have the influence may resist the attempt to set aside the contract by showing that the weaker party did in fact exercise a free judgement in making the contract. A person who has undue influence is presumed to have used it but this is rebuttable. In rebuttal it is usually necessary to show that the person, otherwise subject to undue influence, was advised by an independent adviser to whom the material facts were fully disclosed *and* that adequate consideration was given: *Inche Noriah v Shaik Allie bin Omar 1929.*

*Case: Lloyds Bank v Bundy 1975*
On facts very like those of *Williams v Bayley* above (except that the son was in financial difficulty and the bank required additional security for its loan to him) a customer gave the bank a charge over his house.

*Held:* the bank could not itself give independent financial advice to a customer on a matter in which the bank was interested as a creditor. Since the bank had not arranged for the customer to have independent advice the charge in favour of the bank would be set aside.

5.8 However, there may still be found to be undue influence even where the defendant tries to rebut the presumption by showing that the plaintiff has refused independent advice.

*Case: Goldsworthy v Brickell 1987*
G, an 85 year old man, entered into an agreement to give tenancy of a farm to B, who had been helping him run it. The terms were highly favourable to B, but G had rejected opportunities to consult a solicitor. G sought for the agreement to be rescinded.

*Held:* although there had been no domination (see *Morgan's case* below), the fact that the agreement's terms were clearly unfair and that G placed trust in B meant that the presumption could not be rebutted by showing that free exercise of judgement was allowed. G could rescind.

## Manifest disadvantage

5.9 A transaction will not be set aside on the ground of undue influence unless it can be shown that the transaction is to the manifest disadvantage of the person subjected to undue influence.

*Case: National Westminster Bank v Morgan 1985*
A wife (W) signed a re-mortgage of the family home (owned jointly with her husband H) in favour of the bank, to prevent the original mortgagee from continuing with proceedings to repossess the home. The bank manager told her in good faith, but incorrectly, that the mortgage only secured liabilities in respect of the home. In fact, it covered all H's debts to the bank. W signed the mortgage at home, in the presence of the manager, and without taking independent advice. H and W fell into arrears with the payments and soon afterwards H died. At the time of his death, nothing was owed to the bank in respect of H's business liabilities. The bank sought possession, but W contended that she had only signed the mortgage because of undue influence from the bank and, therefore, it should be set aside.

*Held:* The House of Lords, reversing the Court of Appeal's decision, held that the manager had not crossed the line between explaining an ordinary business transaction and entering into a relationship in which he had a dominant influence. Furthermore, the transaction was not unfair to W. Therefore, the bank was not under a duty to ensure that W took independent advice. The order for possession was granted.

5.10 An influence stopping short of a dominant one may be sufficient to allow the court to set the contract aside on the basis of undue influence. Once trust has been shown to have existed, it is then necessary to demonstrate manifest disadvantage rather than that the position of trust has been abused and exercised as a dominating influence: *Woodstead Finance Ltd v Petrou 1986.*

5.11 The case below identifies what is and is not 'manifest disadvantage'.

*Case: Bank of Credit and Commerce International v Aboody 1988*
Mrs A purchased the family home in 1949 and it was registered in her sole name. Mr A ran a business in which his wife took no interest but in 1959 she became a director of his company on the understanding that she would have to do nothing. Between 1976 and 1980 she signed three guarantees and three mortgages over her house. Mr A deliberately concealed matters from his wife. The company collapsed due to Mr A's fraud and the bank sought to enforce the guarantees against Mr and Mrs A.

*Held:* There had been actual undue influence over his wife by Mr A but Mrs A had suffered no manifest disadvantage since, at the time she signed the documents, her husband's business was comfortably supporting her and there was no indication that it would not continue to do so. She had benefited from the business which she secured and could not be said to have suffered manifest disadvantage in that sense.

**Loss of the right to rescind**

5.12 The right to rescind the contract (or gift) for undue influence is lost if there is delay in taking action after the influence has ceased to have effect.

*Case: Allcard v Skinner 1887*
Under the influence of a clergyman, A entered a Protestant convent and in compliance with a vow of poverty transferred property worth about £7,000 to the order. After ten years A left the order and became a Roman Catholic. Six years later she demanded the return of the unexpended balance of her gift.

*Held:* it was a clear case of undue influence since, among other things, the rules of the order forbade its members to seek advice from any outsider. But A's delay of six years (after leaving the order) in making her claim, debarred her from setting aside the gift and recovering her property. (This is an example of the equitable doctrine of 'laches' or delay.)

5.13 The right to rescission is also lost if the party affirms the contract by performing obligations without protest, or if an innocent third party has acquired rights.

## 6. CONCLUSION

6.1 The binding nature of contract usually means that, once a contract comes into existence, both parties to it must fulfil their obligations in line with the agreement. In this chapter, however, we have seen how a contract may be found not to be binding where it is *void* as *non est factum* or *voidable* for misrepresentation, duress and undue influence. Where a contract is voidable the person is bound until such time as he exercises his right (which can be lost) to rescind it.

6.2 A bank must beware of the effects of *non est factum*, misrepresentation, duress and undue influence.

(a) *Non est factum* is an issue when a person is blind or illiterate and commits himself to something which he innocently and non-negligently believed to be something else. Because it usually arises when the bank is unaware of the customer's handicap, it can only be guarded against in the same way as misrepresentation - that is, the bank must take care not to misrepresent its terms and conditions and should try to ensure that customers take independent advice.

(b) Misrepresentation is significant when:

   (i) the bank misrepresents its terms and conditions, however innocently;
   (ii) a customer misrepresents his or her status or resources when seeking loan facilities;
   (iii) the bank misrepresents a customer's status when replying to a banker's reference.

(c) Duress is rarely an issue, but could be said to exist if the bank pushes too hard for, say, additional security to prevent it from sending in receivers. This would be *economic duress*.

(d) Undue influence is a problematic issue for banks. Although it is not presumed to exist in a normal banker/customer relationship, it can be shown to exist where the bank and its customer were closely linked. In addition, the bank must beware of becoming implicated in the undue influence of a person acting as its agent - say, where a husband takes away a security document to be executed by his wife. We shall return to this topic in Part D of this text.

## TEST YOUR KNOWLEDGE
*The numbers in brackets refer to paragraphs of this chapter*

1  Explain *non est factum* and illustrate how it may affect a legal document. (2.1-2.3)

2  What is a misrepresentation and how does it differ from a statement of opinion? (3.2, 3.6)

3  When may silence be construed as misrepresentation? (3.7)

4  What are the three different kinds of misrepresentation? (3.11)

5  What are the remedies available to a party who has been misled by negligent misrepresentation by the other party to the contract? (3.14, 3.15)

6  In what circumstances may a party misled by misrepresentation by unable to rescind the contract? (3.18)

7  Distinguish between duress and undue influence. (4.2, 5.2)

8  What is the significance of ensuring that the other party to the contract has independent professional advice in deciding whether to decide to enter into the contract? (5.7)

9  How may the right (based on undue influence) to rescind the contract be lost? (5.12, 5.13)

*Now try question 9 at the end of the text*

*Chapter 6*

# STATUTORY INTERVENTION IN CONTRACTS

This chapter covers the following topics.

1. The purpose of statutory intervention in contracts
2. The Unfair Contract Terms Act 1977
3. The Consumer Credit Act 1974
4. The Supply of Goods and Services Act 1982
5. Standard form contracts

## 1. THE PURPOSE OF STATUTORY INTERVENTION IN CONTRACTS

1.1 The relative sizes of contracting parties – Mr Bloggs v Vast Multinational Corporation plc – means that there may be, and very often is, inequality of bargaining power. Whilst Parliament and the courts will not remedy a bad bargain purely because it is bad, they have intervened in unfair ones. For your syllabus, the two most important statutes of this type are the Unfair Contract Terms Act 1977 and the Consumer Credit Act 1974.

## 2. THE UNFAIR CONTRACT TERMS ACT 1977

2.1 Liability for financial loss arising from a bank's negligence in a contract *may* be expressly excluded in the contract's terms, but only if the 'exclusion' (or 'exemption') clause satisfies a test of reasonableness set out in the Act. An exclusion clause is often called a 'disclaimer of liability'.

2.2 The Act uses two techniques for controlling exclusion clauses – some types of clauses are void, whereas others are subject to a test of reasonableness. The main provisions of the Act as they affect banks are as follows.

*Exclusion of liability for negligence (s 2)*

2.3 'Negligence' covers breach of contractual obligations of skill and care, of the common law duty of skill and care and of the common duty of occupiers of premises under the Occupiers' Liability Act 1957.

(a) A person cannot, by reference to any contract term, restrict his liability for death or personal injury resulting from negligence.

(b) In the case of other loss or damage, a person cannot restrict his liability for negligence *unless the term is reasonable.*

*Standard form contracts and consumer contracts (s 3)*

2.4 The person who imposes the standard term, or who deals with the consumer, cannot *(unless the term is reasonable):*

(a) restrict liability for his own breach of contract; or

(b) claim to be entitled to render substantially different performance or no performance at all.

*Case: George Mitchell v Finney Lock Seeds 1983*
The plaintiff, a farmer, ordered 30 pounds of cabbage seeds from the defendants, who were seed merchants. The purchase price was about £200. The defendant's standard term contract limited their liability to refunding the amount paid by the plaintiff. The wrong type of cabbage seed was delivered; it was planted over a wide acreage, but when the crop came up it was not fit for human consumption. The plaintiff claimed about £92,000 (damages plus interest).

*Held:* at common law the exemption clause would have protected the defendant, but the court decided in favour of the plaintiff, relying exclusively on the statutory ground of reasonableness.

2.5 Standard form contracts used by banks are discussed at the end of this chapter.

*Unreasonable indemnity clauses (s 4)*

2.6 A clause whereby one party undertakes to indemnify the other for liability incurred in the other's performance of the contract is void if the party giving the indemnity is a consumer, *unless it is reasonable.*

*The requirement for reasonableness (s 11)*

2.7 The term must be fair and reasonable having regard to all the circumstances which were, or which ought to have been, known to the parties when the contract was made. The burden of proving reasonableness lies on the person seeking to rely on the clause (ie the bank). Statutory guidelines have been included in the Act to assist the determination of reasonableness. The court will consider in relation to contracts under (e) above:

(a) the relative strength of the parties' bargaining position and in particular whether the customer could have satisfied his requirements from another source;

(b) whether any inducement (eg a reduced price) was offered to the customer to persuade him to accept limitation of his rights and whether any other person would have made a similar contract with him without that limitation;

(c) whether the customer knew or ought to have known of the existence and extent of the exclusion of liability clause (having regard where appropriate to trade custom or previous dealings between the parties);

(d) if failure to comply with a condition (eg failure to give notice of a defect within a short period) excludes or restricts the customer's rights, whether it was reasonable to expect when the contract was made that compliance with the condition would be practicable (Unfair Contract Terms Act 1977 Sch 2).

*Case: Walker v Boyle 1981*

The vendor of a house was asked if she was aware of any boundary disputes. Using a form containing a general exclusion of liability clause she replied, through her solicitor, that she was not aware of any disputes. In fact she was aware of a dispute which she did not disclose. A contract which also contained an appropriate exclusion clause was later made.

*Held:* the exclusion clause in the contract was invalid since it did not satisfy the 'fair and reasonable' test imposed by the 1977 Act.

2.8 With regard to all of the above sections of UCTA 1977, the test of reasonableness for an exclusion of liability clause looks at:

(a) the resources which the party who seeks to restrict liability has available for the purpose of meeting the liability if it arises; and

(b) how far that person could cover himself by insurance.

2.9 It is up to the person who is aiming to rely on the clause's reasonableness - ie the bank - to prove that it is reasonable.

*Case: Smith v Eric Bush 1989*

A surveyor prepared a report on a property which contained a clause disclaiming liability for the accuracy and validity of the report. In fact the survey was negligently done and the plaintiff had to make good a lot of defects once the property was purchased.

*Held:* in the absence of special difficulties it was unreasonable for the surveyor to disclaim liability given the cost of the report, his profession of skill and care and his knowledge that it would be relied upon to make a major purchase.

*Case: Phillips Products v Hyland 1984*

The plaintiff hired a JCB digger and a driver (the defendant). An exclusion clause in the contract stated that 'a driver shall be under the direction and control of the hirer. Such drivers shall for all purposes in connection with their employment in the working of the plant be regarded as their servants'. The defendant made it clear that he would not tolerate any 'interference' from the plaintiff. He then drove negligently and caused £3,000 worth of damage to the plaintiff's building.

*Held:* the exclusion clause was not reasonable.

*The definition of consumer (s 12)*

2.10 A person deals as a consumer if:

(a) he neither makes the contract in the course of a business, nor holds himself out as doing so; and

(b) the other party does make the contract in the course of a business; and

(c) the services are of a type ordinarily supplied for private customers.

Hence most private customers of a bank are dealing as consumers with the bank.

2.11 Trade practices, other than exclusion of liability clauses, which prejudice the rights of consumers are regulated by the Fair Trading Act 1973. Under this, the Secretary of State may prohibit certain practices by statutory instrument; breach of these rules may lead to fines for contempt of court.

## Banks and the Unfair Contract Terms Act 1977

2.12 The important areas of this Act for banking are highlighted above. Banks are keen to be seen as organisations which act in a fair and reasonable manner and therefore they take due care to ensure that any bank contracts are within the law and unlikely to be challenged under the Act.

2.13 However customers do not always understand the nature of their contract with the bank and some of its mysteries, particularly the clearing system and the status of ATM transactions. Banks are now publicising 'charters' describing the terms of the relationship, and the final non-statutory Code of Banking Practice achieves 'transparency' in the relationship regarding charging and the system of bankers' references, for instance. Until such time as greater transparency is achieved, however, it is likely that banks will continue to attract the sort of heavy criticism made by consumer bodies, the Banking Ombudsman and the Director General of Fair Trading in 1991.

## 3. THE CONSUMER CREDIT ACT 1974

3.1 The Consumer Credit Act 1974 and the many regulations made under it seek to protect debtors who enter into credit agreements such as loans or hire purchase transactions. Such agreements are nearly always standard form contracts and it is necessary to ensure that the consumer's rights are protected.

3.2 The Act sets out provisions regarding *regulated agreements*. Broadly speaking, these are agreements made to non-corporate customers where credit of less than £15,000 is provided in a number of different ways. A regulated agreement must comply with many different requirements:

(a) the agreement must be written in a particular form and formalities as to completing and signing the form must be complied with to the letter;

(b) certain items of information, in particular as to the total amount of credit, the cost of credit and the names and right of the parties involved, must be spelled out in the agreement;

(c) adequate numbers of copies of the agreement must be provided for the debtor;

(d) some agreements are cancellable by the debtor, and the latter's rights in this respect must be properly set out.

If the bank fails to comply with these requirements then the agreement is unenforceable.

3.3 In addition, the provider of credit is liable for any misrepresentations made by 'negotiators' on his behalf to the debtor and in some circumstances may have 'connected lender liability' for breach of contract with a dealer in goods under a regulated agreement.

3.4 The Act set up a *licensing system* to regulate the providers of credit. A licence covers all activities lawfully done in the course of business by the licensee or his agent, but may be restricted by the Director-General of Fair Trading.

3.5 Orally soliciting an individual to enter into a credit agreement is known as *canvassing*. There is no harm in doing this on the creditor's or debtor's trade premises, but canvassing off trade premises is severely restricted:

(a) canvassing certain agreements off trade premises - such as cash loans - is a criminal offence: s 49. It will still be an offence even if made in response to a request *unless* that request is in writing and signed;

(b) canvassing other regulated agreements off trade premises can only be done under a licence expressly authorising such activity: s 23.

3.6 Canvassing off trade premises by making representations to induce a customer to enter into a regulated agreement involves:

(a) making oral representations during a visit by the canvasser for that purpose; *and*

(b) making that visit to somewhere other than the business premises of the canvasser, creditor, supplier or consumer; *and*

(c) *not* making that visit in response to a request made on a previous occasion.

The fact that the visit must be made *for the purposes* of canvassing exempts a casual conversation at, say, a squash game which leads to a loan being recommended.

3.7 Regulations made under the Act control *advertisements* aimed at providing credit or goods on hire to non-business customers. The objective of these regulations is to ensure that consumers have a fair impression of the product offered and a means of comparison between different products. He or she must therefore have adequate and sufficient information. The advertisement must be phrased so as to fall into one of the following three categories - simple, intermediate or full.

(a) A *simple* advertisement neither specifies a price nor contains an indication that credit or hire products are available.

(b) An *intermediate* advertisement must, at the very least, contain an indication as to where full written credit details can be obtained.

(c) A *full* advertisement must contain a great deal of information, the most important of which is the annual percentage rate (the APR).

3.8 Finally, the Act makes it an offence to solicit a minor aged 17 or under to enter into a consumer credit agreement.

**Overdraft lending**

3.9 An overdraft occurs when a customer is allowed to overdraw on his or her current account at the bank. It is a flexible form of lending:

(a)  interest rates fluctuate over the life of the borrowing;

(b)  the debtor is usually trusted to pay off the borrowing as and when he or she can;

(c)  it is not of a fixed sum but a maximum amount is normally stipulated; and

(d)  the lending is not restricted as to when it is drawn upon.

3.10  Overdraft lending is regulated by the Consumer Credit Act 1974. But in fact, because overdraft lending is so widespread, it is to some extent released from the rigours of the Act:

(a)  there is no ban on canvassing off trade premises and no need for specific authorisation in the licence in the case of overdrafts; and

(b)  overdrafts are wholly exempted from the formalities necessary in forming a regulated agreement provided it is on current account and is not linked to a transaction such as an HP agreement. This exception has been made because frequently a bank will pay a cheque which takes the customer into the red even though there is no prior agreement for this. It is unrealistic to expect every such agreement to satisfy all the requirements for formalities.

3.11  It is common practice to include in a facility letter for an overdraft a power to the bank to vary the rate of interest in line with the bank's prevailing general rates. The general statutory rule for regulated agreements within the scope of the Act is that a variation does not take effect until the lender gives notice of it to the borrower: s 82.

3.12  To relieve banks of the need to write to every customer who has an overdraft whenever the rate of interest is varied it is provided that publication of a notice of the variation suffices if it is published in at least three national newspapers and it is prominently displayed in the part of the bank's premises to which the public has access - that is, the banking hall. The notification procedure is restricted to variation of interest on the daily amount of a fluctuating overdraft. For a loan of fixed amount, even if repayable by instalments at intervals, actual notice to each individual borrower is required. That is also the rule if the terms of a facility are varied in any respect other than the rate of interest.

## 4.    THE SUPPLY OF GOODS AND SERVICES ACT 1982

4.1  Where a contract is wholly or substantially for the provision of services, such as the contracts entered into by a bank, the 1982 Act implies a number of terms.

(a)  Where the supplier of the service is acting in the course of a business, there are implied terms that he will carry out the service with reasonable care and skill (s 13) and within a reasonable time (s 14).

(b)  Where the consideration is not determined by the contract, there is an implied term that the party contracting with the supplier will pay a reasonable charge (s 15). This section obviously allows a bank to charge a 'reasonable amount' for the services supplied, if not previously agreed.

4.2  These terms are always implied. But they are not conditions of strict liability, and may be excluded so long as such an exclusion complies with the 'reasonableness' requirement of the Unfair Contract Terms Act 1977: s 16 SGSA 1982.

## 5. STANDARD FORM CONTRACTS

5.1 You have seen from your study of basic contract law that there is presumed to be a bargain which develops from offer, acceptance, consideration and intention. All this involves an element of negotiation and it will not have escaped your attention that the express terms of many contracts entered into by your bank - such as guarantees and mortgages - are not negotiated as such. They are pre-printed on a standard form which is signed by the bank and its customer.

5.2 These standard terms are often long and expressed in difficult prose. Even if the customer does read them it is unlikely that, as a layman, he could instantly understand them. Hence the opportunity is there, and is often taken, to design the forms to the benefit of the bank.

5.3 The advantages of standard form contracts are that:

(a) administration costs are minimised since the information given is easily identified;

(b) each party knows the terms in advance of the final agreement; and

(c) lengthy negotiations on remote possibilities are kept to a minimum but are still catered for.

5.4 The problem with standard form contracts is that equality of bargaining power is reduced, so that the party with most resources (the bank) can dictate terms. Since the law has always been based on the principle of freedom to bargain, statutory intervention in the form of the Consumer Credit Act 1974 and the Unfair Contract Terms Act 1977 seeks to redress the balance.

5.5 So the bank is restricted by these Acts, discussed above. In addition, the bank will not want to be seen to be exploiting its position, since customers can choose to obtain, say, the mortgage or other loan elsewhere. Hence public relations also serve to ensure that, while there is never equality in bargaining power, rarely is there total unfairness.

5.6 We shall return to the bank's standard form contracts in Chapter 9.

## 6. CONCLUSION

6.1 Because banks make a great deal of use of standard form contracts, and because there is inequality of size and resources between a bank and most (if not all) of its customers, banking contracts are affected a great deal by statutory intervention. The Consumer Credit Act 1974, in particular, greatly affects banking business as it requires complex formalities and affords significant rights to the consumer (excluding companies).

## 6: STATUTORY INTERVENTION IN CONTRACTS

6.2 The three main statutes affect the bank in the following ways:

| Statute | The bank's procedures |
|---|---|
| Unfair Contract Terms Act 1977 | Cannot disclaim liability for death or injury caused by negligence (say, in banking hall) |
| | Can disclaim liability, *provided it is reasonable*, for loss or damage caused by negligence, for breach of contract, and for no performance of contract |
| | Can seek indemnity from customer *if the term is reasonable* |
| Consumer Credit Act 1974 | Imposes a great deal of paperwork for many types of lending to individual customers! |
| Supply of Goods and Services Act 1982 | Requires the bank to act with reasonable skill and care, at a reasonable time, and at a reasonable charge |

---

### TEST YOUR KNOWLEDGE
*The numbers in brackets refer to paragraphs of this chapter*

1  When may a bank exclude liability for negligence giving rise to financial loss? (2.1 - 2.3)

2  What will the court consider when applying the test of reasonableness set down in UCTA 1977 s 11? (2.7, 2.8)

3  Define a consumer in terms of UCTA 1977. (2.10)

4  What provisions in the Consumer Credit Act 1974 affect regulated agreements? (3.2)

5  How is a bank's lending on overdraft to an individual customer affected by the 1974 Act? (3.9)

6  What terms are implied by the Supply of Goods and Services Act 1982 into a contract for services? (4.1)

7  What are the advantages of standard form contracts? (5.3)

---

*Now try question 10 at the end of the text*

*Chapter 7*

# BREACH OF CONTRACT

> **This chapter covers the following topics.**
>
> 1. How a contract comes to an end
> 2. Breach of contract
> 3. Remedies available for breach of contract
> 4. Damages
> 5. Injunction
> 6. Limitations to actions for breach

## 1. HOW A CONTRACT COMES TO AN END

1.1 A party who is subject to the obligations of a contract may be discharged from those obligations in one of four ways. The agreement is then at an end. The four ways are:

(a) performance;
(b) agreement;
(c) breach; and
(d) frustration.

1.2 The vast majority of contracts are discharged by virtue of the fact that each party does what he said he would do. This is *performance* of the contract. The parties may *agree* to terminate the contract, perhaps in order to replace it with a new contract. *Frustration* occurs when the contract becomes impossible to perform. The final means of discharge of contract listed above, breach of contract, is the situation most likely to give rise to a conflict between the parties to the contract. In this chapter we consider what gives rise to a breach and the available remedies for breach.

## 2. BREACH OF CONTRACT

2.1 If one party breaks a condition (a fundamental term of the contract), the other may treat the contract as breached and at an end (repudiation): *Poussard v Spiers 1876*. The injured party may, however, prefer (the option is his) to treat the contract as still continuing despite a breach of condition and merely claim damages for his loss.

2.2 A party is said to be in breach of contract where, *without lawful excuse*, he does not perform his contractual obligations precisely. This may be because he refuses to perform them, he fails to perform them, he incapacitates himself from performing them or he performs them defectively.

2.3 A person has a lawful excuse not to perform primary contractual obligations (that is, what he promised to do under his side of the bargain) where:

(a) performance is impossible;

(b) he has tendered performance but this has been rejected;

(c) the other party has made it impossible for him to perform; and

(d) the contract has been frustrated (by, for example, government intervention or destruction of the subject matter of the contract).

2.4 Breach of contract gives rise to an obligation to pay damages to the other party (discussed later) but usually the primary obligation to perform the contract's terms remains.

## 3. REMEDIES AVAILABLE FOR BREACH OF CONTRACT

3.1 There is strict liability for breach of contract, and a party may apply to the court for a number of remedies when the other party is in breach.

(a) Damages - compensation for loss caused by the breach (see Section 4 of this chapter).

(b) Action for the price - here the breach is failure to pay.

(c) *Quantum meruit* - payment for the value of what he has done.

(d) Specific performance - a court order to the defendant to perform the contract.

(e) Injunction - a court order for the other party to observe negative restrictions (see Section 5 of this chapter).

## 4. DAMAGES

4.1 Damages are a common law remedy and are primarily intended to restore the party who has suffered loss to the same position he would have been in if the contract had been performed. They are *not* meant to be a punishment, which is a criminal, not a civil, measure. In addition, they should not allow the party to whom they are awarded to profit, nor to achieve a better result - the law will not make up for a bad bargain.

4.2 As a general rule *the amount awarded as damages is what is needed to put the plaintiff in the position he would have achieved if the contract had been performed.* If, for example, there is failure to deliver goods at a contract price of £100 per ton and, at the due time for delivery, similar goods are obtainable at an available market price of £110 per ton, damages are calculated at the rate of £10 per ton (Sale of Goods Act 1979 s 51(3)).

4.3 More complicated questions of assessing damages can arise. The general principle is to compensate for *actual* financial loss.

*Case: Lazenby Garages v Wright 1976*
W agreed to buy a car from L at a price of £1,670 (L had previously bought the car for £1,325).
W refused to accept and pay for the car. Shortly afterwards L sold the car to another buyer for
£1,770. L claimed £345 (£1,670 - £1,325) from W as the profit which they would have made on a
sale to W.

*Held:* L's claim must fail since L had suffered no loss. The argument that L might have sold a
different car to the other buyer and so made profits on two sales was rejected.

4.4 It is necessary to consider the following points in relation to how damages are measured.

(a) Non-financial loss - how far this can be recovered.

(b) Mitigation of loss - the court will look at whether the plaintiff took reasonable measures
to reduce a foreseeable loss.

(c) Liquidated damages and penalty clauses.

*Non-financial loss*

4.5 At one time damages could not be recovered for any *non-financial loss* arising from breach of
contract. In some recent cases, however, damages have been recovered for mental distress where
that is the main result of the breach. But it is uncertain how far the courts will develop this
new concept.

*Case: Jarvis v Swan Tours 1973*
Contract for holiday accommodation at a winter sports centre. What was provided was much
inferior to the description given in the defendant's brochure. Damages on the basis of financial
loss only were assessed at £32.

*Held:* the damages should be increased to £125 to compensate for disappointment and distress.

*Mitigation of loss*

4.6 In assessing the amount of damages it is assumed that the plaintiff will take any *reasonable*
steps to reduce or *mitigate* his loss.

*Case: Payzu v Saunders 1919*
Under a contract for the supply of goods to be delivered and paid for by instalments. The
purchaser failed to pay for the first instalment when due, one month after delivery. The seller
declined to make further deliveries unless the buyer paid cash in advance with their orders. The
buyer refused to accept delivery on those terms.

*Held:* the seller was in breach of contract, he had no right to repudiate the original contract.
But the buyer should have mitigated his loss by accepting the seller's offer of delivery against
cash payment. Damages were limited to the amount of the buyer's assumed loss if he had paid in
advance, which was interest over the period of pre-payment.

*Liquidated damages*

4.7　To avoid complicated calculations of loss or disputes over the amount the parties may include in their contract a formula *(liquidated damages)* for determining the damages payable for breach. The formula will be enforced by the courts if it is 'a genuine pre-estimate of loss' (without enquiring whether the actual loss is greater or smaller if it appears to be a bargain to settle in advance what is to be paid).

*Case: Dunlop v New Garage & Motor Co 1915*
The contract (for sale of tyres to a garage) imposed a minimum retail price (re-sale price maintenance was then legal). The contract provided that £5 per tyre should be paid to the buyer if he re-sold at less than the prescribed retail price or in four other possible cases of breach of contract. He did sell at a lower price and argued that £5 per tyre was a 'penalty' (see below) and not a genuine pre-estimate of loss.

*Held:* as a general rule when a fixed amount is to be paid as damages for breaches of different kinds, some more serious in their consequences than others, that is not a genuine pre-estimate of loss and so it is void as a 'penalty'. But the general rule is merely a presumption which does not always determine the result. In this case the formula was an honest attempt to agree on liquidated damages and would be upheld, even though the consequences of the breach were such as to make precise pre-estimation almost impossible.

*Case: Ford Motor Co (England) Ltd v Armstrong 1915*
The defendant had undertaken not to sell the plaintiff's cars below list price, not to sell Ford cars to other dealers and not to exhibit any Ford cars without permission. A £250 penalty was payable for each breach as being the agreed damages which the plaintiff would sustain.

*Held:* since the same sum was payable for different kinds of loss, it was not a genuine pre-estimate of loss and was in the nature of a penalty. (Unlike the *Dunlop* case, the figure set was held to be excessive.)

4.8　As indicated above, a contract term designed as a penalty to discourage breach is void and not enforceable. The court will disregard it and require the injured party to prove the amount of his loss. Relief from penalty clauses is an example of the influence of equity in the law of contract.

4.9　If a clause for liquidated damages is included in the contract it should be highlighted as an *onerous term*. In the following case, the defendant did not plead that the clause in question was a penalty clause and hence void, but it is probable that they could have done.

*Case: Interfoto Picture Library Ltd v Stiletto Visual Programmes Ltd 1988*
47 photographic transparencies were delivered to the defendant together with a delivery note with conditions on the back. Included in small type was a clause stating that for every day late each transparency was held a 'holding fee' of £5 would be charged. They were returned 14 days late. P sued for the full amount of £3,783.50.

*Held:* the term was onerous and had not been sufficiently brought to the attention of the defendant. The court reduced the fee to 50p per transparency per day (one tenth of the contractual figure) to reflect more fairly the loss caused to the plaintiff by the delay.

## 5. INJUNCTION

5.1 In this context an injunction is a discretionary order, requiring the defendant to observe a negative restriction of a contract. An injunction may even be made to enforce a contract of personal service for which specific performance would be refused.

*Case: Warner Bros v Nelson 1937*

N (the film star Bette Davis) agreed to work for a year for WB (film producers) and not during the year to work for any other film or stage producer nor 'to engage in any other occupation' without the consent of WB. N came to England during the year to work for a British film producer. WB sued for an injunction to restrain N from this work and N resisted arguing that if the restriction were enforced she must either work for WB (ie indirectly it would be an order for specific performance of a contract for personal service which should not be made) or abandon her livelihood.

*Held:* the court would not make an injunction if it would have the result suggested by N. But WB merely asked for an injunction to restrain N from working for a British film producer. This was one part of the restriction accepted by N under her contract and it was fair to hold her to it to that extent. But the court would not have enforced the 'any other occupation' restraint. Moreover, an English court would only have made an injunction restraining N from breaking her contract by taking other work in England.

---

## Exercise

To what is the injured party entitled in the event of:

(a) breach of a condition by the other party; and

(b) breach of a warranty by the other party?

### Solution

(a) He may treat the contract as discharged, and rescind or terminate the contract, or alternatively he may go on with it and sue for damages.

(b) He may claim damages only.

---

## 6. LIMITATIONS TO ACTIONS FOR BREACH

6.1 The right to sue for breach of contract becomes statute-barred after six years from the date of the breach (or twelve years if the breach is by deed) under the Limitation Act 1980. The plaintiff's rights merely cease to be enforceable at law. A right to a liquidated sum may, however, be revived by acknowledgement in writing or part-payment on the part of the debtor even if made after the limitation period has expired.

6.2 In two situations the six year period does not begin at the date of the breach but later.

(a) If the plaintiff is a minor or under some other contractual disability (eg of unsound mind) at the time of the breach of contract, the six year period begins to run only when his disability ceases or he dies, whichever is the earlier. If it has once begun to run it is not suspended by a subsequent disability.

(b) If the defendant or his agent conceals the right of action by fraud (which here denotes any conduct judged to be unfair by equitable standards) or if the action is for relief, from the results of a mistake the six year period begins to run only when the plaintiff discovered or could by reasonable diligence have discovered the fraud, concealment or mistake.

*Case: Applegate v Moss 1970*
In 1951 A bought a house built for M (a developer) by builders employed by M. In 1965 A discovered that the foundations were defective and not in accordance with specification. A sued M who pleaded that A's claim was statute-barred.

*Held:* the builders, as agents of M, had concealed the state of the foundations and therefore the right of action in respect of the defects of them. Time only began to run when the relevant facts were discoverable - when the bad foundations became evident by the damage resulting from them.

6.3 Where the claim can only be for the equitable reliefs of specific performance or injunction, the Limitation Act 1980 does not apply. Instead, the claim may be limited by the equitable doctrine of delay or 'laches' (failure of a person to assert his or her rights): *Allcard v Skinner 1887.*

6.4 The limitation period may be extended if the debt, or any other certain monetary amount, is either acknowledged or paid in part before the original six (or twelve) years has expired: s 29. Hence if a debt accrues on 1.1.83, the original limitation period expires on 31.12.88. But if part-payment is received on 1.1.87, the debt is reinstated and does not then become 'statute barred' until 31.12.92.

(a) *Acknowledgement.* The claim must be acknowledged as existing, not just as possible, but it need not be quantified. It must be in writing, signed by the debtor and addressed to the creditor: s 30.

(b) *Part-payment.* To be effective, the part-payment must be identifiable with the particular debt, not just a payment on a running account.

## 7. CONCLUSION

7.1 Although there are a number of ways in which a bank's contracts may come to an end, the way in which termination is most likely to result in serious consequences is when there is fundamental or anticipatory breach of contract. The rules on damages, particularly as regards financial as opposed to non-financial loss, are very important since most claims for breach of contract are settled in this way.

**TEST YOUR KNOWLEDGE**

*The numbers in brackets refer to paragraphs of this chapter*

1     In what ways may a party to a contract be discharged from his obligations under it? (1.1)

2     What are the alternatives open to the innocent party if the other declares in advance that he will not perform his obligations? (2.2)

3     Name five remedies available for breach of contract. (3.1)

4     What is the duty to 'mitigate loss' and on whom does it fall? (4.7)

5     What is the difference between liquidated damages and a penalty for non-performance? (4.8, 4.9)

6     What is an injunction? (5.1)

7     What is meant by 'limitation' and to what periods does it apply? (6.1) How may a limitation period be extended? (6.4)

*Now try question 11 at the end of the text*

# PART C
## THE BANK'S CONTRACTS

*Chapter 8*

# ESSENTIALS OF THE BANKER-CUSTOMER CONTRACT

---

**This chapter covers the following topics.**

1. Definitions of 'bank' and 'customer'
2. The essential features of the banker-customer relationship
3. The contractual relationship
4. The bank's duties to the customer
5. The customer's duties to the bank
6. The rights of the bank

---

## 1. DEFINITIONS OF 'BANK' AND 'CUSTOMER'

1.1 Before considering details of the banker-customer contract, we first have to look at what is meant by 'bank' and 'customer'. The facts of the *United Dominions Trust* case (which are given shortly) illustrate how important it is to a bank to be recognised as such. Much of the essential relationship between bank and customer is concerned with cheque transactions - payment of the cheques drawn by the customer and obtaining payment for him of cheques drawn or endorsed to him by others. But banks also provide other services to customers on request. In the next chapter we examine the standards to which a bank should conform and the conditions applied in these other situations. In this area banking law and practice often coincide - a bank discharges its obligations (under the law) to the customer if it conforms to good banking practice.

1.2 When examination questions are set on the banker-customer contract they may be very general in their terms (a test of knowledge) or they may bring in the obligations to which a bank is subject in acting as agent for its customer. You should note particularly the obligation of a bank to keep in confidence what it knows about the affairs of its customer and the pitfalls of replying to applications for a 'banker's reference' (and how they may be avoided).

**'Bank'**

1.3 It is not, and never has been, easy to define a bank, or even a banker. The problem is a vexing one from a legal point of view, since on that definition rests the duties and liabilities of the parties in law.

*Case: United Dominions Trust Ltd v Kirkwood 1966*
A finance house (UDT) sued K to recover payment of a commercial loan. K argued that the loan contract was void since he asserted that UDT was not a bank but an unlicensed money-lender. Evidence was given that UDT provided current account services to customers and was recognised by other banks.

*Held:* UDT was a recognised bank and the loan contract was valid.

1.4 This case laid down three basic rules to be applied in determining whether an institution is a bank. These stipulate that a bank should:

(a) keep running accounts for customers;
(b) honour cheques drawn on the business; and
(c) collect cheques on customers' behalf.

It was stressed that this was not a static definition and that current practice should be taken into account in assessing whether an institution is a bank.

1.5 Since the enactment of the Banking Act 1987, which repealed the 1979 Act, the words 'bank' or 'banker' are restricted to institutions which:

(a) are authorised by the Bank of England; and
(b) have paid up capital and undistributable reserves of more than £5 million.

1.6 It is important to identify a bank as a bank because:

(a) some legislation (such as the Cheques Act 1957 and the Bills of Exchange Act 1882) applies only to banks; and

(b) the relationship is characterised by certain elements which do not arise in, say, a normal debtor/creditor or agency relationship.

1.7 It is fair to say that a number of facilities are expected of an institution by customers and regulatory authorities before it is considered to be a bank. These are:

(a) a debtor/creditor relationship;
(b) the maintenance of current accounts;
(c) the honouring of cheques or other mandates;
(d) the issuing of cheque forms and the collection of cheques;
(e) the lending of money at a profit;
(f) the acceptance (generally) of any person as a customer;
(g) a relationship of confidence and secrecy; and
(h) the reputation generally as a banker.

### 'Customer'

1.8 'Customer' is not clearly defined either, although the term frequently appears in legislation. In particular it is important to identify a person as a customer since a collecting bank is only protected by s 4 of the Cheques Act 1957 when it acts for a customer. This is examined further in the chapter on the protection of banks.

1.9 Clearly there is a link between defining a bank and defining its customer. If one were to say 'that is a bank because it issues cheque forms and collects them' then one can also say that the person who receives a cheque form and on whose behalf cheques are collected is a customer. So too a current account-holder and a loan debtor would be customers.

1.10 But it is easy to see that a deposit account-holder, a person in overdraft (where the debtor-creditor relationship is reversed) and a person for whom the bank holds jewellery in safe custody are also customers, even though the facilities they enjoy fall outside those listed in paragraph 1.7 above.

1.11 A person becomes a customer in respect of cheque transactions as soon as the bank opens an account for him *(Ladbroke v Todd 1914)* or, in any other situation such as giving investment advice, as soon as the bank accepts his instructions and undertakes to provide a service. This may be the running of a full commercial current account or the provision of just a credit card. But a 'casual service', such as the cashing of another bank's cheques backed by a cheque guarantee card, does not initiate the relationship: *Great Western Railway Co v London and County Banking Co Ltd 1901.*

1.12 A customer then is a person who has a contractual relationship with the bank. But a bank may well have duties to non-customers, such as the common law duty of occupiers of premises, and the duties owed by both sides may vary from relationship to relationship.

## 2. THE ESSENTIAL FEATURES OF THE BANKER-CUSTOMER RELATIONSHIP

2.1 As noted above, the relationship is essentially a contractual one and it may take many forms. But a bank's liability may be more extensive and the relationship might comprise elements of:

(a) contract only;
(b) a debtor/creditor relationship;
(c) agency;
(d) bailment;
(e) contract and trust;
(f) a mortgage agreement; and
(g) contract and tort.

We shall deal with each of these matters in turn.

2.2 The existence of a contract means that there are:

(a) express and implied terms in the agreement;
(b) obligations (or duties) owed by the bank to the customer; and
(c) obligations (or duties) owed by the customer to the bank.

2.3 The nature of the contractual relationship is examined in more detail in the rest of this chapter, and in the next chapter we consider the other matters identified in paragraph 2.1.

## 3. THE CONTRACTUAL RELATIONSHIP

3.1 The general obligations of the contract are not usually expressed in writing but are implied. This may seem surprising since banks deal with very large amounts of money on behalf of customers. The explanation is that over many years it has become well understood and established in banking practice that a bank renders certain services and is bound by certain obligations in its relationship with customers. It is therefore considered unnecessary to express these matters in a long document. When the parties take for granted something which is essential to the contract between them and normal in practice, it is readily implied that they have tacitly agreed that it should be part of the contract. But, as we saw in the earlier chapter on statutory intervention in contracts, it is true to say that many customers are *not* aware of the contract's terms nor that the terms are binding. The Code of Banking Practice addresses this issue in part but, following severe criticism of banks and in particular of their attitudes to small businesses in Summer and Autumn 1991, many individual banks are also setting out the terms in their own customers' charters. The Code of Banking Practice is examined in more detail in the chapter on the bank account; its 'terms and conditions' clauses are as follows.

(a) 'Written terms and conditions of a banking service will be expressed in plain language and will provide a fair and balanced view of the relationship between the customer and bank or building society (3.1).

(b) Banks and building societies will tell customers how any variation of the terms and conditions will be notified. Banks and building societies will give customers reasonable notice before any variation takes effect (3.2).

(c) Banks and building societies should issue to their customers, if there are sufficient changes in a 12 month period to warrant it, a single document to provide a consolidation of the variations made to their terms and conditions over that period (3.3).

(d) Banks and building societies will provide new customers with a written summary or explanation of the key features of the more common services that they provide (3.4).

(e) Banks and building societies will not close customers' accounts without first giving reasonable notice (3.5).'

3.2 In theory bank and customer are always at liberty to substitute some express term to replace what would otherwise be implied. If, for example, a bank makes a loan to a customer it is implied that the bank is entitled to charge a reasonable rate of interest. However, there will often be an express agreement to fix the rate of interest on the loan - since both parties prefer certainty. *An express term always prevails to exclude any term otherwise implied* (except in limited circumstances, usually governed by the Unfair Contract Terms Act 1977).

*Case: Stewart Gill Ltd v Horatio Meyer & Co Ltd 1992*
There was an express term in the contract purporting to exclude one party's right of set-off.

*Held:* under the Unfair Contract Terms Act 1977 such a clause was unreasonable.

### Implied terms of the contract

3.3 The relationship between bank and customer arises from a contract between them. The customer deposits his money with the bank and so the bank becomes a debtor to the customer (if of course the customer is overdrawn the debtor/creditor relationship is reversed). The essential implied terms of this relationship were stated in *Joachimson v Swiss Bank Corporation 1921* as follows:

(a) 'the bank undertakes to receive money and collect bills for its customer's account';

(b) 'the bank borrows the proceeds and undertakes to repay them';

(c) 'the bank will not cease to do business with the customer except upon reasonable notice' (so that there is time for his outstanding cheques to be presented before the account is closed – the same rule applies to withdrawal of overdraft facilities);

(d) 'the bank is not liable to pay until he (the customer) demands payment from the bank', but it will repay at the customer's branch during banking hours; and

(e) the customer 'on his part undertakes to exercise reasonable care in executing his written orders so as not to mislead the bank or to facilitate forgery'.

3.4 Most of these features are implied terms of the contract. When an account is opened, the contract is formed by the bank offering to open an account, and the customer accepting. Funds are then paid in, but the exact terms expressed in the *Joachimson* case are not stated explicitly.

3.5 New customers are normally asked to sign a mandate on opening an account which is a standard form contract and contains some of the major terms, although it will not cover special features such as credit cards, loan accounts or safe deposits. It is a basic principle of contract law that a person who signs a contract knows its terms, whether he has read and understood them or not.

*Case: L'Estrange v Graucob 1934*
A sold to B, a shopkeeper, a slot machine under conditions which excluded B's normal rights under the Sale of Goods Act 1893. B signed the document without reading the relevant condition.

*Held:* the conditions were binding on B since she had signed them. It was not material that A had given her no information of their terms nor called her attention to them.

3.6 If, however, misleading explanations are given by the person who puts forward the documents for signing, then its contents will not be binding.

*Case: Curtis v Chemical Cleaning Co 1951*
X took her wedding dress to be cleaned. She was asked to sign a receipt on which there were conditions by which the cleaners disclaimed liability for damage however it might arise. Before signing X enquired what was the effect of the documents and was told that it restricted the cleaner's liability in certain ways and in particular placed on X the risk of damage to beads and sequins on the dress. The dress was badly stained in the course of cleaning.

*Held:* the cleaners could not rely on their disclaimer since they had misled X as to the effect of the document which she signed.

3.7 Thus while a mandate is effective if it sets out the basic terms of the contract, it may be faulty in the following circumstances.

(a) If misleading explanations are given, its terms will not be enforceable.

(b) If there are ambiguities, they are normally interpreted *against* the bank since it is deemed to have a dominant position.

(c) Any express terms considered to be unreasonable by the court in the light of the Unfair Contract Terms Act 1977 will be ineffective. Generally these are terms which purport to exclude liability for loss or damage caused by the bank's breach of duty of care (negligence) or breach of contract.

(d) Similarly, any exclusion of a customer's rights which arise by implication must be clearly notified and be reasonable.

*Clayton's case*

3.8 Certain terms are implied into the basic banker-customer relationship. One of the most important is that where neither the debtor nor the creditor allocate (or appropriate) an amount paid in to a particular outstanding debt and there is an unbroken current account, then the rule in *Clayton's* case *(Devaynes v Noble 1816)* is assumed. The rule is that, in the absence of any specific appropriation by bank or customer:

(a) where a current account continues or goes into credit, the first payments into the account are reduced by the first payments out; and

(b) where a current account continues or goes into debt, the first payments out of the account are reduced or repaid by the first repayments in.

3.9 This rule can be illustrated by an example. Assume that Alex and Clive are in partnership. They have a partnership bank account which shows a £10,000 overdraft. Alex dies, but the account continues to be operated. In the weeks following Alex's death, Clive pays in credits of £8,000 and there are debits of £7,000. The rule means that of the total debt now outstanding of £9,000, only £2,000 is enforceable against the estate of Alex.

3.10 It can be seen from this example that, although under normal circumstances the rule is of little consequence, in the event of death or insolvency of a party or of notice of a second charge, it will operate to the disadvantage of the bank.

3.11 There are two ways in which the bank can overcome the effect of *Clayton's* case.

(a) Open a separate account on notice of death, insolvency etc. In the example above this would have resulted in a new account with a credit balance of £1,000 and the total debt of £9,000 being enforceable against the estate of the deceased.

(b) Insert a clause which expressly excludes the operation of the rule. The validity of a clause of this type was confirmed in *Westminster Bank v Cond 1940*.

3.12 Out of the contractual relationship certain other terms or duties are inferred, both of the bank and of the customer. The list below shows that rather more duties are owed by the bank!

3.13 The bank's duties are as follows.

*Paying bank*

(a) To honour a customer's cheques
(b) Not to pay without authority
(c) To obey customer's countermands
(d) To tell customer of forgeries

*Collecting bank*

(e) To collect cheques

*All banks*

(f) To retain customers' confidence (duty of secrecy)
(g) To inform customers of the state of his account
(h) To exercise skill and care in the operation of the account

3.14 The customer's duties are the following.

(a) To exercise care in drawing cheques
(b) To tell bank of known forgeries

## 4. THE BANK'S DUTIES TO THE CUSTOMER

*Duty to honour cheques*

4.1 This is one of the more fundamental duties of a banker arising from the fact (established in *Foley v Hill 1848*) that the banker/customer relationship is essentially that of debtor and creditor. The bank should not refuse to make payments which the customer has authorised (to the limit of his credit balance or of any agreed overdraft facility), and it will be liable to the customer for defamation if, by its unjustified refusal to pay, the customer's reputation is damaged.

4.2 The duty to honour cheques only exists if the customer requires his own branch, within banking hours by means of a written and clear mandate, to pay. A bank is only justified in refusing to pay a customer's cheques when presented as above if:

(a) payment has been countermanded by the customer;

(b) there are insufficient funds available in the customer's account, ie that there is not:

   (i)   a sufficient credit balance; or
   (ii)  an agreed overdraft facility;

(c) the cheque is defective in some way or is 'stale' (ie drawn over 6 months previously); or

(d) there is a legal bar on payment, such as a garnishee order; or

(e) the bank has received notice that the customer has died, is insane or is insolvent.

4.3   When a cheque is paid without authority but the payment discharges a legal debt of the customer, the bank can rely on 'subrogation' to the creditor to offset its lack of authority. This means that the bank is entitled to 'stand in the shoes of' the creditor to whom the debt was paid so as to assume the right to be reimbursed payment by the debtor.

*Case: B Liggett (Liverpool) Ltd v Barclays Bank Ltd 1928*
The bank was authorised to pay cheques drawn on the company's account only if signed by both directors. One director persuaded the bank to honour cheques signed only by him on the ground that damage to the company's interests would result if he withheld the cheques from creditors while he obtained the signature of the other director. The company later denied that these payments could be debited to its account.

*Held:* the bank's money had been used to discharge the legal debts of the company and the bank was entitled (by subrogation to the company's creditors) to recover the money from the company.

4.4   *Liggett's* case illustrates the risk taken by a bank which does not comply strictly with instructions or customary procedures over payment of cheques drawn on that bank. There are similar risks where a bank does not follow the correct procedure in collecting payment of a cheque for its customers.

*Case: Forman v Bank of England 1902*
The cheque delivered to the bank for collection was payable at the paying bank's branch either in London or in Norwich. Contrary to recognised custom the cheque was sent to Norwich thereby causing delay. Forman's cheque drawn against it was dishonoured for lack of funds.

*Held:* the customer could recover damages for his loss.

4.5   Because non-payment of a cheque can damage a trader's reputation, a trader may claim damages for breach of mandate without proof of the actual loss if his cheque is wrongly refused payment. A private customer, however, will only recover nominal damages for breach of contract unless he can prove actual loss.

*Case: Gibbons v Westminster Bank Ltd 1939*
G paid in to her bank a cheque of an amount sufficient to meet her rent and drew a cheque payable to her landlord for the rent. The bank by mistake credited the cheque paid in by G to another account and refused to pay the cheque presented by the landlord. The landlord insisted that G should in future pay her rent in cash. But G did not claim special damages on that ground.

*Held:* as G a private customer had not proved special damage, she was entitled only to nominal damages of £2.

4.6   In returning a cheque unpaid the drawee bank would, in accordance with banking practice, add to it a brief note of the reasons for its refusal. In this the bank may be exposed to the risk of a claim by the customer for libel (damage to his reputation). This is a tort for which damages may be awarded without proof of loss (and it is quite distinct from breach of contract explained above). The bank should therefore choose its words with care.

4.7   The reason for refusing payment may be such that the customer cannot complain of prejudice by disclosure. As examples:

'words and figures differ'
're-present on due date' (on a post-dated cheque)
'drawer deceased'.

4.8 The problem usually arises when the bank indicates that it does not have sufficient funds available to the customer to meet the cheque.

(a) To state that a person has issued a cheque which he should know will be dishonoured can amount to defamation. Thus to mark a cheque 'not sufficient' and return it may be libellous (if there were or should have been sufficient funds in the account).

(b) The words *refer to drawer* are of themselves innocuous. They could be taken merely as advice to the holder to make his own enquiries of the drawer as to the reasons for non-payment of his cheque. There are earlier decisions that this phrase is not libellous. But that is no longer the law. In an action for libel the court is concerned with how the statement was *understood* by those to whom it was communicated. The public has come to interpret 'refer to drawer' as an innuendo that the cheque is refused payment owing to insufficient funds. In the main decision *(Jayson v Midland Bank 1968)* it was held that this phrase was libellous.

4.9 A customer who is not a trader may well prefer to base his claim on defamation since substantial damages can be awarded without proof of special damage.

*Duty not to pay without authority*

4.10 This duty overlaps with the duty to honour cheques. The bank should only make such payments as the customer has duly authorised and may not normally debit his account with unauthorised payments (but see *Liggett's* case). Unauthorised payments may arise as a result of:

(a) fraud;
(b) forgery of signature or endorsement;
(c) unauthorised endorsement;
(d) lack of authority of agent signing for principal; and
(e) alterations on a cheque or bill invalidating it.

4.11 The bank's duty to pay cheques drawn on the customer's account and its right to debit his account with payments made terminates in any of the following circumstances.

(a) *Countermand* of payment: s 75(1) Bills of Exchange Act 1882 (see paragraph 4.15 below).

(b) Notice to the bank of the customer's *death*: s 75(2). This must be a reliable report, such as from relatives or a newspaper. Banks usually request a copy of the death certificate.

(c) Notice of the customer's *insanity*, which terminates his authority to the bank to act as his agent.

(d) Receipt of a court order to stop payments. This is usually a *garnishee order* made to enforce payment of a judgement debt of specified amount. The effect is to 'freeze' the entire account. But if the credit balance exceeds the debt specified in the order, the bank may decide to pay cheques out of the surplus (after making a reserve for the debt and incidental expenses). The bank may also be prohibited by injunction (a court order) from making a particular payment or any payment from the account while matters in dispute (such as the ownership of the balance in the account) are decided.

(e) On notice of the customer's *bankruptcy* since the making of a bankruptcy order in effect vests his assets in his trustee: Insolvency Act 1986 s 306. The bankruptcy order also renders void any disposition by the bankrupt of his property from the date of the petition for his bankruptcy. But this does not entitle the trustee to claim from a person to whom the debtor transferred his property, say by drawing a cheque, if the recipient took it in good faith, for value and without notice of the presentation of the petition: Insolvency Act 1986 s 284. As soon as the bank receives notice of the presentation of a petition for a customer's bankruptcy therefore it would be advisable to stop the account.

(f) On notice of commencement of *winding up* of a company customer.

(g) If the bank becomes aware that the person claiming payment of the cheque is not entitled to it. The statutory protection of various kinds given to a bank is limited to payments made in good faith - without *knowledge or suspicion of fraud:* ss 60 and 8 Bills of Exchange Act 1882.

(h) If the bank becomes aware that the payment will amount to *breach of trust* or even if the bank is merely aware of circumstances indicating a misappropriation.

4.12 Note that the general principle underlying all these specific instances is *knowledge* of the relevant event on the part of the bank. The bank should not act on mere rumour or an unreliable report. This can present difficulties since a cheque is due for payment as soon as it is presented. But brief delay, an explanation of the reason for it (in suitably cautious terms) and rapid enquiries (perhaps by telephone) may extricate the bank from its problem.

4.13 The bank may defend itself against a claim from a customer that it paid without authority if it can show that it asked the customer to confirm that all was well and this he did: *Brown v Westminster Bank Ltd 1964*. If it then transpires that the bank paid when all was not well, the customer is estopped (prevented) from claiming that the bank was in breach of its duty. The bank may also be protected if it can show that the customer was in breach of his own duty to the bank.

*Duty to obey customer's countermands*

4.14 Effectively this is an instance in which a bank has a duty not to pay without authority. A countermand withdraws the authority which had been given - it is often known as 'stopping a cheque'. Sometimes a bank may find that its two duties - to honour cheques and to obey countermand - conflict.

4.15 As dishonour of a cheque may have serious consequences, the bank is entitled to a countermand in unambiguous terms and in writing. If the customer countermands by telephone the bank is justified in postponing payment pending receipt of written confirmation which it would normally request.

4.16 The countermand must be complete and correct in its details such as payee's name and the amount and serial number of the cheque.

*Case: Westminster Bank Ltd v Hilton 1926*
The countermand to the bank referred to cheque no 117283 (it should have been 117285) with correct information of the payee's name and the amount. The customer failed to mention that it was a post-dated cheque dated 4 days later. On the due date, cheque 117285 was presented and the bank paid it assuming that it was a duplicate for 117283 issued after the countermand of the earlier cheque. If the bank had searched its records it would have discovered that cheque 117283 (specified in the countermand) with a different payee's name and amount had already been paid. But it made no search.

*Held:* the serial number of a cheque is the one certain means of identification. As the customer had given a wrong number he had not effectually countermanded payment.

4.17 Since a bank is at risk in refusing payment of a customer's cheque, any countermand of payment by him is effective only when it comes to the actual notice of the branch of the bank on which the cheque is drawn.

*Case: Curtice v London City and Midland Bank Ltd 1908*
C drew a cheque for £63 in payment for goods. As the goods were not delivered on time, C sent a telegram to the bank to countermand payment of the cheque. The telegram was put through the bank's letterbox at 6.15pm after it had closed. On the following day the telegram remained unopened and the cheque was presented and paid. On the day after that, C's letter of confirmation was received and the telegram was found in the letterbox. In his action against the bank C claimed return of £63 paid without his authority.

*Held:* at the time when the cheque was paid there had been no effective countermand. The claim must fail. (C might have claimed for negligence but he would have recovered no damages for it since the cheque served to pay the price of the goods for which he was presumably still liable.)

4.18 If the bank pays a cheque after receiving effective countermand it cannot usually debit the customer's account. But it can seek to recover the money from the payee: *Barclays Bank Ltd v W J Simms Son and Cooke (Southern) Ltd 1979*. It may also have other remedies (described later in the chapter).

4.19 There can be other adverse consequences for the bank. As an example, suppose that a customer (A) has a credit balance on his account of say £1,000. He first draws and then countermands payment of a cheque for £800. The bank fails to act on the countermand, pays the cheque, debits the account and so the balance is reduced to £200. The customer, in ignorance of this situation, believes that his balance still stands at £1,000 and issues a cheque for £500 which the bank refuses to pay because there is no agreed overdraft facility. The bank is in breach of contract over the dishonour of the £500 cheque. It has made a mistake in debiting an unauthorised payment (£800) to the account but that is no defence to a claim relating to the non-payment of the other (£500) cheque.

*Duty to tell customer of forgeries*

4.20 This arises from the duty not to pay without authority. A forged mandate is no mandate. The bank should tell the customer because of the risk that other frauds may also be carried out against him.

*Duty to collect cheques*

4.21 Broadly, the collecting bank should collect only in accordance with any crossings and within a reasonable time. It should credit amounts collected to the customer's account.

*Duty of confidentiality*

4.22 The case below sufficiently illustrates the general principle that a bank should keep in confidence what it knows.

> *Case: Tournier v National Provincial (and Union Bank of England) 1924*
> T, who had incurred betting losses, was overdrawn on his account with the defendant bank. He promised to pay off his overdraft by weekly instalments but he failed to do so. The bank then telephoned T's employer, with whom he had a temporary job, to find out his private address. The bank manager mentioned to the employer that T had been gambling. When the three months' period of his employment expired the employer refused to extend T's employment. T sued the bank for slander and for breach of an implied contract not to disclose the state of his account and his transactions.
>
> *Held:* the bank was liable for breach of contract. The court distinguished four circumstances (none of which applied in this case) in which a bank may make disclosures.

4.23 These four exceptions to the duty of secrecy are as follows:

(a) Where the bank is *required by law* to disclose:

    (i) by court order, for example under the Bankers' Books Evidence Act 1879;

    (ii) where there is no legal compulsion to disclose information but where a failure to do so may amount to a criminal act, for example to facilitate insider dealing investigations under s 177 of the Financial Services Act 1986, or where there is a duty to disclose under the Drug Trafficking Offences Act 1986 or the Prevention of Terrorism Act 1989. In these instances, there is statutory protection from an action for breach of contract; or

    (iii) on an official request by the DTI or the Inland Revenue where they are acting on powers conferred by various statutes.

(b) Where there is a *public duty* to disclose - for example, if the bank is aware that the customer's transactions are damaging to the national interest (such as trading with the enemy in time of war).

(c) Where the *interest of the bank* requires disclosure - for example, when the bank sues a customer to recover what he owes, or where the bank does not wish to commit an offence under s 24 of the Drug Trafficking Offences Act 1986 (which makes it an offence for a person to know or suspect a person of drug trafficking and yet put funds at that person's disposal).

(d) Where the customer has given *express or implied consent* - for example, by inviting a third party to apply to the bank for a 'banker's reference' or by sending an employee to collect a bank statement.

4.24 The Code of Banking Practice repeats these exceptions but extends the scope of the 'bank's interests' exception to situations where information is disclosed within the banking group to prevent loss or fraud.

'(a) Banks and building societies will observe a strict duty of confidentiality about their customers' (and former customers') personal financial affairs and will not disclose details of customers' accounts or their names and addresses to any third party, including other companies in the same group, other than in the four exceptional cases permitted by the law, namely:

   (i) where a bank or building society is legally compelled to do so;
   (ii) where there is a duty to the public to disclose;
   (iii) where the interests of a bank or building society require disclosure;
   (iv) where disclosure is made at the request, or with the consent, of the customer (6.1).

(b) Banks and building societies will not use exception (iii) above to justify the disclosure for marketing purposes of details of customers' accounts or their names and addresses to any third party, including other companies within the same group. (6.2)'

*Customer's express consent*

4.25 A customer who requires credit from a third party or who is about to assume large financial obligations (for example, taking a lease of office premises) may be asked by the other party to the transaction to demonstrate that he (the customer) has sufficient financial resources. He is likely to refer the enquirer to his bank. In dealing with such requests for information (banker's references or status enquiries) the bank has obligations both to the customer and to the other party who asks for the information.

4.26 In authorising the other party to make enquiry of his bank, the customer expressly consents to the bank replying to the enquiry. But the bank should be careful to disclose no more than is necessary to satisfy the enquirer. It may suffice (it depends on the circumstances) to express the opinion that the customer has adequate resources to discharge the relevant liability and/or is believed to be careful in avoiding commitments beyond his capacity to pay. If it is necessary to express an adverse or qualified opinion the bank should be careful to avoid words which are capable of being defamatory.

4.27 Since disclosure of the state of an account is an action fraught with difficulty, most banks require written confirmation from the customer that disclosure is authorised. Telephone requests (for instance, a customer ringing up to ascertain the balance on his current account) are also treated cautiously, with many banks refusing to give an answer.

*Customer's implied consent*

4.28 The customer may give *implied consent* to disclosure, for example by drawing a third party into his own discussions with the bank. But the bank cannot substitute its own judgement for that of the customer by arguing that in the bank's view it was 'in the interests of the customer' to make a disclosure and so the customer would have consented if he had been consulted. In *Tournier's* case the judge considered and rejected that argument - though it is sometimes used by a bank for lack of any better attempt at justification of an unauthorised disclosure.

4.29 A better argument is that in opening a bank account the customer, by implication, consents to an established practice of banks either because he is aware of it or because he accepts that a bank will treat him like any other customer in accordance with normal routine, even if he is not actually aware of this particular practice.

4.30 The Jack Committee's report was particularly concerned with what it saw as the erosion of the bank's duty of confidentiality to its customer by both new legislation (drug trafficking etc) and banking practice itself. One area of disquiet pinpointed in the report was the supply by banks of information on customers to credit reference agencies and internally for marketing purposes with the customer's 'implied consent' - consent being implied because it had not been expressly refused since it had never been asked for!

4.31 The report categorically stated that banks should ask for the customer's express consent before passing 'white' credit information (about customers who are not in default) to credit reference agencies. But this is a recommendation not taken up in the Code of Banking Practice, which lays down the following in respect of references.

'Banks and building societies will on request:

(a)  advise customers whether they provide bankers' references or bankers' opinions in reply to status enquiries made about their customers;

(b)  explain how the system of bankers' references works (7.1).'

4.32 Note that there is not a problem over passing information on customers 'in the red' because the bank is simply protecting its own interests in doing so.

4.33 A different type of problem arises when a customer who is aware of the practice of giving 'status opinions' or bankers' references about customers to other banks expressly objects to it and expressly instructs his bank not to do so except with his prior express consent. In such a case the bank may choose not to proceed with the account, since there is a danger that the instruction will be overlooked.

*Duty to inform customer of the state of his account*

4.34 There is an implied term that a customer is entitled to receive a statement of his account, either in loose-leaf statement form or as a passbook. Both are only *prima facie* evidence of the true state of affairs however; either the bank or the customer may show them to be incorrect.

4.35 If a bank is in error over the statement then it may be estopped (prevented) from reclaiming funds paid out of that account where the customer relied upon the bank's statement of fact and changed his circumstances. An instance would be where the bank overcredits an account and the customer, acting in good faith, draws upon that balance. But if the customer did know, or should have known, of the error then he may be liable - in addition, he may be guilty of a criminal offence under s 1 Theft Act 1968.

4.36 The bank may correct any overcredit to its customer's account, provided the customer has not altered his position (used the money) as a result of having been misled by the bank's misrepresentation.

*Case: United Overseas Bank v Jivani 1976*
One credit was passed to J's account, making a balance of $21,000. He raised a cheque for $20,000 to pay towards a business asset. The written confirmation of the original telex transfer was incorrectly treated as another credit. J then paid another $11,000 towards the asset. Were the error corrected, this would make him $10,000 overdrawn.

*Held:* J had been misled by the bank's misrepresentation but had not altered his circumstances as a result, since he could have paid the $11,000 out of other funds. Hence the bank could correct the error.

4.37 Note that the customer does not have a duty to check his bank statements: *Tai Hing Cotton Mill Ltd v Liu Chong Hing Bank Ltd and Others 1986* (discussed below).

*Duty to exercise skill and care*

4.38 This duty is implied into any contract of service, and therefore into banking services, by the Supply of Goods and Services Act 1982, which was discussed in the chapter on statutory intervention in contracts.

## 5. THE CUSTOMER'S DUTIES TO THE BANK

5.1 A noted above, the customer has no duty to check his bank statements - in fact, the following decision (decided in a Hong Kong case by the Privy Council) shows that the customer's duties are few.

*Case: Tai Hing Cotton Mill Ltd v Liu Chong Hing Bank Ltd and others 1986*
The plaintiff ran accounts with three different banks, all of whom had mandates to honour cheques bearing particular signatures. The company had a long-serving employee whom it trusted, maintaining no supervision or financial control over him. Over six years the employee forged over 300 cheques worth $5.5 million. All the banks in question had written terms stating that monthly statements should be deemed correct unless Tai Hing informed the bank of an error within a short space of time. The terms required Tai Hing to examine the statement and sign a confirmation slip that all was in order, silence being deemed to be assent.

*Held:* in the Privy Council, that:

(a) even by express terms, bank statements are not conclusive evidence;

(b) the customer was not estopped by its own negligence from asserting that the bank acted without authority;

(c) the customer has no duty to inspect statements;

(d) the customer has no duty to supervise employees so as to prevent forgeries; and

(e) the customer only owes a duty to draw cheques with care and to inform the bank of known forgeries.

*Duty to exercise care in drawing cheques*

5.2   He must take those precautions in drawing a cheque which are usual. But it is not a duty to take every possible precaution.

*Case: London Joint Stock Bank Ltd v Macmillan & Arthur 1918*
A dishonest clerk presented to his employer for signature a bearer cheque on which £2 had been inserted as a figure (but so that space was left for another digit before it) and no amount at all in words. After the cheque had been signed the clerk altered '£2' to '£120' and inserted that amount in words and obtained payment. The employers denied the bank's right to debit £120 (as distinct from £2) to their account.

*Held:* the employer owed a duty to take usual precautions against alteration and had failed in that duty. The bank might debit the full £120 to the account.

*Case: Young v Grote 1827*
A customer provided his wife with a number of signed blank cheques. She gave one to a clerk who filled out false details and obtained payment.

*Held:* the customer was liable for the loss since he had not exercised due care and so was estopped from denying that the bank had authority to debit his account.

*Duty to tell bank of known forgeries*

5.3   If the customer becomes aware that his signature has been forged on a cheque, he should notify the bank as soon as possible to enable the bank to protect itself if it can. If the customer fails to do this and the bank suffers prejudice thereby, the customer may be estopped from denying to the bank that his forged signature is genuine.

*Case: Greenwood v Martins Bank Ltd 1933*
A husband discovered that his wife had been drawing on his account by forging his signature on cheques. He did not tell the bank. The wife later committed suicide. The husband claimed from the bank £410 which was the amount of the forged cheques.

*Held:* by his non-disclosure the husband had represented to the bank that the forged cheques were genuine and he was estopped from denying that they were signed by him. The bank had suffered loss because under the law at that time its right to claim the money from the wife was terminated by her death. In any future case a bank would probably have to show as in this case that its position had been prejudiced by the customer's non-disclosure.

5.4   Difficult questions may arise over a joint account (say in the names of two executors or trustees) when one forges the signature of the other on a cheque and adds his own. Obviously the forger cannot hold the bank accountable. The current view is that the bank owes a duty to each customer separately only to pay cheques which he (among others) has signed. Hence the innocent account-holder can deny the bank's right to pay a cheque which he has not signed: *Jackson v White and Midland Bank 1967*.

5.5   In normal circumstances the customer can deny the bank's right to debit his account with an unauthorised payment. But the bank may still be able to avoid loss and recover its money, either by subrogation to the rights of the customer's creditor who has been paid, or by a claim against the recipient of the payment if he was not entitled to it.

5.6    If there is no valid claim against the customer, the paying bank seeks to recover from the person who presented the cheque or his agent (the collecting bank) as payment under a mistake of fact.

*Case: Barclays Bank Limited v W J Simms Son and Cooke (Southern) Limited 1979*
R, a customer of the bank, issued a cheque for £24,000 in payment for work done by the defendants. R countermanded payment because a dispute arose over the contract for the work but the bank by oversight paid the cheque when presented. The bank claimed to recover £24,000 from the defendants.

*Held:* the real issue was whether R was liable to make payment. The bank, which was not involved in that dispute, was entitled to recover money paid under a mistake of fact to the defendants – the mistake being that R had given authority for the payment which was still in force.

*Case: National Westminster Bank Ltd v Barclays Bank International Ltd 1974*
The plaintiff bank had paid a crossed cheque on which its customer's signature had been skilfully forged, and sought to recover the money from the collecting bank which still had it.

*Held:*

(a)   the paying bank's failure to detect the forgery at the time of payment did not prevent it (by estoppel) from asserting later that it was a forgery;

(b)   the collecting bank was accountable for the money (and so must repay it) so long as it had the money;

(c)   if the collecting bank had paid the money over to its customer it would (under principles of agency law) cease to be liable to account for it. But the paying bank could still seek to recover it from the customer.

## 6.   THE RIGHTS OF THE BANK

6.1    The duties of the customer might also be seen as rights of the bank. The bank has a number of other rights in addition to these.

*Commission*

6.2    The bank may charge reasonable commission for services to customers. This is in addition to interest charged on loans.

*Repayment on demand*

6.3    The bank is entitled to repayment on demand of any overdraft, unless it is stated or implied that a reasonable period of notice should be given to the customer. For example if the bank has expressed that the facility is available for a specified period, it may not demand early repayment: *Williams and Glyn's Bank Ltd v Barnes 1980*.

## Indemnity

6.4 The bank has a right to be indemnified for any expenses or liabilities incurred in acting for its customer.

## Lien

6.5 The bank has a right of lien over its customers' securities which are in the bank's possession. This right can be exercised to enforce a debt. The right does *not* extend to items held in safe custody for the customer.

## Disposal of customer's money as it pleases

6.6 Amounts deposited are not held on trust for the customer, and so the bank has a right to do what it likes with the money, as long as it repays the customer when he demands it: *Foley v Hill 1848*. Of course, the bank must in the meantime honour its customer's cheques.

## Combination or set-off

6.7 Where a customer has two different accounts with the same bank, the bank has a right to combine them without giving notice to the customer. This right exists even if the accounts are held at different branches of the bank. It enables the bank to settle an overdrawn account by transferring money from another account.

## 7. CONCLUSION

7.1 In this chapter, we have seen how both 'bank' and 'customer' are defined by activities rather than by law. Banks are regulated by the Banking Act 1987 which provides for supervision by the Bank of England. But it is by its facilities to customers that a bank is recognised as such.

7.2 While there is usually a written contract between the parties, this does not preclude important terms being implied by law. A bank must honour and collect cheques, not pay cheques without authority, retain confidentiality and give its customers true statements of account. Failure to observe these duties is a breach of contract. The rule in *Clayton's* case is another very important term implied by law.

7.3 Note that the customer's duties are limited to taking care in writing cheques and informing the bank of known forgeries. He has *no* duty to check statements of account.

## TEST YOUR KNOWLEDGE
*The numbers in brackets refer to paragraphs of this chapter*

1　The provision of which facilities enables an institution to be identified as a bank? (1.4, 1.7)

2　How does the Banking Act 1987 restrict the use of the words 'bank' or 'banker'? (1.5)

3　When does a person become a customer? (1.11)

4　What is the effect of a mandate signed by a customer when opening an account? (3.6)

5　What duties are owed to the customer by:

　(a)　a paying bank;
　(b)　a collecting bank; and
　(c)　all banks? (3.13)

6　How may a paying bank recover funds paid without authority? (4.3)

7　When does a bank's duty to pay cheques end? (4.11)

8　At what stage and with what consequences is a bank affected by its customer's death? (4.11)

9　When may a bank disclose details of its customer's affairs? (4.23)

10　Name the duties owed by a customer to his bank. (5.2, 5.3)

*Now try questions 12 and 13 at the end of the text*

*Chapter 9*

# OTHER FEATURES OF THE BANKER-CUSTOMER RELATIONSHIP

---

This chapter covers the following topics.

1. Banker-customer relationships
2. The debtor/creditor relationship
3. The relationship of principal and agent
4. The relationship of bailor and bailee: safe custody
5. Banks and trusts
6. Mortgagee and mortgagor
7. A special relationship
8. The bank's duty of care: banker's references
9. The bank as data user

---

## 1. BANKER-CUSTOMER RELATIONSHIPS

1.1 In the last chapter, we examined the concept of the banker-customer relationship and in particular the contract which is formed between the two parties. This contract gives rise to legal rights and duties on both sides and these implied terms are the principal means by which the behaviour of each party is governed.

1.2 At the heart of the contract is the relationship of debtor (the bank) and creditor (the customer). These roles are reverted when an account is overdrawn. The range of services which a typical bank provides also gives rise to a number of other possible legal relationships between the parties. A bank may also be:

(a) an agent;
(b) a bailee;
(c) a trustee;
(d) a mortgagee; or
(e) an advisor, in a special relationship.

## 2. THE DEBTOR/CREDITOR RELATIONSHIP

2.1 When an account is in credit the bank stands as the customer's debtor, and the customer as the bank's creditor. Hence when the customer demands his funds, the bank must pay. But in the meantime the bank may use the funds (lending etc) as it wishes and keep the profits. Customer deposits are a source of finance; the bank is neither trustee nor agent for them (although it is the customer's agent regarding collection of cheques).

2.2 Certain consequences arise from the fact that the bank and its customer stand in a debtor/creditor relationship, as follows:

(a) in the absence of contrary agreement, the bank's right to appropriate payments (that is, to allocate payment to particular outstanding debts) is affected by the rule in *Clayton's* case (see previous chapter);

(b) the customer's right to repayment of a credit balance is subject to limitation; in some cases, a debt which has been unacknowledged and outstanding for over six years is 'statute-barred';

(c) the bank may *set off* or combine accounts (eg a credit against a debit balance) so as to arrive at a net balance owed or owing; and

(d) many lending transactions are affected by the Consumer Credit Act 1974 (see Chapter 6).

## 3. THE RELATIONSHIP OF PRINCIPAL AND AGENT

3.1 A bank acts as agent for its customer in a number of circumstances, for example:

(a) when it collects cheques on the customer's behalf;

(b) when it undertakes to arrange the buying and selling of shares; or

(c) when if offers advice on investments, such as life assurance and pensions.

3.2 Under general principles of agency law the bank, when acting as the customer's agent, owes the following duties to the customer as principal:

(a) a duty to complete the task;

(b) a duty to comply with instructions;

(c) a duty to show a proper standard of skill and care in carrying out its functions (note that this is also a requirement of the Supply of Goods and Services Act 1982);

(d) a duty of personal service - the bank may not delegate its performance of obligations as agent, except:

(i) where this is normal practice: for example, a bank acting as executor of a deceased customer may employ a solicitor to draft legal documents, or commence legal proceedings;

(ii) where it is clear from the facts that both parties intended to delegate - for example, when a bank is instructed to sell listed securities and employs a stockbroker to do so;

(e) a duty to account to the customer - it must supply full information of transactions and account for money paid and received;

(f) a duty to avoid a conflict of interest - this may arise where, for instance, a bank acts as banker to both parties in a takeover battle; and

(g) a duty to disclose rewards or benefits received - such as commission from a third party.

3.3 When a bank undertakes to deal with or to advise on a customer's investments, there is an implied duty (as a term of the contract to provide the service) to show proper skill and care. The bank may delegate to a broker those transactions which, under the regulations, must be carried out by an authorised person: the giving of investment advice is regulated by the Financial Services Act 1986 and must only be undertaken by a suitably authorised person.

3.4 You should note that a customer may give authority to an agent to operate his account. This is a separate matter and is dealt with in the next chapter.

## 4. THE RELATIONSHIP OF BAILOR AND BAILEE: SAFE CUSTODY

4.1 A bank has no implied obligation (arising from the banker-customer relationship) to accept a customer's documents or valuables for safe custody. But unless the property is bulky, dangerous or objectionable the bank will usually agree to a customer's request for this service. Unless he requires a safe deposit box the bank does not ordinarily raise an additional charge for this service. On accepting a customer's property the bank has an obligation:

(a) to take proper care to safeguard it against damage or loss; and

(b) to re-deliver it to the customer or to some person authorised by him and not to deliver it to any other person (but see below on competing claims).

4.2 In law, this arrangement is a contract of 'bailment'. There is a bailment whenever one person (the bailor) delivers personal property to another person (the bailee) on the basis described above. There can be many other forms of bailment, for example, delivery of an article to be repaired or the loan of an article for use by the borrower. Although a customer parts with possession of his property on depositing it with his bank (and can have claims against the bank) he is well advised to insure it. Insurers sometimes insist that valuable property such as jewellery must always be deposited at a bank when not in use.

4.3 At one time the law made a distinction (in the required standard of care) between a bailee for reward and a gratuitous bailee (an unpaid bailee). But there is now in practice probably one standard only for all bailments:

(a) the bailee must show the standard of care demanded by the circumstances of the case; and

(b) if the property is lost or damaged, the burden of showing that he took proper care rests on the bailee.

4.4 It is questionable whether a bank could claim to be a gratuitous bailee in which case it would only need to demonstrate the duty of care shown by a normal person to his own property. But this is not an important distinction, as banks generally accept that if there is any difference (in the standard of care) they should conform to the higher standard by taking all the precautions which good banking practice requires. When there is loss or damage the bank is likely to be liable for it unless it can demonstrate that:

(a) its system of precautions was adequate; and
(b) the loss etc did not result from any failure to operate the system as laid down.

The paragraphs below deal with particular situations of loss or damage of property while in the bank's charge.

*Theft from the bank*

4.5 Property may be stolen from the bank, for example by a break-in to the bank strongroom. The bank is liable for the loss unless its precautions against burglary conform to good modern practice and have been properly observed. This often requires elaborate and expensive improvements to strongrooms.

*Theft, loss or damage by an employee*

4.6 Property may be stolen by a dishonest bank employee or lost or damaged by the carelessness of an employee. In general a bailee is responsible for the default of his employees (vicarious liability). In such cases the bank might escape liability if the employee at fault was acting outside the scope of his duties in dealing with the property, and his access to it was not due to lack of precautions on the part of the bank. This question of vicarious liability is the only area where a gratuitous bailee can possibly claim that a less demanding standard is still applied to him than to a bailee for reward. In practice it is difficult for a bank to escape liability in a case of this kind. If the employee at fault was employed on duties connected with the property, the bank is likely to be vicariously liable for the misconduct of an employee acting in the course of his duty. If he was employed on other duties, the bank's working system was defective in allowing him to get access to the property.

*Destruction or damage by fire*

4.7 Property may be destroyed or damaged by fire. Here the question is whether the bank had adequate fire precautions, whether they were properly observed, and whether the cause of the fire was entirely accidental (eg a fire spreading from an adjoining building not owned by the bank) or was due to carelessness (a dropped cigarette end) of bank staff. If the bank or its staff were at fault, the bank is likely to be liable. For purely accidental loss not preventable by ordinary means it may escape liability.

## Conversion

4.8 Dealing with the property of another person in a manner which prejudices his rights of ownership is the tort of conversion under the Torts (Interference with Goods) Act 1977. The following situations can be distinguished in dealings by a bank with property deposited for safekeeping:

(a) To receive property for safekeeping and to return it to the depositor (in ignorance of his lack of title) is not conversion by the bank.

(b) To receive property of a customer and to deliver it (without his proper authority) to a person not entitled to it can be conversion: *Langtry v Union Bank of London 1896.*

(c) To refuse to re-deliver property to the customer or someone authorised by him is conversion unless the bank can justify the refusal.

4.9 The situations in which a bank may be justified in refusing to re-deliver property include the following.

(a) Where there is reasonable doubt over the genuineness of the customer's authority produced by another person. But the bank may only withhold the property for a short time while it makes enquiries.

(b) Where the bank has a lien on the property (discussed in Chapter 15).

(c) Where a third party asserts that he and not the depositor is entitled to the property. The bank should 'interplead' - require the parties to resolve their dispute, if necessary by legal action, on the basis that the bank will deliver the property to the person found to be entitled to it.

(d) Where the customer has died, become bankrupt or become insane (a patient under the Court of Protection). Any of these events terminates a previous authority given by the customer to the bank to re-deliver the property. There are legal procedures - eg an executor obtains probate or the will of a deceased customer or an enduring power of attorney by which another person obtains legal control of the customer's property. The bank should require evidence of the proper authority and may withhold the property meanwhile.

(e) Where property has been deposited by joint depositors, eg trustees or executors, and one of them demands re-delivery on his sole authorisation. Unless the bank has previously received a joint mandate from all depositors to act in this way it should refuse. The most common example is a joint mandate which provides that on death of one of the depositors the survivor(s) shall have control. In that case the bank should require evidence of death and then comply with the mandate. Death of one joint depositor does not affect the authority which he gave in his lifetime.

## 5. BANKS AND TRUSTS

5.1 Trusts may affect a bank in a number of ways, which will be set out in outline here.

(a) Customers may hold funds on trust for someone else. This may mean that the bank should beware of breach of trust (as where a cheque is drawn on a charity fund payable to one of the trustees in a personal capacity) and should be careful to pay in accordance with the correct mandate.

(b) Customers may hold funds which rightly belong to someone else, who may then 'trace' the property into a bank account.

(c) The bank may be a constructive trustee, where it knows that money held is in breach of trust and hence 'becomes' a trustee for that amount (see below).

(d) The bank may hold a Quistclose trust. This derives from the case *Barclays Bank Ltd v Quistclose Investments Ltd 1968* where a company (X) paid in money to an account at B which it had borrowed from Q *specifically* to pay a dividend. When X went into liquidation without paying a dividend it was *held* that B held the funds on trust for Q, since the purpose for which the loan was taken out had not been fulfilled.

5.2 You should note that a bank does not normally act as a trustee for the customer, which would mean having more onerous obligations than arise from a contract: *Foley v Hill 1848*.

5.3 A party who receives and controls money under forged payment orders may be liable as a constructive trustee if it can be shown that he has some knowledge that the transmission of funds may be part of a fraudulent activity.

Data protection Act

*Case: Agip (Africa) Ltd v Jackson and Others 1991*
Z, the chief accountant of A, an oil exploration company, fraudulently altered the payee's name on a company payment order for $½ million to that of an Isle of Man company whose directors, J and G, were among the defendants. The money was then transferred from the latter company's account to a client account of an accountancy firm of which J and G were a partner and an employee respectively. The money was then paid out from this account.

*Held:* A had a right to sue, as the money has been paid under mistake of fact. The defendants' firm had a degree of 'knowledge', having previously received legal advice that payments might involve a fraud on A. They had made no enquiries into this. J and G had assisted in the fraud, and the second partner in the firm, B, was held liable as constructive trustee to A. This was because, as a partner, he was liable for the acts of both partner and employee.

## 6. MORTGAGEE AND MORTGAGOR

6.1 When a customer approaches a bank for a loan, the bank will usually require some form of security. The customer (the mortgagor) may give a mortgage of property to the bank (the mortgagee) as security for the advance. A mortgage is a right (in priority to other creditors) to resort to the property of the borrower to obtain repayment of the loan if the latter defaults. Land is the type of property most commonly mortgaged.

6.2 The law on mortgages is complex; there are different types of mortgage and different categories of land. The rights and duties of the bank as mortgagee and the topic of mortgages generally are covered in the chapter on land as security.

## 7. A SPECIAL RELATIONSHIP

7.1 It was noted earlier that in the banker-customer relationship there is a rebuttable presumption that no undue influence is exerted. Undue influence may be held to arise on the facts of the case. In particular, where there is risk of conflict of interest, a bank may not be able to give *independent* advice. In such cases, it is incumbent upon the bank to ensure that independent advice is received by the customer: *Lloyds Bank v Bundy 1975.*

7.2 The existence of a special relationship gives rise to a strict duty of good faith on the part of the bank.

7.3 A bank may have a strict duty of good faith to advise a provider of security if that person is a personal customer: *Cornish v Midland Bank plc 1985* (described in the chapter on guarantees). However in the case of non-customers, there is no such duty of care.

*Case: Barclays Bank plc v Khaira 1991*
Mr and Mrs K gave the plaintiffs a mortgage over their house. Mr K was declared bankrupt and B sought to take possession. Mrs K disputed the claim and alleged that the bank had been negligent in failing to advise her to seek independent financial advice and to explain the nature of the charge to her.

*Held:* there was no duty to explain to a potential guarantor the nature of a charge, however if an explanation was given, there was a duty not to be negligent in giving it.

7.4  A bank may also in certain circumstances be party to a second type of special relationship. This occurs where the bank is approached for, and gives, a reference to a third party in respect of an existing customer. This relationship is not contractual, but may give rise to liability in tort.

## 8.  THE BANK'S DUTY OF CARE: BANKER'S REFERENCES

8.1  It is often the case that a customer who is entering into dealings with a person who has no prior knowledge of him will allow that person to ask for a banker's reference on the customer from the bank. Usually this request is channelled through the bank of the person seeking the reference. The customer's bank, when sending a reference, has a duty of care to the party making an enquiry for a banker's reference, and an obligation not to mislead by fraud.

*Case: Hedley Byrne & Co Ltd v Heller & Partners Ltd 1963*
HB were advertising agents whose client (E) had given instructions to advertise E's products in the media. By custom an advertising agent is personally liable for contracts of this type. Through its own bank, HB enquired as to the creditworthiness of E. The enquiry came to the defendants (HP) who were merchant bankers acting for E. HP was about to call for repayment by E of its overdraft and HP knew that E might be unable to do this. HP therefore replied to the enquiry 'without responsibility' (they disclaimed all liability) that E was 'a respectably constituted company considered good for its ordinary business engagements. Your figures are larger than we are accustomed to see'. This last sentence was intended to be a warning but HB did not understand it in that sense and went ahead with the advertising. E went into insolvent liquidation and HB incurred £17,000 personal liability on the advertising contracts.

*Held:*  there is (independent of any contract) a duty to take reasonable care in providing information to another person for a known purpose, that is where there is a 'special relationship'; HP was in breach of that duty on the facts, but the disclaimer sufficed to exclude liability. HB's claim therefore failed.

8.2  The decision in the *Hedley Byrne* case has subsequently been refined by the courts. The House of Lords considered the concept of a duty of care, emphasising that it would only arise where there is a sufficient degree of proximity between the parties.

*Case: Caparo Industries plc v Dickman and Others 1990*
C, the plaintiffs, who already owned Fidelity shares, purchased additional shares in Fidelity on the open market, relying on information in the accounts, which showed a profit of £1.3 million. They eventually acquired the company. Later they claimed against the directors (the brothers Dickman) and the auditors, contesting that the accounts should have shown a loss of £460,000. They argued that the auditors owed a duty of care to investors and potential investors.

*Held:*  the auditor's duty of care did not extend to potential investors or existing shareholders. It was a duty owed to the body of shareholders as a whole.

8.3  The House of Lords identified two situations:

(a)  preparation of advice or information in the knowledge that a particular person was contemplating a transaction and was expecting to receive the advice or information in order to rely on it to decide whether or not to proceed with the transaction (a special relationship); and

    (b)  preparation of a statement (in this case the audit report) for more or less general circulation which could forseeably be relied upon by persons unknown to the maker of the statement for a variety of different purposes.

Only in the first situation, and provided that the person making the statement has expertise in the matter, will it be reasonable to impose a duty of care.

8.4  It is clear that in giving a banker's reference on its own customer to another bank for the information of its customer, the bank owes a duty of care and can become liable for negligence (negligent misstatement). There is no comprehensive general definition of negligent misstatement but it can exist where either:

    (a)  a statement is made without reasonable grounds - that is, without sufficient facts or reliable information to support it; or

    (b)  a statement is expressed in such an ambiguous way that the person to whom it is made reasonably understands it in a different sense from the intention of the person who made it. It was in this respect that Heller & Partners failed in their duty to Hedley Byrne. Hence the greatest care is needed in choosing words which can be justified to the customer without misleading the other party. If Heller had replied 'we cannot speak for your figures' they could hardly have been faulted.

8.5  However a bank also runs the risk of defaming its customer if it gives a reference which cannot be justified. When giving banker's references, it is therefore wise to be careful with the wording so that it is not ambiguous yet does not defame. Banks normally also ensure that the reference:

    (a)  contains a disclaimer of liability; and
    (b)  is unsigned.

*Disclaimer*

8.6  Heller & Partners escaped liability by the use of the standard disclaimer. But since that time the general law on disclaimer of liability for negligence has been altered by the Unfair Contract Terms Act 1977 so that a disclaimer of responsibility for a banker's reference is only valid if it is 'reasonable': s 2(2).

8.7  The courts are still exploring and defining how this statutory rule should apply in any given set of circumstances and no decision has yet been given on a banker's reference or any similar statement. However, it appears that where a disclaimer is made and accepted between business concerns which understand its significance, the courts will not readily treat it as unreasonable. At all events, it is still normal - and probably useful - practice for a bank to make the standard disclaimer in giving a reference.

*Unsigned references*

8.8 It does not often happen that a banker's reference is alleged to be fraudulent. If such a case were to arise a disclaimer would not relieve the bank of liability for fraud because the disclaimer is treated as part of the fraud and not as a means of evading liability for it. The relevant case-law, however, must be considered at this point together with the obscurely drafted Statute of Frauds (Amendment) Act 1828 ('Lord Tenterden's Act').

8.9 Firstly, how does fraud differ from negligence? Broadly, negligence in supplying information exists where a statement is made honestly but without reasonable grounds for it or reasonable care in expressing clearly what is intended (as in the *Hedley Byrne* case). The generally accepted definition of a fraudulent statement is that it is made

'knowing it to be untrue or without belief in its truth or recklessly, careless whether it be true or false': *Derry v Peek 1889* (a company prospectus case). Essentially, the distinction is made between deliberate or *reckless* deceit and an honest but *careless* mistake. For a fraudulent statement, the person deceived may sue for damages for deceit.

8.10 A bank should not include in a banker's reference statements which it knows are not true or does not believe to be true. However, banks have occasionally been sued because their banker's reference is alleged to have been written with a reckless disregard of known facts. The disclaimer may not suffice to avoid liability in such a case, but the bank can rely on Lord Tenterden's Act which negatives liability for an assurance given about the credit of another person unless that 'assurance be made in writing, *signed* by the party to be charged therewith'. *An unsigned banker's reference is protected by this statutory rule.*

8.11 In the *Hedley Byrne* case the plaintiffs originally alleged fraud but later relied merely on negligence as the basis of their claim. Such cases where the reference given can hardly be said to reflect the facts known to the bank are very much on the borderline between carelessness (negligence) and recklessness (fraud). The facts of this leading case, decided before the Australian courts, are a warning.

*Case: Commercial Banking Co of Sydney Limited v R H Brown & Co 1972*
At the time when the reference was given, the customer had exceeded its agreed limit for advances and the bank was aware that the customer was making delays in payments to trade creditors because, essentially, it was overtrading. The reference was generally favourable, stating among other points that the customer 'had always met its engagements, is trading satisfactorily . . . and would be safe for its trade engagements generally' . . . The reference was unsigned and there was a disclaimer of liability.

*Held:* in view of the facts known to the bank, the opinion given was reckless and therefore fraudulent. The disclaimer as part of the fraud should be disregarded. The absence of a signature was not raised as a defence.

## 9.  THE BANK AS DATA USER

9.1 In 1984 the Data Protection Act was passed; its objective was to lay down standards for the holding of personal data and to give rights to the individual about whom data is held. The Act affects the bank because it is defined as a 'data user': that is, an organisation which controls the contents of files of personal data and the use of personal data which is processed automatically.

9.2 Under the Act it is necessary for the bank to take the following steps:

(a) to register as a data user (failure to register is an offence) and only to disclose data to recipients disclosed in the registration; and

(b) to follow the data protection principles, which lay down rules for obtaining, processing, holding, using and amending data and allow individual data subjects limited rights of inspection.

9.3 Many banks have addressed the Act's implications by formulating guidelines to be followed regarding the storage and disclosure of data.

(a) The bank should appoint a data protection co-ordinator. The co-ordinator's job is to arrange the bank's registration and to ensure continued compliance with the Act's provisions after registration.

(b) The bank's staff should be informed of the Act's implications. In order to ensure complete and accurate registration and also continued compliance with the Act after registration, all relevant staff must be made fully aware of the Act and be made to realise that the Act will inevitably affect the performance of their work with computers.

(c) The bank's entry in the register should be amended whenever there is a change to the nature of the personal data that is being held and used, in order to comply with the Act. So disclosing data to group companies for marketing purposes should be registered as a particular kind of user.

(d) *Future procedures* should be established. The co-ordinator needs to set systems which will allow him:

(i) to monitor compliance with the Principles;
(ii) to meet subject access requests; and
(iii) to be made aware of any changes in the bank which may require amendment to the registered entry.

(e) The bank should ensure that whenever a new computer system is planned, or a new software package purchased, consideration is given to whether a registration of the system under the Act is necessary. This should be a *formal* step in the system design and development, so that it is never overlooked.

## 10. CONCLUSION

10.1 A customer of a bank has a contractual relationship with it, but this relationship may also contain elements of debtor/creditor liability, tort, bailment and trust.

10.2 As well as taking care as a contractual term, the bank owes a duty of care in tort to avoid negligent misstatement, as set down in the *Hedley Byrne* case.

10.3 A safe custody facility provided by a bank gives rise to a contract of bailment, the bank usually owing the standard of care owed by a paid bailee. There may arise liability for the tort of conversion if the bank is careless in bailment.

---

**TEST YOUR KNOWLEDGE**

*The numbers in brackets refer to paragraphs of this chapter*

1  What terms are implied into the bank's contract with its customer by virtue of the fact that they stand in a debtor/creditor relationship? (2.2)

2  When does a bank act as the customer's agent and what duties does it owe? (3.1, 3.2)

3  What duties are owed by a bank which accepts property for safe custody? (4.1 – 4.3)

4  How may trusts affect a bank? (5.1)

5  Does a bank owe a duty of care to outsiders? If so, in what circumstances will this be breached? (8.1)

---

*Now try question 14 at the end of the text*

# Chapter 10

# OPERATING A BANK ACCOUNT

> **This chapter covers the following topics.**
>
> 1. References and enquiries
> 2. Opening the account
> 3. Standard form contracts
> 4. Customers' agents
> 5. Statements of account
> 6. Bank charges
> 7. Closing the account
> 8. Reform of banking services law

## 1. REFERENCES AND ENQUIRIES

1.1 When a person previously unknown to the bank proposes to open an account, the bank - in its own interest - needs to obtain information about the stranger before accepting him as a customer and opening the account. There are several factors to be considered.

   (a) *Identity* - has the new customer assumed a false name, perhaps for the purpose of obtaining payment through the bank of a stolen crossed cheque?

   (b) *Character references* - is the applicant a person of good character and likely to be a satisfactory customer? Unless a potential customer is very young he or she may well have had an account previously with some other bank. If so, that bank may have found this person to be a troublesome customer. It may occasionally happen that the person who is seeking to open an account has a record of fraud, or is an undischarged bankrupt, etc. The bank therefore needs to obtain satisfactory references before accepting a new customer. The bank should also take precautions against the production of false or forged references.

   (c) *Employment or means of livelihood* - there must always be suspicion when a customer delivers to the bank for collection a cheque payable to his or her employer and endorsed to the customer or drawn by the employer in favour of a third party and similarly endorsed. The bank therefore needs to know the name of the employer in order to identify such cheques. Similar considerations arise if the customer claims to be self-employed and then delivers for collection cheques which are not drawn payable to him or her by name.

1.2 The necessary information can be obtained direct from the customer, but supported by confirmatory evidence, or in the form of references given by third parties. It is therefore normal banking practice to seek information by these means. A cunning rogue is aware of the likelihood of bank enquiries on these lines and may devise means of deception which are not easily exposed. However, a bank which makes no enquiries is very likely to be held to be negligent for failing to carry out normal practice. If it makes enquiries and is deceived it may, depending on the degree of thoroughness and attention which it gives to the matter, avoid being negligent in the legal sense. If it is negligent the bank thereby forfeits the essential safeguards for cheque transactions given by various sections of the Bills of Exchange Act 1882 and the Cheques Act 1957 (discussed in the chapter on the protection of banks).

### Identity

1.3 There is a double risk here. First, the stranger may have assumed a false name for himself. Secondly, on being asked for references, he may name as a referee either himself under his real name or an existing person of that name who knows and vouches for the third party whose identity the fraudulent stranger has assumed in approaching the bank.

1.4 There are thus certain precautions to be taken.

(a) The stranger can be asked to produced documentary evidence of his own identity such as a passport, a driving licence or a season ticket, etc. Preferably it should be something which bears a photograph of the holder. Without a photograph there is much greater risk of deception since a rogue may come prepared to produce stolen or forged documents to support his fake identity.

(b) The bank should make some enquiries to identify and obtain information about any referees who give references. A useful step is to ask for the name of the referee's bank and make an enquiry of that bank about the referee. Alternatively, if the stranger names his employer it may be sufficient to obtain a reference from the employer, especially if the employer is known by reputation at least to the bank, or is vouched for by its own bank or can at least be found at the address given in the telephone directory.

1.5 The following cases illustrate the views taken by the courts in the past on the subject of identification. In every case except *Marfani's*. the bank was held liable to pay damages in conversion to the cheque's true owner.

*Case: Ladbroke v Todd 1914*
The thief opened an account in the name of the payee of a stolen cheque. The bank did not ask for references nor did it make other enquiries.

*Held:* the bank lost its statutory protection because of its failure to take references.

*Case: Guardians of St John's Hampstead v Barclays Bank Limited 1923*
The thief opened an account in the name of Donald Stewart and gave the name of a referee. The reference supplied to the bank in response to its enquiry was a forgery. The bank had taken no steps to verify the standing or identity of the referee. Later the thief delivered to the bank for collection stolen cheques payable to D Stewart & Co, saying that he carried on business under that name. The bank could have discovered from the telephone directory that no individual or firm was present at the address given by the thief.

*Held:* the bank had been negligent in accepting the reference of a stranger.

1.6 A bank cannot be expected to pursue its enquiries to such lengths as to make deception impossible. This would require visiting and making personal contact with referees. It is not required by law. In *Marfani's* case below the bank had not carried through the routine procedure in a thorough manner but contended - successfully - that if it had done so, it would have been deceived nonetheless. It should also be alert in its routine to spot an improbable statement or one which can be checked without extra work. In both *Lumsden's* case and *Marfani's* case below the rogue told the bank that he had recently arrived from abroad. In neither case did the bank ask to see his passport, which would have exposed the deception at once since he had assumed a false name, and the passport, if it had existed in the assumed name, would not have born a recent immigration stamp to record entry into the UK. The better view (applied in *Lumsden's* case but not in *Marfani's*) is that on hearing this story the bank should have asked to see the passport.

*Case: Marfani & Co v Midland Bank Limited 1967*
The thief first manufactured evidence of his false identity by making the acquaintance (under an assumed name) of a customer of the bank. In applying to open the account in the assumed name he said that he had recently arrived from Pakistan but was able to give two references. The bank did not ask to see his passport but wrote to each of the referees. One did not reply. The other, who was the existing customer of the bank, only replied verbally, while at the bank on his own business, to the effect that he had known for some months a person of that name. The bank made no further enquiries. The thief then stole from his employer a cheque drawn payable to the real person whose identity he had assumed. Apart from the passport point there were certain discrepancies and similarities in the cheque itself which, if noticed, might have put the bank on its guard.

*Held:* the bank was not negligent. The sole referee was a good customer who had introduced other satisfactory customers and there was no need for further enquiries.

*Case: Lumsden & Co v London Trustee Savings Bank 1971*
As in *Marfani's* case the thief told the bank that he had only recently arrived in this country but the bank did not ask to see his passport. He gave his own name and address as referee and in that name provided a satisfactory reference. The bank asked for particulars of the referee's bank but did not pursue the matter when the information was not forthcoming.

*Held:* the bank should have followed up the reference, should have checked telephone book entries and should have required proof of identity (eg sight of the passport).

## Character references

1.7 Apart from limited use of references as a check on identity, the new customer should be asked to provide references as a general guide to his suitability as a customer of the bank. Receipt of one satisfactory reference is sufficient as a safeguard but some banks ask for two.

1.8 There is a possibility that a referee named by the applicant will fail to provide a satisfactory reference or not reply at all. Any reply received from a referee needs careful attention. Referees hesitate to make explicit adverse statements and may plead that they do not know enough about the applicant or have been acquainted with him for only a short time. The bank may also obtain information from some other source, such as the applicant's previous bank, that his record renders it unlikely that he will be a satisfactory customer. It is perhaps rather unwise to let drop an enquiry to a referee which produces no answer at all. In *Marfani's* case the bank must be considered fortunate in being absolved from negligence when one referee did not reply and the other gave a most inadequate answer. The referee cannot be pressed for a reply (he has no obligation to respond) but the applicant who named him as referee can be told and asked to put forward another referee in his place.

1.9 To preserve customer goodwill and obtain business in a time of sharp competition from building societies as much as from other banks, it is necessary to pursue these matters tactfully and to avoid any indication of suspicion. In the end however the bank may have to refuse the application if a satisfactory reference or references are not forthcoming.

1.10 Some banks have decided not to take references, but to ask the prospective customer to show identification (eg passport or driving licence). The bank then undertakes its own credit reference search to ensure that the prospective customer has no county court judgements against him, or is not an undischarged bankrupt. As long as the credit reference search is clear, the account will be opened. This is a recent alteration to banks' procedure, and there is no case law to clarify whether or not the courts consider them to be acting negligently in not obtaining references. If they are, they will lose protection under the Bills of Exchange Act 1882 and the Cheques Act 1957.

## Customer's employment

1.11 The bank should ask whether the new customer is employed and if so, obtain particulars of the employer's name and address with - if possible - the customer's agreement that the bank may apply to the employer for a reference. Whether it is necessary to enquire from the employer, as a referee, about his bank and pursue enquiries with that bank must be a matter of judgement depending in the status of the employer. It is not general banking practice to do so. It may be difficult to induce the employer to answer an enquiry addressed to him as referee.

1.12 In addition to the identity of the employer the bank should, if possible, obtain information of the position which the customer holds in his employer's organisation. The main reason for wishing to know the identity of the customer's employer is to make it possible for the bank to identify cheques drawn by, or in favour of, the employer and presented by the customer for collection. In such instances, except where the cheque is drawn by the employer payable to the employee, it may have been stolen at the place of work - where the greatest opportunity of cheque fraud or dishonesty exists. Some employees, such as a cashier or company secretary, must by reason of their duties be in a position to misappropriate cheques. Others have duties which give them little opportunity for dishonesty. Again, such enquiries have to be made with tact but banks - to protect their own interests - should not omit this precaution.

### Case: Savory & Co v Lloyds Bank Ltd 1932
S (a stockbroker) drew bearer cheques to settle with other firms. Two employees of S stole cheques which were paid in to accounts in the names of the employee in one case and his wife (in the other). These accounts were at suburban branches. The cheques were paid in at City branches for credit to the accounts elsewhere. Hence the branches to which the money was credited never saw the cheques. S sued the bank which argued that it had followed normal practice in accepting the cheques at City branches without enquiry and was not negligent. The bank had not followed its own regulations in opening the accounts since no information was then obtained of the identity of the employer (of the customer and the customer's husband respectively) but the bank argued that in the circumstances such information would not have affected the position. The bank also argued that the 'branch transfer system' (described above) was part of the ordinary course of business of banks and the bank had operated it for 40 years. The fraud had remained undetected for several months during which a large number of cheques were stolen.

*Held:* through its branches the bank as a whole was (or should have been) in possession of information sufficient to enable it to detect that these were employers' cheques. What was done in the ordinary course of business could nonetheless be negligent (ie the branch transfer system). On the facts the bank had been negligent (so that the relevant safeguard did not apply) and was liable.

1.13 In this case the main fault of the bank was that it failed to recognise that the sequence of large cheques delivered for credit to the accounts were bearer cheques - which is not the usual method of paying a monthly salary. Lord Wright (in the House of Lords) said: 'bankers fail in taking adequate precautions, if they do not ask the name of his employers. Otherwise they cannot guard against the danger known to them of his paying in cheques stolen from his employers'.

1.14 If the bank's suspicions are awakened by any reasonable indication of possible defalcation at the place of work, it becomes its duty to make thorough enquiries.

*Case: Harding v London Joint Stock Bank Limited 1914*
F was introduced as a new customer to the bank by an existing customer. He wished to open the account by paying in a cheque payable to the firm by which he was employed as cashier. The bank asked F to obtain written confirmation from his employers that the cheque was his property. F wrote a letter to the bank on the firm's notepaper to the appropriate effect and signed the letter in the firm's name, in accordance with normal partnership practice but entirely without authority from the partners. The bank accepted the letter as sufficient confirmation. The firm sued the bank for conversion.

*Held:* in view of its knowledge that the payee of the cheque was the customer's employer the bank had been negligent in permitting the customer to produce the evidence for which the bank had properly asked.

## Married women

1.15 If a married woman opens an account the bank should obtain from her information of her employer, if she has a job, and in any event information of the name of her husband's employer. *Savory's Case* mentioned above illustrates the risk against which this precaution is taken. In view of the Sex Discrimination Act 1975, the bank should make similar enquiries about the wife's employment before opening an account for a married man. However, *Savory's* case came before the House of Lords in 1933 when law and social attitudes were less sensitive to sexual discrimination. There is no modern reported case on the point, though obviously it is an area which requires tact and common sense in dealings with customers.

## Change of employment

1.16 Logic would also suggest that a bank should be diligent in keeping record of an existing customer's change of employment and of the identity of his new employer. However, on this point it has been decided that a bank has no legal duty to enquire and is not at fault if it does know that a customer has changed his employment: *Orbit Mining & Trading Co Limited v Westminster Bank Limited 1963*. In this more tolerant attitude the law recognises that a bank has no opportunity to ask questions of an existing customer such as it can in responding to his request to open an account. It will often happen of course that the bank is aware of the customer's change of job. To take an obvious point his monthly salary cheque or transfer comes from a different source. What the bank actually knows, whether or not it should know it, is information which it must apply in observing the transactions passing through the customer's account.

## 2. OPENING THE ACCOUNT

2.1 Although it may take a short time to obtain the required reference(s) some necessary arrangements can be agreed with the new customer in the course of his first meeting at the bank. The following paragraphs deal with some practical matters which may come up.

2.2 The bank should obtain a *specimen signature* of the customer on its standard signature card and file it for reference. Two related matters may also require attention:

(a)  if it is a joint account the bank will require specimen signatures of all account-holders;

(b)  mandates and other authorisation by the customer to the bank to honour cheques signed by agents of the customer are considered in Section 4 of this chapter. Again specimen signatures of all authorised signatories are required.

2.3 In modern practice the customer may expect to receive (i) a *cash dispenser card*, (ii) a *credit card*, (ii) a *debit card* and (iii) a *cheque guarantee card*. Some banks now issue cards which combine the functions of two at least of these important plastic cards. It is normal practice not to issue a cheque guarantee card to a new customer at the time of opening the account but to wait for say three months and then, if the operation of the account has been satisfactory to the bank, to issue it.

2.4 As the bank's agreement to open the account is conditional on obtaining a satisfactory reference, the issue of a *cheque book* should be deferred until the reference has been obtained. There is no objection to accepting from the intended customer a sum in cash with which to open the account meanwhile. If he hands in a third party cheque for collection and credit of the proceeds to his account some caution is needed since, until the reference is received, the bank might be held to be negligent in collecting a cheque for a person who is technically a customer but of whose character and identity the bank has no information. In *Ladbroke's* case, the bank had no reason to wait because it made no enquiries at all but it was additionally at fault in agreeing to special - rapid - presentation of the first cheque. It is more difficult and risky for a thief to escape detection if the bank at which he opens an account acts with what the US Supreme Court once called 'deliberate speed'. There must be exceptions when sufficient explanation and safeguards are available but the stranger in a great hurry exposes the bank to the risk that he is not what he seems. When the time comes to issue the cheque book it may, depending on the circumstances, be advisable to ensure that the customer has funds (not merely an uncleared cheque) against which to draw.

2.5 The customer will also require a *paying-in book* and there should be sufficient discussion between the bank and the customer of such matters as:

(a)  the sources and frequency of regular payments into the account, eg monthly salary payments;

(b)  the balance he is likely to maintain and the effect that this will have on the bank's charges for maintaining the account (of which the customer should be informed); and

(c)  the intervals at which the customer requires statements of his account.

Agreeing on these matters clarifies for both parties the terms of the contract which has been formed.

2.6 The customer may stipulate that he does not wish the bank to reply to enquiries from other banks about his creditworthiness. If a polite explanation of the difficulties for himself and the bank does not persuade him to withdraw his instructions, the safest course is to decline to accept him as a customer. There is a risk that the bank will later overlook his instructions and reply to the enquiry as normal routine and thereby incur liability for breach of contract.

2.7 Once it has opened the account the bank has a mandate from the customer to act on his instructions. The mandate covers such matters as:

(a) payment of cheques drawn on the account;
(b) countermand of payment;
(c) credit of monies received to the account;
(d) cash advances;
(e) delivery of documents and other property held for safekeeping by the bank; and
(f) revocation of the mandate.

2.8 The Code of Banking Practice sets the following standards on account opening.

(a) 'Banks and building societies will satisfy themselves about the identity of a person seeking to open an account to assist in protecting their customers, members of the public and themselves against fraud and other misuse of the banking system. (2.1)

(b) Banks and building societies will provide to prospective customers details of the identification needed. (2.2)'

## 3. STANDARD FORM CONTRACTS

3.1 We have seen that, in the light of parliament's intervention by way of statute to protect the consumer, such as the Consumer Credit Act 1974, the Unfair Contract Terms Act 1977 and the Supply of Goods and Services Act 1982, it is important to be aware of the implications of these Acts in relation to the bank's standard form contracts.

3.2 In common with many large organisations, the banks design and use their own standard forms of contract particularly for legal and equitable mortgages and contracts of guarantee. These contracts have been drawn up after the bank has sought legal, commercial and technical advice from within its own organisation and from outside bodies, such as solicitors, accountants etc. They are used by banks on a daily basis to standardise procedures and enable the parties to the contract to be fully aware of their respective terms, rights and obligations prior to signing.

---

### Exercise

Try to identify some of these contracts that are used daily in your bank. Think about its standard security documentation, house purchase and personal loan documentation, and the contracts (mandates) used for all forms of automatic banking eg cheques, automated teller machines and credit cards.

---

3.3 It should be noted that the unscrupulous may use standard form contracts to take away the legal rights of the other party. Whilst it is legitimate to use this form of contract to clarify their rights, banks should ensure that their contracts conform to accepted standards of fairness.

## 4. CUSTOMERS' AGENTS

4.1 The customer may wish to give authority to someone else to draw cheques on his account or, less frequently, to deal with the bank on his behalf, eg in the withdrawal of documents or valuables deposited with the bank for safe-keeping. A company customer is obliged to authorise others to sign its cheques since as an abstract person it cannot sign them itself.

In such cases the customer is termed the *principal* and the person acting on his or her behalf is known as the *agent*.

4.2 To understand these matters, which result in the use of mandates and less frequently powers of attorney, it is necessary to grasp the essential features of the law of agency which determines how far one person can validly give authority to another to conduct business for him. We touched on this subject in the previous chapter. The main rules are as follows.

(a) *Personal capacity:* as a general rule any person can appoint an agent to act for him. However, a minor, whose capacity to enter into binding contracts is severely restricted, cannot, through an agent, exceed the limits of his own contractual capacity. The same rule applies to any other person under a legal disability such as a person affected by mental illness. There is no legal restriction on personal capacity to be appointed as agent but there are obvious practical objections to appointing a minor or a mentally disordered person as agent.

(b) *Prohibition on delegation.* Some persons, in particular trustees, have powers which are personal to themselves and which cannot be delegated in the ordinary way, though there are special procedures for doing so. There is no prohibition against trustees appointing a bank to act as their agent in banking matters - Trustee Act 1925 s 23 expressly provides for it - subject to certain conditions. But trustees in their dealings with their bank must usually act collectively so that all must sign a cheque drawn on their account. However, the trust deed may remove this difficulty by providing that one (or two) trustees may act for the rest in signing cheques. We will take a closer look at trust accounts in Chapter 11.

(c) *Limits on agents' authority.* There are two principles here; both are especially important in connection with companies. First, a principal cannot give authority to an agent to do something which is beyond the capacity of the principal. What is *ultra vires* (beyond the powers of) a company is similarly beyond the powers of its agent even if it has purported to give him authority to do it. Secondly, there may be a set procedure for the grant of authority to an agent such as is found in the articles of association of the company or in the Powers of Attorney Act 1971 and the Enduring Powers of Attorney Act 1985. To effect a valid authorisation, that procedure must be correctly followed. Apart from procedure the principal may decide to set limits on the agent's authority. For example, a company in general meeting may authorise its directors to borrow, say, £100,000 but no more.

(d) *Termination of authority.* The authority properly granted to an agent may come to an end, either by revocation on the part of the principal or by the automatic effect of some event such as death of the principal.

You will recognise that the foregoing is only a brief summary of some complicated rules of the law of agency.

4.3 Banking practice in dealings with agents who represent customers seeks to achieve as much certainty as possible for all concerned. The use of mandates, drafted with specific reference to bank transactions, is the mainstay of the system. However, the bank must always keep in view the possible effect of any of the facts mentioned in the paragraph 4.2.

## Mandates for signature of cheques

4.4 When a customer's agent, duly authorised by mandate, signs a cheque drawn on the customer's account it suffices if he simply writes his signature - which should correspond with the specimen signature previously supplied to the bank. The agent may however add words to his signature and the significance of these words should be understood.

4.5 By the mere fact of signature as drawer of the cheque the agent assumes personal liability on it unless he shows that he signs merely as agent for another person: Bills of Exchange Act 1882 s 23. To avoid liability it is usual to add the words 'for and on behalf of' the principal, although this is no longer necessary for a person signing a company's cheque: *Bondina Ltd v Rollaway Shower Blinds Ltd 1986*. The bank is not concerned with these words, or their absence. They merely serve to protect the agent against claims by other parties to the cheque should the principal fail to pay.

4.6 Secondly, an agent may have only limited authority from his principal to sign cheques up to a stated amount or for particular purposes. If he adds to his signature 'per pro' (or less often the full formula 'per procurationem' or the brief 'pp') that gives notice that his authority is limited and relieves his principal of liability if the agent has exceeded the limit: *Morison v Kemp 1912:* Bills of Exchange Act 1882 s 25. However, as between the customer and the bank the mandate has overriding effect - if the cheque is within the authority given by the mandate the bank need not concern itself with the implications of a 'per pro' signature.

## Power of attorney

4.7 A general power of attorney (abbreviated here to 'P/A') is a formal appointment of an agent by deed. The customer giving the power is called the 'donor' in legal contexts and the agent to whom the power is given is called the 'donee'. This power is usually in a form prescribed by the Powers of Attorney Act 1971, although it may be an enduring power of attorney which is given by a person approaching senility in order to allow the donee to exercise powers as a P/A of the donor once mental incapacity has overtaken him or her.

4.8 A mandate is, from the bank's point of view, a much simpler and more satisfactory method of obtaining a customer's authority to honour cheques, deliver documents, etc. The mandate is an authority, on a printed form prepared by the bank to cover the relevant points, given by the customer *to the bank*. By contrast a P/A is a legal document prepared by the customer's legal advisers, with reference to various acts of the agent, and given *to the agent* so that he may produce it to the persons, including the bank, with whom he does business on behalf of his principal. If a customer proposes to execute a P/A (for example, because he is going abroad for a time) it is much better to obtain from him a mandate giving authority to his agent in the latter's dealings with the bank. However, the bank may not have the opportunity of asking for a mandate but may find itself confronted with a P/A which it *must* recognise since it is legally valid.

4.9 The bank must examine the P/A to ensure that it is valid and executed as a deed, and that the power is operated strictly in accordance with its terms. In addition, it will need to identify the donee, who may not be known to the bank. This can be done by way of a banker's reference from the donee's personal bankers or by introduction by the donor.

*Revocation of powers of attorney*

4.10 Just as he can give a power the donor can cancel it by revocation. To protect himself the donor would usually recover the P/A from the donee and cancel or destroy it. Revocation does not invalidate acts of the donee up to that point.

4.11 Revocation may also result automatically from various events.

(a) If granted for a specified time or to effect a specified transaction, the P/A ends when the period expires or the transaction is completed (this is termination, not revocation).

(b) Death, mental incapacity or bankruptcy of the donor usually revokes the P/A automatically except where is has been given under the Enduring Powers of Attorney Act 1985. That is also the result if the donor is a company which goes into liquidation or is dissolved. Death or incapacity of the donee must obviously terminate his authority.

(c) The donor may revoke the P/A by implication, for example by executing a new power of attorney.

## 5. STATEMENTS OF ACCOUNT

5.1 It is an implied term of the contract between a bank and the customer that the bank shall render a statement of account by supplying periodic statements, in a sheet which can be held in a loose-leaf folder. There are additional statutory requirements on the supply of periodic statements (Consumer Credit Act 1974 s 78(4)) to individual but not to company customers.

5.2 A prudent customer on receiving his statement of account examines it and draws the attention of the bank to any errors which he may detect. However, it is well established that *the customer owes no duty to the bank to check his statement nor in consequence to draw attention to errors: Tai Hing Cotton Mill Ltd v Liu Chong Hing Bank Ltd 1986.* Even if he does check his statement and the bank has reason to believe that he accepts it as correct he is entitled nonetheless to dispute its accuracy later.

*Case: Chatterton v London & County Bank 1890*
C collected his pass-book together with the paid cheques from the bank at weekly intervals. He went through the entries and ticked them off before returning the pass-book to the bank. After 11 months he discovered that 25 cheques bore signatures forged by his clerk who had been able to deceive him in the checking process also. He denied the right of the bank to debit these cheques to his account and the bank relied, among other defences, on his apparent confirmation of the debit entries.

*Held:* a customer has no duty to his bank to examine his pass-book, nor to draw its attention to errors.

5.3 The situation in *Chatterton's* case would not recur in modern practice since the customer no longer returns his pass-book to the bank nor provides other indications that he accepts the statement of his account as correct. But from the *Tai Hing* case it can be seen that even where there is an express term that the statement shall be conclusive evidence in the absence of objections by the customer, he is still not said to have accepted it. In practice, when the bank or the customer discovers the error, the necessary correction is often made without dispute. However, there can be more difficult situations as the cases mentioned below will show.

### Customer's account shows too large a credit

5.4 The statement may show a larger credit than it should because either a sum has been wrongly credited to it or a debit has been omitted. In either case the error is likely to be the result of an error in dealing with another customer's account - the entries have got into the wrong accounts. This is a mistake of fact (the identity of the customer to whose account the entry belonged).

There is a general right in law to recover money paid in error; moreover in these circumstances it is a book-keeping error rather than a payment. However, the bank's normal right to reduce the credit balance to the correct figure, by entry in its records and notice to the customer, is qualified in one respect. By sending to the customer a statement showing too large a credit balance, the bank may have induced the customer to believe that he had more in the account than he was really entitled to. If the customer honestly relied on the statement and altered his position accordingly, the bank is prevented from correcting its mistake by reducing the balance.

*Case: Lloyds Bank Limited v Brooks 1950*
B was entitled to dividends paid on certain preference shares held in trust. Owing to an error in its records, the bank paid to B both the dividends to which she was entitled and also dividends on another trust shareholding which should have been received by another beneficiary. Over a considerable period of years the overpayments to B accumulated to a total of £1,108 which the bank then sought to recover. B had spent the money which she believed was her income.

*Held:* the bank was prevented (estopped) from asserting its claim to recover the money from her.

*Case: British & North European Bank v Zalstein 1927*
A bank manager deliberately transferred £2,000 to the account of Z whom he had permitted to exceed his overdraft limit. This was done to conceal the size of the overdraft from the auditors. Later the manager transferred the money out of Z's account to re-establish the correct position. Z was unaware at the time of these entries in his account but later relied on them to resist the bank's claim in respect of his correct overdraft balance.

*Held:* the bank had not misled Z nor, in consequence, had Z relied on information given by the bank which was not estopped from asserting the true position. A similar result occurred in *United Overseas Bank v Jivani 1976* (see Chapter 8).

5.5 In any well-managed business of a customer, the bank statement will be examined and the balance 'reconciled' with the accounts by normal accounting procedure. Except in circumstances such as *Chatterton's* case it would be difficult for a business customer to be misled. But even where it is misled, as a result of it not supervising an employee responsible for reconciling accounts, a business customer may still claim against a bank: *Tai Hing* case.

5.6 A private customer would find it difficult to persuade a court that he had failed to note an incorrect credit entry, though he might more easily be misled by the omission of a debit entry. The customer would normally assume that the payee of a cheque not yet debited to his account was merely being slow in presenting it. He too would have difficulty in showing that the statement misled him and that he relied on it. The key feature of the *Brooks* case was that B was genuinely entitled to income from a trust investment and she had no obvious means of discovering that it was inflated by mistake.

5.7 In *United Overseas Bank v Jivani 1976* it was laid down that, in order to be able to claim an amount wrongly credited, the customer must show that:

(a) the bank had misrepresented the state of the account;
(b) he had been thereby misled; and
(c) as a result he had altered his position so that, in equity, he should not have to repay.

**Customer's account is over-debited**

5.8 This may result from (1) debiting to the account an item which should properly be debited to some other account (2) failing to credit payment received because it is wrongly credited to someone else or (3) debiting to the account a cheque or cheques on which the customer's apparent signature is a forgery.

5.9 It may be possible to settle the affair in cases (1) or (2) by making a correction when the error is discovered. The bank may not assert that the customer should have discovered the bank's error by examination of the statement when received: *Tai Hing* case.

5.10 More serious consequences, however, ensue if the customer draws a cheque in reliance on the amount of correct balance and the bank dishonours the cheque because the balance in the bank's books at the time of presentation of the cheque is insufficient to meet it. This situation is illustrated by *Gibbons v Westminster Bank Limited 1939* in Chapter 8. As a result the customer, if a trader, may recover substantial damages for breach of contract causing detriment to his creditworthiness. There is also the risk that, in returning the dishonoured cheque marked 'refer to drawer' or 'not sufficient', the bank may become liable for defamation by innuendo.

5.11 When a forged cheque has been paid the bank cannot usually debit the payment to the customer's account. When the forgery is discovered, the debit must be reversed by a corresponding credit to the account. The only exception is where the customer, on becoming aware of the forgery of his cheque, has withheld the information form the bank which in consequence has lost its opportunity of pursuing a claim against the payee: *Greenwood v Martins Bank Limited 1932*.

5.12 The Code of Banking Practice includes the following in respect of availability of funds.

'Banks and building societies will provide customers with details of how their accounts operate, including information about:

(a)  how and when they may stop a cheque or countermand other types of payments;

(b)  when funds can be withdrawn after a cheque or other payment has been credited to the account;

(c)  out of date cheques.' (10.1)

## 6.  BANK CHARGES

6.1  There are normally no grounds on which a dispute will arise over the bank's general right to make charges, since it is consideration given by the customer to the bank for the services provided. It is a matter of good practice to ensure that the customer is also aware of the exact basis of the charge made and, it has recently been argued, of the amount and timing of each charge before it is debited. We have seen that s 15 Sale of Goods and Services Act 1982 provides that a reasonable charge for services rendered may be made.

You will be aware, however, that a great many customers are no longer charged for bank services provided they stay in credit; it can be argued that by making funds continuously available to the bank the customer is thereby providing consideration for the bank services he receives.

6.2  In connection with some specific task undertaken at the customer's request or some service given, eg a loan, the bank give to the customer *advance* notice of its commission or other charges. By continuing with the matter he impliedly agrees to the charge - if indeed he is not required to say so explicitly.

6.3  Customers are aware that banks raise periodic charges for maintaining an account unless either it is in credit at all times above the prescribed minimum or it is an account subject to a particular agreement that charges are not levied. In view of the volume of criticism of routine bank charges it is now the practice to advise customers of the scale of charges or (usually by way of pre-printed leaflets) to exhibit a statement of the scale in banking halls. It would therefore be difficult nowadays for a customer to assert credibly that he was entirely unaware of the general practice. If he has been a customer for some time it can be argued that by 'course of dealing' he became aware of and thereby consented to paying charges (if any) on the scale currently in force from time to time. However, this fact may not suffice to avoid dispute if the charge raised is more than he expected, if the scale has recently been increased or if the timing of the debit is unusual *and* causes the customer great inconvenience. It should therefore be the practice to send a circular to customers whenever the scale is altered; banks are now also under pressure to be more open about charges generally, especially to business customers.

6.4  Where it cannot be shown that the customer has agreed to pay charges at the current rate, the bank may have to rely on the argument that in using the bank's services the customer agreed to pay 'reasonable' charges. This principle is well established in dealings between professional people, such as accountants or solicitors, and their clients. In these circumstances there is usually no published scale of charges and the bill is calculated when the work is completed by reference to records of working time expended on the client's affairs. It is a practice less appropriate to banks' dealings with customers but there is no reason why, in the absence of an agreed rate of charge, a bank should not assert that it is entitled to raise charges which are 'reasonable' - since this is an implied term of the contractual relationship.

6.5 The Code of Banking Practice includes the following standards in relation to charges and interest.

(a) 'Banks and building societies will provide customers with details of the basis of charges, if any, payable in connection with the operation of their accounts. These will be in the form of published tariffs covering basic account services which will

    (i) be given or sent to customers:

        (1) when accounts are opened;
        (2) at any time on request;
        (3) before changes are made; and

    (ii) be available in branches. (4.1)

(b) Charges for services outside the tariff will be advised on request or at the time the service is offered. (4.2)

(c) Charges on charges. Banks and building societies will disregard the charges to be applied to customers' accounts for any charging period if those charges were incurred solely as a result of the application of charges for the previous charging period. The foregoing shall not apply when customers have effectively been notified in advance of the charges and given a reasonable opportunity to fund their accounts. (4.3)'

## 7. CLOSING THE ACCOUNT

7.1 The relationship between banker and customer in its many forms can be terminated by certain actions by either party or automatically on the occurrence of certain events.

7.2 Either the bank or the customer may decide to close the account. This may be because of practical problems - eg moving house - or because the relationship has run into difficulties.

7.3 If the customer closes the account, the bank should obtain an explicit statement in writing that this is the case, so as to avoid misunderstandings regarding outstanding cheques.

*Case: Wilson v Midland Bank Limited 1961*
There was a conflict of testimony between the bank manager and the customer as to whether there had been a telephone conversation in which the customer stated that he was closing the account. The bank took action to close the account and this led to confusion and the dishonour of a cheque drawn by the customer and returned by the bank marked 'no account'. The customer sued the bank for breach of contract and for libel.

*Held:* the bank was liable on both counts. Substantial damages for libel were awarded.

7.4 If the bank decides to close the account, it must give the customer 'reasonable notice' of the decision.

*Case: Buckingham & Co v London and Midland Bank Limited 1895*
B had a credit balance of £160 on current account and a loan account in debit for the amount of £600 for which security had been given. The bank informed the customer of its decision to close the accounts immediately because it had become anxious about the value of the security. The bank told B that it would no longer honour his cheques or pay his accepted bills of exchange. On the following day two cheques and two bills were dishonoured.

*Held:* the bank was not entitled to withdraw *without notice* the established facility by which the current account (in credit) was to be kept separate from the loan account. B was awarded £500 damages (a lot of money then).

*Case: Prosperity Limited v Lloyds Bank Limited 1923*
P developed a business of a controversial nature. Essentially, it was a 'pyramid' scheme in which each participant member of the public would secure a profit to himself by finding, within a year, 10 more subscribers to make similar payments. The business was lawful and P explained its *modus operandi* to the bank manager of the bank when P opened its account. Later, the more senior management of the bank decided that it would be prejudicial to the bank's reputation to be associated with P as its banker. The bank gave P one month's notice that it would cease to maintain P's account, in which there was a credit balance of £7,000, at the end of that period. P sued for a declaration that he was entitled to reasonable notice before the account could be closed and an injunction to prevent the closure of the account at the end of the month.

*Held:* a customer is entitled to reasonable notice and in the circumstances of this case one month was insufficient. The injunction however was refused. The general test of 'reasonable notice' for closing an account in credit was the time which the customer requires to make alternative arrangements.

7.5 The banker–customer relationship also terminates in the following circumstances:

(a) death of the customer;

(b) mental incapacity of the customer;

(c) the customer's bankruptcy/liquidation or voluntary arrangement; and

(d) certain legal orders (which deprive the customer of control of his funds but do not terminate the relationship as such) such as garnishee orders, sequestration, injunctions and restraint orders.

## 8. REFORM OF BANKING SERVICES LAW

8.1 Developments in modern banking have rapidly gathered pace in the last ten to twenty years. In particular, the legal basis of the banker/customer relationship has become clouded by events. As a result of this, a report was issued in February 1989 by the Commission on Banking Services, Law and Practice, chaired by Professor Robert Jack. This report and the consequences of it (to October 1992) are summarised here.

**The Jack Committee (February 1989)**

8.2 The central field of study of this report was the banker–customer relationship in all its forms, ranging from traditional aspects such as the banker's duty of confidentiality, to the sometimes abstruse issues thrown up by the new banking technology.

8.3 Underlying the report were four major principles:

    (a)   the need to achieve fairness and transparency in the banker-customer relationship;

    (b)   the need to maintain confidence in the banking system, as the threat of fraud becomes graver;

    (c)   the need to promote the banking system's efficiency; and

    (d)   the need to preserve and consolidate the banker's duty of confidentiality to his customer.

8.4 The Committee made a total of 83 recommendations, which fell under two main headings - the need for a voluntary code of practice and the need for new legislation (on electronic banking, cheques, bank payment orders and negotiable instruments in particular). In addition, it recommended that the Bank Ombudsman's office should be a statutory one.

*Confidentiality*

8.5 The Committee was particularly concerned with preserving and consolidating the banker's duty of confidentiality to his customer, which it saw as being eroded by:

    (a)   the increasing number of statutes requiring disclosure;
    (b)   the tendency of banks to use customer information for marketing purposes; and
    (c)   the provision of credit information by banks to credit reference agencies.

8.6 It recommended that the duty of confidentiality should be a statutory duty applying to all providers of banking services. It should:

    (a)   be based on the *Tournier* exceptions (discussed in detail in Chapter 8);

    (b)   consolidate all the current statutory exceptions;

    (c)   exclude the 'public duty' defence;

    (d)   permit disclosure in 'the interests of the bank' only as regards:

        (i)    court actions;
        (ii)   intra-group disclosure for prudential, *not marketing*, purposes; and
        (iii)  sale of the bank;

    (e)   exclude disclosure by 'implied consent'; and

    (f)   permit disclosure to credit reference agencies only in the event of default.

*Cheques*

8.7 One of the most important areas at which the review looked was the possibility of reducing fraud in the use of cheques and payment orders. It proposed to bring in:

    (a)   a single standardised *crossing* on cheques to make them non-negotiable and payable only through a banker;

(b) a new payment instrument which is neither negotiable nor transferable to cut out cases where a bank is liable because of a forged endorsement. This would be called a Bank Payment Order and could be paid only to the payee, through a bank account;

(c) truncation of cheques so the paying bank is sent the necessary details electronically and does not need to see the cheques themselves; and

(d) a new Negotiable Instruments Act to cover all negotiable instruments, including those outside the 1882 Act, which would provide legal rules on screen-based transfers and de-materialisation of bills.

8.8 The Committee's report was generally welcomed at the time of its publication and, up to November 1991, has led to three positive moves which should see some, at least, of its recommendations being implemented. These are:

(a) the publication of a Government White Paper in April 1990 entitled *Banking Services: Law and Practice* outlining new statutory provisions; and

(b) the issue of a draft Code of Banking Practice in December 1990, followed by the publication of 'Good Banking', the Code of Banking Practice, in December 1991;

(c) the only piece of *legislation* in response to the review, the Cheques Act 1992.

**Government White Paper (April 1990)**

8.9 The White Paper states that most banking issues can and should be dealt with by the Code of Banking Practice. It proposes that new legislation should only be made where:

(a) it will aid competition;
(b) it will correct areas where the law is inadequate or out of date; or
(c) it is the only means of ensuring that consumers are protected.

8.10 The White Paper's proposals will necessitate the following changes to the law:

(a) the £50 customer liability limit on credit cards will be extended to all plastic cards (ATM cards, debit cards);

(b) the ban on unrestricted mailing of credit cards will be extended to all plastic cards, including cheque guarantee cards;

(c) if the bank fails to block off the unwanted part of a multifunction card, it will be liable for any loss arising to the customer;

(d) contributory negligence on the part of a customer drawing cheques will be made a statutory defence by the bank (though not for some time);

(e) the bank will be liable for losses arising out of a failure in its Electronic Funds Transfer equipment;

(f) banks will be allowed to handle truncated cheques - meaning that, instead of cheques being moved physically from collecting to paying bank, the information on them only can be transferred by computer.

8.11 It is interesting to note the Jack Committee's proposals which have *not* been taken up by the White Paper:

(a) it is not proposed that the Bank Ombudsman scheme should be put on a statutory footing;

(b) the proposal for a non-negotiable, non-transferable Bank Payment Order is turned down on the grounds that it would lead to confusion;

(c) the proposed Negotiable Instrument Act, aimed at tidying up the law on bills of exchange, has been turned down; and

(d) the proposed Banking Services Act has been shelved in favour of the Code of Banking Practice - but it is still a possibility if the Code does not operate well.

**The Code of Banking Practice**

8.12 The Code of Banking Practice was drawn up jointly by the British Bankers' Association, the Building Societies Association and APACS. The Code was issued in December 1991 and became effective from 16 March 1992. It sets out the standards of good banking practice to be observed by banks, building societies and card issuers in their dealings with personal customers in the UK. It is acknowledged that individual institutions may, if they wish, observe higher standards than those set out in the Code.

8.13 It should be noted that the Code is not *law*. However it is likely that it will affect banking law to a considerable extent.

(a) It will affect banking *practice*. As we have seen, most of the terms of the banker-customer contract are *implied* terms. Changes in practice may affect these implied terms and consequently the legal positions of banker and customer alike.

(b) As noted earlier, the Banking Ombudsman will consider whether or not banks have complied with the Code when he is reviewing customer complaints. Similarly the courts, in considering what is normal banking practice, may look to the Code for a summary of normal practice. In either case, failure to adhere to the requirements of the Code could count against banks.

8.14 A key feature of the code is an introductory section which sets out four overriding principles of fairness which banks and others should observe. These were included in response to severe criticism by Laurence Shurman, the Banking Ombudsman, of the draft Code, which did not include any such statement.

8.15 The full text of the Code of Banking Practice is included as Appendix 1.

*Cheques Act 1992*

8.16 The Cheques Act 1992 gives legal meaning to the words 'account (or a/c) payee' written on a crossed cheque. Cheque crossings are discussed in Part E of this text. This Act is to date the only change in the law to have been made following the Jack Committee's report.

8.17 The draft Code of Banking Practice pulls back from some of the proposals advocated by the Jack Report and by the Government White Paper.

   (a)   It does not set out to restrict the marketing activities of banks and building societies. The working party and the government felt this to be better tackled by regulations under the Consumer Credit Act 1974, since they will then apply to *all* providers of credit.

   (b)   The Code is general in its restrictions as to marketing of credit: much is left up to the judgement of individual banks.

   (c)   It proposes to extend the £50 liability limit on credit cards to *all* cards; this proposal is likely to be enacted in the replacement to the 1974 Act as well.

   (d)   It does not take up the proposals as to informing customers in advance of interest and charges debits. It simply proposes that the customer should be in a position to be aware of them.

   (e)   It does not accept that customers should only be allowed to use cards once they have notified the bank of safe receipt of both card and PIN.

8.18 The above summary of legal and practical reforms as at October 1992 is an indication of how far banking practice has moved in the last few years. The particular areas of concern are covered more fully in the relevant sections of this text - but you should keep an eye out in *Banking World* for any further developments.

## 9.   CONCLUSION

9.1 The opening, conduct and closing of a bank account are practical matters which have many legal implications. The problems as to references and enquiries on opening an account are particularly important, since failure to take up references may mean that the bank is considered negligent. This can lead to it losing protection under the Bills of Exchange Act 1882 and the Cheques Act 1957.

9.2 Standard form contracts are legitimately used a great deal in banking, but you should be aware they are regulated by the Unfair Contract Terms Act 1977.

9.3 A bank account may be operated by the customer's agent, so that the banker must be aware of the giving and nature of an agent's powers. Signatures on cheques by agents present particular problems since a 'per pro' signature indicates that there are limits on authority but not the extent of them.

9.4 A customer's account showing too large a credit may not be changed by the bank if the customer was misled by the statement into altering his position. This is because the bank has misrepresented the state of the account. Wrongful debiting of the account may also have dire consequences since it may lead to wrongful dishonour of a cheque, which could result in a claim for breach of contract and/or defamation.

## TEST YOUR KNOWLEDGE
*The numbers in brackets refer to paragraphs of this chapter*

1   On what matters concerning an unknown new customer does a bank seek information before opening an account for him? (1.1)

2   How may evidence be obtained to confirm the identity of a new customer? (1.4)

3   Why is it useful to know what kind of work is done by a customer in his job? (1.12)

4   Describe three arrangements to be settled with the customer in opening a new account. (2.2, 2.3)

5   What is the significance of:

(a)   'for and on behalf of'; and
(b)   'per pro' following the drawer's signature on a cheque? (4.5, 4.6)

6   What is a general power of attorney? (4.7)

7   How is a P/A terminated? (4.11)

8   Has a customer any obligation to examine the statement of his account when received from the bank and does it affect his relationship with the bank if he does so? (5.2, 5.3)

9   Is the bank entitled to eliminate an error in a statement of account so as to reduce a customer's balance to the correct amount? (5.4)

10   If a customer disputes his liability to pay bank charges, on what grounds may the bank rely to justify its charges? (6.2 - 6.4)

11   What action should a bank take over closing an account:

(a)   on the customer's telephone instructions; and
(b)   as a result of withdrawing an overdraft facility? (7.3, 7.4)

*Now try questions 15 to 17 at the end of the text*

*Chapter 11*

# SPECIAL TYPES OF BANK ACCOUNT

---

**This chapter covers the following topics.**

1. Minors as bank customers
2. Joint accounts
3. Partnership accounts
4. Accounts of unincorporated clubs and societies
5. Executors and administrators
6. Trustee accounts

---

## 1. MINORS AS BANK CUSTOMERS

1.1 In Chapter 4 we saw how minors had only limited general capacity. We shall now look at how this may affect a bank.

1.2 A bank will not usually open an account for a minor who is still a young child. He does not need to make payments since a parent or other adult pays for his living expenses and education - even if the money is derived from income received for the child's benefit. If a child needs a bank account for the receipt of income his parent, guardian or other adult in charge of his affairs may open an account in the adult's name as trustee. It would be unsafe for a bank to have direct dealings with a young child since it might be held that he was too young to understand the effect of the transactions and so the bank would not obtain a valid discharge for money paid to him or on his behalf. Much would depend on the circumstances. There is no case on the point but trustees - for the same reason - do not usually make payments of trust money to beneficiaries who are minors. If, however, it were clear that the bank had made a payment in a straightforward case to or on the instructions of a minor who was a customer, the minor would be unlikely to persuade a court that he should be bound by the payment.

1.3 There is no inherent legal difficulty in the acceptance of a minor's instructions by cheque or otherwise to make a payment from the balance on his account. It is expressly provided by the Bills of Exchange Act 1882 s 22(2) that the holder of a cheque drawn by a minor is entitled to receive payment. Hence banks do, in practice, agree to open accounts for minors who are within a year or two of majority. A minor who is a customer has enforceable rights against his bank, for example if a cheque drawn by him were wrongly dishonoured.

1.4 Nonetheless a bank in its own interest must recognise that a minor is a special type of customer and, in particular, avoid *lending* money to him, the contract for which would be unenforceable. There is the possibility that to avoid this restriction the minor may overstate his age. If he does so and thereby obtains a loan, he commits the tort of deceit. In principle a minor is not immune from liability for his torts but it is well settled that a lender cannot enforce a void contract to repay borrowed money by claiming damages for deceit over the borrower's age: *Leslie v Sheill 1914.* Hence it is wise in opening an account for a youthful-looking customer who states that he is 'just 18' to obtain evidence of his age if only from his referee, who would not enjoy any immunity if he deceived the bank.

1.5 However, a bank may wish to obtain a guarantee for the loan to a minor, since the Minors' Contracts Act 1987 expressly states that such a contract is enforceable even though the primary contract (the loan) is not. The bank will also be protected under this Act in that the minor may be required by the court to repay any money lent or property acquired under the loan agreement.

1.6 Banks do not usually issue cheque guarantee cards to minors since any overdraft thus created is unenforceable. Again, however, the 1987 Act allows a bank to sue for return of property acquired with the proceeds of an overdraft.

## 2. JOINT ACCOUNTS

2.1 A joint account is essentially an arrangement made between the bank on one side and two or more customers on the other for the opening and operation of a bank account in the names of the joint accountholders. The most common example is where husband and wife use a single account to make their income available to them both for common domestic purposes.

2.2 As explained earlier, the bank acts on the instructions of all the account-holders: either

(a) by obtaining cheques and other written authorisations signed by them all; or

(b) by obtaining from them all written authority by mandate to act on instructions given by any one or two of them, or whatever other arrangement is convenient.

For simplicity, we will assume that there are only two joint account-holders.

**Mandate for a joint account**

2.3 In opening the account, the bank may provide a standard form of 'mandate for joint account' to cover the various contingencies likely to arise. *Each operative part of the mandate provides for authority to be given by both or either of the account-holders.* They may well, of course, opt for a mixed authorisation so that some transactions (eg drawing cheques) require only one signature but others (eg re-delivery of property deposited for safekeeping), require the signature of both account-holders. The forms of mandate in use by different banks vary in their detail, depending on what sort of persons will operate the account. You should obtain copies of some of your own bank's forms and identify the important parts of the contract.

2.4 The bank is mandated to act on the signature of one or both account-holders as the case may be in such matters as:

(a) payment of cheques drawn on the account;
(b) advances;
(c) delivery of documents, property etc in the safekeeping of the bank;
(d) disposal of any credit balance by the survivor following the death of either;

(e)  any joint account-holder may revoke the mandate;

(f)  any joint account-holder may countermand payment of a cheque.

2.5  A mandate on a joint account is terminated by the bankruptcy or mental incapacity of one or more parties. The account must be stopped (a line drawn) and opened in the survivor's name. This overcomes the rule in *Clayton's* case. In the event of death of one party, the mandate would also be terminated at common law, but a clause will usually be included in the mandate expressly permitting withdrawals to be made by the survivor.

2.6  The mandate will guide the bank as to the disposal of any credit balance by the survivor following the death of either, and will state that either or any joint account-holder may revoke the mandate.

## Joint and several liability

2.7  By the terms of the mandate, the joint account-holders agree to be jointly and also severally liable to the bank for any liability which they may incur to the bank. The simple and obvious case is liability to repay a loan or overdrawn current account. The bank could claim repayment from both holders together or from one or other of them. If the claim against one does not succeed, the bank may then claim successively against the other(s) until the debt is paid.

2.8  It is generally accepted that if the liability of each account-holder was merely joint, his death would release him and his estate from liability to the bank which would thus lose the advantage of holding more than one customer liable for a single debt. With several liability, death does not terminate the bank's claim against the estate of the deceased.

2.9  There is also a positive advantage to the bank in connection with set-off by establishing that joint account-holders have several liability on the joint account. Each is then separately liable for the joint debt and the bank can set off a credit balance on his personal account against the debit balance on joint account for which he is individually as well as jointly liable.

## Forged signature of a joint account-holder

2.10  The safeguard of requiring that cheques shall be signed by both account-holders, which is normal in connection with a trust account in joint names, may be defeated if one signatory signs the cheque and forges the signature of the other.

2.11  In *Brewer v Westminster Bank Limited 1952* the bank argued successfully that the two account-holders only had rights against the bank exercisable by them jointly. As one, the forger, had disentitled himself from denying the bank's authority to pay a cheque which he had presented, the other, whose signature he had forged, could not *acting by himself* deny the validity of the cheque merely because his apparent signature, required by the mandate, was not genuine. This argument seems neither logical nor fair.

2.12 Although one High Court decision at first instance does not overrule another, there is a general disposition to accept as correct the later case of *Jackson v White and Midland Bank Limited 1967*, where the decision on essentially similar facts went the other way - the innocent joint account-holder could hold the bank liable.

2.13 The judicial reasoning in *Jackson's* case was that by the terms of the mandate the bank was answerable to each joint account-holder to make payment only if he had signed the cheque. That requirement was not satisfied - since a forgery is a nullity - and so the innocent joint account-holder in his own right could deny the bank's authority to pay the cheque and debit the account.

## 3. PARTNERSHIP ACCOUNTS

3.1 Partnership is defined by the Partnership Act 1890 s 1 as 'the relation which subsists between persons carrying on a business in common with a view of profit'. From that definition follow a number of important consequences.

(a) There must always be at least two partners and so the partnership bank account must always be a joint account; most professional firms are exempt from the legal maximum of 20 partners.

(b) A partnership is merely two or more persons who have agreed to carry on a business together. The partnership is the partners *as a group*. In this a partnership differs essentially from a company which is a separate entity from its shareholders.

(c) A partnership carries on a business which for this purpose includes a professional practice or other gainful activity.

(d) Although the partners' purpose is to make profits, they may incur losses. If they do they are all (with the very rare exception of a limited partnership) liable without limit for the debts of their business.

3.2 The following incidental points are worth noting.

(a) *Name:* it is usual for a partnership to adopt a 'firm name' as a collective description and, rather confusingly, the name may end with the word 'company' - eg 'Smith and Company'. But the firm name may never end with the word 'limited' which is reserved to registered limited companies. If, as is usual, the firm name is not the surnames (plus if desired their initial, etc) of *all* the partners, the firm is using a 'business name' to which certain statutory requirements apply: Business Names Act 1985.

(b) *Firm and partnership:* these two words are interchangeable since they have the same meaning. There are two mistakes to be avoided:

(i) it is not correct to use the word 'firm' for a registered company, though newspapers often do so; and

(ii) it is not correct to use the word 'company' for a firm or partnership even though its name may end with that word.

(c) *Agency:* in their dealings with third parties, the partners are agents of each other so that within the limits of his authority each partner can commit the firm (eg under an arrangement with the bank).

(d) *Formal constitution:* most partnerships have a written partnership agreement but there is no legal requirement that they should do so. The law treats as a partnership any arrangement, even a temporary or informal one, which satisfies the legal definition given above.

(e) *Management:* every partner has, unless otherwise agreed, a right to participate in the management of the firm's business. But a joint proprietor of a business can be a 'sleeping partner' - one who does not take part in managing the business.

(f) *Employees:* a senior employee of a firm, who may often be qualified in the same profession as the partners, is not automatically a partner by reason of his duties as a manager. If, however, it appears to persons dealing with a firm through one of its managers that he is a partner, for example, because his name is shown on the firm's letterheads (which is or was common practice in professional firms), the creditors may treat the manager as a partner liable for the firm's debts even though within the firm he is not a partner.

(g) *Individual and corporate partners:* it is possible for companies to enter into partnerships but in practice the partners are usually all individuals. A minor may be a partner but the firm's debts are unenforceable against him.

(h) *Limited partners:* it is possible to form a partnership registered under the Limited Partnership Act 1907 in which some but not all partners have limited liability. However, this type of partnership is extremely rare since a limited company formed under the Companies Act is a much more convenient means of obtaining limited liability.

## Partners' authority

3.3 Except in the case of a small firm of two or three partners, a bank is unlikely to have dealings in person with all the partners. The bank may of course insist that an important document such as a loan agreement be signed by all the partners. Alternatively, the partner(s) with whom the bank deals may produce written authority from the other partners for the transaction with the bank with the bank. Note that if the transaction involves the execution of a deed (eg a legal mortgage of the firm's premises to the bank as security for an overdraft), then either all the partners must join in executing the deed (which is the normal practice) or those who do not do so must execute a Power of Attorney which the bank will inspect. For routine transactions, such as the issue of cheques drawn on the firm's account, the bank obtains a mandate which incidentally defines the extent of a partner's authority in dealings with the bank.

3.4 Nonetheless, the bank is sometimes obliged to rely on the general legal rules of partnership law in asserting that an individual partner was the apparent representative of the firm in a transaction with the bank. The Partnership Act 1890 s 5 states that every partner is an agent of the firm which is bound by what he does. But this general principle is restricted by four conditions.

(a) The partner must be acting *on behalf of the firm* and in its name. For example, a solicitor who is a partner in his firm (a customer of the bank) may be the secretary of a company which is a client of his firm. He writes to the bank in the latter capacity to withdraw title deeds of the company deposited by the firm but the bank should require him to make his request as a partner of the firm acting for its client. If the withdrawal was unauthorised it cannot be treated as an act of the firm.

(b) The transaction must be one which is *business of the kind carried on by the firm*. The test here is what a person dealing with the firm would reasonably believe was its business. He is not concerned with any narrower definition of the firm's business agreed between the partners but unknown to him: *Mercantile Credit Co Limited v Garrod 1962* (dealing in cars is part of the normal range of business of a small garage).

(c) The partner must appear to be carrying on the firm's business *in the usual way* – within the accepted limits of a single partner's authority.

(d) The bank can only rely on the apparent authority of a partner, as defined above, if the bank is *unaware of any actual restriction set on that authority by the partners*. The mandate will sometimes have that effect (eg when it provides that cheques for amounts above £X must be signed by at least two partners).

3.5 Case law establishes what a single partner has apparent authority to do in connection with the firm's business. The partnership's bank is concerned with the following:

(a) *signature of cheques* is a normal function of a single partner but that principle can be overruled by the terms of the mandate requiring two or more partners to sign cheques;

(b) *signature of other bills of exchange* as drawer, acceptor or endorser is a normal function of a single partner *only if* the partnership carries on a trading business (that is, it trades in buying and selling goods);

(c) *borrowing money* and giving security for loans – as under (b) above;

(d) *receiving payment of debts* due to the firm and issuing receipts is a normal function of a partner of any firm, as is buying and selling goods (in a commercial firm) and engaging employees;

(e) *executing a deed* for the firm is NOT within the normal authority of a single partner of any firm;

(f) *giving a guarantee* for the firm is NOT within the normal authority of a single partner unless the ordinary business of the firm includes giving guarantees – which is unusual;

(g) *submitting a dispute to arbitration* or *accepting property (such as shares) in satisfaction of a debt owed to the firm* are also NOT within a single partner's powers.

3.6 In any of the cases where a partner acting alone does NOT have normal implied authority as agent of the firm, it is always possible for the other partners to give him that authority by the terms of a mandate to the bank, or a Power of Attorney (essential for executing a deed) or by other express authorisation. Unless they have done so all must join in the transaction.

### Opening a partnership account

3.7 As the partnership bank account will be a joint account to which some special procedures apply, the bank should obtain a suitable mandate. The mandate signed by the partners serves incidentally to give the bank the required written agreement of all partners to the opening of the account.

3.8 Under the 1890 Act partners have joint and several liability only for torts (such as deceit or conversion). Liability for all the firm's debts etc is merely joint under the statute; hence a bank which failed to reclaim funds from one partner could not then claim against another, since without several liability the first action exhausts the claim.

3.9 In practice therefore, banks require a mandate establishing joint and several liability, so that they can make claims against both partnership and partners should either become bankrupt, and can set off a partner's private account against the partnership account.

3.10 Some particular points applicable to a mandate for a partnership joint account are as follows.

(a) *Identity*. Unless the partners are already customers of the bank in another capacity, the bank should make the same enquiries as in opening an account for a sole customer.

(b) *Firm name;* the account should be in the designated firm name. An account in the name of a single partner but for the firm is unusual and can give rise to problems if that partner only makes the arrangements. It is not within his authority to do so: *Alliance Bank Limited v Kearsley 1871.*

(c) *Changes in the partnership* must be notified to the bank as soon as they occur. A new partner will be asked to give his formal assent to the mandate unless a new mandate is given.

(d) *Signatures*. It is usual for individual partners to sign cheques in the firm's name. For example, all the partners of 'Smith & Co' sign 'Smith & Co' rather than write their individual signatures. This is recognised by the Bills of Exchange Act 1882 s 23 as a signature on behalf of all partners. However, the bank will need specimen signatures of 'Smith & Co' as written by each individual partner in his handwriting.

(e) *Revocation* of the mandate must be an express communication to the bank with the required signatures. Death of a partner, change of the firm name, etc, do not operate as revocation.

## 4. ACCOUNTS OF UNINCORPORATED CLUBS AND SOCIETIES

4.1 Like a partnership, an unincorporated club or society is merely a group of people who are associated by agreement. But whereas a partnership is a compact small group with a defined business activity and a statutory legal framework (the Partnership Act 1890), a club or society often has a large membership which is constantly changing. It often has an income (eg from membership subscriptions or charges for goods and services supplied to members). It may own premises such as a clubhouse or a sports ground and incur expenditure on upkeep. Sometimes it trades; for example, the bar profits or green fees paid to a golf club by visiting players are an important element in its finances. Clubs and societies obviously must have bank accounts.

4.2   It is not possible for a bank to require the formal participation - eg in giving a mandate - of all the members. There are usually office-holders, such as a secretary or treasurer, or a management committee who in fact administer the finances of the club or society. The bank can recognise these representatives as agents of the general body of members and as informal trustees of the income and property without being unduly perplexed by the imprecision of their powers.

4.3   The situation becomes more difficult, however, if the club or society, through its management, obtains a loan or overdraft facilities from the bank. The management are personally liable to the bank, either because they have made a binding contract for the members including themselves or, if the contract is not binding on members, because they have misrepresented their authority. This is liability for 'breach of warranty of authority'. In the latter case, the bank can have no claim on the general body of members. The uncertainty on this point may, however, be resolved by reference to the membership rules or bye-laws.

4.4   The following are the main points of practice to be observed.

(a)   In opening an account for a club or society, the bank should obtain an explicit statement of its name, which will form part of the title of the account, and should also ask for a copy of the written rules of by-laws of the club or society, ensuring that the copy given is up-to-date.

(b)   It should be clear from the rules or by-laws whether, as is usual and inevitable, the conduct of the affairs of the club or society is in the hands of office-bearers and/or the members of a committee. Those individuals should sign the mandate.

(c)   The extent of any borrowing powers delegated to the managing body should be ascertained from the rules or by-laws.

(d)   An undertaking should be obtained from the club's managing body that the bank will be informed promptly of any change in the club's membership, rules or bye-laws.

4.5   If the club or society applies to the bank for a loan or overdraft facility, the bank should consider two points of procedure (if it is willing to accede to the request).

(a)   *Is there a prescribed method* - eg passing a resolution at a general meeting of members - by which the members, under their own rules or by-laws, approve and accept responsibility for the loan? If there is a prescribed procedure, the bank should insist on obtaining evidence (eg a certified copy of the resolution) that proper authority has been given. The bank can then probably assert a claim against the assets of the club or society and against its members individually since, on becoming members, they have accepted that liability can be imposed on them in this way.

(b)   *Is any security offered?* It may take the form of a guarantee, including an indemnity, given by a member or members who are persons of substance. Alternatively, the club or society may have property such as premises which can be mortgaged as security. However, any such property must necessarily be in the legal ownership of trustees. Even if it is vested in certain office-holders without any formal trust deed, they are trustees and difficult questions may arise as to whether they are legally competent to create a mortgage.

4.6 If the bank is really satisfied that the borrowing is properly authorised and that the bank will have effective resort against individuals or property of substance in case of default, it may be safe to make the loan. But if there is uncertainty it will be wiser to decline the proposition.

## 5. EXECUTORS AND ADMINISTRATORS

5.1 When an individual dies, it is necessary to pay his debts out of his property, so far as it suffices, and then to distribute what remains in accordance with the instructions given in his will or, if there is no will (a situation called 'intestacy'), to his next of kin.

5.2 If the deceased leaves a will, he names one or more persons as 'executors' (the feminine form of executor is 'executrix') to pay his debts and distribute his estate. If, however, he leaves no will or the executors appointed by the will are unable or unwilling to accept appointment under it, the next of kin apply to the court to appoint 'administrators' to his estate. The term 'personal representatives' (abbreviated to 'PR's') is used to describe executors or administrators as the case may be.

5.3 In most respects personal representatives are a special type of trustee (see Section 6 below). Like trustees, PRs have legal ownership of property under binding obligations to apply it for the benefit of others. Unlike trustees, however, a PR may act separately, for example in drawing cheques. PRs have a special task - to wind up and distribute an estate - which can usually be completed within a year or two of the death.

5.4 It is possible to appoint a single executor. Alternatively, the will may appoint two or more executors but only one of them applies for 'probate' and, on obtaining it, he alone has authority over the estate since it is the grant of representation which gives legal powers to him. Since there is more than one PR in charge of an estate they normally deal with the banks as joint accountholders. But a corporate body, in particular a trust corporation, may be appointed executor alone or jointly with others.

## Bank accounts of executors and administrators

5.5 On receiving notice of the death of a customer, the bank 'freezes' the account since there is no person with authority to operate it. The account is 'frozen' until such time as the PRs have obtained a grant of representation carrying legal authority to deal with the bank.

5.6 Often the bank holds the will in safekeeping. Although relatives or solicitors may be allowed to inspect the will, it should not be handed over except against a receipt. Property, such as jewellery or title deeds, should not be handed over until probate is obtained.

5.7 PRs usually open a bank account soon after the death. Although they cannot sell assets until they have a grant, they may have money found in the possession of the deceased at his death which they wish to put in a safe place or they may receive income, for example dividends from estate assets. The PRs need not, though in practice they usually do, open the account at the branch of the same bank at which the deceased had his only or main account. If the executors are strangers to the bank they should have no difficulty in arranging an introduction to the bank through their solicitors. Otherwise it may be necessary to ask for references in the usual way.

5.8 The bank will ask to see a copy of the death certificate as soon as it is first informed of the customer's death. In opening the account, the bank will give it an appropriate title – ie the names of the PRs and their descriptions, for example 'Paul Evans and Mary Brown, executors of Henry Evans deceased'.

5.9 The PRs should sign a joint account mandate. There is no legal objection to a mandate by which the bank is authorised to pay cheques signed by any one of the PRs. It is, however, better to obtain a mandate by which cheques are signed by all PRs. *They may, later, become trustees of the estate and joint signatures will then be essential.* It avoids difficulty at that later stage if they begin as they must later continue. Although PRs can authorise each other to sign cheques by a sole signature, they may not delegate authority to sign cheques to anyone who is not a PR.

5.10 The mandate will provide that the PRs are to be jointly and severally liable to the bank. This is important since it is likely that they will need a temporary advance to pay inheritance tax, to operate the deceased's business or to pay administrative costs.

## 6. TRUSTEE ACCOUNTS

6.1 Personal representatives may, on completing the administration of the estate, continue to hold the residue or some part of it in trust as trustees. If the property which they hold includes land, it may be necessary to make the transition from personal representative to trustee status by a formal document called a 'vesting assent'. In other cases, no formality is required. But because there are small but significant differences (eg signature of cheques by a single trustee when there are two or more is generally not permissible), the bank is well advised to obtain a mandate suitable for a trust account when the account is first opened (as noted in paragraph 5.9 above).

6.2 It may be arranged that one person has legal ownership of property, including the credit balance in a bank account, under a binding obligation to deal with it for the benefit for others or (in the case of a charity) for the benefit of the community. Arrangements of this kind are very flexible and have been adapted to provide for the disposal of estates of deceased persons and the settlement of claims by creditors of an insolvent person.

6.3 The above is a general description of a trust. There is no entirely satisfactory definition of a trust, but those offered by various textbook writers bring out the essential nature of a trustee. Property is in the legal ownership of a trustee or trustees under a binding obligation to apply it for the benefit of beneficiaries, for charitable purposes or for the benefit of creditors.

6.4 Note that whereas a contract is not, as a general rule, enforceable by third parties, a trust may be enforced by a beneficiary who is not a party to the instrument creating the trust.

### Opening a trustee account

6.5 A bank may find that it has a number of trust accounts even though they were not opened in that description. Since a trust exists where one person has legal title to property which he undertakes to apply to another person's benefit, an account such as 'L Oliver, Portsmouth

Amateur Dramatics account' is a trust account. The situation may also arise by operation of law, as where a person holds funds as constructive trustee for the benefit of another person.

6.6 All trustees must sign the mandate opening an account and, since trustees may not delegate, all would usually have to sign cheques etc.

6.7 While trustees may operate a bank account, they have no implied power to give a valid charge over property or to borrow - the trust instrument must expressly allow this. Obviously a bank would require a copy of the trust instrument before entering into this type of transaction.

6.8 One of the most significant points about trusts for a bank is that it may be liable if it unwittingly or negligently facilitates a breach of trust by a trustee. This may arise where a bank allows a trustee to use trust property as security for a personal overdraft for which the bank pressed repayment, as where it allows a trustee to use trust funds for paying what are clearly personal debts.

*Testate - how to distribute*
*Intestate - who to distribute*

## 7. CONCLUSION

7.1 In this chapter we have seen how different legal principles affect the bank accounts operated for various types of customer (excluding companies, which are covered in the next chapter).

7.2 The rules relating to joint accounts, particularly joint and several liability and the number of signatures required under a mandate, are especially important since they also affect partnership, PR and trustee accounts.

---

**TEST YOUR KNOWLEDGE**

*The numbers in brackets refer to paragraphs of this chapter*

1   Why do banks allow minors to open accounts, and what problems may arise? (1.3, 1.4)

2   What matters will be covered by a mandate opening a joint account? (2.4)

3   What is joint and several liability? (2.7)

4   What is a partnership? (3.1)

5   What may a single partner do in connection with the firm? What may he not do? (3.5)

6   What problems do unincorporated bodies present to a bank? (4.2 - 4.5)

7   How should executors conduct a bank account? (5.7 - 5.10)

8   What is a trust? (6.2, 6.3) What powers and liabilities of trustees would affect a bank? (6.6 - 6.8)

---

*Now try questions 18 and 19 at the end of the text*

*Chapter 12*

# COMPANY ACCOUNTS

> **This chapter covers the following topics.**
>
> 1. What is a company?
> 2. The characteristics of a company
> 3. Types of company
> 4. Formation of a company
> 5. Opening a bank account for a company
> 6. The memorandum of association
> 7. The articles of association
> 8. Company directors

> *Statutory references in this chapter are to the Companies Act 1985 unless otherwise stated.*

## 1. WHAT IS A COMPANY?

1.1 A registered company is only one of several types of **corporate body** (also called 'corporations'). A corporate body (which is a legal entity distinct from its members) may be formed in any of three ways.

    (a) By grant of *royal charter* of incorporation from the Crown. This procedure is now reserved for special cases such as the Chartered Institute of Bankers: an ordinary trading concern would not be granted a charter.

    (b) By passing a *special Act of Parliament* - for example, to form railway and canal companies in the 19th century or to constitute local authorities. This method of forming companies is little used since it is slow and expensive. Its advantage is that the Act can confer on the particular corporation any special legal powers which it may need (eg. to acquire land compulsorily). A commercial body formed in this way is sometimes called a 'statutory company'.

    (c) By *registration* under the Companies Act as described below. This is the normal method of incorporating a commercial concern. It is also available to non-commercial bodies such as a charity or a research association which may need corporate status as a convenient method of, for example, owning property. Any body of this type is properly called a 'company' though the media sometimes apply to it the term 'firm' (which ought to be reserved to unincorporated partnerships). This category is best distinguished (if there is doubt) by describing it as a 'registered company'.

# 12: COMPANY ACCOUNTS

1.2 The essential feature of any corporate body is that it *exists as a legal entity (or 'person') distinct from its members.* All types of corporate body described above have at least two members and they are classified as *'corporations aggregate'.* This distinguishes them from some public offices which exist separately from the individual who for the time being holds the office. This latter category is called a *'corporation sole'* since only one person fills the office at one time. The Archbishop of Canterbury and the Public Trustee are examples of a corporation sole.

1.3 The Companies Act limits the word 'company' where it appears in the Act to a company registered under the Act: s 735. This text follows that usage.

## The veil of incorporation

*tax – They are taxed as individuals corporation tax*

1.4 The distinction between a company and its members (called 'the veil of incorporation') was authoritatively established by the House of Lords in the important case described below.

*Case: Salomon v Salomon Ltd 1897*
S transferred to a company the business of making boots and shoes which he had carried on successfully as a sole trader for the previous 30 years. S, his wife, 4 sons and a daughter each took one share of the company at its formation but the others held their shares as nominees of S. The company bought the business for £39,000 and issued to S £20,000 £1 shares and a debenture for £10,000 secured by a floating charge on the assets (the balance was paid in cash). The business became insolvent and a liquidator was appointed. The trade creditors argued that the company and S were indistinguishable and that his debenture (which gave him a priority entitlement to the remaining assets) was void since a man cannot be a creditor of himself.

*Held:* the creditors' argument was false. It is possible for the sole owner of a company to assert rights against it as a secured creditor since a company is a separate person distinct from its members.

1.5 There are a number of exceptions to the principle of *Salomon's* case - situations (called 'lifting the veil of incorporation') in which the company is identified with its members or its directors. One of the most important exceptions is that for some purposes (it is not automatic) a holding company is identified with its subsidiaries as a single entity. The holding company must, for example, produce 'consolidated accounts' in which the assets, liabilities, profits, or losses of each subsidy are attributed to the holding company. Exceptions are also made as sanctions against breaches of company law or to prevent fraud.

## 2. THE CHARACTERISTICS OF A COMPANY

2.1 A company's status as a separate legal entity has a number of important implications for its constitution and management.

2.2 *Limited liability.* The company is liable without limit for its own debts. However, it obtains its capital from and distributes its profits to its members. It may be - and usually is - formed on the basis of limited liability of members. In that case they cannot be required to contribute (if the company becomes insolvent) more than the amount outstanding (if any) on their shares (or if it is a company limited by guarantee, the amount of their guarantee).

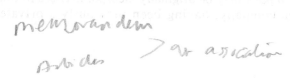

*memorandum*
*Articles } of association*

2.3 *Transferable shares*. The interests of members as proprietors of the company is a form of property (measured in 'shares') which they can transfer to another person (subject to any restrictions imposed by the constitution of the company).

2.4 *Perpetual succession*. A change of membership or the death of a member is not a change in the company itself. It is a separate person which continues unaffected by changes among its members since these are not changes in the company itself (compare with partnership).

2.5 *Assets, rights, liabilities etc*. The assets and liabilities, rights and obligations incidental to the company's activities, are assets etc of the company and not if its members.

*Case: Macaura v Northern Assurance Co 1925*
M, a landowner, sold the timber on his estate to a company of which he was the sole owner. Before the sale to the company, he had insured the timber in his own name. He did not transfer the insurance policy to the company name. Two weeks later almost all the timber was destroyed by fire. He claimed for the loss under his policies but the insurers denied liability.

*Held:* since the plaintiff no longer owned the property he could not have a valid contract of insurance covering the property. The company could not claim the benefit of the policy as it was not a party to the contract of insurance.

2.6 *Capital*. The sums paid to the company by its members in return for their shares comprise the company's capital. If it is a company with limited liability, it may not ordinarily distribute capital to them (but must retain it as a fund to meet its own debts).

2.7 *Management*. A company cannot, as an artificial person, manage itself. It must therefore have managers (called 'directors'). But the members have no claim to be directors though they usually have power to appoint the directors (and may appoint themselves). For the same reason, a member as such has no inherent power to make contracts for the company as its agent. The distinction between members (proprietors) and directors (managers) is extended to require that:

(a) the directors as a body (the *board of directors*) shall have defined powers of management delegated to them by the company; and

(b) the members as a body shall meet as a *general meeting* of the company to decide those matters (including the appointment and removal of directors) which are not delegated to the directors.

2.8 *Written constitution*. A company has no mind of its own to decide what it will do. The structure of divided control described above must be clearly defined. For these and other reasons a company must have a written constitution in the form of memorandum and articles of association.

## 3. TYPES OF COMPANY

### Public companies

3.1 A *public company* may be originally incorporated as a public company or it may have re-registered as a public company, having been previously a private company.

3.2 A public company is such because the Registrar of Companies (referred to as 'the registrar') has issued a certificate that the company has been registered or re-registered as a public company: s 117. The registrar will not grant this certificate unless:

(a) the name of the company identifies it as a public company by ending with the words 'public limited company'or 'plc' or their Welsh equivalents (for a Welsh company): s 25; and

(b) the memorandum of association of the company states that the company is to be a public company: s 1(3);

(c) the authorised capital of the company is not less than £50,000 (or such other sum as the Department of Trade and Industry may prescribe later): s 11; and

(d) it is a limited company with a share capital.

## Private companies

3.3 Although a *private company* is the residual category (any company which is not a public company), and so need not satisfy any special conditions, many private companies were incorporated before 1980; under the previous law a private company was one which included three restrictions in its articles:

(a) the right to transfer shares was restricted;
(b) the maximum number of members (exclusive of employees) was 40;
(c) the company might not offer its shares or debentures to the public.

3.4 A private company need no longer be subject to these restrictions in its articles (though rule (c) is now imposed on private companies by statute - s 170 Financial Services Act 1986). But many private companies do still retain these restrictions in their articles. The lifting of the maximum number of members is particularly important since this restriction, when it was obligatory, required non-trading companies with a large membership, such as some chambers of commerce, to register as public companies. Companies of that type (with share capital usually well below £50,000) are now free to register as private companies (and may remove from their articles the restriction on membership numbers).

3.5 A private company may have a share capital of any size - there is no minimum and it may be a private company even if its share capital greatly exceeds £50,000.

## Public and private companies compared

3.6 The main reason for distinguishing between public and private companies is that private companies are generally small enterprises in which some if not all shareholders are also directors and *vice versa*. Ownership and management are thus combined in the same individuals. In that situation, it is unnecessary to impose on the directors complicated restrictions to safeguard the interests of members, and so the whole structure of the company can be simplified. Accordingly many statutory rules apply only to public companies.

3.7 Companies generally become public companies because they may then offer shares to the public – to people who are 'strangers' to the enterprise. This may be done in a number of ways, and can be an offer to subscribe for shares or debentures. A public company will use the following intermediaries.

(a) **The Stock Exchange** – it applies for a full listing of its securities on the Exchange, by issuing listing particulars in line with the Exchange rules (the Yellow Book – given statutory force in the Financial Services Act 1986).

(b) **The Unlisted Securities Market (USM)** – it obtains a 'quote' on this market (run by the Stock Exchange) by preparing a prospectus in accordance with its rules which must be registered with the Registrar of Companies before any investment advertisement may be issued.

3.8 *A public company does not have to be listed or quoted* – the term 'public' is not synonymous with 'listed' or 'quoted', but there is little point in being public if the increased marketability of securities is not utilised. Public companies are subject to stricter accounting and financial rules and the inconvenience of these would only be adopted for a real purpose.

## Limited and unlimited companies

3.9 The majority are companies limited by shares. This means that once the company has received the agreed amount to be subscribed for the shares which it issues, it cannot call on its shareholders to contribute any more towards the payment of the company's debts.

3.10 There are, however, two other kinds of company

(a) *A company limited by guarantee.* In this case the members may be required (but only when the company goes into liquidation) to contribute up to a specified amount per member (their guarantee) towards the payment of its debts. A company limited by guarantee does not usually have a share capital. This type of company is often a non-trading company such as a research association, a tenant's company in a block of flats or a chamber of commerce. It serves as a common organisation to provide a service; the members' guarantee is a sort of reserve fund.

(b) *An unlimited company.* This is suitable when the company merely holds assets and has no liabilities. Its main advantage is that (with some exceptions) an unlimited company is not required to deliver a copy of its annual accounts to the Company Registry (for public inspection).

## 4. FORMATION OF A COMPANY

4.1 A registered company is formed by delivering to the registrar of companies (see paragraph 4.6 below) the following documents (and paying a fee):

(a) memorandum of association;

(b) articles of association (or a statement that the statutory model articles (Table A) will be the articles of the company);

(c) particulars of:

    (i)   the first director(s) of the company;
    (ii)  the first secretary; and
    (iii) the address of the registered office;

The persons named as director(s) and secretary must signify their consent by signing this form;

(d) a statutory declaration – a sworn statement by a solicitor or by one of the persons named in (c) (i) or (ii) – that the relevant requirements of the Companies Act have been complied with.

### Certificate of incorporation

4.2 If these documents are found to be in order, the registrar (after an interval of about two weeks) issues a certificate of incorporation. This is the company's 'birth certificate' and cannot be cancelled once it has been issued.

4.3 As a company comes into existence only when the certificate of incorporation is issued, it cannot adopt (ratify) a contract made on its behalf before incorporation:

*Case: Kelner v Baxter 1866*
B and two others agreed on behalf of a company yet to be formed to purchase trade stock for its business. Later, the company was formed and accepted the trade stock and used it in its business. But it failed to pay for these goods. K (as vendor) sued for the price.

*Held:* the company was not liable since it could not ratify a pre-incorporation contract with retrospective effect to a date before the company existed. No new contract had been made by the company since its incorporation (no novation). B and his friend were liable to pay. Their liability arose from breach of warranty of authority. Under s 36 the defendants would now be treated as liable under a contract to which they became parties (as agents for a non-existent company). But the amount (the price of the goods) which they have to pay is the same under either principle.

4.4 A *private company* may commence business, including borrowing money, as soon as its certificate of incorporation has been issued.

4.5 A *public company* formed as such may not commence business until it has obtained an additional certificate from the registrar issued under s 117. Pending the issue of a certificate, a public company which receives money for shares issued may pay it into a bank account. But it may not enter into any other business transaction or borrow money until the certificate has been obtained. If it does so, the transaction is valid but the company and its officers may be fined. In addition, the third party may call on the directors to obtain a certificate; failure to do so within 21 days means they must indemnify him for any loss. Finally, if a public company fails to obtain a certificate within one year, it may be compulsorily wound up: s 122 Insolvency Act 1986.

**Companies registry**

4.6 The registry (its full title is the Companies Registration Office) is a branch of the Department of Trade and Industry headed by the Registrar of Companies ('the registrar'). The registry for England and Wales is at Cardiff but documents may also be inspected at the branch in London. The registry for Scotland is in Edinburgh.

4.7 When he issues a certificate of incorporation for a company, the registrar allocates to it a serial number which must appear on all documents relating to that company delivered to the registry. He also opens a file and encloses in it a copy of all documents which he issues and the original documents received relating to that company. These include the memorandum and articles of association, the annual accounts and annual return, notices of events such as a change of directors and copies of special, extraordinary and some (but not all) ordinary resolutions passed at general meetings of the company's members, and particulars of registered charges over the company's property.

4.8 Any member of the public (including a bank) may, on payment of a small fee, inspect the contents of any company file. In current practice the documents are produced for inspection in microfiche form. He may also have copies on payment of a fee. Banks will usually make thorough enquiries by inspecting the file and this is generally accepted as being a reasonable expectation of a bank.

## 5. OPENING A BANK ACCOUNT FOR A COMPANY

5.1 In dealing with an application to open a bank account for a company customer, the bank would require to see the following:

(a) the certificate of incorporation to ensure that the company is an existing person;

(b) if the certificate of incorporation discloses that the company was formed as a public company, the registrar's certificate issued under s 117 (unless the company merely wishes to pay in subscription money at that stage);

(c) the memorandum and articles of association certified by the company secretary (see Sections 6 and 7 of this chapter);

(d) a certified copy of a resolution of the board of directors, whereby they appoint the bank to be the company's bank; and

(e) a mandate (usually provided by the bank) covering the operation of the account, and showing which people are authorised to sign cheques and all other matters arising between the company and the bank.

5.2 The bank must scrutinise the memorandum and articles with care since these would disclose the company's permitted *objects* (the business which the company may properly carry on), the limits of the directors' borrowing powers and any requirements for signing bills of exchange, guarantees etc. This was mentioned briefly in Chapter 5 and is discussed below at Section 6.

## 6.   THE MEMORANDUM OF ASSOCIATION

6.1   This is in printed or other permanent written form. The first memorandum of association must be signed by at least two persons who agree to be the first members and to subscribe for 'subscription shares' (conventionally one share each). Their signatures are witnessed by another person and dated. The first articles of association (discussed in Section 7) are similarly signed by the subscribers to the memorandum, witnessed and dated.

6.2   The memorandum of association sets out the basic structure of the company, partly for the information of the public. The articles of association are its internal bye-laws. But the articles are very important to a bank since they define the powers of the directors to act for the company.

6.3   The memorandum of association of a private company limited by shares must contain a minimum of five substantive clauses showing:

(a)   the name of the company (ending with 'plc' if it is public or 'limited' if it is private);

(b)   the situation of its registered office (in England and Wales or in Scotland). This fixes the company's country of domicile and hence the legal jurisdiction under which it operates. The actual address of its registered office is contained in a notice at the registry. This is its legal address at which writs, summonses or notices should be delivered in order that the company may not then dispute receiving them;

(c)   its objects;   *operations intended*

(d)   that the liability of members is limited;

(e)   the authorised share capital - the maximum amount of share capital which the company may issue, divided into shares of specified value.

6.4   The memorandum of association of a public company includes a sixth clause (placed second in order) which states that the company is a public company. The memorandum of association of a company limited by guarantee states the maximum amount which each member undertakes to contribute towards the payment of the company's debts.

6.5   There are statutory rules which require a company to display its name (in its correct form) on business documents, and at business premises: s 349. The business documents include bills of exchange such as cheques.

### The objects clause

6.6   The purpose of the objects clause is to define the business of the company - such as a car hire business or the manufacture of soap. The company has legal power to carry on that business and to enter into whatever transactions are incidental or conducive to it (for example to employ staff, to occupy premises, or to buy goods for the purpose of the business).

6.7 Companies vary greatly in the wording and breadth of their objects clauses.

(a) Some older companies may have a very specific clause - such as 'the acquisition of a patent to manufacture coffee from dates': *Re German Date Coffee Co 1882*. The drawback to being so specific is that, if the object fails, the company can be wound up under s 122(1)(g) Insolvency Act 1986 (as happened in this case).

(b) Most modern objects clauses contain the company's original objects in one paragraph plus two or three paragraphs expressed in more general terms. The only restriction on such practices is that the registrar will not issue a certificate of incorporation to a company with illegal objects. A clause such as the following is not uncommon:

'to carry on any other business, trade or enterprise which may be advantageously carried out, in the opinion of the directors, in connection with or ancillary to the general business of the company'.

(c) A company can register an objects clause stating that its object is to 'carry on business as a general commercial company': s 3A. The Act specifically states this to mean that:

(i) 'the object of the company is to carry on any trade or business whatsoever; and
(ii) the company has the power to do all such things as are incidental or conducive to the carrying on of any trade or business by it.'

6.8 Point (c) above may well mean that long, complex objects clauses are a thing of the past, although it remains to be seen whether members of companies are willing to give this degree of commercial freedom to their directors, or whether the draughtsmen of objects clauses consider the wording sufficient to encompass all the express powers which would otherwise have been included.

*Alteration of the objects clause*

6.9 Where a company has an old-style objects clause and wishes to borrow money for a purpose which is not within the objects, the normal procedure is to ask it to alter its objects clause accordingly. This used to be rather complicated since there were only seven prescribed reasons for alteration, but the 1989 Act now provides that a company can alter its objects for any reason whatsoever: s 4(1) Companies Act 1985. This has a number of effects:

(a) a dissenting minority of the company cannot object on the grounds that the alteration is not for one of seven prescribed reasons; and

(b) any objection must be raised by more than 15% of the members together (previously a *single* member could object).

## Ultra vires

6.10 Since a company's capacity is defined in its object clause it follows that, however widely this is drawn, some acts must go 'beyond' its capacity or 'power'. The Latin term for this is *ultra vires*; in principle, the law will not allow such an act to be legally enforceable due to lack of capacity, rather as a minor is restricted. However, the Companies Act 1989 has radically changed this position.

6.11 S 35(1) now provides as follows:

'the validity of an act done by a company shall not be called into question on the ground of lack of capacity by reason of anything in the company's memorandum.'

6.12 One possible way in which a company could seek to avoid s 35(1) would be to plead that, since the authority of the directors must also be limited by the objects of the company, an act beyond the company's capacity which is validated by s 35(1) should nevertheless be *invalidated* on the grounds that the directors had no authority to make it. S 35A(1) is introduced to close this loophole. It provides that:

'in favour of a person dealing with a company in good faith, the power of the board of directors to bind the company, or authorise others to do, shall be deemed to be free of any limitation under the company's constitution.'

6.13 There are two points to note about this new provision.

(a) In contrast with s 35(1), *good faith* is required. It is up to the company to prove the other party's lack of good faith, however, and this may turn out to be quite difficult. Constructive notice of the provisions of the memorandum or articles can no longer be imputed to the bank, and s 711A specifically excludes constructive notice of documents registered at the Companies Registry. Even where the bank has *actual* notice that the act is outside the company's capacity (and directors' authority), s 35A(2)(b) provides that this fact alone will not be enough to establish bad faith. Clearly the implication is that *some* actions or knowledge can constitute bad faith, but it is likely to be a very rare case indeed where the company can establish this of a bank.

(b) The section covers not only acts beyond the capacity of the company, but also acts beyond 'any limitation under the company's constitution'. S 35A(3) makes it clear that this includes not only the memorandum and articles, but also resolutions of the members and other agreements made by them. Examples would include a stipulation that a particular power will only be exercised by the directors with the prior consent of the members in general meeting, or perhaps that a director who is interested in a transaction should not be counted towards the quorum.

6.14 As mentioned above, s 35A(1) operates to protect the person dealing with the company (that is, the bank), not the company itself. However, the company acquires a right under s 35(3) to ratify the acts of its agents and to enforce the contract if it wishes to do so. Such ratification must be by *special* resolution (75% majority).

6.15 As can be seen, the combined effect of the 1989 legislation is virtually to abolish the effect of the *ultra vires* rule in relation to acts done between a company and its bank. In future almost all such acts will be capable of validation, at the instance of either party.

## 7. THE ARTICLES OF ASSOCIATION

7.1 The articles of association deal with such matters as the allotment and transfer of shares, general meetings of the company, and the appointment and powers of the directors.

7.2 Each successive Companies Act has provided a standard model set of articles (Table A) which a company may adopt as its own articles (with any modifications desired). Most companies still have articles based on Table A of the Companies Act 1948. But the current Table A was introduced in 1985 and so references in this text are to the 1985 version unless otherwise stated. For the purpose of banking, the most important difference between the 1948 and 1985 versions of Table A is that the 1948 version includes a *limited* delegation to directors of the company's powers to borrow money but the 1985 version permits the directors to borrow - for a proper purpose - without a limit (if the company itself has unlimited capacity, as is usually the case).

7.3 The articles are a contract between the company and its members, which each may enforce against the other, in respect of rights and obligations of membership: s 14. In this respect the articles are rather like the rules of a club.

7.4 Every company has a general power to alter its articles as it may wish by passing a special resolution (which requires a 75% majority of votes cast). There are certain restrictions on the power of alteration. For example, the articles must always be in accordance with obligatory rules of company law and the memorandum of association prevails over the articles if there is discrepancy between them.

7.5 The power of a majority of members to alter the articles by passing a special resolution is restricted by the principle that the majority may not use that power simply to discriminate against a minority in order to secure advantage to themselves. This principle is expressed by the formula that an alteration is invalid unless it is made in good faith and in the interests of the company as a whole. It does not often affect the position.

## Company's borrowing powers

7.6 The company's borrowing powers are normally vested in the directors, although these may be limited by the articles. Article 79 of the 1948 Companies Act limited the power of directors to borrow to the nominal amount of the company's issued share capital unless the consent of the company in general meeting was obtained. Table A of the 1985 Companies Act does not contain a similar limit.

7.7 In practice, a bank should ensure that it always has an up-to-date copy of the memorandum and articles of association of a company customer. These documents define (among other things) what transactions the company is legally competent to undertake and what powers have been delegated to the directors to enter into transactions so as to bind the company. As well as having the documents, the bank should always ensure that they are also understood.

## 8. COMPANY DIRECTORS

8.1 Since a company is not a living being, its affairs are conducted by human agents. The bank must ensure that those people are validly appointed and have adequate powers if it is to be protected in its dealings with them.

8.2 The first directors are named in the formation documents and are automatically appointed as soon as the certificate of incorporation is issued. Any subsequent appointment of directors is made in whatever ways are specified in the articles of association. A private company must have at least one director and a public company at least two: s 282. There is no statutory maximum number of directors, but the articles of association usually fix a maximum. A director may be removed by a simple majority (50%) of the members: s 303.

## Powers of directors

8.3 There are two general principles regarding directors' powers.

(a) Powers of management are given to the directors as a group to be exercised by collective decisions at board meetings. Hence an individual director (other than a managing director) has no apparent authority as agent of the company, though he may be given actual authority by delegation from the board.

(b) The collective powers of the directors are such (no more and no less) as are given to them by the articles of association.

8.4 The articles of association of most companies follow the model of Table A Article 70 in conferring on the directors general power to do anything which the company is competent to do (anything which is not *ultra vires* the company) unless:

(a) the Companies Act requires that the transaction shall be sanctioned in general meeting; the Act, for example, requires that an alteration of the objects clause or of the articles of association shall be made by special resolution passed in general meeting; or

(b) the articles of association reserve the decision to the company in general meeting; or

(c) the company in general meeting gives directions by passing a special resolution.

Neither (b) nor (c) enable the members in general meeting to invalidate any prior act of the directors which was valid at the time when they did it.

## The rule in Turquand's case – 'indoor management' rule

8.5 An outsider (including a bank) may assume that a company has complied with its own internal procedure for giving authority to its directors.

8.6 This is sometimes called the 'indoor management rule'; the facts of the case below illustrate how the rule works.

*Case: Royal British Bank v Turquand 1856*
The articles of association authorised the directors to borrow only such sums as might be sanctioned by resolution passed in general meeting. A resolution was passed but it did not specify any amount – it merely authorised the directors to borrow. It was therefore valueless. Acting on this authority, the directors borrowed £2,000 from the Royal British Bank. Later the bank sued the liquidator of the company (Turquand) to enforce repayment. The issue was whether the directors had made a binding contract with the bank although they lacked actual authority for it.

*Held:* under the principle of constructive notice of the articles (since repealed), the bank was aware that the directors would only borrow such amounts as were authorised in general meeting. But the bank was entitled to assume that internal procedure (which it had no means of investigating since most ordinary resolutions are not sent to the Registrar) had been correctly implemented. On that basis the directors appeared to have authority and the company was bound by the loan contract.

8.7    There are, however, a number of situations to which the rule does not apply.

(a)    A person who *actually* knows that the directors lack authority cannot assert that he believed they had it: *Howard v Patent Ivory Manufacturing Co 1888.*

(b)    A person who *might* know of the director's lack of authority, either because he is himself an insider with access to the company's records and transactions, or because there are suspicious circumstances which he fails to investigate, cannot rely on his ignorance of the true position: *Hely-Hutchinson v Brayhead 1968.*

(c)    The principle does not apply to a document which is a forgery or issued without authority. It is not the act of the company: *Kreditbank Cassel v Schenkers Ltd 1927.*

(d)    The principle only applies to the collective authority of the board of directors. There is no presumption that the board has delegated its powers to a single director (unless he is or appears to be a managing director).

(e)    If there are suspicious circumstances which put the outsider under a duty to enquire and he fails to do so, then the principle does not apply.

*Case: A L Underwood Ltd v Bank of Liverpool and Martins Ltd 1924*
A customer of the bank paid into his personal account cheques drawn payable to a company of which he was the only director and principal shareholder; he endorsed the cheques on behalf of the company. The bank was unaware that the company had its own account at a branch of another bank.

*Held:* the bank was put on enquiry and was not entitled to assume that the customer had authority.

## Statutory protection of a person dealing with directors

8.8    We saw in paragraph 6.12 that s 35A protects a third party, such as the bank, who is dealing in good faith with a board of directors. No limitation under the company's constitution can affect it. It is interesting to note that, if the situation in *Turquand's* case arose again today, the problem would be dealt with by the changes in the Companies Act 1989 - s 35 and the fact that an outsider is only expected to make reasonable enquiries concerning a company's internal management (he is no longer deemed to have 'constructive notice' of all details contained on the company's file).

## Managing director

8.9 A director may also be an employee of the company, for example a finance director or a sales director. He then has a dual status (director and employee). This of itself does not alter his apparent authority as a director. As a manager he may act for the company as its agent (under authority given by the board) just like a manager who is not a director. But as director he has no greater powers than as a manager.

8.10 However, if the articles of association provide for it (as in fact they always do), the board of directors may appoint one or more directors to the office of managing director. In doing so the board can give to a managing director such actual authority as they deem fit. *But the mere fact of his appointment as managing director gives him apparent authority to enter into commercial contracts on behalf of the board of directors whose delegate he is.*

8.11 The board of directors cannot, of course, give to a managing director any greater actual authority than the board itself derives from the articles of association. They cannot therefore give him authority to enter into a contract which the board itself could not make, being:

(a) an illegal or *ultra vires* contract; or

(b) a contract within the company's capacity but beyond the delegated powers of the board, for example, to borrow money in excess of the board's borrowing powers as defined and restricted by the articles of association.

But what the board is authorised to do, it can delegate (the articles of association are expressed to permit delegation of powers) to a single agent. A managing director by virtue of his position has apparent authority to make commercial contracts.

## Signatures on company cheques

8.12 Any agent who signs a cheque in accordance with the mandate should still add words to indicate that he signs for or on behalf of his principal, for example:

```
                  J Smith, Manager
                 for and on behalf of
                    A Best & Co
```

He is not then personally liable on the cheque. But if he merely specifies his position:

```
                  J Smith, Manager
                    A Best & Co
```

he is treated as signing in a personal capacity and is liable accordingly: s 26 Bills of Exchange Act 1882.

8.13 But a *director* or *other person* (such as a manager) signing a company cheque in accordance with the mandate is treated as signing in a representative capacity even if this is not made clear in the signature.

*Case: Bondina Ltd v Rollaway Shower Blinds Ltd 1986*
The company's printed cheque form supplied by the bank contained its printed name. A printed line of figures gave the cheque number, the branch sort code and the account number. Two directors signed a cheque in their own names only. Payment was not made by the company and the payee sought payment instead from the directors.

*Held:* by signing the cheque the directors adopted all the writing on it, including the company's name and account number. The drawer of the cheque was the company, not the directors.

8.14 A company is required by s 349 Companies Act 1985 to have its name in legible characters on all cheques. The same section states that a director is liable on any cheque not paid by the company if he signs it at a time when the company's correct name is not on it.

*Case: Durham Fancy Goods Ltd v Michael Jackson (Fancy Goods) Ltd 1968*
A creditor drew a bill of exchange on the company and wrote on it a form of acceptance which did not state the correct name of the company ('M Jackson' instead of 'Michael Jackson' in full). The defendant signed the acceptance for the company.

*Held:* the defendant was not liable since the error had been introduced by the plaintiff. But for that fact it would have been liable.

8.15 This rule raises the question as to what is and is not the correct name of a company.

(a) In an old case *(Penrose v Martyr 1858)* a company secretary incurred liability because the word 'Limited' had been omitted from the company name.

(b) In *Hendon v Adelman 1937* a signatory was liable because the sign '&' had been omitted from the company's name.

(c) The use of 'Co' instead of 'Company' *is* acceptable: *Banque de L'Indochine et de Suez SA v Euroseas Group Finance Co Ltd 1981.*

## 9. CONCLUSION

9.1 Most of a bank's bigger customers are companies, and the vast majority of commercial activities are undertaken by corporate bodies. This means that the banker needs to be very aware of the special legal environment which surrounds companies.

9.2 The most important principles to bear in mind are that, in the case of a limited company, the company has separate legal identity from its members and that the *members'* liability for debts is limited whilst the *company* retains full liability.

9.3 The doctrine of *ultra vires* used to be a source of real difficulty to banks because they were often exposed to the risk of making a loan which became unenforceable when used for an *ultra vires* purpose. Transactions entered into beyond the directors' powers were also problematic. The amended Companies Act 1985 ss 35 and 35A greatly reduces this exposure.

**TEST YOUR KNOWLEDGE**

*The numbers in brackets refer to paragraphs of this chapter*

1   How may a corporate body be formed? (1.1)

2   What is meant by 'the veil of incorporation' and when may it be lifted? (1.4, 1.5)

3   What is the significance of:

(a)   limited liability; and
(b)   perpetual succession? (2.2, 2.4)

4   What condition must be satisfied before the registrar of companies will grant a s 11 certificate to a public company? (3.2)

5   Name the markets available for a public company's shares. (3.7)

6   What documents must be given to the registrar on forming a company? (4.1)

7   Which documents should a bank see before opening a new company account? (5.1)

8   What is the memorandum of association? (6.1, 6.2)

9   What is the significance of the objects clause? (6.6)

10   What is the effect of a transaction which goes beyond a company's stated objects? (6.11 - 6.13)

11   What do the articles of association represent? (7.1)

12   How may the directors' general powers be restricted? (8.4)

13   When does the indoor management rule *not* operate? (8.7)

14   What is the liability of a director who signs a company cheque 'A N Other, Anonymous Ltd'? (8.13)

*Now try question 20 at the end of the text*

# PART D
# PROPERTY AND SECURITY

*Chapter 13*

# LAND

---

**This chapter covers the following topics.**

1. Land law
2. Rights over land
3. Legal estates
4. Legal interests
5. Equitable interests
6. Unregistered land
7. Transfer of unregistered land
8. Registered land
9. Transfer of registered land

---

*Land law was modernised in 1925 by a group of statutes of which the Law of Property Act 1925 (referred to as LPA) is the most important here. Statutory references in this and the following chapter are to this Act unless otherwise noted. The other major statute is the Land Registration Act 1925 (LRA).*

---

## 1. LAND LAW

1.1 The framework of land law is supported by a system of registers to which the public has access. The main elements are as follows.

(a) *Registered title.* Some (but not yet all) land ownership in England is based on a system of entries in public registers maintained in District Land Registries at main centres (with a principal registry in London). A person who wishes to inspect an entry must usually obtain the prior consent of the owner of the land comprised in that entry, but once the Land Registration Act 1988 is brought into force, anyone may inspect the register without permission. The right of inspection carries a right to have a copy (on payment of a fee).

(b) *Registered charges.* Some (but not all) types of mortgage and other rights and incumbrances over land are protected by entry in a Land Charges Register (maintained at Plymouth for all parts of England). The standard procedure for investigating title to land requires that a search should be made in this register (usually by postal application and official certificate of search). If the land is owned by a registered company it may also be necessary to make a search at the Companies Registry (in Cardiff). Most charges over company land require registration at that registry.

(c) *Local authority registers.* Local authorities (county councils, borough and district councils etc) have statutory powers to regulate and to promote land development, say by planning restrictions. Orders, decisions etc of local authorities may affect particular areas or specific plots of land. The local authorities maintain registers in which these matters are recorded. It is part of the standard procedure in land transactions to apply to the local authorities of the area in which the land is situated for copies of entries in their registers (or answers to specific questions). In legal jargon these entries are called 'local searches'.

### What is land?

1.2 The term 'land' includes any building or structures on it and rights over land (including mining below the surface and to some extent the air above it). There are borderline categories.

(a) *Fixtures* are things attached to land or to a building as part of it. But movable things (eg pictures hung on a wall) are not fixtures. Land includes any fixtures attached to it.

(b) *Growing crops* are usually not part of the land if they are to be severed from it in the course of harvesting.

1.3 Some mineral rights (particularly over coal) have been taken into public ownership. Aircraft have a statutory right to fly over land at a safe height.

1.4 For historical reasons the law distinguishes between:

(a) *real property* (also 'realty') which is land owned under freehold (perpetual) title; and

(b) *personal property* (also 'personalty') which is all other property, including rights of ownership over land under a (terminable) lease.

This is an unsatisfactory distinction. For most purposes the law treats freehold and leasehold property in land in the same way. Leaseholds are sometimes called 'chattels real' which adds to the confusion since they are neither realty nor chattels (which are moveable things, such as personal possessions).

*Freehold*

## 2. RIGHTS OVER LAND

2.1 For historical reasons land law relates to *rights over land* rather than to land itself. For example, when a customer mortgages his freehold land to the bank as security he encumbers (restricts) his freehold rights of ownership by giving to the bank rights over his land in the form of a legal or equitable mortgage. The land is still land but the rights over it have been altered and divided.

2.2 The law draws a most important distinction between rights which are legal and rights which are equitable. *A legal right is valid against anyone* (but priorities may depend on notice, as we shall see shortly). For instance, if a purchaser of land later discovers that someone has legal rights over the land of which he was previously unaware, he is bound by those rights. The person who has legal rights cannot (without his consent) be deprived of them (except by a public authority acting under an Act of Parliament, for example, a compulsory purchase order made by a local authority).

## Equitable rights

2.3 *Equitable rights are valid against anyone who has notice of them, actual or constructive, at the time of the relevant transaction.* But a purchaser of land without notice of equitable rights over it usually acquires the land free of those rights. The person who has the equitable rights does of course have safeguards. He can:

(a) *register* his rights at the Land Charges Registry, thereby giving constructive notice to *everyone* who may thereafter have dealings with the land; or

(b) transfer the equitable rights over land which is sold so that they become rights over the proceeds of sale (a 'trust for sale') which the seller receives and holds in trust for the person with equitable rights. This system is called *over-reaching* equitable rights.

2.4 The reason for the distinction between legal and equitable rights is that by this means a purchaser of land can limit the expensive investigation of the seller's title to discovering whether there are legal rights over it. He can then strike a bargain with the persons who own those rights for their sale to him. As regards equitable rights the purchaser makes searches in the register. If he thereby discovers rights which affect the land he can deal with them as he sees fit. But he need not make any further investigation to discover equitable rights since if there are any more of them and they are not registered or can be overreached they do not concern him. (The above explanation is a slightly simplified summary which suffices to bring out the main points.)

## Legal rights

2.5 Legal rights over land are classified as legal estates and legal interests.

(a) An *estate* is that kind of right of ownership which carries an entitlement to possess - to occupy the land.

(b) A legal *interest* is a right over land given to a non-owner. But it is valid against everyone and gives a right to something less than possession.

For example, freehold ownership of land is a legal estate but a permanent 'right of way' over a neighbour's land is a legal interest. If one has that legal interest one may cross the land but not take possession of it.

## Co-ownership

2.6 It is possible for more than one person to own land. If land is purchased or transferred to two or more persons, these persons become either 'joint tenants' or 'tenants in common'.

(a) *Joint tenancy* is legal and equitable co-ownership, arising where two or more people acquire land but no words of 'severence' are used. This means that the transfer does not state what share in the land each person has. The land is merely 'held by X and Y'.

(b) *Tenants in common* represent equitable co-ownership, whereby the co-owners have shares in the land. For instance, a conveyance may state that the land should go to 'P, Q and R equally' - each then owns one-third of the interest.

2.7 The importance of the distinction is that, if a joint tenant dies, his interest lapses and the land is owned wholly by the survivor(s). He may not pass his legal interest on by will, although he may pass on his equitable rights. The advantage is that only a limited number of interests can exist. The disadvantage is obviously the unfair fact that survival decides ownership. With tenants in common, each tenant can bequeath his interest which means that a house owned by tenants in common (A, B and C equally) will, if C dies and leaves his interest to D, E, F and G, be owned by A, B (one third part each), D, E, F and G (one twelfth part each). Whilst being fairer, this can be cumbersome!

2.8 LPA achieved a compromise by providing that, where land is owned by two or more persons, then no more than four of those persons hold the *legal* estate as joint tenants and trustees, for the benefit or *equitable* interest of themselves and other co-owners in a 'trust for sale', so that all the owners get fair shares.

## 3. LEGAL ESTATES

3.1 LPA recognises only two legal estates in land (before 1926 there were several more). They are:

(a) *freehold ownership* called 'fee simple absolute in possession'; and
(b) *leasehold ownership* of the type called 'term of years absolute'.

Essentially the difference between them is how long they last (their 'tenure').

### Freeholds

3.2 In freehold ownership 'fee simple' means that the owner can transfer ownership at death to whomsoever he pleases. 'Absolute' means that there are no overriding conditions limiting the ownership. 'In possession' means that the owner has a right *now* to occupy the land or, if it is let to a tenant, to receive the rent.

### Leaseholds

3.3 In leasehold ownership the expression 'term of years' is misleading. There can be very long leases, eg for 999 years, or for a very much shorter period such as a weekly tenancy. 'Term of years' simply indicates that it is an estate for a defined or terminable period. There is an elaborate definition of 'term of years' which excludes a lease for a lifetime or a lease which covers a period beginning more than 21 years ahead. But these are not important distinctions here. Leaseholds are created by executing a deed but if the tenure is less than three years then just a written or even an oral lease will be binding.

3.4 The essential distinction between freehold and leasehold rights of ownership is that a freehold continues for ever but a leasehold can (in most instances must) end. Obviously the owner of freehold land may not continue in ownership of it for ever. If he is an individual he will die or perhaps sell or give away the land in his lifetime. A company also may dispose of its freehold land. But if this happens the perpetual *right* of ownership continues to exist and passes to the next owner - and so on.

3.5 Leasehold ownership is a much more complicated concept. Because land itself is indestructible there must always be an owner of the perpetual freehold estate from which the leasehold estate has been carved out for a period of time. Even a lease for 999 years must come to an end when 999 years have passed. The land will then revert to the *possession* (it is already subject to the existing *ownership)* of the freeholder.

3.6 As leases are usually granted in return for a rent payable in money (or a large initial down payment called a 'premium' or both premium and rent) the freeholder will be entitled to money payments while the lease continues in addition to his ultimate right to resume possession.

### Terms in leases

3.7 A lease is also a contract made between lessor and original lessee. In principle the terms of the lease can be whatever they may agree upon. The lease will describe and define the property let (and any rights attached to it), state for how long it is to last (say for a year or indefinitely until terminated by a month's notice), state what rent is payable and at what intervals, and impose obligations on lessor and lessee. In particular a lease may restrict the use to which the tenant may put the leasehold premises. This is particularly common in leases of commercial premises such as shops. The terms of leases are often varied or restricted by statutes, such as the Rent Acts, enacted to protect tenants.

3.8 In general a leasehold is transferable on the basis that the new tenant is bound by its terms. The lease itself may give the lessor or his successor a limited right to withhold consent to any transfer (called 'assignment') of the entire lease, and to any sub-letting.

3.9 A person to whom a lease is transferred is said to have 'privity of estate' with the lessor (or any person to whom the lessor on his part has transferred his reversionary rights). This expression means that although the present lessee was not a party to the lease when it was first made (as a contract) he does now own the legal estate (the lease) and this puts him into a direct relationship (rights and obligations) with the present owner of the reversion.

3.10 A lessee may sub-let all or part of the leasehold property for all or part of the unexpired period of the lease (subject to any veto retained by the lessor). It is usual then to call the lease granted by the freehold owner the 'head lease' and the sub-letting a 'sub-lease'. The lessee is also a landlord or lessor (as regards the sub-lease).

### Termination of a lease

3.11 A lease may come to an end in a variety of ways:

(a) expiry of a fixed period;

(b) termination by notice; or

(c) 'forfeit' - where the lease's contractual terms are breached by default in payment of rent, bankruptcy, company liquidation or receivership.

3.12 If the lessor acquires the lessee's leasehold title or the lessee acquires the lessor's right for possession to revert to him (his 'reversion'), the freehold and leasehold are merged and the latter ceases to exist.

3.13 The Leasehold Reform Act 1967 gives a lessee who holds property under a lease granted for more than 21 years a right to purchase a lessor's reversion or to have it extended by 50 years. But this right applies only to house property in respect of which the tenant must have satisfied certain rules governing occupancy.

## 4. LEGAL INTERESTS

4.1 There are five legal interests in land recognised by LPA:

(a) an easement, right or privilege over land of another person; *(handwritten: sharing driveway)*

(b) a charge by way of legal mortgage (see Chapter 14); → *(handwritten: can be registered)*

(c) a rentcharge - a right (not arising from a lease) to receive an annual payment from the owner of land. (This type of legal interest is being extinguished over a long period of years by the Rentcharges Act 1977);

(d) a charge imposed on land by law; and

(e) a right of entry - a right to resume possession given to a lessor of a lease or a person entitled to a rentcharge if there is default.

Only (a) and (b) have any practical importance nowadays.

4.2 An *easement* is typically a right to do or to have something which restricts the rights of an owner of other land. As examples, one plot of land may carry a right of way over another, or a right of support (as when semi-detached houses share a party wall) or a right of light (which prohibits creating an obstruction to the passage of light to windows). It is also possible though less common that one piece of land gives to its owner a right to go on the land of another and remove something from it (fishing or shooting rights, or the right to collect firewood or to graze cattle). This right to take away something is called a *profit à prendre*.

## 5. EQUITABLE INTERESTS

5.1 It is possible to have interests in land which are equitable - interests which are not legal estates or legal interests as described above. *Equitable* interests are valid against a purchaser of the land for value if he has notice of them, but if they arise from a trust and can be over-reached (see paragraph 2.3) the law does not permit him to be so affected by them. Important types of equitable interest are:

(a) *the equity of redemption*. This gives a mortgagor the right to redeem his property or the sale proceeds thereof once the principal and outstanding interest have been paid. This interest is discussed further in the following chapter;

(b) *equitable charge*. An interest in land may be given as security for, say, a loan without creating a formal legal charge. Again, we shall look at this in more detail later;

*(handwritten: deed money)*

(c) *restrictive covenants* are promises made by one person to another to place limits on property. An example might be an agreement to prevent land being used for the purposes of entertainment, such as a cinema next to a church; and

(d) *estate contracts*. These are in the nature of a preliminary contract for the transfer of land, such as where the vendor and purchaser in a house-sale have exchanged contracts but have not yet completed the deed. No legal interest has passed but the equitable interest is enforceable.

## 6. UNREGISTERED LAND

6.1 The system of registered title to land was introduced a hundred years ago on a limited scale. In recent years it has been progressively extended throughout the country, with priority for built-up areas. But even in an area of compulsory registration there may still be unregistered titles since registration becomes compulsory only on transfer of freeholds and some leaseholds. The intention is that eventually all land ownerships (other than short leases) shall be registered.

*Voluntary registration*

6.2 Title to unregistered land is denoted by possession of title deeds (the owner will hold these when the land is charged). Title deeds comprise:

(a) abstracts of title - prepared by a solicitor to indicate past transactions whose documentation is not included with the deeds;

(b) conveyances - documents conveying title to another person;

(c) mortgages - creating charges over the property;

(d) releases of mortgages - signifying that the charges are discharged;

(e) search certificates;

(f) assignments - transferring leasehold interests; and   *deed of assignments*

(g) a schedule listing the documents included.

### Registrable interests

6.3 To simplify the rules on notice it is provided that certain interests in land may be registered at the Land Charges Registry. These registrable interests include some legal interests and some equitable interests. If they are registered, the registration operates as constructive notice to everyone, whether or not he actually knows of them. If they are not registered these interests are void against a third party even if he actually knew of them. Accordingly it is standard procedure to search the registers at the Land Charges Registry when buying *unregistered land* only.

6.4 The registrable charges over land are divided in the Land Charges Registry register into classes. The most important classes are:

*Classes C and D* - (which we will consider in more detail) and

*Class F* - the right of a spouse to occupy a house owned by the other spouse - very important to a mortgagee since the mortgagee will wish to sell (if he sells) with vacant possession. This subject is explained in Chapter 14 on land as security.

### Class C land charges

6.5 The following charges over land are registrable in Class C of the Land Charges Register:

(a) *a legal mortgage* (typically a second or later mortgage) if not protected by deposit of title deeds - called a *'puisne* mortgage' - explained in Chapter 14;

(b) *a limited owner's charge* - typically when a life tenant of settled land (which he does not own outright) has paid from his own resources a liability which should have been paid out of trust capital - he becomes in effect a mortgagee with security on the land for his outlay;

(c) *a general equitable charge* such as an equitable mortgage (which is not, as mentioned above, a legal interest) - explained in Chapter 14;

(d) *an estate contract* - a preliminary contract for the sale of land or the grant of a lease - explained at paragraph 6.7.

### Class D land charges

6.6 The following charges over land are registrable in Class D:

(a) a charge for inheritance tax (payable on the death of an owner);

(b) a *restrictive covenant* - a restriction on the use of land imposed after 1925 for the benefit of other land - but such a restriction in a lease is not registrable (as it is disclosed through inspection of the lease);

(c) an *equitable easement* created after 1925 - an easement which does not qualify as an overriding legal interest may nonetheless be protected by registration which gives notice of its existence.

6.7 If a registrable charge is not registered, a purchaser of the land is generally not affected by it. A 'purchaser' includes a mortgagee such as a bank lending on security. But a Class D land charge and an estate contract (in Class C) will, if unregistered, be valid and binding on a purchaser unless he acquires a legal estate in the land. This last rule can prejudice a bank which takes an equitable mortgage only.

*Case: McCarthy and Stone Ltd v Julian S Hodge Ltd 1971*
A builder entered into a contract - an 'estate contract' - to sell a house, but this was not registered as a charge. The builder then gave an *equitable* mortgage to the bank by deposit of title deeds (explained later in this text).

*Held:* the estate contract, although unregistered, must prevail over a subsequent *equitable* interest.

6.8 Some equitable interests (claims to financial benefits from trust property rather than direct rights to land) are by law not capable of registration. But interests in that category pass (by overreaching) from the land (when it is sold) to the sale proceeds in the hands of the vendor (in a trust for sale).

### Companies registry

6.9 A company is required within 21 days of creating charges to register the charge at the Companies Registry: s 398 Companies Act 1985. Failure to do so renders the charge, but not the debt it secures, unenforceable. The categories of company charges to be registered in this way include a charge on land or any interest in land. This registration requirement is in addition to the registration of land charges as such. If, therefore, a company creates a mortgage - a fixed charge - over its unregistered land, it should register the charge both at the Land Charges Registry and at the Companies Registry. But a floating charge is registrable only at the Companies Registry.

### Beneficial interests in unregistered land

6.10 Overriding interests in registered land are described at paragraph 8.5 below. A similar system operates for unregistered land, whereby a person may have a beneficial interest in the land of which others have constructive notice. This is particularly relevant with regard to matrimonial homes and rights of occupation, which are dealt within in Chapter 14.

## 7. TRANSFER OF UNREGISTERED LAND

7.1 An owner of land transfers his ownership by deed - by a written transfer. A transfer is usually a sale. Before he pays the price, the purchaser (and any mortgagee who is lending part of the price) investigates the seller's title and other matters affecting the land and its value.

### Freehold land

7.2 The usual sequence of action for transfer of *unregistered freehold land* is as follows.

   (a) Vendor and purchaser agree upon the sale - the essential terms such as the price - but stipulate that their agreement is 'subject to contract' (neither is yet bound and either may withdraw).

   (b) The purchaser makes 'local searches' (he may also make a land charges search) and he addresses a questionnaire (preliminary enquiries) about the property to the vendor. The vendor puts forward a draft contract which is usually a standard printed form (containing numerous conditions) adapted to the particular transaction.

   (c) Vendor and purchaser each sign a copy of the contract and deliver it to the other. The contract usually requires that ten per cent of the price is to be paid at this stage. Each party is now bound by the contract. In equity the purchaser is now the owner of the property, which he may mortgage. If he defaults at this stage, the vendor resumes equitable ownership and any mortgage is invalid. The property is at the purchaser's risk - if it is burnt down he must pay the agreed price for the smoking ruins! He therefore insures his interest in the property.

(d) In accordance with the contract, the purchaser investigates the vendor's title deeds and may require information or action (requisitions on title). The purchaser prepares a transfer (a 'conveyance') to himself to be executed by the vendor, and he makes all necessary searches for charges over the land.

(e) At completion, the vendor delivers the conveyance (and his title deeds) in exchange for payment of the balance of the price, usually by banker's draft. If there is to be a mortgage to raise all or part of the purchase price, the purchaser as mortgagor will at the same time execute the mortgage and deliver it to the mortgagee (lender) together with the conveyance to him and the previous title deeds. These documents are retained by the mortgagee until the mortgage is paid off. The mortgage must be signed by the mortgagee.

This sequence of action is usually handled by solicitors acting for the parties. The above is merely an outline of what can be a prolonged series of exchanges between solicitors.

7.3 The vendor is required by the contract to 'deduce' - demonstrate his title - by showing:

(a) that he is the owner of the land (to the extent described in the contract);

(b) how he acquired it from the previous owner; and

(c) what have been the sequence of previous dealings (including earlier changes of ownership) over a period of years.

7.4 If the sequence of documents (title deeds) raises no doubts (or if they can be removed), and no one is challenging the present owner's rights, the purchaser is reasonably safe in buying those rights of ownership from him.

7.5 It is normal practice to require that proof of title shall begin from a transaction at least 15 years before (called 'the root of title'). If, for example, the latest transaction is about to be completed in 1992 the vendor would specify a suitable event, usually a previous sale, before 1977 and produce the deeds covering the devolution of the property from that event down to his own purchase. If during that period there have been events such as mortgages or leases, the vendor demonstrates that they are no longer in force (or if they continue that he has provided in the contract for sale subject to them). The period of 15 years can be varied by mutual agreement.

7.6 Proof of title is like testing the strength of a chain by examining each link. The chain is only as strong as its weakest link. But if the chain is sound throughout its length a good root of title (at one end of the chain) establishes that the present owner's title also is good. If there is a weakness in the chain of title, the owner's rights are likely to be challenged within the recent past by someone else who has rights (so he asserts) over the land. Hence undisputed and valid title for a period of 15 years or more is a reasonable proof that the owner's title is indeed valid.

7.7 To prove his title over the required period, the vendor supplies either a lengthy summary (an abstract of title) of the original title deeds or (more common in these days of photocopies) he supplies copies of the title deeds. The purchaser is given an opportunity to check the abstract or copies against the originals (which may still be held by the vendor's mortgagee).

*Leasehold land*

7.8 The general sequence of action in transfer of *unregistered leasehold land* is broadly the same as for a transfer of unregistered freehold land. But here the vendor's title is the lease granted to him (or to his predecessor). He discloses the ownership and dealings with it for the previous 15 years. He must at completion assign the lease (by deed) and hand over the lease itself and the relevant earlier documents.

7.9 The terms of the lease often require that the lessor's consent to a transfer (called an 'assignment' of a lease) shall be obtained. It may also be necessary to obtain the lessor's consent to a change of use of commercial premises or alterations to the building.

## 8. REGISTERED LAND

8.1 The purpose of the system of registered title is to simplify the transfer of ownership of land. When unregistered title is converted to registered title, the title deeds are delivered to the District Land Registry for the area in which the land is situated. The Registry extracts and summarises the relevant particulars which are entered together in the register as follows.

(a) *Property Register* - a description of the land and the owner's rights supplemented by reference to a general map or filed plan which shows the boundaries and the position of the land in relation to adjoining properties.

(b) *Proprietorship Register* - this states:

  (i)   the class of title (described at paragraph 8.8);

  (ii)  the name, address etc of the registered proprietor - on each change of ownership the particulars of the new owners are inserted so that from the time of registration onwards the sequence of ownership is visible on the register (but this is not material - it is only the latest entry which counts);

  (iii) any restrictions on the registered owner's right of disposal (say, because of bankruptcy proceedings).

(c) *Charges Register* - particulars of mortgages, charges, leases and other incumbrances other than 'overriding interests' and 'minor interests' (explained below). Occasionally it is necessary to supplement this data by retaining a copy of a document.

8.2 All these particulars are generally typed on two sides of one large page in the register. An exact copy of the entries is issued to the registered proprietor as evidence of his title. This copy (authenticated by the Registry seal) is called the *Land Certificate*. The old title deeds are returned to the owner but are endorsed to the effect that the title has been registered (so that the deeds cannot be used in a fraudulent sale as an unregistered title).

8.3 To keep the burden of maintaining the register within manageable limits, registration (in an area of compulsory registration) is compulsory:

(a)  on sale of a freehold;

(b)  on grant of a lease for a term of 21 years or more;

(c)  on sale of an existing lease if, at the time of sale, it has at least 21 years unexpired.

Note that a lease of less than 21 years cannot be registered.

8.4  The above rules relate to land in those areas (mainly built-up) to which compulsory registration has so far been extended. There is no general obligation or right to registration of title in a non-compulsory area. But in exceptional circumstances registration may be permitted (after due investigation of title) in a non-compulsory area. For example, if title deeds have been lost or destroyed but other evidence (photocopies etc) exist, registration might be allowed as the most convenient method of establishing ownership and the right to transfer land.

*Overriding interests*

8.5  Overriding interests are not registered but nonetheless bind anyone who acquires an interest in the land (for example, by purchase). Overriding interests (such as those of a spouse - see Chapter 14) can be discovered by enquiry of the occupier (and so the intending purchaser is expected to make this enquiry for himself). They include such interests as leases not exceeding 21 years and legal easements such as rights of way.

*Case: Hodgson v Marks 1971*
H transferred her house into the name of her lodger (E) solely to prevent her nephew turning E out of the house. H remained in occupation. E sold the house to another person who mortgaged it to a building society.

*Held:* although H was not a party to the later transaction she was in 'actual occupation'. Her transfer to E had given her certain equitable rights against E (a resulting trust in her favour). These rights were an overriding interest and valid against the subsequent registered owner.

*Minor interests*

8.6  Minor interests in registered land can be protected by presenting to the Registry a notice, caution, inhibition or restriction (these different documents arise in different ways and from different sources). Some can be entered in the Minor Interests Index. A prospective purchaser is concerned mainly with those minor interests which are protected by entry in the *Proprietorship* (not Charges) Register to restrict the proprietor's personal rights of disposal. These interests become apparent to a purchaser when he obtains a copy of the complete entry in the Land Register. If he acquires the land for value without notice of them he is not bound by them.

8.7  An interest may be protected by making entries in the Proprietorship or Charges Register as follows.

(a)  *Restrictions* - forbid certain dealings with the land, and are applied for by the registered proprietor.

(b)  *Inhibitions* - are often used in bankruptcy cases, being court orders which forbid certain dealings, particularly by the registered proprietor.

    (c) *Cautions* – are entered into by a person with an interest in land (in the Proprietorship Register) or a charge (in the Charges Register). The effect of a caution is that the Registrar must inform the person who lodged the caution of any attempt by a person to deal with the land or charge in such a way as to affect the register. That person then has 14 days in which to act. Lodging a caution does not require production of the Land Certificate. It gives only a right of objection, not priority, unless the registrar failed to inform and a purchaser knew of the caution – in such a case, the purchaser would take the title subject to the interest protected by the caution.

    (d) *Notices* – are entered in the Charges Register if the person giving them has the Land Certificate, or if the latter is on deposit at the Land Registry. A purchaser takes title subject to the notified interest. The usefulness of a caution is that a mortgagee would be informed of any attempt to sell, and could then enter a notice since the purchaser would produce the Land Certificate.

    (e) *Notices of deposit* are also entered in the Charges Register, signifying that a Land Certificate has been deposited. It is a form of caution, giving no priority but enabling the person receiving notice to act on it.

### Classes of registered title

8.8 The Proprietorship Register describes the title of the registered owner as one of four categories.

    (a) *Absolute Title* – this is a state-guaranteed title limited only by:

        (i)    what may appear from the register itself;
        (ii)   any overriding interests; and
        (iii)  any minor interests of which the person affected has notice.

    (b) *Possessory Title* – this is a provisional title which is not guaranteed. It is the category used in cases of doubt. But after 15 years a registered owner of freehold land held under possessory title may have it upgraded to absolute title. A leaseholder may similarly progress to good leasehold title after 10 years. Possessory title is a holding operation – the proprietor fails at the outset to establish his title beyond doubt but if time passes without challenge being made he achieves absolute title.

    (c) *Qualified Title* – this is rare. It is a registered title qualified by explicit limits or reservations on it.

    (d) *Good Leasehold Title* – this guarantees a leasehold title but it does not guarantee that the leasehold was granted out of a guaranteed freehold title. After 10 years, however, it may be upgraded to absolute title.

## 9.   TRANSFER OF REGISTERED LAND

9.1 The procedure is the same as for unregistered land except that the transferor completes a printed form of transfer as a deed. This transfer and the transferor's Land Certificate are delivered to the District Land Registry. The particulars of the transferee are entered in the Proprietorship Register. A new Land Certificate is then issued to the transferee as registered proprietor.

9.2 The main difference between transfer of registered and unregistered land is that the vendor proves his title merely by producing his Land Certificate. As the Land Certificate may not show entries made on the register since the Land Certificate was issued or last up dated it is usual to send the Certificate in for updating when the sale is agreed or to apply to the Registry for a copy of the entries on the register (relating to the land to be sold). But in proving title, suitable evidence of what the register now contains is all which the vendor must produce and which the purchaser need concern himself with. There are of course complications to be kept in view, such as possible overriding interests. But in essentials registered title reduces to a minimum the task of extracting information about the rights and interests in the land of the registered proprietor and any third parties.

9.3 A purchaser of registered land takes his title subject to overriding interests, even though they have not been registered and/or he does not know of them. These may be:

(a) rights of persons in occupation (*excluding* a spouse's statutory right of occupation);
(b) rent leases of less than 21 years;
(c) duties to repair (for example, sea walls); and
(d) legal easements and *profits à prendre*.

The most common problem encountered by a bank in relation to overriding interests derives from (a) above. This is covered in Chapter 14.

---

## Exercise

Describe how an owner proves title to:

(a) unregistered land; and
(b) registered land.

### Solution

(a) Title to unregistered land is shown by possession of title deeds. The vendor must demonstrate title by showing a good 'root of title' going back at least 15 years.

(b) Title to registered land is shown by issue of a land certificate by the District Land Registry. Title deeds are endorsed to show that the land has been registered.

---

## 10. CONCLUSION

10.1 This chapter lays the groundwork for the next on land as a security for bank lending. One can only understand the intricate rules on mortgages if one also understands what rights the owner of land has at his disposal to offer as security for his borrowing.

10.2 In this subject area it is important for you to learn the different categories of ownership - legal estates and interests in land, and the distinction between legal and equitable rights (leading to the elaborate administrative arrangements for giving notice of rights and incumbrances by registration at the Land Charges Registry where land is unregistered).

10.3 You should master the basic elements of registered title which is the dominant form of land ownership, and which will continue to expand in your working lifetime until it covers the whole of English land. Registered title is in its essentials very simple. The land, the owner of it, and the rights of non-owners over it are summarised in a public register. Any charge is generally void or invalid unless it is entered in the register. But registered title is only a summary of the essentials. One has to remember that overriding interests and minor interests over land can exist without appearing on the register (though the more significant minor interests appear as limits imposed on the owner in the Proprietorship Register).

10.4 You may find this brief summary of differences between registered and unregistered land useful.

| | Unregistered land | Registered land |
|---|---|---|
| *Title* | Demonstrated by title deeds | Demonstrated by Land Certificate produced by Land Registry |
| *Interest in land* | Registered at Land Charges Registry | Some can be notified for inclusion on the Charges Register part of the entry at the Land Registry |
| *Transfer* | 15 years 'proof of title' required. Transfer effected by conveyance and transfer of title deeds | Form of transfer executed as deed. Delivered to District Land Registry with Land Certificate (latter updated) |

10.5 Transfer of land is of much practical importance to banks as lenders on the security of land. If a borrower defaults and the bank enforces its security by sale of the land, it can usually offer a prospective purchaser only as good (or bad) a title as the borrower previously obtained on his previous acquisition of the land. When a bank or a building society lends money towards the price of buying a house, the lender as much as the purchaser has to be satisfied on all the relevant points of title. Solicitors acting for a mortgagee tend to take a tough line on debatable points of title. For that reason the existence of a legal mortgage (later discharged) in the past history of dealings in a property is considered reassuring to a later purchaser.

**TEST YOUR KNOWLEDGE**

*The numbers in brackets refer to paragraphs of this chapter*

1   At what registries can information be obtained about rights over land? (1.1)

2   What are the main differences between:

  (a)   real and personal property; and
  (b)   legal and equitable rights? (1.4, 2.3)

3   What protection is given to the owner of equitable rights against the risk that the legal estate in land may be transferred by sale to a purchaser who is unaware of those rights? (2.3)

4   Describe the two possible ways in which people can co-own land. (2.6)

5   What are the legal estates and interests in land?  (3.1, 4.1)

6   Compare freehold and leasehold estates in land. (3.2, 3.3)

7   What is an easement? (4.2)

8   Describe three types of equitable interest. (5.1)

9   What are Class C and Class D Land Charges?  (6.5, 6.6)

10   Describe in outline how a sale of unregistered freehold land is carried through. (7.2)

11   What information is entered (in respect of a registered title) at the District Land Registry? What may *not* be entered on the register?  (8.1)

12   What are the categories of registered title as described in the Proprietorship Register?  (8.8)

13   What is the procedure for transfer of registered land? (9.1, 9.2)

*Now try question 21 at the end of the text*

# Chapter 14

# LAND AS SECURITY

---

**This chapter covers the following topics.**

1. Mortgage law
2. What is a mortgage of land?
3. The form of a legal mortgage
4. The form of an equitable mortgage
5. Mortgages of unregistered land
6. Mortgages of registered land
7. Second mortgages
8. Taking a mortgage
9. Taking a mortgage of unregistered land
10. Taking a mortgage of registered land
11. Discharge of a mortgage
12. Remedies of a legal mortgagee
13. Remedies of an equitable mortgagee

---

## 1.  MORTGAGE LAW

1.1  For a number of reasons the law of mortgages (of land) is a complicated subject.

(a)  The lender is usually in the stronger position and so in earlier centuries the Court of Chancery applied principles of equity to redress the balance and assist the borrower. This appears in the principle of 'the equity of redemption'.

(b)  Mortgages can be either 'legal' or 'equitable'. Broadly the distinction here in practice is between a formal, long-term mortgage (which is usually legal) and an informal, usually short-term equitable mortgage. The more theoretical distinction is between a legal interest in the property (valid against everyone) and a personal right (in equity) against the mortgagor and other persons who acquire an interest in the land with knowledge of the prior mortgagee. The procedure for creating each type of mortgage is different. There is also an obsolescent method of creating legal mortgages which takes the form of granting a lease to the lender.

(c)  A borrower is not restricted to creating one mortgage of the same property. If there is surplus value he can create a second or later mortgage to rank after a first mortgage (in most cases). The borrower may also mortgage different properties to the same lender as security for one or for several loans.

(d)  Occasionally a secured lender may wish to transfer his rights as mortgagee or to use them as security (by a sub-mortgage) for his own borrowing.

211

1.2 Either freehold or leasehold land may be used to provide security by means of a mortgage. Because they are different types of legal estate, the mortgage procedure is slightly different. Equitable interests in land may also be subject to a mortgage which in this case must be in the form of an equitable mortgage.

1.3 The *legal* problems of mortgages of land must be a main theme in this text on the legal environment of banking. But the law is only a part of the total situation when a bank lends on this security. The bank must also consider the value of the property (how much money it is likely to recover if it has to enforce its security by sale) and whether or not the property is readily marketable. This aspect requires some form of valuation. In answering questions set in this paper remember that they are designed to test your knowledge of mortgage *law*.

## 2. WHAT IS A MORTGAGE OF LAND?

2.1 The essential feature of a secured loan (other than a collateral security by guarantee) is that the borrower (called the 'mortgagor') gives to the lender (called the 'mortgagee') a right in priority to other creditors to resort to the land of the borrower to obtain repayment of the loan (and/or interest due on it) if (but only if) the borrower defaults.

2.2 The mortgagee usually enforces his right by sale of the land (though there are alternative remedies, as we shall see in this chapter). He therefore has or can obtain by court order a power of sale of the land. This power (and his other remedies) does not make the mortgagee the owner of the land. He can dispose of the land by sale in order to repay himself what is owing. But the surplus (if any) arising from a sale belongs to the mortgagor (subject to the rights of any other mortgagees to whom the mortgagor may have given subsequent mortgages of the same land).

### The equity of redemption

2.3 In the normal case a mortgagor borrows money from the mortgagee, such as a bank, and undertakes to repay the loan at a specified date or on demand and to pay interest (at specified dates) until the principal is repaid. This is a loan contract. The mortgage is the security for the mortgagor's due performance of the contract.

2.4 If the mortgagor duly performs his contract he is, under the terms of the contract, entitled to have his mortgage discharged by release of the land from the mortgagee's rights over it (with a legal mortgage those rights are a legal interest in the land). He is also freed from his personal obligations to the mortgagee.

2.5 However, if the mortgagor fails to repay the loan when it falls due he no longer has any contractual right (since he is in breach of contract) to redeem his security by payment at a later date. But to relieve this hardship the Court of Chancery in mediaeval times gave him a right at any time after the contractual date of repayment had passed to repay the loan and redeem his security. He must however give notice (usually six months) or pay six months' interest instead. Since this additional right is an equitable principle it was called 'the equity of redemption.'

(a) *'All monies' clause* - the mortgage covers all liabilities of the mortgagor to the bank existing at any time and on any account. This includes interest due and any expenses incurred by the bank in enforcing its security.

(b) *Repayable on demand* - the mortgagor undertakes to repay *on demand* what he owes at any time. Without this clause his liability to repay would begin at the time when the mortgage is created. The bank's right to sue for the debt would then become statute-barred after twelve years (as it is a debt based on a deed) under the Limitation Act 1980. By making the debt repayable on demand the limitation period does not begin to run until payment is actually demanded. This is the main point of difference between a bank and a building society mortgage. The latter is usually stated to be for a fixed term, with the mortgagor covenanting to repay by fixed instalments. Since it is not repayable on demand, a building society mortgage may only be exercised as security when the customer defaults in making payment.

(c) *Continuing security* - the mortgage secures whatever the borrower owes to the bank at any time and not just the original loan. Without this clause, the bank would be prejudiced by the effect of the rule in *Clayton's* case (payments into a running account are repayment of the earliest outstanding debits). Hence the amount which the customer owes when he gives the mortgage would be gradually repaid by sums credited even if subsequent drawings maintain the balance owing at the same or a higher level. A continuing security clause makes the mortgage into security for sums borrowed *after* the mortgage is created (as well as sums borrowed previous to it while outstanding). But additional action must be taken if the bank is informed of a later mortgage (described in Section 9 of this chapter).

(d) *Covenants to maintain the value of the property* - the mortgagor covenants:

   (i)   to keep the buildings on the land in good repair;
   (ii)  to keep the buildings insured against fire and other damage and to apply any insurance moneys received in making good the damage (or repaying the loan);
   (iii) to observe the provisions of his lease if the mortgaged property is leasehold - otherwise the lessor could terminate the lease by forfeiture.

(e) *Exclusion of certain provisions of the LPA 1925* to improve the position of the bank (see below).

*Statutory power of sale: ss 101-103 LPA*

3.8 Every mortgage made by deed gives to the mortgagee a statutory power to sell or appoint a receiver: s 101. But, unless modified by agreement, the mortgagee's statutory powers become exercisable only if:

(a) demand for repayment has been properly made and three months have elapsed without compliance by the borrower; or

(b) some interest on the loan remains unpaid for at least two months after the due date; or

(c) the mortgagor has broken some other term of the mortgage (s 103).

3.9 Defaults (a) or (b) are the most likely events: each imposes an unacceptable period of delay between default and action to enforce the security. Bank mortgages (and most other standard forms used by lenders) therefore exclude the statutory conditions and authorise sale or appointment of a receiver immediately *on default* (or after a much shorter period, say one month after demand for payment). A mortgagor has the right to apply to the court to suspend the mortgagee's right to take possession of the mortgaged property (with a view to sale). This may not apply where the loan is repayable on demand, though it does exist if the mortgage loan is repayable by instalments (as provided by a building society or bank long-term loan). This point has a bearing on a bank loan given for a different purpose but secured by a mortgage on the customer's house and repayable on demand.

### Consolidation: s 93 LPA

3.10 The bank may have made more than one loan to the same borrower on the security of mortgages over different properties. Under general mortgage law (s 93) the mortgagor could exercise his right to redeem selectively and in doing so repay the loans where his equity of redemption is most valuable. But the bank form of mortgage (like most standard forms of mortgage) entitles the bank to 'consolidate' its mortgages (created by the same mortgagor) so that if he wishes to redeem one he must redeem all. This is done by a clause which provides that s 93 shall not apply.

### Leasing: s 99 LPA

3.11 The mortgagor remains the legal owner of the mortgaged property and normally remains in possession with the right to give possession to someone else by the grant of a lease. This right is regulated by statute (s 99) so as to limit the duration of such leases to a maximum of 50 years (or 999 years for a building lease). But it could be prejudicial to the bank, if it enforced its security, to be bound by the rights of a tenant under a lease granted by the mortgagor for a long period of years. A landlord's reversion, although it yields income (rent) is less marketable and therefore less valuable than an unencumbered right of an owner to possession. Hence the bank form of mortgage prohibits the mortgagor from granting (or accepting surrender of) leases without the bank's consent. But it is not possible to deprive a mortgagor of his statutory power to grant a lease of agricultural land under s 2 Agricultural Holdings Act 1948.

## 4. THE FORM OF AN EQUITABLE MORTGAGE

4.1 In some circumstances it is not possible, or not convenient, to complete the formalities of a legal mortgage. The alternative is an equitable or informal mortgage, which may be created in any of the following ways.

(a) *Agreement* – a borrower may agree with a lender that in consideration of the loan the borrower will execute a legal mortgage if ever requested to do so. Such an agreement is now unlikely to be actionable since the 1989 Act requires the creation of a charge to be in writing, signed by both parties, before it is actionable.

(b) *Deposit of title deeds or land certificate* – there is a mortgage if the person who makes the deposit intends to hand over his document to the lender *as security*. But if the deposit is merely for safekeeping it does not create a mortgage. To remove any doubt the mortgagee usually insists on obtaining from the mortgagor a written *Memorandum of Deposit* which the latter signs (or sometimes executes as a deed) to express the intention and terms of the arrangement. This method may of course be combined with (a) by including in the memorandum an undertaking to create a legal mortgage. The memorandum is merely evidence of intention. Even if nothing is put in writing a mortgage by deposit is created when the intention to do so is clear, but it is not actionable unless it is in writing and signed by both parties.

(c) *Equitable charge* - the mortgagor states in writing that, in consideration of the loan, specified property which he owns is to be security for the loan. If the bank needs to enforce the security, it must apply to the court for an order to sell.

4.2 When a bank takes an equitable mortgage, it usually requires a customer to sign its standard Memorandum of Deposit including an undertaking to execute a legal mortgage if called on to do so. At the same time the bank obtains possession (if it does not already have it) of the title deeds etc. We shall come back to this procedure in more detail later in this chapter.

4.3 Taking a written Memorandum of Deposit is particularly important in the light of s 2 of the Law of Property (Miscellaneous Provisions) Act 1989 which provides that no action may be brought on a contract of disposition of land (including equitable and legal mortgages) unless it is made in writing and signed by the person charged *and* by the bank. Merely taking deposit of the deeds therefore may create a mortgage but this mortgage will not be actionable.

## Bank forms of equitable mortgage

4.4 Bank forms of Memorandum of Deposit contain the same standard clauses as the forms of legal mortgage (see paragraph 3.7 above) except that there is no express power of sale or for appointment of a receiver (for which a mortgage by deed is required). Instead there is an undertaking by the mortgagor (on request by the bank) to execute a legal mortgage.

4.5 Sometimes, however, the bank Memorandum of Deposit is in the form of a deed. As a deed it can include an irrevocable power of attorney giving the bank power to sell or appoint a receiver: s 101. Alternatively the deed can declare that the mortgagee is trustee of the land (with power for the bank as mortgagee to appoint itself as trustee - to exercise a trustee's power of sale).

---

## Exercise 2

Which provides better security to the mortgagee, a legal mortgage or an equitable mortgage? Give reasons for your answer.

**Solution**

A legal mortgage is a better security than an equitable mortgage for two reasons.

(a) It gives *greater security* - the mortgagee acquires a legal interest in the mortgaged land. That interest is valid against anyone to whom the borrower may sell or mortgage the land (provided that a legal mortgage not protected by deposit of title deeds is registered).

(b) It provides *better remedies* - the legal interest of the mortgagee in the land gives him better remedies, in particular a power of sale.

Note however that a legal mortgage does not take priority over an existing equitable mortgage if, at the time when the legal mortgage is created, the legal mortgagee has notice of the existence of an equitable mortgage.

An equitable mortgage is less safe and less easy to enforce. But an equitable mortgagee can usually sell the property with the sanction of a court order. An equitable mortgage is more convenient if the borrower requires only a short-term loan such as a 'bridging loan' to pay the price of a new house pending the sale soon afterwards of the borrower's old house. It is also less expensive in fees than a formal legal mortgage.

## 5. MORTGAGES OF UNREGISTERED LAND

5.1 The owner of unregistered land which is unencumbered by any mortgage has possession of the title deeds. This is one of the normal rights of ownership.

5.2 If the owner creates a mortgage over his land the mortgagee requires him to hand over the title deeds which the mortgagee retains until the mortgage debt is discharged. The mortgagee obtains the title deeds to prevent the mortgagor from selling the land (for which the vendor must produce the deeds) or from creating another mortgage without giving notice of his mortgage (since the other mortgagee would demand the deeds).

5.3 If it is a legal mortgage then the mortgagor must execute a deed.

5.4 Since the owner of land subject to a mortgage is unable to produce his deeds, the fact that he does not have them operates as notice to any purchaser from him (or another mortgagee) that there is an existing mortgage. But if the owner is left in possession of his title deeds by a mortgagee, then the mortgagee has failed to give notice of his mortgage by the best available means and may on that account be held (it is not however an automatic result) to have misled others about the existence of his mortgage. He is then ranked in priority behind a purchaser for value.

5.5 If a mortgagee has possession of the title deeds it is not required to register its mortgage (to give notice of it) because it effactually gives notice by taking possession of the deeds.

5.6 These general principles are applied and extended as follows.

(a) An *equitable mortgage* can be created merely by obtaining possession of the deeds without the formalities of a legal mortgage, but it will not be actionable unless it is in writing and signed by both parties.

(b) A *first mortgagee* in possession of title deeds should take precautions if he is asked to release them.

(c) An *intending purchaser or mortgagee* should always enquire at the outset whether the owner has possession of the deeds. If the enquiry is not made (and followed by delivery of the deeds on completion of the sale or mortgage) the purchaser or mortgagee is deemed to have notice of an existing mortgage and is bound by it.

(d) A *second mortgagee* cannot protect his mortgage by obtaining possession of the title deeds. He is therefore required to register his mortgage in order to give notice of it by registration at the Land Charges Registry as Land Charge Class C. A legal second mortgage is registered as a *puisne* mortgage (since it is not protected by deposit of title deeds) and an equitable second mortgage as a general equitable charge. Both are Land Charges Class C.

## 6. MORTGAGES OF REGISTERED LAND

6.1 The same general principles apply to the procedure for creating a *legal mortgage* of registered land. But the registration requirements are different because a registered title (Part C) itself records mortgages etc. Contrast this with a mortgage of unregistered land which is registered at a different registry (Land Charges Registry) in those cases where registration is a necessary safeguard.

6.2 The mortgagee (when it is a first mortgage) obtains possession of the mortgagor's Land Certificate and sends it with the executed mortgage deed to the District Land Registry for registration as a 'charge' on the land. The particulars of the mortgage are entered in the Charges Register part of the registered title. The Registry then issues a *Charge Certificate* which comprises:

(a) the contents of the former Land Certificate now enclosed in a different cover which is plainly labelled 'Charge Certificate'; plus

(b) the new mortgage over the land.

6.3 By these means no one can be in doubt that he is dealing with a registered title which is subject to a registered charge. Unless it is registered in the Charges Register within two months it ceases to be a legal mortgage and become an equitable mortgage - the mortgagor has no legal right.

6.4 Registering a charge in this way:

(a) gives the transferee good title, free of minor interests (unless they are overriding);

(b) determines priority, normally in the order of entry in the register subject to other agreement and some statutory charges.

6.5 An *equitable mortgage* of registered land is usually a deposit with the mortgagee of the mortgagor's Land Certificate with or without a suitable Memorandum of Deposit. It is not actionable unless it is in writing and signed by both parties.

6.6 An equitable mortgage is a 'minor interest' in registered land, unless it is protected on the register within two months of creation. So too is a legal mortgage which is not properly registered on the Charges Register. Failure to register and/or protect means that a purchaser or mortgagee can acquire title free of minor interests. Refer back to Chapter 13 Section 8 to see how a minor interest in registered land can be protected.

6.7 It is usual but not essential in sending in a notice of deposit of the Land Certificate to return the Land Certificate to the Registry so that the same note of the deposit may be entered on the Land Certificate as is made in the title registered at the Land Registry.

6.8 When a bank takes a customer's Land Certificate as an equitable mortgage by deposit, it may require him at the same time to execute a legal mortgage. But the bank then gives notice to the District Land Registry merely of the deposit of the Land Certificate as described above. The legal mortgage is held back (to save registration fees) until it is needed (if ever that occurs). There is of course 14 days in which to send in the legal mortgage for registration under the caution procedure described above.

6.9 If there is delay in securing the Land Certificate (say because the title to the land has to be registered for the first time and no Land Certificate yet exists), a notice of intended deposit of a Land Certificate can be given.

6.10 A *second mortgage* of registered land cannot usually be protected by deposit of the Land Certificate since the Certificate will have been delivered to the first mortgagee. In that situation the second mortgagee delivers to the District Land Registry a 'caution' supported by a statutory declaration. This also serves to give the mortgagee the 14 day protective period described in Chapter 13.

## Overriding interests

6.11 A purchaser of registered land takes his title subject to overriding equitable interests, even though they have not been registered and/or he does not know of them. These may be:

(a)  rights of persons in occupation (*excluding* a spouse's statutory right of occupation);
(b)  rent leases of less than 21 years;
(c)  duties to repair (for example, sea walls); and
(d)  legal easements and *profits a prendre*.

The most common problem encountered by a bank in relation to overriding interest derives from (a) above. This is covered in Section 8 of this chapter.

## Exercise 3

Explain the steps which should be taken by a bank in addition to searching for changes at land registries if the prospective mortgagor is a company.

### Solution

Any type of mortgage created by a company must be registered at the Companies Registry within 21 days: Companies Act 1985 s 398. This gives rise to some duplicate registration but certain company charges over land are registered at the Companies Registry only - and so it is essential always to search at that registry if the prospective mortgagor is a company. Charges not registered at land registries and so only discoverable at the Companies Registry are:

(a) floating charges; and

(b) a charge on unregistered land created by a previous owner and taken over with the land when acquired by the company.

(Charges are discussed further in Chapter 15.)

---

## 7. SECOND MORTGAGES

7.1 As already explained, a mortgagor is free to create a second or later mortgage which (if the holder of the first mortgage has taken the normal steps to protect his interests) ranks after the first or prior mortgages. In effect the mortgagor uses his equity of redemption (of the first mortgage) as security for further borrowing. The procedure for registration of a second mortgage of *unregistered land* is covered at paragraph 5.6.

7.2 A second mortgage of *registered land* is registered at the Land Registry. The holder of a legal second mortgage obtains a Charge Certificate from the Registry (to show that his title is entered against the title in the Charges Register). An equitable second mortgagee lodges a 'caution' which is noted in the register.

7.3 There are disadvantages inherent in the position of second mortgages.

(a) The security may be *inadequate in value*. The first mortgage may sell at a time when the market value has fallen to less than the aggregate of the two mortgage loans.

(b) *No possession of title deeds* - but registration and notice to first mortgagee improve the second mortgagee's position.

(c) *Risk of tacking* by first mortgagee.

*Tacking*

7.4 To illustrate the effect of tacking, consider the following example of successive mortgage transactions by X (as mortgagor) over the same land.

| | |
|---|---|
| 1 July | X borrows £50,000 from Y on the security of a first mortgage on property valued at £80,000. |
| 1 August | X borrows £20,000 from Z on the security of a second mortgage to Z. |
| 1 September | X borrows an additional £10,000 from Y whose mortgage secures 'all moneys owing'. |
| 1 December | Y sells the mortgaged property (following default by X). It realises £60,000 as the market value has fallen sharply and this is a forced sale. |

7.5 The question is whether Y can retain the entire £60,000 since X owes him that amount or whether Y keeps only £50,000 and Z can recover £10,000 out of the £20,000 owed to him since the loan on second mortgage cam earlier (in time) than the second advance (of £10,000) by Y. A first mortgagor can 'tack' - treat a later advance as an addition to his previous loan - and (in the example) keep the entire £60,000 if any one of the following conditions are satisfied:

(a) if the second mortgagee (Z) agrees; or

(b) if the first mortgagee (Y) has *no notice* of the second mortgage (to Z) at the time when Y makes his further advance (of £10,000 in the example); or

(c) if the first mortgage *obliges* the mortgagee (Y) to make further advances up to an agreed limit: LPA s 94(1).

7.6 An intending second mortgagee therefore takes two precautions against tacking:

(a) before agreeing to lend on this security he finds out by enquiry from the first mortgagee whether he is obliged to make further advances (situation (c) above) and can tack them on to his original loan on that account; and

(b) he gives notice of his second mortgagee to the first mortgagee so as to preclude tacking by lack of notice.

7.7 Note that when the first mortgagee is a bank the 'continuing security' clause of its mortgage forms merely extends the mortgage as security for whatever further advances the bank may decide to make. It does not *oblige* the bank to make such advances and so does not permit them to be 'tacked' on.

### Position of first mortgagee when second mortgage is created

7.8 What then are the risks to a bank which holds a first mortgage as security for an overdraft on a customer's current account when it receives notice of a second mortgage?

(a) The customer's drawings after the creation of the second mortgage are new loans made subsequent to that mortgage; and

(b) the sums paid in to the credit of the account would, if the rule in *Clayton's* case applies, be repayment of the amount owing to the bank as advances made before the second mortgage is created.

## 8. TAKING A MORTGAGE

8.1 It is now necessary to bring together the general principles of mortgage law as they affect a bank which intends to take a mortgage as security for a loan or other indebtedness of a customer to the bank. Obviously the distinctions between legal and equitable mortgages, unregistered and registered land, and first and subsequent mortgages lead to differences of working procedure in particular transactions.

## 14: LAND AS SECURITY

### Valuation and title

8.2  With respect to undertaking a professional *valuation* of the land, note that:

(a)  it is not a legal requirement, but a matter of commercial prudence;

(b)  the value of a leasehold is affected by that facts that (i) it declines over a period of years as the lease runs out and (ii) there may be onerous obligations of repair in the lessee's covenants;

(c)  a valuation obtained by a customer means that the bank has no contractual relationship with the valuer. Hence if a bank suffers loss because of over-valuation, it can only sue in tort (under the *Hedley Byrne* principle) and not in contract.

8.3  If a bank is acquiring unregistered land, it will obtain a report on title through a solicitor, who searches the Land Charges Registry and local authority registers. With registered land, where the seller has a Land Certificate showing Absolute or Good Leasehold title, only local searches need be made. If it shows any other title then a full report would be obtained. The Land Certificate should be updated.

8.4  Obviously, where a bank is lending on a mortgage of property acquired by its customer, it may choose to depend on the customer's own searches and report.

### Rights of occupiers: mortgages of matrimonial homes

8.5  As the banks expand their house mortgage loan business they are increasingly concerned with mortgages of the matrimonial home of the borrower and his or her spouse. The law gives to a spouse (usually the wife) protection against sudden eviction from the home. But this protection can be a serious problem for a bank which wishes to enforce the mortgage by sale of the house with vacant possession. A bank as mortgagee has therefore to consider that there may be:

(a)  joint ownership of the home by both spouses;

(b)  a registered interest (a land charge Class F or a caution); and

(c)  the right of a person in occupation as an overriding interest under s 70(1)(g) Land Registration Act 1925.

Each situation is examined in turn below.

*Joint ownership by both spouses*

8.6  If a house is owned in the joint names of both spouses, the bank can see immediately from the title deeds that any mortgage must be executed by both spouses. But there can still be surprises.

*Case: First National Securities Ltd v Hegarty 1984*
Mr Hegarty signed a mortgage form over his matrimonial home which was registered in the joint names of him and his spouse. He then forged his wife's signature on the same form and as a witness for both signatures used the girlfriend he was currently living with.

*Held:* Mr Hegarty was liable for the mortgage but his wife was not. By signing the form he created a charge over his equitable interest, but not over his wife's. The plaintiffs obtained a valid charge on his interest.

8.7 An equitable mortgage by deposit of title deeds by one joint tenant without the other's assent does not bind the co-tenant, who is entitled to return of the deeds: *Thames Guaranty Ltd v Campbell 1984.* Thus the bank, when taking a mortgage by deposit of deeds, should always insist on a written acknowledgement from *all* joint tenants.

### Registering an interest

8.8 Under the Matrimonial Homes Act 1983 where one spouse owns, or has an interest (say as tenant) in the matrimonial home, the other spouse has a right of occupation (which can only be terminated by order of the court). This right of occupation is an equitable charge which prevails over the rights of a purchaser or mortgagee *only if* it has been protected by registration *before* the date of the purchase or mortgage as:

(a) a Land Charge Class F at the Land Charges Registry (if the house is unregistered land); and
(b) a caution (if the house is registered land).

*It is not, ipso facto, an overriding interest – it is a minor interest.*

8.9 The entries give a right of occupation whatever the wishes of the other spouse or the mortgagee.

8.10 When such a charge has been so registered the bank's routine searches before taking the mortgage will disclose the existence of this incumbrance. In such cases the bank can insist (as a condition of the loan) that the spouse so protected either waives his or her right altogether or undertakes (in writing) that it shall not be enforced (by remaining in occupation) against the bank as mortgagee if it wishes to sell the house. It should be added that in a stable marriage situation the wife does not usually think it necessary to protect herself by registration. If the bank takes a mortgage it is not prejudiced by the wife's *subsequent* registration of her rights. A husband has the same rights in respect of a house owned solely by the wife.

### Overriding interest of a person in occupation

8.11 The Land Registration Act 1925 s 70(1)(g) has, since 1980, caused the banks much anxiety. This section protects 'the rights of every person in actual occupation of the land or in receipt of the rents and profits thereof, save where enquiry is made of such person and the rights are not disclosed'. Effectively, actual occupation gives constructive notice of the occupier's beneficial interest.

8.12 Note that there must be *proprietory rights* as well as *actual occupation*. If a wife acquires an interest in the house by contributing to its cost, her occupation (jointly with her husband) operates as constructive notice of her interest – it is then an overriding interest.

*Cases: Williams & Glyn's Bank Ltd v Boland 1980*
Mrs Boland had contributed to the cost of her matrimonial home (which was registered (under registered title) in the name of her husband) by virtue of the fact that she worked and the previous home was in joint names. Mr Boland, without his wife's knowledge, had granted a mortgage to the bank. Mrs B had not sent a caution to the District Land Registry to protect her equitable (minor) interest in the house. In taking the mortgage the bank had made no enquiries and had no actual knowledge of the circumstances on which Mrs B's interest was founded. Was the bank bound by constructive notice of Mrs B's interest?

*Held:* Mrs B's interest could (as an equitable interest under a trust) be treated as a minor interest to be protected by notice on the register. But her actual occupation of the house was also a potentially overriding interest under s 70(1)(g) LRA 1925 which a purchaser could discover by inspection. The bank should have enquired whether the owner's wife was in occupation with him and if so whether she had any equitable interest arising from making a contribution to the purchase price. Although this decision related to registered land, by analogy it applies also to unregistered land.

8.13 This decision, together with that in *Williams and Glyn's Bank Ltd v Brown 1980*, has led to the banks instituting procedures whereby:

(a) properties are inspected for actual occupation of persons other than the mortgagor;

(b) the equitable interests of those persons are either postponed by means of a Deed of Postponement or themselves mortgaged to the bank; and

(c) the bank advises them to take independent legal advice.

8.14 The difficulty for banks arises out of the concept of notice, since such interests are by definition not registrable. A husband and wife occupying the home, whose bank accounts at the same bank show that both contributed to the property, does not necessarily mean that the bank has constructive notice of the wife's beneficial interest: *Caunce v Caunce 1969*. But if there are other people occupying (children or lodgers as in *Hodgson v Marks 1971*) then the bank ought to enquire.

*Case: Kings North Trust v Tizard 1986*
The matrimonial home was in the sole name of the husband, although the wife had contributed towards its purchase. The couple experienced marriage problems and the wife moved out, but visited the property daily to look after the children and stayed in the property when the husband was away. The husband applied for a loan through a broker and arranged for the valuer to visit the property at a time when the wife would not be there, having concealed all traces of her occupancy. The loan was subsequently granted, but repayments lapsed when the husband left the country.

*Held:* the bank had not made adequate enquiries (in particular because it had pre-arranged the time of the visit) and the wife's visits constituted occupation. The bank was not able to obtain possession.

8.15 But if the cohabitee as equitable owner assents to the legal owner's mortgage then this prevents him or her from getting priority over a legal mortgagee: *Bristol & West Building Society v Henning 1985*.

8.16 Similarly there may be *implied* consent to a second mortgage.

> *Case: Equity and Law Home Loans Ltd v Prestidge 1991*
> P and B paid £40,000 for a house in 1987. B contributed £10,000 and the balance was raised by P by means of a mortgage. (B remained off the title deeds, having taken legal advice concerning other financial problems which she had at the time.) In 1988 P remortgaged the property for £43,000, paying off the original loan and keeping the balance. B was unaware of this. The new mortgagees, the plaintiffs, were not told of B's interest in the property. They sought to enforce the charge when P defaulted.
>
> *Held:* B had consented to the creation of the second mortgage because she had intended there to be a mortgage over the property and had consented to this. However her consent was held to be limited to £30,000.

8.17 When a mortgage is taken over a home which is jointly owned by husband and wife, the bank should be careful not to exercise undue influence in securing the co-operation of the wife as joint mortgagor: *National Westminster Bank plc v Morgan 1985*.

8.18 The *Boland* principle in practical situations very much depends on the facts of each particular case.

(a) The equitable interest must not be too remote.

> *Case: Winkworth v Edward Baron Development Co Ltd 1986*
> Mr and Mrs W occupied a property bought by a company. They sold their other home and used the funds to pay off the mortgage; £8,600 remained in the company's name. The plaintiff took a mortgage over the house from the company; the charge was sealed by the company, Mr W added his own signature as director and forged his wife's as co-director. The company defaulted and the plaintiff sought a possession order.
>
> *Held:* by the House of Lords (overruling the Court of Appeal) that the payment of £8,600 by Mrs W to the company did not create an overriding equitable interest because the payment was too remote from the company's original purchase of the house.

(b) It is difficult to see that anything less than direct contribution to the purchase price will be sufficient to create the beneficial interest.

> *Case: Lloyds Bank Ltd v Rossett 1990*
> A property was purchased in the sole name of the husband. The wife did not live in the house but daily performed decorating work while builders did major renovations. Her husband, without her knowledge, executed a legal charge over the house.
>
> *Held:* for the purposes of s 70(1)(g) LRA her contribution to the work was not enough to create an equitable interest.

(c) The person claiming an overriding interest must be in *actual occupation* at the time of the transfer of land or creation of charge - that is, when the contracts are completed (at which time the mortgage money has normally already been advanced by the lender): *Abbey National Building Society v Cann 1990*.

*Case: Midland Bank Ltd v Dobson 1985*
The matrimonial home was purchased by Mr D and his mother, and registered in his name only. His wife, Mrs D, resided there and contributed to the general family budget from her earnings. Mr D mortgaged the house without her knowledge and the bank sought a possession order.

*Held:* Mrs D had not made sufficient contributions to assert that she had acquired an equitable interest in the house.

(d) A person who does not disclose his equitable interest when given the opportunity to do so is estopped from asserting that it takes priority.

*Case: Midland Bank Ltd v Farmpride Hatcheries Ltd & Willey 1980*
The defendant company owned a farm which it charged to the bank, who later sought a possession order. W, a director of the company and occupier of the manor house on the farm on a rent-free licence, claimed an equitable interest as occupier under the *Boland* principle, and also claimed that the bank had had constructive notice of the licence.

*Held:* W should have disclosed his interest as occupier during negotiations for the charge with the bank. His silence prevented his claim from succeeding.

8.19 Where property is held in joint names and each tenant is a trustee of the sale proceeds for the other, payment of loan monies to two of the trustees gives a good receipt to the lender and his rights overreach the interests of the joint tenants: *City of London Building Society v Flegg 1987*. The rights of a third person in occupation do not prevent the overreaching interest. The recourse of that third person is against the two joint tenants who give a receipt to the lender.

## 9. TAKING A MORTGAGE OF UNREGISTERED LAND

9.1 The bank's form of *legal mortgage of unregistered freehold land* should be executed as a deed by the owner(s). Remember that the signatories must be identified (if necessary) and it must be signed on behalf of the bank. If this is a first mortgage the title deeds, if not already in the possession of the bank, should be handed over with the completed mortgage deed (and also a fire insurance policy).

9.2 If the bank holds the title deeds to freehold land, the mortgage need not be registered at the Land Charges Registry, because if the mortgagor later attempts to sell or mortgage the property his inability to produce the title deeds will alert the purchaser to the need to make enquiries. For the same reason the bank should not (while the mortgage is outstanding) allow the deeds to pass out of its possession unless there are safeguards.

9.3 If the mortgagor is a company the mortgage must be registered at the Companies Registry within 21 days: Companies Act 1985 s 398. Otherwise it is void against other creditors of the company or its liquidator (though late registration by leave of the court may remedy the omission).

9.4 The procedure for taking an *equitable mortgage of unregistered land* by deposit of title deeds (to freehold or leasehold land) has already been described, in particular the need for it to be in writing and signed by both parties in order to be actionable. An equitable mortgage not protected by deposit of title deeds is registrable at the Land Charges Registry as a general equitable charge.

*Second mortgages*

9.5  If the bank takes a second or subsequent mortgage the preliminary procedure is different in some respects.

    (a)  Valuation relates to the gross value of the property less the amount outstanding on the prior mortgage(s).

    (b)  The title deeds will be in the possession of the first mortgagee. If that mortgagee is likely to have investigated the title thoroughly (a building society for example) the bank may decide to abbreviate or waive its own investigation. The first mortgagee has the same interest as the bank - that the mortgagor has good title.

    (c)  The bank makes enquiries of the first mortgagee (and any other prior mortgagee) about his prior mortgage, as to:

        (i)   the amount outstanding, the rate of repayment, whether there are any arrears etc;

        (ii)  is the prior mortgagee entitled to tack further advances or to consolidate other mortgages?

These enquiries are usually made by a standard questionnaire - try to find a copy of your bank's form for these purposes.

9.6  At completion the bank obtains the mortgage deed duly executed but not the title deeds. It should therefore protect its legal *puisne* mortgage (a Land Charge Class C) by registration at the Land Charges Registry; an equitable second mortgage should be registered as a general equitable charge. This is essential to give the bank priority for its charge over any subsequent charge created over the same property. The person who takes the subsequent charge either discovers the bank's charge by a search at the Registry or is deemed to have constructive notice if he makes no search.

9.7  The bank should also give written notice of its second charge to the first mortgagee and obtain his acknowledgement (by asking him to sign and return a duplicate copy of the bank's notice). There are two reasons for this:

    (a)  it may prevent tacking; and

    (b)  it ensures that if the first mortgage is repaid the first mortgagee must hand the title deeds to the bank as second mortgagee and not to the mortgagor.

9.8  Any prospective mortgagee of unregistered land may send a *priority notice* of his intention to register a charge. This should reach the Land Charges Registry at least 15 days before the charge is registered. If the charge is registered within 30 days of the notice it takes effect (giving priority over other charges) as if registered on the actual date when the charge is executed. Banks seldom follow this procedure, however, since an official search certificate is usually an adequate safeguard. In making its own search the bank may of course obtain notice that another prospective mortgagee has protected himself by giving a priority notice.

9.9 An *insurance policy* (on land or buildings) is often required. This is usually a contract between the insurers and the owner of the property. The bank as mortgagee is not a party to the contract but can give notice to the insurers in advance of its prospective interest. But to avoid much paperwork the banks and insurance companies (the British Insurance Association) have agreed that notice need not be given of a mortgage of a private dwelling insured for £70,000 or less.

## 10. TAKING A MORTGAGE OF REGISTERED LAND

10.1 The essential difference when taking a *mortgage of registered land* is that the bank as mortgagee:

    (a) obtains information of the owner's title and of the interests (if any) of other persons in the land from the District Land Registry; and

    (b) protects its position as holder of a legal charge by registering it at the District Land Registry.

10.2 At completion of the mortgage, the bank obtains the mortgage executed as a deed by the mortgagor and (if it is a first mortgage) his Land Certificate. The mortgage should be signed by the bank as well. These documents (plus some Land Registry forms and a fee) are sent to the District Land Registry. In addition to the original mortgage (which is bound into the Charge Certificate and returned) the bank supplies a copy of the completed mortgage which the registry retains (so that it is on record and available in case of a search by another person later).

10.3 If the mortgagor is a company, the original mortgage is sent to the Companies Registry first so that it may be registered there within the 21 day period. The certificate issued by the Registrar of Companies is sent, with the original mortgage, to the Land Registry, which returns it with its own Charge Certificate.

10.4 The charge when registered at the District Land Registry takes priority over all other legal or equitable charges which may be registered later. There is no material difference in the procedure between registration of a first charge over freehold and over leasehold land. The differences lie in the preliminary steps.

10.5 Taking and registering a *second mortgage* differs mainly in the fact that the bank will never see or have possession of the Land Certificate. But the bank may (and this is a routine procedure) apply to the District Land Registry for an 'office copy' of the mortgagor's registered title. This is in effect a duplicate copy of the Land Certificate and is sent back with the second mortgage to the registry when that is registered (as a charge on the Charges Register when the second mortgage is legal; where it is equitable it is noted as a caution).

10.6 As with a second mortgage of unregistered land, the bank gives notice of its charge to the first mortgagee. It is only possible to register a second mortgage if the first mortgage has also been registered and a Charge Certificate issued in respect of it.

*Company debentures and registered land*

10.7 If a company gives a secured debenture to the bank, the debenture usually requires the company to deposit with the bank any Land Certificate(s) of registered land which is now charged to the bank by the debenture. The bank then gives notice of deposit of the Land Certificate.

10.8 However, if the bank requires a registered *land* charge it must ensure that the debenture specifies the property charged (including the registered title number(s) at the Land Registry). This is because the Land Registry cannot trace the property subject to a mortgage without these particulars. The bank then registers its mortgage (the debenture) as a charge and obtains a Charge Certificate in the usual way.

10.9 A floating charge over company land cannot be registered at the District Land Registry since it does not specify the land charged. But it can be protected by notice of deposit of the Land Certificate.

## 11. DISCHARGE OF A MORTGAGE

11.1 Any mortgage may be discharged in the following ways.

    (a) *By redemption* - the mortgagor or any other person who has an interest in the property may redeem it. A bank mortgage is repayable on demand, or at the mortgagor's option. This right of redemption (or 'equity') is only lost if:

        (i)    the mortgagor releases it to the mortgagee (see below);
        (ii)   the mortgagor defaults and the mortgagee sells or agrees to sell;
        (iii)  the mortgagee forecloses; or
        (iv)  the mortgagee takes and retains possession for 12 years.

    Anything restricting the right of redemption is normally unenforceable, though companies may have irredeemable debentures and there are certain other limited restrictions.

    (b) *By release* - for example, House B may substitute for House A, in which case the mortgage on House A is released. The reducing balance of the debt may permit some of the property to be released as security.

    (c) *By lapse of time* - if the mortgagee does not act to enforce the mortgage or receive the loan for 12 years, it is discharged.

**Unregistered land**

11.2 If the mortgage discharged was a first legal mortgage supported by a deposit of title deeds with the bank, the bank returns the receipted mortgage together with the title deeds to the mortgagor. In any subsequent transaction he includes the mortgage in the particulars of his abstract of title but he only has to produce the receipted mortgage as evidence that the mortgage has terminated. It will not have been registered since the bank held the title deeds.

11.3 In the case of a second mortgage not protected by possession of the title deeds or an equitable mortgage (without deposit of title deeds), the bank will have registered the mortgage at the Land Charges Registry as a *puisne* mortgage or a general equitable charge. The registered charge is cleared from the register by sending a form (signed by an authorised officer of the bank) to notify the registry of the discharge. Otherwise the procedure is as described for a first legal mortgage.

11.4 It has so far been assumed that the bank receives payment from the mortgagor and has no actual notice of any mortgage ranking after its own. But if that is not the case:

(a) receipt of repayment from a third party operates to transfer the mortgage to him. The deeds are therefore handed to him;

(b) the bank has no obligation (as it has if it sells the land) to make a search at the Land Charges Registry for subsequent mortgages. But if it knows of one (the second mortgagee will probably have given notice previously) the bank must hand over the deeds to the second mortgagee since he now moves to the advantageous position of first mortgagee.

### Registered land

11.5 On discharge of a mortgage of registered land, the bank as mortgagee sends to the District Land Registry (i) its Charge Certificate and (ii) a form (Form 53) duly signed giving notice of discharge. The Land Registry notes the discharge in Part C of the registered title, transfers the contents of the Charge Certificate (less the mortgage) to the Land Certificate cover and sends the Land Certificate and mortgage to the bank for disposal to the person entitled. For a second mortgage, written confirmation of the charge's deletion suffices.

11.6 The same procedure applies to discharge of an equitable mortgage. If that mortgage has been entered on the Land Certificate, the certificate must be returned for deletion of the entry.

## 12. REMEDIES OF A LEGAL MORTGAGEE

12.1 While a mortgage is still in force, the legal mortgagee has the following rights over the property.

(a) *Documents of title* - the first mortgagee of unregistered land is entitled to hold these; with registered land he will have a Charge Certificate.

(b) *Possession* - this is immediate on the mortgage's creation - there need not be default. It is a risky right and seldom used.

(c) *Grant/surrender leases of less than 50 years* - only if there is possession.

(d) *Tacking*.

(e) *Protection of property* - the mortgagee is impliedly or expressly allowed to restrain deliberate damage, insure against fire and perform necessary repairs.

(f) *Additional property* - such as added fixtures (for instance, a patio), a new lease or a freehold reversion on a leasehold, are included in the original mortgage.

12.2 If the mortgagor defaults, the legal mortgagee has five remedies and may pursue any of them at the same time or in sequence (but not so as to recover more than the full debt).

(a) *Action for debt*. This is an action against the debtor *personally* to enforce his obligation to pay. On obtaining judgment for his debt the creditor may enforce it by seizure of the debtor's property or by obtaining a court charging order on it. He may also go on to petition for bankruptcy of an individual debtor or compulsory winding up of a company. This remedy is available to unsecured as well as secured creditors. It has nothing to do with mortgage law.

(b) *Sale* of the mortgaged property (see paragraph 12.3).

(c) Appointment of a *receiver* (see paragraph 12.14).

(d) *Foreclosure* - transfer of the mortgaged property by court order into the outright ownership of the mortgagee. Many conditions impede and restrict foreclosure. It is rarely used.

(e) *Taking possession* of the property. This is risky to the mortgagee. If he fails to obtain the maximum income from the property while in his possession he must account for the deficit. Again mortgagees rarely resort to this remedy.

*Case: White v City of London Brewery Co 1889*
The brewery took possession of the plaintiff's public house and let it to a tenant as a 'tied house' (the tenant had to buy his beer from the brewery). If let as a 'free house' the rent would have been higher.

*Held:* the brewery were accountable to the plaintiff for the loss of rent resulting from its method of letting the property.

## Sale of the property

12.3 Any mortgage made by deed, whether legal or equitable, confers on the mortgagee a power to sell and in doing so to transfer to the purchaser the entire estate and interest in the property of the mortgagor, free of the mortgage and any mortgages subsequent to it (but not free of mortgages (if any) which rank ahead of the mortgage under which the sale is made): s 101.

12.4 A bank can only sell if the power has arisen by reason of the mortgage debt becoming due for payment. It has been explained earlier that a bank's standard form of mortgage gives to the bank as mortgagee the right to sell (following default by the mortgagor) with the minimum of delay. Sale is the usual remedy if the mortgaged property can be sold without difficulty or delay.

12.5 A court order for possession may be required if: *(county court)*

(a) the loan is a regulated agreement under the Consumer Credit Act 1974; or

(b) there are people resident in the property or the mortgagor's chattels remain there. An eviction order may even be required.

12.6 The court may postpone the making of a possession order in the case of a private home if it is satisfied that the mortgagor has a reasonable prospect of repaying the loan.

12.7 It will be difficult to obtain a court order if the house was occupied by a tenant (still resident there) *at the time* the mortgage was created, since the mortgage is subject to his prior rights: *Universal Permanent Building Society v Cooke 1951*. But if the tenancy was created *after* the mortgage, without the bank's knowledge or consent, the tenancy is void against the bank and a court order may be obtained: *Dudley and District Benefit Building Society v Emerson 1949*.

12.8 In selling, the bank contracts as mortgagee with the purchaser and at completion delivers a transfer or conveyance executed by the bank as mortgagee exercising the statutory power of sale. As soon as the mortgagee has entered into a binding contract to sell, the mortgagor can no longer prevent the sale by repaying the loan.

12.9 In arranging to sell the mortgaged property the mortgagee must:

(a) act in good faith (for instance he cannot buy the property himself);

(b) use reasonable care to realise the true value of the property - a professional valuation should be carried out by a chartered surveyor to ascertain the market value of the property.

*Case: Cuckmere Brick Co Ltd v Mutual Finance Ltd 1971*
The mortgagee advertised the mortgaged property for sale but gave incomplete information of the available planning permission for erecting buildings on the land. The sale did not realise the full amount of the loan.

*Held:* the mortgagee had been negligent. Its claim to recover the balance of the loan failed because it had not obtained the full value of the mortgaged property.

12.10 Note that the test is only one of reasonable care. A mortgagee who sells at a time when property values are low is not at fault merely because by delaying the sale he might have obtained a higher price. It has been said (in the *Cuckmere* case above) that in selling, a mortgagee is not subject to the stringent standards imposed on a trustee. It suffices if he acts honestly and reasonably. To minimise any risk of liability a mortgagee may take such steps as:

(a) enquiring of a subsequent mortgagee whether he is willing to take a transfer of the mortgage by repayment;

(b) obtaining professional advice from a surveyor and estate agent;

(c) offering the property for sale by auction (but the advertised particulars should be drafted with care - see the *Cuckmere* case above).

12.11 On receipt of the proceeds of sale the mortgagee has a duty to apply the money as follows:

(a) to meet the costs of the sale; then
(b) to discharge the mortgage debt and interest; then
(c) to pay the residue to the person entitled.

12.12  If there are no subsequent mortgages, the mortgagee accounts for the surplus proceeds (if any) to the mortgagor. But the mortgagee must (on a sale of *unregistered land*) make a 'surplus proceeds search' at the Land Charges Registry before paying the surplus to the mortgagor. If the search discloses a subsequent mortgage, the money must be paid to the holder of that mortgage as the person entitled. The second mortgagee then repays himself and accounts to the mortgagor (unless there is yet another mortgage disclosed by his search). In the ordinary course of events a second or subsequent mortgage will already have given notice to a prior mortgagee. But a mortgagee who sells cannot rely on the lack of such notice; he *must* make a search to put the matter beyond doubt. A mortgagee who sells registered land need not make a surplus proceeds search since the District Land Registry gives him notice of the registration of any subsequent charge on the land when it occurs.

### Appointment of a receiver

12.13  A mortgagee may, as an alternative to exercising his statutory power of sale, appoint a receiver.

12.14  The appointment of a receiver is a standard and appropriate procedure to enforce a company floating charge over its undertaking. Banks do not usually appoint a receiver to enforce a mortgage of land. But it could happen if the mortgaged land produces income (such as a block of flats) or the mortgagor is a company which has given its bank a fixed charge on its land as well as a floating charge on its assets generally. If the mortgagor is a company, the bank in appointing a receiver must within 7 days give notice of the appointment to the Companies Registry.

12.15  The receiver must be appointed in writing. He applies the income from the property as follows:

(a)  in payment of outgoings such as rates and taxes; then

(b)  in payment of interest on prior charges (if any); then

(c)  in payment of insurance premiums (if required by the mortgage or by law) and his own commission; then

(d)  in payment of the interest on the mortgage; then

(e)  in repayment of the mortgage debt if the mortgagee so directs (as in practice a bank always does); and

(f)  the residue goes to the persons entitled to the property.

## 13.  REMEDIES OF AN EQUITABLE MORTGAGEE

13.1  An equitable mortgagee has rights against the mortgagor if he defaults (it can sue for debt), but he has no legal interest in the land to enable him to sell it as mortgagee.

13.2  An equitable mortgagee can get round this difficulty if he takes his mortgage in the form of a deed (s 101) or if he obtains from the mortgagor:

    (a)  an irrevocable power of attorney which authorises him to sell the land as agent of the mortgagor; or

    (b)  a declaration of trust.

13.3  If these devices are used, the bank sells as agent or as trustee and is not impeded by its lack (as equitable mortgagee) of power to sell arising from the mortgage.

13.4  However, if the equitable mortgage is not in the form of a deed (with the elements mentioned above) the equitable mortgagee may:

    (a)  require the mortgagor to execute a legal mortgage if he has previously undertaken to do so; or

    (b)  apply to the court for an order for sale.

But remember that no charge is actionable unless it was made in writing and signed by both parties.

13.5  An equitable mortgagee can only appoint a receiver if:

    (a)  the mortgage is by deed (so that s 101 – right of sale – applies); or
    (b)  the mortgage expressly confers a power to appoint a receiver.

---

## Exercise 4

Although land is very frequently taken as security for loans, it may not in all circumstances be the best form for a bank. What are the advantages and disadvantages of land as security?

**Solution**

Land has the following *advantages* as security.

    (a)  Land normally appreciates in value, although this may be a long-term phenomenon – certainly in the past five years land has decreased in value generally.

    (b)  A mortgage over land is normally the safest form of security a bank can obtain in that land never completely loses it value.

    (c)  Valuation of domestic properties is relatively simple compared with, say, valuation of private company shares.

Land also has *disadvantages* as security.

    (a)  Factories, shops and offices are difficult to value accurately for security purposes.

    (b)  Land is not a readily realisable security. Completion and realisation of land can be costly.

(c) The effect of various planning requirements may reduce desirability of property, eg road widening, etc.

(d) Any tenancy created by the mortgagor may mean that property is only attractive to investors as vacant possession cannot be given.

(e) With an equitable mortgage, unless under seal, the bank would have to approach the court before realisation could take place.

(f) The bank has to obtain a court order for possession unless the mortgagor will voluntarily vacate property. This procedure may result in damaging bad publicity.

---

## 14. CONCLUSION

14.1 The best and most practical way of mastering this mass of detail is to visualise the sequences of matters with which you would be dealing if you were handling a mortgage transaction on behalf of your bank.

(a) *What kind of property* (registered or unregistered land, freehold or leasehold, legal or equitable estate or interest) is offered as security?

(b) *What type of mortgage*, legal or equitable, is appropriate? If the security is a legal estate, a legal mortgage is usually preferable. But for a short-term transaction or equitable property as security, an equitable mortgage may be the only practicable type which can be used.

(c) Is it to be a *first or subsequent mortgage* over the same property? For a second or subsequent mortgage special safeguards are applied.

(d) How does the *bank's appropriate type of mortgage form* meet the requirements of the case?

(e) What is the *current procedure* for obtaining that type of mortgage over that type of property so that the bank obtains a satisfactory and marketable security? What about other occupiers?

(f) What *follow-up action* should be taken after the mortgage transaction has been completed, to protect the position of the bank? Some steps are standard; some apply only to particular situations. What is appropriate in this case?

(g) On *repayment* of the mortgage loan by the borrower, what action does the bank take? Has it any obligations to anyone other than the customer who has repaid the loan?

(h) If there is *default* by the borrower, what steps can the bank take to enforce the security and recover its money? Much depends on the type of mortgage. Must the bank consider the rights of third parties?

## TEST YOUR KNOWLEDGE

*The numbers in brackets refer to paragraphs of this chapter*

1   What is the equity of redemption? (2.3)

2   What is a legal mortgage by charge? (3.3)

3   What is found in the standard forms of legal mortgage used by banks? (3.7)

4   How may an equitable mortgage be created? (4.1)

5   Why should a first mortgagee insist on holding the title deeds? (5.1, 5.2)

6   What is the procedure for obtaining and protecting a mortgage of registered land? (6.2 - 6.4)

7   What is meant by 'tacking' and when is it possible? (7.4)

8   How may a husband or wife have rights of occupation of the matrimonial home? (8.6 - 8.13)

9   What is the procedure on taking a second mortgage of unregistered land? (9.5)

10  What notices should the bank give on taking a second mortgage of unregistered land? (9.8)

11  How is a mortgage of registered land entered on the land register and what other action is taken? (10.1 - 10.3)

12  What additional procedure applies when a company mortgages registered land? (10.7 - 10.9)

13  How are mortgages of unregistered and registered land discharged? (11.1)

14  What remedies are available to a legal mortgagee? (12.1)

15  What are the rules which determine how and when a mortgagee may sell mortgaged property? (12.3 - 12.12)

16  How must a receiver apply income from property? (12.15)

*Now try questions 22 to 24 at the end of the text*

*Chapter 15*

# OTHER FORMS OF SECURITY

> This chapter covers the following topics.
>
> 1. Lien
> 2. Pledge
> 3. Guarantees
> 4. Representations by the bank when taking a guarantee
> 5. Stocks and shares
> 6. Life assurance policies
> 7. Debentures given by companies

## 1. LIEN

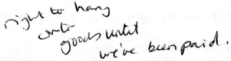

*right to hang onto goods until we've been paid.*

1.1 Any *possessory lien* is the right to retain property belonging to another person until a debt due from the owner of the property to the possessor of the property (the holder of the lien) is paid. By this, the actual ownership of the property is left undisturbed, but the lender has possession. Generally, the lender has no right to sell the property - the lien only has a 'nuisance' value.

1.2 A possessory lien can either be *particular* or *general*. For example, take the case of a warehouse keeper with a number of articles in store for the same customer, for which the customer pays individual storage charges to the warehouse keeper. If, by the terms of his contract, the warehouse keeper must release each item as the storage charge is paid, then the warehouse keeper cannot have a lien over articles which may remain in the warehouse on which the storage charge has been paid, only over the items on which the storage charge has not been paid. On these items he will have a *particular* lien. If he had a *general* lien, he could retain *all* the items in his warehouse until all the storage charge was paid.

1.3 This distinction could be important to a bank if it has taken a charge over a customer's goods which are in the warehouse.

### Banker's lien

1.4 However, the most important lien for bankers is, not surprisingly, a *banker's lien*, which is a general lien over such of a customer's property as comes into the hands of the bank in the normal course of business.

# 15: OTHER FORMS OF SECURITY

1.5 A banker's lien is an exceptional lien in that it gives to the bank the *right of sale* of the item involved after reasonable notice to a customer. Of course, the lien only exists if the customer owes the bank money.

*Case: Brandao v Barnett 1846*
The plaintiff, a Portuguese merchant, had a London agent who used to buy exchequer bills for his principal, collect the interest for him and exchange the bills at the proper times. The agent kept his account with Barnett, the defendant banker, and used it to lodge at the bank a box containing the bills and other bills. The box was kept locked. However, the agent became bankrupt and Barnett claimed a lien on the exchequer bills in his possession. The plaintiff sued Barnett for return of the bills.

*Held:* there was an implied agreement that the bills be kept for safe-keeping which was inconsistent with lien. The banker had to surrender the bills.

1.6 Both the property itself and the reasons why it was handed to the banker are critical factors in establishing whether a banker's lien exists. The usual items over which a banker has a lien are negotiable securities, such as bills of exchange, or cheques paid in for collection. But if a security has been realised in the form of cash, the bank is then owner of the funds and so cannot have a lien over its own property. Its right then is to appropriate those funds to a particular debt.

1.7 However, where property is handed to the bank for a particular purpose, *the banker does not have a lien*. So if a customer hands to his banker shares to be sold through a broker, the banker will not have a lien, nor will he have a lien over property placed into his hands for safe custody. Similarly, property belonging to a third party cannot be subject to a lien.

1.8 A bank which successfully claims that it has a lien is deemed to have given value (Bills of Exchange Act 1882 s 27(3)) and it is therefore a holder in due course (a term explained in Part E of this text) and can recover from any party to the cheque, provided it has retained possession of the cheque.

1.9 The right of lien of banks has been looked upon favourably in recent years and may be upheld in two situations:

(a) where an account is overdrawn when a cheque is paid into the bank, the bank may be deemed to have a lien for the amount of the cheque or the overdraft, whichever is the lower (provided there is no agreement to the contrary); or

(b) where an account has insufficient or no funds or is overdrawn when a cheque is collected and then returned unpaid, the bank may be deemed to have a lien for any part of the amount of the cheque which cannot be debited to the customer's account.

*Case: Re Keever 1966*
Mrs Keever, a customer of Midland Bank, was made bankrupt on 30 November 1962. A cheque for £3,000 was paid into her account on 15 November. The trustee in bankruptcy contended that Midland Bank should not apply the money in reduction of Mrs Keever's overdraft of £1,350.

*Held:* Midland Bank had a lien on the cheque as it had given value and was unaware of her impending bankruptcy. It was a holder in due course until such time as the cheque was cleared.

1.10 A lien letter is sometimes signed by a customer where a credit balance on one account is regarded as security for a debit balance on another account. The lien letter usually forms an agreement that the credit balances will not be reduced below a certain figure and that the bank can combine the accounts without notice. This letter enables the bank to dispose of the requirement of notifying the customer.

1.11 There are certain problems with the banker's lien.

(a) The bank has a duty to its customer to present a cheque for collection within a reasonable time, meaning that a lien could not be held for very long. The bank's right of appropriation of the cheque's proceeds is actually more important than the lien, but conversely this could not arise if the bank was not a holder in due course and so holder of a lien.

(b) If the customer exercises his right to appropriate the proceeds to whatever items he sees fit, the bank loses its lien – since it arises by operation of law and is confounded by contrary agreement.

(c) If a cheque paid in for collection is dishonoured, the banker destroys his lien if he returns the cheque to the customer. When the customer returns it to the bank so it can sue for payment, this is not the ordinary business of banking and the bank is not holder in due course. Hence no lien arises: *Westminster Bank Ltd v Zang 1966*.

## 2. PLEDGE

2.1 A pledge is a deposit with the bank, as security for an advance, of goods or documents of title to them, or of negotiable instruments. The borrower retains ownership of the items but the bank has possession. The bank will ask the customer to execute a letter of pledge in respect of each transaction or may ask for a general letter of pledge covering a number of transactions. It is thus an express agreement between pledgor and bank; a pledge cannot arise automatically as can a banker's lien.

## 3. GUARANTEES

3.1 The concept of a guarantee is simple – it is a promise to discharge the debt of another person. But the legal rules on guarantees, mainly developed by case law, are technical and complicated. The purpose of these rules is mainly to protect the *guarantor* (also called the 'surety' if he gives some form of principal security such as a cash deposit) against the risk inherent in assuming liability for a transaction between two other persons (the *principal debtor* and the *creditor*) about which he may be inadequately informed and over which he has no control. A guarantee is therefore strictly interpreted to relate only to the exact terms of the guarantor's promise.

3.2 For a bank, a personal guarantee is a useful form of security since it gives the bank a possibility of recovering its debt from two persons instead of one. But a guarantee (unless the guarantor supports it by giving security over his property) is only as good as the financial resources of the guarantor. A guarantee given by a 'man of straw' is an illusion. Hence (unless the guarantor gives security) it is advisable to make enquiries about his financial position in taking the guarantee and at intervals while it is in force. Banks usually undertake status enquiries on the guarantor on an annual basis.

3.3 Obtaining a guarantee is usually simple compared with other forms of security. The banks use elaborate forms of guarantee which include a variety of clauses to ensure that the guarantee 'holds' despite changes in circumstances.

## What is a guarantee?

3.4 To constitute a guarantee there must be three persons and two liabilities (on two contracts). The three persons are the *principal debtor*, the *creditor* and the *guarantor* (or surety). The principal debtor has a debt or liability to the creditor. The secondary liability is that of the guarantor who undertakes to discharge the debt of the principal debtor to the creditor. To be enforceable the guarantee's terms must at least be evidenced in writing: Statute of Frauds Act 1677. This means it must be a written agreement signed by the guarantor, or a signed note or memorandum of terms if it was originally given orally.

## Guarantee and indemnity

3.5 It is important to distinguish a guarantee from an indemnity.

(a) In a *guarantee* there are two distinct contracts - the primary debt owed by the principal debtor alone and the guarantor's secondary undertaking to pay another person's debt.

(b) A person who gives an *indemnity* accepts a primary liability for the debt (or he undertakes to be responsible for making good any loss even though the debt may arise from a transaction in which he has no part). It is not always easy to distinguish guarantee and indemnity in practice. But if the person liable says 'I will pay' or 'I will see you paid' he is assuming a direct liability which is an indemnity and not a guarantee of another person's debt.

3.6 The distinction between guarantee and indemnity is important in two respects.

(a) A guarantee is unenforceable unless it is given in writing or, if given orally, unless it is supported by written evidence such as a letter of confirmation. This point is not of much practical importance to banks since it is their standard practice always to obtain a *written* guarantee. But if the promisor receives some sort of payment in return then it is likely that it will be construed as a guarantee.

(b) The effect of a guarantee is that the guarantor undertakes that the debtor (customer) will discharge his debt or other obligation to the creditor (bank). If the primary contract between debtor and creditor is void (for example, because there was a fundamental mistake as to the subject-matter of the contract) the guarantee also is void because the debtor has no enforceable obligation to perform.

*Case: Associated Japanese Bank (International) v Credit du Nord 1988*
A rogue, B, entered into a sale and leaseback agreement with the plaintiff to fund the purchase of four machines, identified by serial numbers. The defendant guaranteed the transaction as a leasing agreement. The plaintiff advanced £1m to B, who made one quarterly repayment before being arrested for fraud, and adjudged bankrupt. The machines did not exist, and so the plaintiff sued to enforce the guarantee. The defendant claimed the underlying contract was void for mistake because of the non-existence of the machines.

*Held:* the non-existence of the machines in the principal contract (the lease) on which the secondary contract (the guarantee) relied was so fundamental as to render the guarantee 'essentially different'. Hence there was a common mistake - the guarantee was void and could not be enforced.

3.7 An indemnity is a promise by the person who gives it that the creditor will not suffer loss. It is not dependent on the validity of the primary debt.

The practice of banks is to include in their form of guarantee an indemnity by the guarantor to safeguard the bank against loss if its claim against the customer is unenforceable.

### Consideration for a guarantee

3.8 Although consideration is required for a guarantee (unless it is in the form of a deed), the written guarantee need not specify what consideration has been given. In practice however the guarantee does specify the consideration.

3.9 Consideration for a guarantee must satisfy the normal rules of contract. An existing debt (past consideration) is not of itself consideration for a guarantee of that debt. But a further advance or even forbearing to demand repayment of an existing debt is sufficient consideration. In a doubtful case the bank can formally demand repayment; the guarantor then offers his guarantee if the bank will withdraw its demand. Alternatively the guarantee can be executed as a deed under seal so that consideration is not required.

3.10 Although it is not legally necessary to state the consideration, a bank form of guarantee always does specify it in general terms (such as 'making advances to the debtor or otherwise giving credit', or 'continuing the account'). Even though this is not normally consideration given to the guarantor, it does move from the creditor (the promisee) and so is good consideration for the guarantee. These general words are preferable to expressing the consideration as a loan of specific sum, as it is then necessary to show that the bank has lent that exact amount.

### Capacity to give a guarantee

3.11 Under the normal rules of the law of contract:

(a) the guarantee is void unless the guarantor has legal capacity to give the guarantee. This rule is important if a guarantee is obtained from a minor, a partnership or a registered company (although a guarantee of a minor's loan is enforceable against an adult guarantor); and

(b) a guarantee obtained by duress or undue influence is voidable. We have considered these areas of contract law in Chapter 6, and will relate them specifically to guarantees below.

### Joint and several guarantees

3.12 Two or more persons may guarantee the same debt. Two points then arise:

(a) each guarantor's liability is conditional on the other guarantor(s) acceptance of his share of the burden; and

(b) the effect of the guarantees depends on whether they are 'joint', 'several' or (as is usual) 'joint and several'.

3.13 A bank should not make an advance until all the proposed guarantors have signed.

*Case: National Provincial Bank of England Ltd v Brackenbury 1906*
Four persons agreed to give a single joint and several guarantee. Three signed and the bank made the advance in the expectation that the fourth would sign later. But he died before doing so.

*Held:* the three guarantors were discharged since their liability was conditional on that of the fourth and they had not consented to dispensing with it.

*Case: James Graham & Co (Timber) Ltd v Southgate-Sands 1985*
A joint guarantee was given by three people but when it came to be enforced it was found that one of the signatures had been forged. The plaintiff tried to enforce it against the other two signatories.

*Held:* it was part of the contract that all three parties should be liable on the guarantee; the fact that one was not meant that the other two also escaped liability.

3.14 The same result follows if A signs a separate guarantee under an agreement with B that B will also give his separate guarantee and B fails to do so. So also a joint and several guarantee is void if in signing it one of the guarantors limits his liability to less than the previously agreed amount.

3.15 If there is more than one guarantor the modern practice is to obtain a guarantee which imposes *joint and several liability* for the entire debt. By this means the creditor (the bank) obtains maximum flexibility in enforcing the guarantee against all or any of them.

(a) A *joint* guarantee means that each party is liable for the whole amount guaranteed, it being a single liability which is shared.

(b) A *several* guarantee is one where each party is separately liable for the debt, it being several liabilities (though obviously it can only be satisfied up to its full amount).

(c) A *joint and several guarantee* combines the above features. If one guarantor is required to pay the full amount of the debt he is entitled to claim a proportionate contribution from his co-guarantors. (They may of course by the terms of their guarantee expressly limit their respective shares - if not they share the burden equally).

3.16 Under general law, if the creditor releases one guarantor, that act releases them all unless otherwise agreed. But bank guarantee forms often permit the bank to release a guarantor without prejudice to its rights against the other.

3.17 Although death of a guarantor (under a joint and several guarantee) does not release his estate from liability accrued up to that time, notice of his death to the creditor terminates the guarantee for the future unless the guarantee has been expressed to bind his personal representatives.

## 4. REPRESENTATIONS BY THE BANK WHEN TAKING A GUARANTEE

4.1 Under general principles of the law of contract a distinction is made between:

(a) mere non-disclosure of information even if the information would have affected the individual's judgment; and

(b) misrepresentation – an untrue statement which induces the individual to give the security.

4.2 Non-disclosure and misrepresentation are a particular problem since guarantees are complex by nature and unlikely to be understood at all by the individual or in full by bank staff. Three areas of information need to be examined:

(a) disclosure of the guarantee's terms;
(b) disclosure of the principal debtor's affairs; and
(c) disclosure of information on the guarantor's risk.

*Disclosure of the guarantee's terms*

4.3 The nature and terms of a guarantee may not be instantly appreciated by an individual. Good practice would dictate that a bank should explain the contents of legal documents, particularly to people with limited business experience, but it has no legal duty to do so to a non-customer: *O'Hara v Allied Irish Banks 1985.*

4.4 Whether a bank has a duty to explain the terms to a customer giving a guarantee is a little unclear, but it will be liable for any misrepresentation by its agents.

*Case: Cornish v Midland Bank plc 1985*
C, the plaintiff, signed a mortgage at her bank to secure her husband's borrowings on a joint account. She was given to understand that she was signing a guarantee of up to £2,000. A clerk told her that it was a second mortgage like a building society one, but in fact it secured 'all borrowings'. She left her husband and went to live abroad; to the bank's knowledge, he remarried. He was advanced up to £16,000 and the property was sold, leaving C with nothing. She sued the bank for negligent misstatement and misrepresentation.

*Held:* the mortgage was valid but the bank was liable to indemnify her for her loss arising out of misrepresentation on the void guarantee. Although the decision was not made on a bank's duty, the House of Lords stated in an *obiter dictum* that the bank did have a duty to explain the nature and effect of the document. This comment was confirmed in *Midland Bank plc v Perry 1987.*

*Case: Lloyds Bank plc v Waterhouse 1990*
The bank obtained a guarantee from a father as security for a loan to his son to buy a farm. It also took a charge over the farm. The father did not read the guarantee because he was illiterate (which he did not tell the bank) but he did enquire of the bank about the guarantee's terms. As a result he believed that he was guaranteeing only the loan for the farm. In fact he signed an 'all monies' guarantee, securing *all* the son's indebtedness to the bank. The son defaulted and the bank called on the father's guarantee for that amount of the debt which was not repaid following the farm's sale.

*Held:* the father had made adequate attempts to discover his liability by questioning the bank's employees (he was not careless). They had caused him to believe he was signing something other than he believed.

*Case: Barclays Bank plc v O'Brien 1991*
O'B wished to increase the overdraft facility of a company in which he had an interest to £135,000, so arranged to provide security in the form of his matrimonial home, in which he and his wife had an equity of £100,000. A legal charge was signed by both spouses. No explanation of the effect of the documents was given to Mrs O'B and she was not advised to take independent legal advice. O'B misrepresented to his wife that the charge was limited to £60,000 and pressurised her into signing. The bank sought to enforce the charge.

*Held:* the bank had not taken reasonable steps to explain the documents to Mrs O'B, and she had misunderstood their effect. The charge was only enforceable against her as to £60,000.

4.5 Best practice would dictate either a full and complete explanation (possibly by providing written details in plain English), or advice that the customer should obtain legal explanation because the document is so complicated. Since this line is often taken in practice, courts may construe it as being the bank's duty, or at least the measure of a bank's competence. The Code of Banking Practice lays down the following.

'Banks and building societies will advise private individuals proposing to give them a guarantee or other security for another person's liabilities that:

(a) by giving the guarantee or third party security he or she might become liable instead of or as well as that other person;

(b) he or she should seek independent legal advice before entering into the guarantee or third party security.

Guarantees and other third party security forms will contain a clear and prominent notice to the above effect. (12.1)'

4.6 Even an honest mistake made in supplying information may render the guarantee invalid:

*Case: Mackenzie v Royal Bank of Canada 1934*
By mistake the bank told M incorrectly that unless she gave a guarantee in respect of an account it would be necessary to realise certain investments.

*Held:* the guarantee was void for misrepresentation.

*Disclosure of the principal debtor's affairs*

4.7 A contract of guarantee is not a contract of extreme good faith *(uberrima fides)*. There is no general obligation on the creditor to disclose what he knows about the debtor's affairs.

*Case: Cooper v National Provincial Bank Ltd 1945*
C gave a guarantee to the bank in respect of the account of Mrs R. The bank did not disclose to C that Mrs R's husband was an undischarged bankrupt to whom Mrs R had given authority to sign cheques drawn on her account, nor that a number of cheques had been issued and then countermanded by the drawer. C argued that non-disclosure of these facts entitled him to repudiate his guarantee.

*Held:* the bank had no duty to disclose these facts. On the contrary they comprised information about the customer's account which the bank had a duty to keep in confidence.

4.8 There are a number of decisions to the same effect. The bank has no duty to disclose:

(a) that the debtor's account is already overdrawn, that he has previously had unsecured loans or that he is using this account for particular purposes such as payment of gambling debts: *Hamilton v Watson 1845;*

(b) that previous lending to the customer had been made available on an unsecured basis: *Westminster Bank Ltd v Cond 1940; nor*

(c) that there had been any change in the circumstances of the principal debtor: *National Provincial Bank of England Ltd v Glanusk 1913.*

4.9 Nonetheless there can be exceptional cases where the bank *does* have a duty of disclosure about the customer.

(a) It has been said that if the arrangements between the bank and the debtor customer are 'different from that which the guarantor might naturally expect' he is entitled to be informed: *Hamilton v Watson 1845.* It is not easy to suggest an illustration of this formula. It would only apply in an extreme case where the bank realises that the guarantor totally misapprehends the customer's situation or intentions.

(b) A half-truth can amount to misrepresentation. If information is given, usually in reply to the guarantor's questions, it should be full and fair: *Royal Bank of Scotland v Greenshields 1914.*

4.10 In the situation of either (a) or (b), the bank should remember its duty of confidentiality to the customer. It is difficult to know, at the time, which facts may be relevant. The best solution is to call a meeting of all three parties to reveal certain agreed facts. If any inconsistencies appear, these may be discussed. Doubts which persist may lead to the guarantee not being taken.

*Disclosure of the guarantor's risk*

4.11 After the guarantee has been given, the position changes somewhat. The guarantor is at risk and he is entitled to know the amount of his risk. It is now information about his own affairs which the bank has an obligation to give whenever he asks for it. This obligation must still be balanced against the bank's duty of confidentiality about the customer's affairs. The situation yields the following rules of banking practice.

(a) If the guarantor asks the amount of his liability under his guarantee then:

(i) he is given the exact figure if the customer's liability is less than the financial limit set on the guarantee; for example, if the guarantee is limited to £5,000 and the customer's overdraft is £4,550 that figure is disclosed to the guarantor;

(ii) if the customer's liability exceeds the limit of the guarantee (eg. a £5,550 overdraft in the example above) the bank replies that it 'relies fully' on the guarantee but gives no figure.

(b)   If the guarantor enquires about transactions in the customer's account, the bank declines (unless the customer consents) to reply.

(c)   The bank has no right or duty to volunteer information to the guarantor about any change in the relevant circumstances of the guarantor, such as that he is not using the account for the circumstances intended when the guarantee was given: *National Provincial Bank of England Ltd v Glanusk 1913*.

4.12  It is usual to include in the bank's form of guarantee a clause that the bank's statement of the amount due under the guarantee shall be conclusive – the guarantor shall have no right to investigate how the figure is calculated.

## Undue influence

4.13  There is a clear distinction between (i) not supplying information to a guarantor when he is entitled to it or giving him information which is inaccurate or misleading; and (ii) exerting pressure on him to an improper extent to prevail on him to give a guarantee or security without genuine consent. This is undue influence as discussed in Chapter 5 and if it is used the guarantee is voidable – it may be set aside by the guarantor if he wishes to do so (and if he takes his decision within a reasonable time after the influence ceases to operate on him).

4.14  If undue influence on the part of the bank is alleged by the guarantor the following general principles apply.

(a)   Undue influence is overbearing a person's free will – the guarantor should prove more than persuasion. A bank is not presumed to be in a position of undue influence.

(b)   If the *dealings* between one person and another disclose that one is stronger than the other and is exerting that strength in the course of persuasion or negotiation, undue influence is likely to be attributed to the stronger party. Here the bank is vulnerable if it presses too hard to obtain a guarantee.

4.15  A bank may very rarely be in a position of undue influence in obtaining a guarantee if:

(a)   the bank indicates that unless the guarantee is given it will have to take other steps to reduce or eliminate a risk of loss; and

(b)   the guarantor has a close relationship with the debtor and possibly with the bank so that he is disposed to give way to save the debtor from financial embarrassment or insolvency: *Williams v Bayley 1866*.

This is not to suggest that a bank cannot obtain a valid guarantee in these circumstances. But it should take proper steps to avoid an imputation of undue influence.

4.16  The standard precautions taken by banks are:

(a)   to include in the guarantee a 'free will' clause by which the guarantor declares that he (or she) signs voluntarily and with full knowledge of the nature of the obligation; and

(b) to invite the guarantor's professional adviser, usually a solicitor, to witness the guarantor's signature with an attestation clause to the effect that he has explained the nature and contents of the document to the guarantor.

4.17 The guarantor may of course refuse to bring in his or her professional adviser (because of the cost of paying a fee for the service). It may then be prudent to have evidence (such as a letter from the bank) that the suggestion was made and its value explained. But remember that the decision in *Goldsworthy v Brickell 1987* means that if there is manifest disadvantage the contract may still be voidable for undue influence even though the guarantor was offered, and refused, independent legal advice.

4.18 A bank may be implicated in and affected by undue influence in a guarantee if its agent exerts undue influence. This may happen where the bank allows a principal debtor or his solicitor to take the guarantee form away in order to obtain the guarantor's signature, and in doing so the principal debtor or his solicitor exerts undue influence. In such a case the principal debtor or the solicitor acts as the bank agent, and hence the bank itself is deemed to have exerted undue influence: *Avon Finance Co Ltd v Bridger 1985* (bank gave form to principal debtor) and *Kings North Trust Ltd v Bell 1985* (bank gave form to solicitor). The moral of the story is to exercise great care to avoid a guarantee being signed elsewhere than in the presence of bank officials.

---

## Exercise

What do you think are the advantages and disadvantages of guarantees as security?

### Solution

The main *advantage* of a guarantee as security is simplicity. It is only necessary to obtain a signature on a standard form. It is not necessary to investigate ownership and previous dealings with assets nor to register the guarantee. If it becomes necessary to enforce the guarantee the bank sues the guarantor on his personal covenant to pay. Admittedly the complications of mortgage law enter into the arrangement if the guarantor gives security in support of his guarantee, but generally a guarantee may be enforced immediately by the court.

The *disadvantages* of a personal guarantee as security are that:

(a) the guarantor may be unable to discharge his liability - banks should make enquiries as to the financial circumstances of the guarantors at yearly or other intervals;

(b) in spite of the clauses included in the standard forms of guarantee to protect the banks, it is possible to fall into traps - for example, the guarantee may become invalid by reason of some apparently insignificant change of circumstances;

(c) court action may be necessary to recover money - which is costly and time-consuming.

But since a guarantee may be taken from several parties under joint and several liability, it often serves as a useful form of security for a loan to a business which is just starting up and so has no assets as such.

## 5.   STOCKS AND SHARES

5.1   Security may be taken by the bank in the form of registered stock or shares in a company, particularly in a listed company.

5.2   A share certificate (unlike the title deeds of unregistered land or a bill of exchange) is not a document of title transferable in its own right. A share certificate merely purports to be a formal statement by the company of particulars contained in its register of members at the date of issue of the share certificate.

5.3   The company is nonetheless 'estopped' (prohibited) from denying (in normal circumstances) that the share certificate which it has issued is correct. It should have been a correct extract from the company's register when it was issued. The company insists that the certificate is surrendered for cancellation before the company will enter in its register a transfer of the shares to which the certificate relates.

5.4   This principle is the foundation of all mortgages of shares to a bank by way of security. Neither a legal nor an equitable mortgage can be completed and made effective unless the customer hands over his share certificate. Once he has done so it is extremely difficult for him, and for anyone who might forge his name on a transfer of the shares, to dispose of the shares to anyone else. The company normally refuses to register a transfer unless the transferor's share certificate is surrendered to it.

5.5   Because listed companies' shares are more marketable by virtue of their Stock Exchange quotation, this type of share offers good security for lending. They are readily realisable and can be valued easily.

### Transfer of shares

5.6   Transfer of shares which are listed on the Stock Exchange is effected under a modified procedure by which the transferor delivers a transfer to a Stock Exchange holding agency (SEPON) which in turn delivers to the transferee a transfer of the shares to which he is entitled. This system (called 'Talisman') permits the pooling of all transfers of shares of a company effected within the two week dealing period of the Stock Exchange. No share certificate is issued to SEPON since it is merely a temporary shareholder, but the company will have received the transferor's share certificate at the time when he delivered his transfer to SEPON.

### *De-materialised transfers of shares*

5.7   In 1993 the Stock Exchange plans to introduce a system which will enable quoted shares to be transferred without the need for share certificates or forms of transfer to be submitted. This system will be known as TAURUS (Transfer and Automated Registration of Uncertificated Stock) and is the means by which dematerialised or paperless trading will be facilitated.

5.8 Central to the TAURUS system are commercial and company TAURUS Account Controllers (TACs) who will be able to provide shareholders with statements of their holdings. When the TAURUS system goes live a legal mortgage will most likely be effected by submitting a 'transfer of entitlement' to the TACs to give the bank control of the shares. Alternatively, the mortgagor's share account can be transferred into the name of the bank or its nominee.

### Legal mortgage of shares

5.9 Under a legal mortgage, the customer transfers his shares to be registered in the name of the bank, or its nominee, as registered shareholder until the mortgage is discharged.

5.10 The banks have nominee companies; often one such company is created for the convenience of branches of the bank in each local district. The branch arranges for shares mortgaged to it by a customer to be registered in the name of the local nominee company. It is still necessary for the nominee company to remit to the branch dividends received in respect of the shareholding, so that each dividend may be credited to the customer's account.

5.11 A legal mortgage gives maximum protection to the bank. Its nominee company is the registered shareholder and has possession of a share certificate in its name. The company which issued the shares is prohibited by law from recognising any claim of a third party - the customer - to an interest in the shares: Companies Act 1985 s 360.

5.12 The customer can obtain from the court a 'stop notice' and serve it on the company whose shares have been mortgaged. This prevents registration of any further transfer of the shares without first giving eight days' notice to the customer. In banking practice, stop notice procedure is infrequent and therefore unimportant.

5.13 When the mortgage is discharged, the branch instructs the bank nominee company to re-transfer the mortgaged shares back to the name of the customer to whom a new share certificate is issued by the company in which he is again a registered shareholder.

5.14 In addition to transferring his shares to the bank as security, the customer usually - it is not however legally necessary - signs a Memorandum of Deposit prepared by the bank on a standard form. The form usually provides that:

(a) the shares and all dividends and other rights, in particular to bonus issues, are charged as security to the bank;

(b) the security is a continuing security for all sums owing to the bank (since the original debt may be paid off under the rule in *Clayton's* case);

(c) the debt is repayable on demand. If the customer does not repay on demand being made, the bank is authorised without further notice to sell the shares in order to recover what is owing;

    (d)   in cases where it is appropriate the customer may undertake:

        (i)     to provide additional security when necessary to maintain a specified margin, say 20 per cent, of value of security over amount owing. This is a safeguard against a fall in the value of the shares;

        (ii)    to repay to the bank any sum which the bank has to pay on the shares. This is only necessary if the shares are not fully paid;

    (e)   on discharge of the mortgage, the bank is to re-transfer the same number of shares (not necessarily the identical shares) back to the customer;

    (f)   appropriate terms on bank interest, dividends on the shares etc as agreed between the bank and the customer.

*Advantages and disadvantages of a legal mortgage of shares*

5.15 The *advantage* of taking a legal mortgage is that the bank or its nominee becomes the legal owner of the shares with all the protection which legal ownership gives.

5.16 But there are *disadvantages* as follows:

    (a)   A listed company must always register a transfer of shares if (i) a 'proper instrument of transfer' duly stamped and the share certificate are presented and (ii) the shares are fully paid. From the bank's point of view partly paid shares, leaving aside the theoretical risk of refusal of the transfer by the company, are unsatisfactory since the customer's debt to the bank will be increased if the bank has to pay the call, when made, on the shares for the balance due.

    (b)   By a legal mortgage by registered transfer the customer may lose his position as director of the company if its articles require each director to be the registered holder of a number of shares as qualification for being a director. However, the number of shares prescribed as a qualification is usually small. If an equitable mortgage of the entire shareholding is not acceptable security, the bank may be content to take a legal mortgage of all the shares held by the mortgagor except those which he must retain in order to continue as a director. The latter can be made subject to an equitable mortgage.

    (c)   If the bank takes a legal mortgage and presents for registration a transfer to itself, it warrants to the company that the transferor's signature is genuine and must compensate for the company if it is a forgery: *Sheffield Corporation v Barclay 1905*.

5.17 The bank should know whether a signature on a transfer is that of its own customer. However, it is a standard precaution to invite a customer who is mortgaging shares to the bank to attend at the bank to sign the transfer and other documents. The bank should never permit one joint shareholder to take the transfer away to get it signed by the other.

**Equitable mortgage of shares**

5.18 This is an informal mortgage by which the customer deposits his share certificate with the bank. To create an equitable mortgage it is sufficient that the customer intends his deposit of the certificate to constitute a security for his debt to the bank: *Harrold v Plenty 1901*. For obvious reasons the bank's normal practice is to obtain a signed Memorandum of Deposit on the same lines as under a legal mortgage but without any reference to re-transfer of the shares on discharge of the mortgage.

5.19 The one advantage obtained by giving notice of deposit of the share certificate to the company is that the bank thereby obtains priority over any claim which the company itself might later have against the customer if he were indebted to the company, for example for unpaid calls on his shares: *Bradford Banking Co Limited v Henry Briggs Son & Co Limited 1886*. However, Stock Exchange Listing Agreement rules and the Companies Act 1985 s 150 prohibit a public company from making such claims except on partly-paid shares. It is therefore of little importance since shares are normally fully paid.

5.20 Apart from the risk that the customer might cheat the bank by obtaining a duplicate share certificate, or contrive somehow to get a transfer to a third party registered without producing his share certificate (held by the bank), the bank should be prepared for the more likely eventuality of default by the customer, perhaps in course of bankruptcy, and the sale of the shares by the bank to realise its security.

*Blank transfers*

5.21 Under an equitable mortgage, the bank has no rights as owner of the shares, since it is not on the company's register of members. If it sells the shares it can deliver a share certificate (in the customer's name) but not, unless the customer cooperates, a transfer signed by him. To obviate that difficulty it is common practice in taking an equitable mortgage by deposit to obtain a 'blank' transfer from the customer.

5.22 A *blank transfer* is a transfer signed by the customer and complete except for (i) the date and (ii) the name and other particulars of the transferee. The date is omitted since there are penalties if a transfer is presented for stamping more than 30 days after its date. The transferee's name is omitted so that the name of the purchaser may be inserted at the time of sale by the bank. If it becomes necessary to sell the shares to enforce the security, the bank inserts a current date and delivers the transfer, signed by the customer previously, together with his share certificate. The purchaser inserts his own name as transferee, has the transfer stamped and delivers transfer and share certificate. (The Talisman/SEPON procedure is essentially similar though there are differences of detail.)

5.23 There is, however, a potential difficulty over reliance on a 'blank transfer' to be used in this way. Have the bank and the purchaser any authority to insert on the transfer material particulars which were omitted when the customer signed as transferor? The law implies that they have authority to complete the transfer by reason of the delivery of the transfer by the customer. If, however, it is executed under seal as a deed it is doubtful, for technical reasons, whether any such authority is so *implied*.

5.24 The individual customer invariably signs and does not seal a share transfer. A company either applies its common seal or authorises one or more individual officers of the company to sign the transfer. Hence the bank should, in taking a blank transfer from a company customer, arrange that, by board resolution in appropriate terms, it is signed and not sealed.

5.25 As an alternative to the above procedure, on obtaining a blank transfer the bank can ask for a power of attorney from the customer authorising the bank to complete the transfer. Yet another alternative solution is to obtain a complete transfer, duly dated, to the bank as transferee, have it stamped but then withhold it until, if ever, the bank needs to sell the shares. It then presents the transfer and the old share certificate and is registered as the new holder of the shares. As a second stage, it can then complete a transfer, supported by its new share certificate, and present it to the purchaser.

*Advantages and disadvantages of an equitable mortgage of shares*

5.26 The *advantage* of an equitable mortgage by deposit is that it avoids the work and expense incidental to a transfer (to the bank) followed by a second transfer later by the bank to the customer.

5.27 The main *disadvantages* of an equitable mortgage are that a dishonest customer may use his status as registered shareholder to cheat the bank and that some care and documentation (blank transfers) are required to enable the bank to sell the shares without difficulty. There are two particular risks of deception.

(a) The customer may not be the beneficial owner of the shares. He may, for example, hold the shares as trustee or nominee for someone else. The interests of that third party prevail, since they are earlier in time, over the interests of the bank if the bank contents itself with an equitable mortgage only. The only safeguard against that risk is to take a legal mortgage. If the bank, in ignorance of third party rights, becomes the registered shareholder, it has a *legal* title to the shares which prevails even over existing prior equitable interests (unless known to the legal mortgagee when his mortgage is created).

(b) The company may make a bonus issue of shares by capitalising reserves to pay up and issue additional shares to registered shareholders. For example, suppose that X creates an equitable mortgage by deposit of the share certificate of 5,000 shares of Y plc, valued at £5 per share. Later Y makes a bonus issue on the scale of 1 new share for each share held. X now has 10,000 shares, worth perhaps only £2.50 per share. Unless he hands over the new share certificate to the bank, as he has undertaken to do in the memorandum of deposit, the bank's security has been halved in value. Bonus issues of listed companies are announced in the newspapers some time before they send a letter of allotment of share certificate to the shareholders for their new shares. The bank should be alert to notice such impending events and perhaps obtain from the customer written authority for the bank as his agent to receive the document of title when issued.

## 6. LIFE ASSURANCE POLICIES

6.1 A life assurance policy is a contract (called a 'policy') by which an *insurer* undertakes to the *policyholder* (who pays the premium) to pay a sum of money on the death of the *life assured* or, if it is a policy of endowment assurance, on his attaining a specified age or at his death before that age, to an identified *beneficiary*. It is conventional to refer to such policies as 'life *assurance*' in contrast to *insurance* against the risk of loss or damage to property, which is a contract of indemnity by which the amount paid is related to the loss suffered.

6.2 Like most other forms of property, the benefit – the right to receive the sum payable at maturity – can be transferred either outright or as security for, say a loan. A transfer is in this case called an 'assignment'. Assignment of a life policy is one of the forms of security which a customer may offer to his bank.

## Insurable interest

6.3 The law requires that a contract of insurance shall relate to a risk or event in which the policyholder has an insurable interest: Life Assurance Act 1774. The effect of this principle on life assurance is that:

(a) an individual has an insurable interest (for any amount) in respect of the life of himself or his wife or husband – one may always insure one's own life or the life of a spouse;

(b) other persons may demonstrate that they have an insurable interest in the life of another person. As examples:

| Persons who may insure | Life assured |
|---|---|
| (i) Creditor (eg bank) | Debtor* (eg customer) |
| (ii) Guarantor | Principal debtor* |
| (iii) Employer (who may be a company) | Employee |

*The insurable interest is limited to the amount of the debt.

6.4 Apart from husband and wife, relatives have no insurable interest in each other's lives unless there are special circumstances. But a parent may insure the life of a child who supports him and *vice versa*. Anyone may insure the life of another person if he can demonstrate that he has a financial interest in the survival of the life assured. The list given above is not exhaustive.

6.5 For life assurance it is sufficient that the policyholder has an insurable interest; he need not be the person entitled to the money at the death of the life assured (that is, the beneficiary). For example, H insures the life of W (his wife) for his own benefit and later assigns the benefit of the policy to his bank as security. The bank has no insurable interest in the life of W (she is not a debtor to the bank) but it is entitled as beneficiary to the insurance monies at W's death. The same principle permits a person to insure his own life (in which he has an insurable interest) on trust to pay the monies to someone else.

## Uberrima fides

6.6 Insurance is a contract of extreme good faith *(uberrima fides)*. Each party, but especially the policyholder in making his proposal, has a duty to disclose what he knows insofar as it is material to the contract. Unlike most pre-contract negotiations, one cannot safely hold back information merely because the other party did not ask for it. The insurer may avoid it and refuse to pay if material facts are not disclosed.

6.7 The obligation to disclose is confined to what is *material* – what would influence a prudent insurer:

(a) in deciding whether to insure the risk; or
(b) in fixing the rate of premium.

## 15: OTHER FORMS OF SECURITY

### Types of life assurance policy

6.8 To help you identify the better forms of policy for security, we shall look at three important types:

(a) *whole life policy* - in which the sum insured is payable only on the death of the life insured, and the policy is to continue until his death;

(b) *endowment policy* - which matures at a given date or earlier death;

(c) *trust policy* - this is commonly a policy issued under Married Womens Property Act 1882 ('MWPA') s 11 to a husband for the benefit of his wife and/or children or (less often) to a wife for the benefit of her husband and children;

A *mortgage protection policy* is a policy under which the amount payable is the sum, reduced year by year, owed by the mortgagor if he dies before repayment in full of his mortgage. This is an indemnity for the bank as mortgagee; such policies are rarely taken as security in themselves.

6.9 *Whole life policy* - the drawback to this type of policy (as a security) is that the bank cannot know how long the life assured will live and so how long the premiums (if the bank takes over the policy) will be payable. But such a policy is less expensive in premium than an endowment policy and it provides a useful safeguard against the premature death of a customer who lacks capital but hopes to repay his loan out of future earnings. Moreover it builds up a surrender value and it can be converted into a paid-up policy.

6.10 *Endowment policy* - this is a more acceptable security since it covers the risk of premature death of the life assured and there is a fixed maturity date at which the money is paid if the life assured is still alive. In addition it soon has a surrender value and can be made paid up. But it is more expensive in premium than a whole life policy.

6.11 *Trust policy* - this involves at least two different persons - the policyholder who takes out the policy (normally with his own life as the life assured) and holds it on trust, and the person or persons who are beneficially entitled to it under the trust (the beneficiaries). If such a policy is offered as security, the beneficiaries as well as the trustee must join the assignment since the assignment is a transfer of the benefit as well as the legal title. This is only possible if all the beneficiaries are *aged at least 18. If they include young children the policy cannot be assigned as security.*

6.12 A second problem is to *identify* the beneficiaries whose participation is required to effect a valid assignment. If the benefit is given to identified persons (for example, 'on trust for my wife Mary and my children John and Jane') those individuals (even if minors) take an immediate vested interest (which passes to their heirs if they die before the policy matures). There is in this situation a clearly defined group of beneficiaries. But if the policy is held 'in trust for my wife and children' this means the persons who are the wife and children living at the death of the life insured. If his first wife dies or there is a divorce and he re-marries 'my wife' is his second wife and 'my children' are any children (alive at his death) of either marriage: *Re Browne's Policy 1903.*

## 15: OTHER FORMS OF SECURITY

**Legal assignment of a life policy**

6.13 There are two ways in which a legal assignment of a life assurance policy may be effected.

    (a) Under the Policies of Assurance Act 1967 the assignment transfers legal ownership to the bank, subject to the fact that it must reassign the policy once the sum secured is repaid. Either the policy is endorsed by the policyholder or a separate written assignment is made. The assignor's signature must be witnessed, and notice of the date and effect of the assignment must be given to the insurer.

    (b) Under s 136 LPA the assignment must simply be in writing, with written notice to the insurer (which need not be acknowledged).

6.14 Banks use an elaborate form of assignment of life assurance policies. The bank forms have much in common with their forms of legal mortgage of land - because the bank requires similar safeguards and powers.

*Remedies of a legal assignee*

6.15 *If the policy moneys have become payable* by reason of the death of the life assured (or maturity of an endowment policy at the agreed date), the legal assignee produces to the insurer a death certificate as proof of the death (if that is the relevant event) and demands payment.

6.16 *If the policy moneys are not yet payable* but the bank as legal assignee seeks to realise the security and repay the loan, it can:

    (a) surrender the policy; or

    (b) obtain a loan from the insurers against the policy (this requires the policyholder's co-operation in applying for the loan and authorising payment to the bank); or

    (c) sell the policy; or

    (d) convert the policy into a paid up policy.

**Equitable mortgage of a life policy**

6.17 The mere deposit of a policy with the intention that it shall be a security for advances is sufficient to create an equitable mortgage. In practice banks obtain a signed Memorandum of Deposit (if it is given by deed the bank then has a power of sale on default):

    (a) to establish that the policy has been deposited as security;

    (b) to declare that it is a continuing security;

    (c) to authorise the bank to pay the premiums if necessary; and

    (d) to obtain an undertaking from the borrower that he will execute a legal assignment if requested to do so.

6.18 The bank's possession of the policy is usually a sufficient safeguard against the insured charging the policy to another person. But the disadvantage of an equitable mortgage of a life policy (like an equitable mortgage of land by deposit of title deeds) is that the mortgagee requires the cooperation of the borrower in obtaining the policy moneys from the insurers or in disposing of the policy. The remedies of an equitable mortgagee are inferior to those of a legal assignee. For that reason, banks usually insist on obtaining a legal assignment.

6.19 Notice of deposit should be given to the insurer to preserve the bank's priority over any person who later obtains an equitable interest.

6.20 Whether the policy moneys are payable or not, the bank with an *equitable assignment* only would probably call on the policyholder to execute a legal assignment (as provided by the Memorandum of Deposit). Otherwise the bank must obtain the co-operation of the policyholder or apply to the court for an order for sale or foreclosure.

**Advantages and disadvantages of a life policy as security**

6.21 The *advantages* of this form of security are as follows:

  (a)  Legal assignment of a policy can be effected simply and a perfect title easily obtained.

  (b)  Policies of the type accepted by the bank as security have normally an increasing value provided the premiums are paid.

  (c)  The security can be realised immediately the customer defaults.

  (d)  The policy proceeds are due immediately the assured dies or at earlier maturity.

6.22 But the *disadvantages* are that:

  (a)  Since life policies are *uberrimae fidei* (of the utmost good faith), non-disclosure by the insured enables the insurer to avoid liability. They may also have exclusion of cover clauses for where the policyholder indulges in dangerous activities.

  (b)  The proposer must have an insurable interest otherwise the contract is void.

  (c)  The policy's value is linked to the policyholder's ability to keep up the premiums.

  (d)  Many policies are linked to the stock market through unit trusts - and the stock market can go down as well as up!

## 7.  DEBENTURES GIVEN BY COMPANIES

7.1  Any document which states the terms on which a company has borrowed money is a debenture: s 744 Companies Act 1985. It may create a charge over the company's assets as security for the loan. But a document relating to an unsecured loan is also a debenture in company law (though often called an unsecured loan note in the business world to distinguish it from a secured debenture).

## Charges

7.2 A debenture is normally secured by a charge over assets of a company. This gives to the bank prior claim (over other creditors) to payment of its debt out of those assets. Charges are of two kinds.

(a) *A fixed or specific charge (legal)* which attaches to the relevant asset as soon as the charge is created. By its nature, a specific charge is best suited to fixed assets which the company is likely to retain for a long period. If the company does dispose of the asset, it will either repay the mortgage debt out of the proceeds of sale so that the charge is discharged at the time of sale, or pass the asset over to the purchaser still subject to charge.

(b) *A floating charge* which does not attach to the relevant assets until the charge crystallises. The nature of a floating charge has been defined (*Re Yorkshire Woolcombers Association 1903*) as:

(i) a charge on a class of assets of a company, present and future .......;

(ii) which class is, in the ordinary course of the company's business, changing from time to time ......;

(iii) and until the holders enforce the charge the company may carry on business and deal with the assets charged.

A floating charge therefore applies to current assets such as book debts or stock in trade but is not limited to them. A floating charge over 'the undertaking and assets' of a company (the most common type) applies to fixed as well as current assets. But it does not attach to *any* assets (point (iii) above) until crystallisation. It is an equitable charge.

7.3 A fixed charge must be created by the procedure appropriate to the type of asset over which the charge is created. Hence land or shares may be subject to a legal mortgage, as may book debts.

7.4 Events causing crystallisation - the point at which a 'floating' charge is treated as if it had been created as a 'fixed' charge - are specified in the debenture document. On crystallisation there is a specific charge on the assets owned by the company at that time. It usually occurs when:

(a) the company ceases to carry on its business: *Re Woodroffes (Musical Instruments) Ltd 1986*;

(b) the company goes into liquidation or an administration order is made;

(c) a creditor enforces his security by the appointment of an administrative receiver;

(d) the holder of the charge takes action, for which the debenture gives him authority, to convert the floating charge to a fixed charge on the relevant assets: *Re Brightlife 1987* (where the mortgagees exercised a right, given by the debenture, to serve notice on the mortgagors of the conversion of the charge); or

(e) when another floating charge crystallises, if it causes the company to cease business.

7.5 In some floating charge contracts there is a clause which provides for 'automatic crystallisation'. This means that the charge crystallises on the occurrence of a certain event (such as breach of the contract) *whether or not* the charge-holder knows of the event and *whether or not* it wishes to enforce the charge. Such clauses expressly stating that the charge has crystallised are valid and effective (*Re Brightlife 1987*) but clauses providing only that, when a particular event occurs, the company can no longer deal with the assets charged are not effective: *Edward Nelson & Co Ltd v Faber & Co 1903*.

7.6 A fixed charge is usually the more satisfactory form of security since it confers immediate rights over identified assets. A floating charge has some advantage in being applicable to current assets which may be easier to realise than fixed assets subject to a fixed charge. For example, if a company becomes insolvent it may be easier to sell its stock in trade than its empty factory premises. But for the reasons given above the holder of a floating charge cannot be certain, until the company fails, what assets will form his security.

7.7 A second disadvantage to the holder of a floating charge is that even when his charge has crystallised over an identified pool of assets, he may find himself postponed to the claim of other creditors.

(a) A judgement creditor or landlord who has seized goods and sold them may retain the proceeds if received before the appointment of the debenture holder's receiver: s 183 IA.

(b) Preferential debts (mainly arrears of wages) must be paid out of assets subject to a floating charge unless there are other uncharged assets available for this purpose: ss 40 and 175 IA.

(c) The holder of a fixed charge over the same assets will usually have priority over a floating charge over those assets even if the floating charge was created before the fixed charge.

(d) A creditor may have sold goods and delivered them to the company on condition that he is to retain legal ownership until he has been paid (a *Romalpa* clause).

(e) If the company goes into liquidation within 12 months of creating a floating charge it may then be invalid as security under s 245 IA 1986 (where a floating charge is created to secure an existing debt). It may also be vitiated under ss 238-240 of the same Act (preferences, undervalues).

(f) Since a floating charge does not prevent disposal of charged assets until it crystallises, those assets may be run down, leaving insufficient available to repay the debt.

*Priority of charges*

7.8 If different charges over the same property are given to different creditors, it is necessary to determine their priority. For example, if charges are created over the same property to secure a debt of £5,000 to X and £7,000 to Y and the property is sold yielding only £10,000, either X or Y is paid in full and the other receives only the balance remaining out of £10,000 realised from the security (he then claims for the amount unpaid as an unsecured creditor of the company but there may be insufficient assets to pay those claims in full).

7.9 The priority of charges is determined by the following principles:

(a) Legal charges rank according to the order of creation. If two successive legal mortgages over the same factory are created on 1 January and 1 February the earlier takes priority over the later one.

(b) A legal charge created before an equitable one has priority.

(c) If an equitable charge is created first and a legal charge over the same property is created later, the legal charge ranks before the equitable charge (under principles of the law of property), unless at the time when the subsequent legal charge is created the creditor to whom it is given has notice of the existing equitable charge. Notice may be given by registration of the earlier charge (discussed below).

(d) If two floating charges are created over the general assets of a company they rank in order of creation. But if a company creates a floating charge over a particular kind of asset (such as book debts) that will rank before an existing floating charge over the entire assets and undertaking.

These rules become easier to grasp if one remembers that a fixed charge attaches when it is created and a floating charge when it crystallises (though there are one or two special situations above which fall outside that general principle).

7.10 It is always possible to vary the rules by agreement between the creditors.

7.11 If a floating charge is created and a fixed charge over the same property is created later, the fixed charge will usually rank first since it attaches to the property at the time of creation whilst the floating charge attaches only at the time of crystallisation. Once a floating charge has crystallised a subsequent fixed charge ranks after it under rule (a) above.

7.12 A charge may become void either for failure to register it (s 399 CA 1985), or in some circumstances if the company goes into liquidation: ss 239-245 IA. A charge which is void is not a charge at all and obviously carries no priority over a valid charge. But even though a charge is void that does not invalidate the debt which it attempted to secure.

7.13 A creditor to whom a floating charge is given may seek to protect himself against losing his priority by including (in the terms of his floating charge) a prohibition against the company creating a fixed charge over the same property which would otherwise take priority. If the company breaks the prohibition, the creditor to whom the fixed charge is given nonetheless obtains priority unless at the time when his charge is created he has *actual* knowledge of the prohibition imposed by the floating charge. Registration of a floating charge, as explained below, is deemed to give constructive notice of the existence of the floating charge but registration does not give notice of the prohibition (sometimes called a 'negative pledge clause'), even though the registered particulars on file at the registry refer explicitly to the prohibition.

**Registration of charges**

7.14 A charge is registered following delivery to the registrar of a statement of the particulars of the charge: s 398(4). Formerly the original of the charge itself had to be produced, but this is no longer necessary.

7.15 The registrar files the particulars in the 'companies charges register' which he maintains (s 397) and notes the date of delivery. He then sends copies of the particulars and of the note of the date of registration to the company and chargee: s 398(5).

7.16 If a company creates a fixed or floating charge (of any of nine types) over its assets, the charge should be registered within 21 days of its creation: s 398(1). The nine types specified in fact cover almost every kind of asset.

7.17 The registrar used to issue a certificate which was conclusive evidence that the charge had been duly registered: *Re C L Nye Ltd 1969*. The Companies Act 1989 changed this position: since the original of the charge is no longer submitted to the registrar, and he merely files the particulars when they are submitted, the registrar will only now issue a copy of the note stating the date on which they were submitted (s 398(5)) and, on request, a certificate of that note, signed and sealed by him: s 397. The effect of this certificate is as follows.

(a) There is an irrebuttable presumption that the particulars were delivered not later than the date shown.

(b) There is a rebuttable presumption that they were delivered not earlier than the date shown.

The registrar's certificate therefore no longer carries any warranty that the registered particulars are *accurate*.

*Delivery of inaccurate particulars*

7.18 The question thus arises as to the effect of delivery of inaccurate particulars to the registrar. Where they are not complete and accurate, the charge will be *void* against an administrator, liquidator or person acquiring rights in the property to the extent that it confers rights which would have been disclosed by full and accurate particulars, when a 'relevant event' takes place, and the court does not intervene to order otherwise: ss 399(2) and 402(1). Particulars are not deemed to be inaccurate merely because there is an error in naming the chargee: s 402(6).

7.19 A *relevant event* is defined in s 402(2). The definition covers the following situations.

(a) *The beginning of insolvency proceedings*, so that the charge is void against an administrator or liquidator unless the court decides that:

   (i) the error or omission is unlikely to have misled an unsecured creditor in such a way as to have materially prejudiced him; or

   (ii) no person became an unsecured creditor in the period whilst the particulars were incomplete or inaccurate: s 402(4).

(b) *The acquisition of an interest in (or right over) the charged property.* The charge will be void against a person who acquires such an interest or right for value unless:

(i) the court decides that the acquirer of the interest did not rely on the incomplete or inaccurate particulars in connection with the acquisition; or

(ii) the acquirer did so subject to the charge.

7.20 Under s 407(1), a charge becoming void because of inaccuracy results in the whole of the sum secured by the charge being payable forthwith on demand.

7.21 Further particulars, supplementing or varying the registered particulars, may be delivered to the register at anytime, provided they are in the prescribed form and are signed by both company and chargee: s 401(2). Registration of them is effected in the same way as for the original particulars, and there is no longer any need for court intervention.

## Time period for delivery of particulars

7.22 The 21 day period for registration runs from the creation of the charge, or the acquisition of property charged, and not from the making of the loan for which the charge is security: s 398(1). Creation of a charge is usually effected by execution of a document. But it may result from informal action.

*Case: Re Wallis & Simmonds (Builders) Ltd 1974*
The company deposited title deeds to secure a loan.

*Held:* the purpose of the deposit was to create a charge. As it had not been registered the charge was void.

## The effect of non-delivery

7.23 As well as the company and its officers being liable to a fine, non-delivery in the time period results in the charge being void against an administrator, liquidator or person acquiring an interest on the happening of a relevant event: s 399. The following further points on relevant events should be noted.

(a) The charge will be void even if insolvency proceedings or the acquisition of an interest in the property occur *within* the 21 days prescribed for delivery, *if* the particulars are not in fact delivered during this period: s 399(1).

(b) Creditors who subsequently take security over property and duly register their charge within 21 days will take precedence over a previous unregistered charge. This will be the case even if the later chargee had *actual notice* of the previous unregistered charge (unless the later charge was expressed as being subject to the previous charge).

7.24 Non-delivery of a charge means that the sum secured by it is payable forthwith on demand, even if the sum so secured is also the subject of other security: s 407(1).

*Late delivery of particulars*

7.25 If the charge was not registered within 21 days, but a relevant event has *not* yet occurred, it is possible to perfect the charge by late delivery under s 400(1), so that it will not be void against an administrator, liquidator or purchaser if a relevant event happens *after* registration. If it occurs on the same day then there is a rebuttable presumption that the relevant event happened first. In contrast with the old system, a court order is *not* required, and the system applies without regard to the reasons for failure to register within the prescribed period.

7.26 Such late delivery will not have a *retrospective* effect to defeat a creditor's rights which have been acquired by the occurrence of a relevant event. Therefore, if proceedings for insolvency have commenced, the unsecured creditors' rights will not be affected by the late delivery of particulars. Priority will also be given to another charge which has been duly perfected by delivery of particulars, and to a charge granted before the unregistered charge which has meanwhile been perfected by registration.

7.27 An example may help. Say that Charge X is created on 1 January, and particulars are delivered on 1 June. Particulars of Charge Y are delivered before 1 June. Charge Y will have priority *whenever* it was created; it may have been created before 1 January, during the first 21 days of January, or at any later time. (This example assumes that Y is not expressed as being subject to X.)

7.28 S 400(2) provides that a charge registered late may be void against an administrator or liquidator if insolvency proceedings begin within certain prescribed periods of late delivery *and* if, at the date of delivery, the company was unable to pay its debts or became so in consequence of the transaction giving rise to the charge. The period varies with the nature of the charge:

    (a)   floating charges generally – one year;
    (b)   floating charges granted to connected persons – two years;
    (c)   other charges – six months.

## Bank debentures

7.29 A bank's debenture is normally a single redeemable debenture taken as security for the debt. The bank would first satisfy itself that the proposed borrowing was within the company's capacity (not *ultra vires*) and the amount (when added to existing borrowing) was within the directors' delegated borrowing powers.

7.30 It is normal practice to include in the articles a limit on the amount which the directors may borrow. If they require to exceed that limit, they should convene a general meeting and either propose an alteration of the relevant article or seek express authorisation from members to borrow in excess of the limit. The limit is usually expressed not as fixed amount but in terms of the issued share capital (plus in most cases the company's reserves). The 1985 Table A has no article imposing a limit on directors' powers of borrowing, with the result that they are authorised to borrow – for a proper purpose – without limit, unless the objects clause puts a limit on the *company's* capacity to borrow.

7.31 The debenture is issued by the company to the bank. But the bank usually provides its own standard form of debenture for this purpose. The form usually contains clauses on the following subjects.

(a) The debenture covers all sums owing from time to time to the bank (an 'all monies' clause).

(b) The company undertakes to repay on demand the whole amount owing.

(c) The debenture is to be a continuing security, in addition to existing ones. *Clayton's* case rules are excluded.

(d) The company undertakes to pay interest (the precise terms on rates, due date etc).

(e) The company grants to the bank fixed and floating charges as security. This means that the disadvantages of each type are counteracted by the advantages of the other.

(f) The company undertakes not to create any charge which ranks before or equally with the charges given to the bank.

(g) The remedies of the bank if the company defaults, including the appointment of a receiver with appropriate powers of management, are stated.

(h) There are various undertakings by the company to maintain the value of the security. These may include a covenant to keep assets adequately insured and in good repair. There is sometimes a covenant that the value of assets or the level of profits shall not fall below a certain level (or multiple of the loan capital or interest) or that the company will not dispose of all or part of the undertaking without the bank's consent. If the level is not maintained the bank is then entitled to appoint a receiver.

(i) An undertaking by the company to deposit with the bank all title deeds etc, relating to land and buildings (including property acquired after the issue of the debenture).

(j) A realisation clause states on what events the debt is repayable and security enforceable.

## The bank's remedies

7.32 Whether it is a secured or unsecured debenture, the bank may exercise the rights of any unsecured creditor on default. It may:

(a) sue in the courts for interest and principal; or

(b) petition for the company to be wound up under s 122 IA - on the grounds of it being unable to pay its debts.

7.33 A debenture secured by a charge, fixed or floating, gives certain powers on default - these may be to sell charged assets, to take possession and continue the business, or to appoint a receiver (part (g) in paragraph 7.31.

# 15: OTHER FORMS OF SECURITY

*Appointing a receiver*

*Debenture-*
*Loan Contracts*

7.34 A receiver appointed by the bank:

(a) must be a qualified insolvency practitioner; and

(b) is the agent of the *company*, not of the bank. Hence the bank is not liable on his contracts nor to pay his remuneration; and

(c) has suitable powers of management and disposal of assets under his charge.

7.35 A receiver has many duties and powers conferred by the Insolvency Act 1986, but one of his most important duties as far as the appointing bank is concerned is the duty of care.

*Case: Standard Chartered Bank Ltd v Walker 1982*
As security for a loan the company gave a floating charge to the bank and two directors gave personal guarantees (limited to £75,000). The bank appointed a receiver under the floating charge at a time when the company's indebtedness to the bank was £88,432. The bank instructed the receiver to realise the security by sale as soon as possible. The sale was held at the wrong time of the year and was inadequately advertised. The property was sold for only £42,800, which was considerably less than it would have realised if sold in more advantageous conditions. The bank then claimed from the guarantors the unpaid company debt (ie after deducting £42,800, much reduced by the sale expenses).

*Held:* the bank (acting through the receiver) owed a duty to the guarantors to take reasonable care to obtain the best possible price. This decision was backed up in *American Express Banking Corporation v Hurley 1986* (concerning mortgages).


## 8. CONCLUSION

8.1 We have seen that there are a great many other forms of security which may be given to a bank than mortgages of land. When revising these topics, bear in mind the following points.

(a) Define the type of property given – is it realty (freehold property), personalty (leasehold land etc), moveable property (jewellery) or intangible property (negotiable instruments, life policy), or is it an undertaking for the future (a guarantee or floating charge)?

(b) In what forms may such a security be given – legal or equitable mortgage, charge, lien, pledge or assignment?

(c) How is the security taken and who must be notified?

(d) What is contained in a bank form for the particular type of security?

(e) What rights has the bank as holder of the security?

(f) Are there any points which may nullify the security – such as lack of capacity, undue influence, lack of insurable interest, forgery of transfers, failure to register a charge?

(g) Lastly, how good is that particular type as security for bank lending? What are its advantages and disadvantages?

---

**TEST YOUR KNOWLEDGE**

*The numbers in brackets refer to paragraphs of this chapter*

1 What is a banker's lien and why is it exceptional? (1.4, 1.5)

2 What is a pledge? (2.1)

3 Define a guarantee and distinguish it from an indemnity. (3.4 – 3.6)

4 Why do banks impose joint and several liability when there is more than one guarantor? (3.15)

5 What problems may be encountered regarding giving information to a guarantor after he has signed the guarantee? (4.11)

6 How does a bank take a legal mortgage of shares? (5.9, 5.10)

7 There are three ways in which a bank can supplement an equitable mortgage of shares by deposit. Name them. (5.22, 5.25)

8 What types of life assurance policy are usually taken as security? (6.9 – 6.11)

9 How is (a) a legal mortgage and (b) an equitable mortgage of a life policy taken? (6.13, 6.18)

10 Define (a) a fixed charge and (b) a floating charge. (7.2)

11 What is crystallisation and when will it occur? (7.4)

12 When will a charge become void? (7.7)

13 What is the effect of the certificate issued by the registrar when a company's charge is registered? (7.15)

14 What happens if a registrable charge is delivered late for registration? (7.23 – 7.26)

15 What remedies has a bank as holder of the debenture of a company which defaults? (7.30, 7.31)

---

*Now try questions 25 to 27 at the end of the text*

# PART E

## CHEQUES AND OTHER MEANS OF PAYMENT

*Statutory references in this Part of the text are to the Bills of Exchange Act 1882 unless otherwise specified.*

# Chapter 16

# CHEQUES

---

**This chapter covers the following topics.**

1. Negotiable instruments
2. Cheques
3. Negotiating a cheque
4. Endorsement
5. Signatures on cheques
6. Capacity to be liable on a cheque
7. Dishonour and discharge of cheques
8. Value for a cheque
9. Holders for value and in due course
10. Liabilities of the parties to a cheque
11. Crossings on cheques

---

## 1. NEGOTIABLE INSTRUMENTS

### Assignment

1.1 It is generally possible to transfer the benefit of a contract, including the right to receive payment of a sum of money. This can be done by the procedure called 'legal assignment' as prescribed by s 136 LPA. This imposes three requirements:

(a) the assignment must be in writing and signed by the assignor;

(b) it must be an absolute (unconditional) assignment of the entire debt;

(c) notice in writing must be given to the debtor (so that he can no longer discharge his liability by payment to the assignor).

1.2 If these conditions are satisfied, the assignee can, in his own name, enforce payment to himself and his receipt is a valid discharge to the debtor. An informal assignment (an 'equitable assignment') is also recognised to some extent. The method of assignment of debts is often used in the business world. For example, a trader may find it advantageous to 'factor' his trade debts by selling the right to collect the debts to a specialist debt collection agency. The price paid is of course rather less than the full nominal amount of the debts and there may be special arrangements relating to debts which cannot be recovered.

1.3 There are two serious drawbacks to legal assignment.

(a) *Formality* - the written transfer must be correct in its form and detail. Evidence must be obtained that the debtor has received notice of the transfer.

(b) *Uncertainty* - the assignee has no better rights than the assignor had. In particular:

(i) the debtor can set up against the assignee any set off (of another debt) or counter claim which was available to him against the assignor;

(ii) the assignor may have had a defective title to the debt - for example it might be tainted by fraud, or invalid because a previous transfer to the assignor was defective.

1.4 Hence the assignee is said to acquire the assignor's rights 'subject to equities' (because at one time the court of chancery dealt with assignment and took account of (i) and (ii) above in dealing with it). The result of all this is that an assignee may have to investigate the past history of the debt before he can safely pay money to acquire it.

1.5 The business world, however, requires *simplicity* and *certainty*. This need arises particularly in providing short-term finance for trading transactions. A may consign goods to B, an overseas customer, on the basis that payment is due 6 months after shipment. But A wishes to transfer the debt at once to C his bank in return for immediate cash (to replenish A's working capital), less a discount on the amount of the debt representing 6 months interest until C receives payment. It can be done, but assignment (which involves obtaining evidence that notice has been given to B and the possibility that B, on receiving the goods, may claim a deduction for shortages or defects) is inconvenient and risky. For a bank which handles many such transactions for many customers assignment becomes unworkable.

## Negotiability

1.6 The solution to the problems outlined above (and others incidental to assignment) is the negotiable instrument, which is a type of 'chose in action'. This broad category of property covers any sort of intangible property, such as shares, a bank balance or a copyright. A person's rights over a chose in action can only be enforced by legal action - hence the name. Due to developments in the legal system, such property became unwieldy because:

(a) each time a chose in action was transferred, such a transfer was only effective if the person liable (the drawer of a payment order) was notified; and

(b) any new owner had the same (possibly defective) rights as his transferor or assignor, even though he had acted in good faith etc.

Hence the concept of negotiability developed.

1.7 By using a negotiable instrument, the rights to a chose in action are embodied in a single document which:

(a) is transferable by delivery plus (in some cases) a signature (endorsement);

(b) gives a full and legal title on such transfer (so that the transferee may exercise all the rights as owner of the instrument; and

    (c)   gives to a transferee who takes it in good faith and for value (as 'holder in due course') title 'free of equities' – he may have better rights than the transferor had and need not concern himself with the transaction's past history.

In addition, the document itself must be:

    (d)   complete and regular on the face of it; and
    (e)   in a deliverable state.

1.8   The system of negotiable instruments was developed by European bankers in late mediaeval and early renaissance times in the course of financing trade and providing banking services across international frontiers. By custom they treated certain documents as 'negotiable' in the sense described above. The custom was absorbed into English law and extended. The important negotiable instruments now are:

    (a)   bills of exchange (including cheques);
    (b)   promissory notes (including bank notes); and
    (c)   Certificates of Deposit (CDs) issued by commercial banks.

By definition these are all examples of the category of intangible property called 'choses in action'. Most of them (but bearer securities are an exception) carry a right to receive a sum of money.

*Transferability*

1.9   There are other sorts of choses in action in the form of a document which may be transferable by delivery but where the transferee gets no better rights than the transferor had. These include:

    (a)   a postal order, money order or a cheque crossed 'not negotiable';

    (b)   a bill of lading or warehouseman's warrant which gives to the person in possession the right to obtain goods from a ship or warehouse;

    (c)   American and Canadian share certificates duly endorsed.

1.10  Other kinds of choses in action (such as registered shares or debentures or government loan stock) are not even transferable by delivery. It is necessary to present a proper form of transfer and have it registered.

1.11  To decide whether any item is negotiable, it should be analysed in line with the features of negotiability at paragraph 1.6.

1.12  Take the example of X who leaves his briefcase in the train. It is found by Y who misappropriates it in circumstances amounting to theft. The contents include a bill of lading and some bank notes. Y sells the bill of lading to Z and spends the stolen money on purchase of goods from Z who is unaware of Y's theft. X can recover the bill of lading from Z since this is not negotiable – it can be transferred by delivery but does not pass free from equities. Since Y had no title to it and he could not pass title to Z. But X cannot recover the banknotes or their value since as negotiable instruments they passed to the ownership of X even though the transferor to him had no title.

*Negotiability and transferability*

1.13 It is very important to bear in mind the difference between these two concepts. To be negotiable, an instrument *must* fulfil the first three criteria in paragraph 1.6. A document may fulfil requirement (1) - transfer by delivery - and (2) - full and legal title - but still not be negotiable.

For instance, a cheque crossed 'not negotiable' is transferable by delivery and, if passed from a true owner to another person in good faith and for value, may give full and legal title, but it gives no better rights than the transferor had. It is *transferable*, not *negotiable*.

1.14 The relationship between various types of transferable intangible property can be summarised as follows:

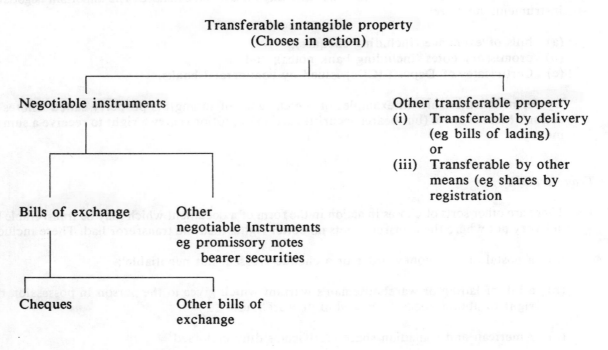

Transferable intangible property
(Choses in action)

Negotiable instruments

Other transferable property
(i)   Transferable by delivery
      (eg bills of lading)
      or
(iii) Transferable by other
      means (eg shares by
      registration

Bills of exchange     Other
                      negotiable Instruments
                      eg promissory notes
                      bearer securities

Cheques               Other bills of
                      exchange

## 2.   CHEQUES

2.1 A cheque is defined by the Bills of Exchange Act 1882 as a bill of exchange drawn on a banker payable on demand: s 73.

2.2 A bill of exchange is defined by s 3(1) Bills of Exchange Act 1882 as:

'an unconditional order in writing, addressed by one person to another, signed by the person giving it, requiring the person to whom it is addressed to pay on demand, or at a fixed or determinable future time, a sum certain in money to, or to the order of, a specified person, or to bearer'.

*These definitions must be learnt.*

2.3 The two definitions of bill and cheque may be combined to describe a cheque as:

An unconditional order in writing addressed by a person *to a bank*, signed by the person giving it, requiring *the bank* to pay on *demand* a sum certain in money to or to the order of a specified person or to bearer.

But this definition does not appear in either the 1882 Act or the Cheques Act 1957.

2.4 If you decide to combine the definitions in answering a question do not forget (this is a common mistake) to omit the words 'at a fixed or determinable future time' included in the definition of an ordinary bill. They are an alternative which is inappropriate to a cheque.

2.5 The core of the definition is that a cheque is *an order to pay money*. The purpose of the other points of the definition is to make a cheque as simple and precise as possible to facilitate dealings with it. A cheque which satisfies the requirements of the definition may be negotiated in the manner and with the rights referred to earlier. If it does not satisfy those requirements it may be transferable but ordinary rules of assignment apply to determine the rights of the transferee. He has no better rights than his transferor had.

2.6 A specimen cheque looks like this:

This cheque includes the obligatory particulars required by the definition (numbered) plus some particulars which are only customary.

2.7 By convention (it is not legally necessary) it may:

(a) be dated (3 January 19X2);
(b) express the amount in both words and figures (£1,000); and
(c) give the address of the drawee bank to whom it is addressed (13 High Street, Anytown).

2.8 There is no objection to these additional particulars provided that they do not infringe the definition: s 3(4). The following paragraphs explain the meaning and importance of the key phrases, numbered (1) to (3) on the above example.

**An unconditional order in writing (1)**

2.9 It must be an *order* to pay though words of politeness ('Please pay') are permitted. But if the order is restricted - eg Pay Jack Jones only - the cheque is not transferable and hence not negotiable: s 8(1).

2.10 Unless it is payable to bearer, a cheque must be payable 'to or to the order of a specified person'. The words 'or order' mean that (unless the contrary is stated) the original payee may, by endorsement, order that payment be made to some other person. This is a necessary element of negotiability. But the words 'or order' are implied if not stated on the cheque: s 8(4).

2.11 It may be *written* on any material, though paper alone is convenient. Banks issue pre-printed numbered forms for use as cheques, but this is merely a convenient arrangement between banker and customer. A cheque may be written in pencil but this obviously facilitates fraud (see Chapter 9 for the customer's duty to obviate fraud).

2.12 It must be *unconditional*. Thus an order 'Pay out of the proceeds of sale of my goods when received' is not a cheque since payment is made conditional on (1) receipt of the goods (2) sale of the goods and (3) sufficient proceeds of sale to meet the payment. Any of these conditions might not be realised. It is permissible to give instructions such as 'Pay and debit my No 1 account' or to refer to the transaction to which the payment relates ('Pay £1,500 being the purchase price of my car'). But neither is usual.

2.13 If the signature of the payee is required this must be expressed as an instruction to him ('the receipt at the foot must be signed') and not as a pre-condition for payment imposed on the person who is ordered to pay.

*Case: Bavins & Sims v London & SW Bank 1900*
Order to pay 'provided that the receipt form at the foot hereof is duly signed'.

*Held:* this made it a conditional order ('provided that') and so not a bill of exchange.

*Case: Nathan v Ogdens Ltd 1905*
The order stated that 'the receipt at the back must be signed'.

*Held:* an instruction to the payee and not a condition. A valid bill.

2.14 In modern practice when a receipt is required a large and prominent letter 'R' is printed in heavy type. This is simply an instruction which is well understood in the banking world.

**Three parties (2)**

2.15 The definition refers to and requires that there shall be three parties to a bill:

(a) *the drawer* - the customer who issues the cheque and whose signature is an essential part of it (Robert Smith);

(b) *the drawee* - the bank on which the cheque is drawn, meaning that the order to pay is addressed to it (National Westminster Bank plc);

(c) *the payee* - the person to whom payment is ordered to be made (Peter Jones). If no payee is specified the cheque may be expressed to be payable to 'bearer', and so it is payable to any person in possession of it. The definition does not require that the payee shall sign but if he wishes to negotiate (transfer the cheque to someone else), he must sign on the back of the cheque to *endorse* it.

A person is only treated as party to a cheque if he or she signs it. Hence a bank is not party to a cheque drawn on it since it does not 'accept' or sign it.

2.16 The three necessary parties need not be different persons.

(a) The drawer may order that payment shall be made to himself ('pay to me or my order' or 'pay self'). Drawer and payee are the same person: s 5(1).

(b) The drawer may order the drawee to pay himself - for example, a customer draws a cheque payable to the bank to reimburse the bank for some expenditure, such as purchase of investments, incurred on his behalf: s 5(1).

*Identity of parties*

2.17 The drawer identifies himself by his signature which is an essential element of the cheque.

2.18 He must also identify the drawee bank and the payee (unless it is a bearer cheque) and do so 'with reasonable certainty'(ss 6-7). A cheque may be drawn payable to the holder of an office ('The Borough Treasurer') or to a person by the name under which he trades ('George Hotel' denotes the proprietor). But an impersonal purpose such as 'Pay cash', 'Pay wages' is neither an order to pay a specified person nor to pay bearer. In fact, it is not legally a cheque at all, though a cheque in that form is an order to a banker to which s 4 Cheques Act 1957 applies.

2.19 If the named payee is either 'non-existent' or 'fictitious' (terms explained in Section 3 in this chapter) the cheque is nonetheless negotiable. Contrary to appearances it is then a bearer cheque: s 7(3). As it appears to be an order cheque it is likely to bear a forged endorsement which, if it were a necessary link in the chain, would prejudice the rights of the person to whom it is transferred. But as a bearer cheque may be negotiated without endorsement, the transferee gets good title.

*Joint parties*

2.20 A cheque may be made payable to joint payees whether jointly or in the alternative: s 7(2). But each must be indicated with reasonable certainty.

2.21 The most common example of joint involvement is where a cheque is drawn by or in favour of a partnership. The form of signature or designation in the firm's name avoids any real difficulty of identification or entitlement.

*Holder*

2.22 The definition of a cheque does not refer to 'holder' but he is a basic part of the system. 'Holder' means the person who:

(a) is in *possession* of a cheque which

(b) is either *payable* to him (as original payee or as endorsee) or is payable to bearer – to anyone in possession: s 2.

Note that a person in possession of a cheque which bears a forged endorsement to himself is not a holder; he merely has possession of a cheque which is not his property.

## Sum certain in money (3)

2.23 The whole system for dealing with cheques is based on the fact that a cheque is an order to pay money. It follows that a cheque must specify the amount to be paid and must not require any transaction other than payment of that sum.

2.24 The definition does not require that the amount to be paid shall be stated in words or in figures or (as is normal practice) in both. But if the amount is stated in both words and figures and they differ, the amount in words prevails: s 9(2). Mechanisation is tending to induce the use of cheques on which the amount is stated only in figures (this is of course legally permissible).

## Value

2.25 A cheque is valid without value having been received so the definition of a cheque makes no reference to value. For example, a cheque given as a birthday present is a valid and negotiable bill which the payee can either present to the drawee bank to obtain payment or negotiate in payment of a debt. However, if no value is ever given for it, the holder has no enforceable rights against other parties.

## Time for payment

2.26 The definition states that a cheque must always be payable on demand. It is payable on demand if no time for payment is expressed.

*Date of issue*

2.27 The definition does not require that the cheque shall indicate the date of *issue*. A cheque is valid even if undated: s 3(4)(a). There are, however, practical and some legal reasons for the standard practice of inserting its date of issue on the cheque.

(a) A cheque payable on demand becomes overdue when it has been in circulation for an unreasonable length of time (a question of fact): s 36(3). When a cheque becomes overdue the holder to whom it is negotiated is not a holder in due course. But the customer's authority to the bank to pay the cheque is not affected unless it is so overdue as to be stale (see para 2.30 below).

(b) A bank may refuse to pay an undated cheque on the grounds that the bank is uncertain of the customer's intentions. It should properly be returned unpaid: *Griffiths v Dalton 1940* (but see para 2.28 below).

(c) A cheque is not invalid if it bears a date before or after the actual date of issue (or if it is dated on a Sunday): s 13. But there are rules on post-dated and 'stale cheques' explained at paragraph 2.30.

2.28 Where a bank receives an undated cheque it may (and, if reasonably satisfied, often does) rely on the statutory rule that any person in possession of a bill 'wanting in a material particular' (an 'inchoate instrument') has authority to fill up the omission in any way he thinks fit: s 20(1). In this event the bank inserts the estimated date of issue and pays the cheque.

2.29 The above rule also gives authority to the payee or other holder of an undated cheque to complete it by inserting a date before presenting the cheque for payment. It may be apparent to the bank (from a difference in handwriting or ink) that the drawer did not insert the date. Unless there are grounds for suspicion the cheque would not be queried on that account.

2.30 A cheque may also be ante-dated (bear a date earlier than the date of issue) or be post-dated (bear a future date which has not arrived) when the cheque is presented for payment: s 13(2). In either case the cheque is valid. But the following additional rules may apply.

(a) *Stale cheques:* the banks consider that the customer's authority to pay his cheque expires after six months from the date of issue - although it would have become 'overdue' long before. After six months the bank would return the cheque marked 'stale cheque' or 'out of date' so that the drawer may either confirm his authority to pay it or (as is the more usual practice) issue a fresh cheque bearing a current date. This practice of banks is covered by the terms of the relationship between bank and customer - the latter cannot claim against the bank since there is no breach of contract in returning a stale cheque.

(b) *Post-dated cheques:* if the cheque is post-dated and presented for payment before the date inserted on it, the bank may (and should) refuse to pay it until the date arrives. But if the bank, usually by oversight, does pay before the due date, the customer is often unable to deny the bank's right to debit his account since the payment usually discharges a debt which the customer owes to the payee. There are, however, risks for the bank in premature payment of a post-dated cheque as follows.

(i) Termination of the bank's authority before the due date for payment of the cheque - the customer may, for example, countermand payment or die before the due date.

(ii) Wrongful refusal to pay other cheques: the premature payment of a post-dated cheque reduces the customer's balance available to meet other cheques. But in issuing those cheques the customer relies on his balance as it should then be and the bank should pay them; he may be expecting to make a later payment to the credit of the account before the post-dated cheque is due.

*Note.* A post-dated cheque is not literally payable 'on demand' but it is a cheque and a negotiable instrument: s 3.

## 3. NEGOTIATING A CHEQUE

3.1 The drawer of a cheque gives it legal effect (as regards himself and others) by issuing it. *Issue of a cheque* is its first delivery, complete in form, to a person who takes it as holder: s 2.

3.2 *Delivery of a cheque* (*voluntary* transfer of possession) is necessary for the negotiation of any cheque. A person who signs or endorses a cheque but retains it does not confer any new rights on anyone else. It remains his property in spite of his presumed intention at some later stage to issue or transfer it by delivery. In addition:

   (a) there can be constructive delivery (eg. A sending to B a letter of authority to collect a cheque held by C to A's order): s 2;

   (b) if a cheque is no longer in the possession of the party who has signed it, unconditional delivery by him is presumed until the contrary is proved;

   (c) in favour of a holder in due course, it is conclusively presumed that every party prior to him made due delivery: s 21.

As an example of (b) and (c), suppose that X steals a bearer cheque drawn by Y and negotiates it to Z in circumstances which make Z a holder in due course. While the cheque is in the hands of X it will be presumed that Y delivered it to him until it is shown that X stole it. But against Z, Y cannot escape liability nor deny Z's title by showing that he did not 'deliver' the cheque to X. It is conclusively presumed that he did.

3.3 *Negotiation of a cheque* is its transfer from one person to another in such a manner as to make the transferee the holder of the cheque: s 31.

3.4 To negotiate a cheque:

   (a) delivery is essential in every case; and
   (b) cheques payable to order must also be endorsed by the previous holder: s 31.

3.5 If the holder of a cheque which is payable to his order transfers it *for value* but without endorsing it:

   (a) the transferee acquires such title to the cheque as the transferor had; and

   (b) the transferee has the right to require the transferor to make the necessary endorsement: s 31(4).

3.6 Apart from the circumstances above, mere transfer of possession of a cheque does not give rights of ownership since the transferee is not the holder, unless it is a bearer cheque (the holder of a bearer cheque is the person in possession of it). Thus the theft of a bearer cheque makes the thief a holder even though there has been no *voluntary* delivery to him. The delivery of an order cheque bearing a forged endorsement gives no rights since there is no valid endorsement - the holder of an order cheque is its valid payee or endorsee.

## Order and bearer cheques

3.7  A cheque is payable either:

(a)  to or to the order of a specified person – an 'order cheque'; or
(b)  to bearer – it is payable to any person in possession if it (a 'bearer cheque').

The importance of the distinction lies in the need to endorse an order cheque as part of the process of transferring ownership.

*Bearer cheques*

3.8  A bearer cheque is one which is either:

(a)  drawn payable to bearer originally; or

(b)  an order cheque bearing a single or last endorsement in blank (explained below at paragraph 4.1); or

(c)  a cheque drawn payable to a non-existent or fictitious payee – it appears to be an order cheque but in reality it is not: s 7 (also explained below).

3.9  A *non-existent* payee is a payee of whose existence the drawer has no knowledge when he draws the cheque: s 7.

*Case: Clutton v Attenborough 1897*
A dishonest employee of C put before him for signature cheques payable to 'Brett', saying that C had trade debts owing to Brett. In fact there were none and C had no dealings with any person named Brett. The clerk then forged an endorsement by 'Brett' and negotiated the cheques to A, who became holder in due course provided that these were bearer cheques and not order cheques (for which a valid endorsement would be required).

*Held:* these were bearer cheques since 'Brett' was non-existent to C. It did not have to be shown that there was no living person named Brett.

3.10  A *fictitious* payee is a payee known to the drawer but to whom he does not intend (when the true facts are known) to make a payment, usually because he owes him nothing.

*Case: Bank of England v Vagliano 1891*
V's clerk drew a cheque on V as drawee and forged a drawer's signature by one of V's customers in favour of a person known to V. V accepted the cheque and the clerk forged the payee's endorsement in order to negotiate the cheque to the Bank of England.

*Held:* the payee, although existing, was fictitious since the drawer did not intend that he should receive payment.

*Case: Vinden v Hughes 1905*
The facts were as in *Clutton's* case above, except that the payees were persons with whom the employer had had dealings in the past, though he owed them nothing. Some cheques were signed before the payee's name was inserted.

*Held:* the drawer intended payment to be made to the payees whoever they might be and so they were not 'fictitious' or unintended payees.

## 4. ENDORSEMENT

4.1 We have seen above that endorsement is necessary to negotiate an order cheque. There are two main types of endorsement: s 34.

(a) *Endorsement in blank* - a simple signature of the holder on the reverse of the cheque. This converts an order cheque to a bearer cheque since it authorises payment to anyone to whom the cheque is delivered.

(b) *Special endorsement* - the holder's signature on the reverse of the cheque plus instructions to pay a particular person (the endorsee).

The cheque remains an order cheque. If the cheque is delivered to H Brown he becomes the holder (and may in turn negotiate it to another person by endorsement - special or in blank - plus delivery). If the cheque comes into the possession of anyone other than H Brown, he is not the holder since it is not payable to the mere possessor (nor is it payable to bearer).

4.2 The person to whom a special endorsement is made is called 'the endorsee'. He himself may later become an endorser to another endorsee.

4.3  A *restrictive endorsement* entitles the endorsee to obtain payment, but denies him the power to negotiate it: s 35(1). Examples – 'Pay X only'; 'Pay X for the account of Y' or 'Pay X or order for collection'. In these latter cases X is clearly only a collecting agent and not the owner of the cheque.

4.4  A restrictive endorsement may contain authority to transfer the cheque: s 35(3). This restores transferability but *not* negotiability. Thus a subsequent transferee takes the cheque subject to the 'equities' existing at the time of the restrictive endorsement.

4.5  Endorsement must always be of the entire amount of the cheque, which is a single order for payment and cannot be divided. An endorsement which requires payment of part of the amount of the cheque or requires a division between two recipients is invalid.

4.6  A *conditional endorsement* (eg 'Pay X on delivery of the goods') is valid to negotiate the cheque: s 33. The drawee may either disregard the condition – and pay the holder without insisting on its fulfilment – or, at his option, insist upon it.

## Form of endorsement

4.7  The above examples show that endorsement requires nothing more than the holder's signature. He can add if he wishes (this is not usually done) 'endorsed'. Endorsement is usually made on the back of the cheque but it can be done on the face of it. There are two rules affecting the position of the endorsement.

(a)  If there is more than one endorsement on a cheque they are deemed to have been made in the order in which they appear – the one below after the one above – unless and until the contrary is proved.

(b)  If there is insufficient space left, a strip of paper (called an 'allonge') may be attached to provide space for additional endorsements: s 32.

### *Irregular endorsement*

4.8  The endorsement should follow in form the order to pay the endorser (as payee or endorsee) which precedes it. If, for example, a cheque payable to 'F Smyth' is delivered to the payee who spells his name 'Smythe' with a final 'e' and he wishes to endorse, he should do so as 'F Smyth' though he may add if he wishes his correct signature (F Smythe) as well: s 32. If there is any discrepancy between the order to pay and the endorsement then the endorsement is 'irregular' and no subsequent holder of the cheque can be a holder in due course (explained in Section 9 of this chapter).

4.9  An irregular endorsement is effective to transfer ownership though not with the benefits of negotiability. A bank in paying a cheque is not usually concerned with any irregularity of endorsement by reason of s 1 Cheques Act 1957 (explained in Chapter 17).

*Endorsement by joint accountholders*

4.10 A cheque may be drawn payable, or later be endorsed, to two or more persons. If they both endorse the rules are as follows.

(a)  Partners may endorse (or sign as drawer) in the firm's name: s 23. The normal practice is that one partner signs in that name as agent for the firm (to the extent of his normal authority to do so).

(b)  Other joint payees or endorsees should *all* endorse unless one is authorised to do so for the others.

4.11 With regard to (b) above, trustees can only authorise one of themselves to sign for all if the trust deed so provides. Otherwise all must sign. But one executor can sign for all - though he should add words to show that he signs on that basis - for example 'For self and co-executors of J Smith deceased'.

*Endorsement on behalf of a company*

4.12 The endorser is necessarily an individual agent who should take precautions to avoid becoming personally liable on the cheque by ensuring that the company's name is correctly spelt. Otherwise he may be liable under s 349(4) Companies Act 1985 (see paragraph 5.6 below).

**Effect of endorsement**

4.13 Endorsement has two legal effects.

(a)  It is a necessary part of the negotiation for transfer of ownership of an order cheque. An invalid endorsement breaks the chain of title.

(b)  Endorsement of any cheque is a guarantee of payment unless the endorser expressly disclaims liability or restricts it.

## 5.   SIGNATURES ON CHEQUES

5.1  The definition requires that a cheque shall bear the drawer's signature. It may later be signed by the payee and any later holder of an order cheque as *endorser* in the course of negotiation. The same general principles apply to any such signature.

5.2  *A person is only liable on a cheque if it has been signed by him (as drawer, or endorser) or by his agent duly authorised.* For example, the holder of a cheque which the drawee bank refuses to pay has no claim against the bank (which has not signed it), though he usually has against the drawer since he has signed it: s 23. The transferor of a bearer cheque who negotiates it without endorsement is not liable on the cheque (since he does not sign it), though he has a limited liability arising from his position of 'transferor by delivery'.

## Forgery of signatures

5.3 A signature which is a forgery (or a signature by an agent who has no authority to sign - for example, a company cheque signed by a cleaner: 'per pro Wonder Ltd, M Mop') has no legal effect: s 24. *The cheque is treated as if there were a blank space where the forged signature is written.* The effect of a forged signature is therefore as follows.

(a) *Drawer's* signature forged - the cheque lacks an essential element and is invalid and worthless. If the bank fails to detect the forgery and pays the cheque it cannot usually debit the payment to the customer's account.

(b) *Endorser's* signature forged - this breaks the chain of title (if endorsement is necessary in the course of negotiation - it therefore does not break the chain if an endorsement is forged on a bearer cheque). The previous holder whose signature is forged can recover the cheque (or its value if it has been paid) from the person in possession of it and the latter (contrary to appearances) is not the holder.

The bank may not debit payment to its customer's account unless the customer failed in his duty to exercise due care in drawing cheques:

## Form of signature

5.4 A cheque may be signed in the name of a firm; it is normal practice for partnership cheques to be signed in this way. This form of signature is equivalent to the signature of all the individual partners: s 23(2). A person may sign a cheque under the business name which he uses or even an assumed name. If he does so he is liable as if he had signed in his personal or real name: s 23(1).

### *Signatures on company cheques*

5.5 We have seen that a director or other person signing a company cheque in accordance with the mandate is treated as signing in a representative capacity even if this is not made clear in the signature. A company is required by s 349 Companies Act 1985 to have its name in legible characters on all cheques. The same section states that a director is liable on any cheque not paid by the company if he signs it at a time when the company's correct name is not on it.

*Case: Durham Fancy Goods Ltd v Michael Jackson (Fancy Goods) Ltd 1968*
A creditor drew a bill of exchange on the company and wrote on it a form of acceptance which did not state the correct name of the company ('M Jackson' instead of 'Michael Jackson' in full). The defendant signed the acceptance for the company.

*Held:* the defendant was not liable since the error had been introduced by the plaintiff. But for that fact it would have been liable.

## Agent's signature on cheques

5.6 An agent who signs a cheque should add words to indicate that he signs 'for or on behalf of' his principal. He is not then personally liable on the cheque. But if he merely specifies his position (such as 'manager'), he is treated as signing in a personal capacity and is liable accordingly: s 26. Note that the *Bondina* case means that this rule no longer applies to company directors.

5.7 An agent who endorses a cheque in a situation where endorsement on behalf of his principal is unnecessary may be treated as a guarantor since this is favourable to the validity of the cheque: s 26(2). This type of liability is described at paragraph 10.6 below.

5.8 A principal is liable on a cheque signed by his agent if the agent had either actual or apparent authority to sign it. If he limits the agent's authority to less than is usual the limitation is only effective if it is disclosed to the other party.

5.9 An agent who makes a procuration signature ('H Brown per pro') discloses that he may have only limited authority. If he is exceeding his actual authority the principal is not usually bound: s 25.

*Case: Morison v Kemp 1912*
A clerk was authorised to sign business cheques drawn on his employer's account and he signed 'per pro'. Using this style he drew a cheque to pay a personal debt to a bookmaker.

*Held:* the employer could recover the money since the payment was in excess of the clerk's authority and the existence of a limit on it had been disclosed.

5.10 The principle above is subject to any overriding authority given expressly by the principal. In modern practice a bank insists that a customer shall supply a mandate to the bank authorising it to pay cheques signed only by the customer's authorised signatories. In giving the mandate the customer represents that any cheque (even if signed 'per pro') signed by an authorised signatory has his authority. He is estopped against the bank from denying it (but he would not be estopped against a third party unaware of the mandate, as in *Morison's* case above).

5.11 A bank may also be able to rely on the rule in *Turquand's* case (described in Chapter 12) if a cheque has been signed on behalf of a company by a director or officer of the company in excess of his actual authority. If the articles of association permit the board of directors to give authority to an individual agent to sign cheques, the bank (or other person concerned) can assert that it was entitled to assume that the authority had been duly given. But this rule is restricted to cases where the signatory held a senior position and the provision for authorisation was known.

*Case: Kreditbank Cassel GmbH v Schenkers Ltd 1927*
A branch manager drew cheques in the name of the company to pay his personal debts. The plaintiff bank to which the cheques were made payable was unaware that the company's articles of association permitted the directors to delegate authority to sign cheques. The company repudiated the cheques.

*Held:* the company was not liable since it was not within the usual and therefore apparent authority of a branch manager (arising from the position which he held) to issue cheques for the company. The bank could not rely on the possibility of authorisation under the articles since it was unaware of that provision. Moreover an unauthorised signature by an agent is equivalent to a forgery and has no effect.

## 6. CAPACITY TO BE LIABLE ON A CHEQUE

6.1 The rules on capacity to assume liability on a cheque are the same as the rules on capacity to make contracts: s 22. As regards minors, apart from contracts for necessary goods (defined by s 3 Sale of Goods Act 1979), contracts are not enforceable unless ratified: Minors' Contracts Act 1987.

   (a) A minor can never be liable on a cheque which he has signed. For example, if a minor draws a cheque to pay for necessaries and the cheque is dishonoured by the bank, no one can sue the minor as drawer of the cheque, though he remains liable to pay for the necessaries.

   (b) If a minor draws a cheque and the bank pays it, the bank may debit his account and the payee may retain the money.

   (c) If a minor endorses a cheque to negotiate it, he has no liability on it as endorser but the endorsement is effective to transfer ownership to the endorsee.

6.2 The capacity of a company is defined by its objects clause supported by the *ultra vires* doctrine and subject to the effect of the s 35(1) and s 35A Companies Act 1985 (explained in Chapter 12). The rules given in (b) and (c) above apply to a company which draws or endorses a cheque when it lacks capacity to do so.

## 7. DISHONOUR AND DISCHARGE OF CHEQUES

**Dishonour of cheques**

7.1 If a cheque is presented for payment at the proper place and is not paid, it is then *dishonoured for non-payment*.

7.2 In case of dishonour by non-payment, the holder should give notice of the dishonour to the drawer and to any endorsers within a reasonable time (normally within 24 hours). If he does not do so the other parties are discharged from their liability on the cheque (except that if the holder at the time of dishonour later negotiates the cheque to a holder in due course, the latter may still sue all previous parties: s 48).

7.3 The rules on notice of dishonour of a cheque are as follows: s 49.

   (a) The holder, or the endorser liable at the time of notice, or their agents, must give notice to the drawer and each endorser (or their personal representatives if known to be dead).

   (b) Failure to give such notice discharges the drawer or endorser: s 48.

   (c) Notice given by the holder or by a liable endorser means that subsequent holders and prior endorsers need not give notice

   (d) Notice should be given as soon as the cheque is dishonoured, or within a reasonable time (on the day if the parties are close at hand, the next business day by post if not).

7.4 Delay in giving notice of dishonour is excused when the delay is caused by circumstances beyond the control of the person who eventually gives the notice. In a number of specified circumstances the duty to give notice is dispensed with altogether (s 50):

(a) when, after exercise of reasonable diligence, the notice cannot be given;

(b) if the person entitled to it has waived it; or

(c) where the drawer has countermanded payment of the cheque.

7.5 The notice may be given orally or in writing: s 49. With dishonoured cheques it is normal practice to return the cheque to the drawer by way of notice. The notice is sufficient if it is accurate when received; it need not be signed.

*Case: Eaglehill v J Needham Builders 1973*
A bill of exchange was due for payment on 31 December 1970 but the acceptor went into insolvent liquidation before that date. The holder posted on 30 December 1970 a notice of dishonour dated 1 January 1971. It reached the acceptor on 31 December 1970.

*Held:* the notice took effect when received and so on these facts it was valid. Notice given and received before dishonour (even if dishonour followed) would be invalid.

7.6 Liquidated damages may be sought under s 57 where a cheque has been dishonoured. This means that only actual, calculable loss may be made up by an award. The amount of the cheque plus interest may be recovered:

(a) by the holder, from any party liable;

(b) by an endorser who has paid, from the drawer or any prior endorser.

## Discharge of a cheque

7.7 A cheque is discharged when no one has any outstanding claims arising from it. If the bank pays the cheque to the holder in good faith and without notice of any defect in his title, that is payment in due course which discharges the cheque: s 59.

7.8 An endorser may be required as guarantor to pay the cheque. He then has rights of recourse against other parties and so the cheque is not discharged.

7.9 A cheque is also discharged if:

(a) the holder (or his authorised agent) intentionally makes an 'apparent' cancellation of it. Any particular party is discharged from liability if the holder intentionally cancels that party's signature: s 63;

(b) there is material alteration of the cheque without the assent of all the parties liable; it is discharged except against the person making the alteration and subsequent endorsers: s 64 (see paragraph 7.11 below).

*Cancellation, alterations and additions*

7.10 It must be apparent that *cancellation* was intended – evidently unintentional, mistaken or unauthorised cancellation is inoperative. But the party who alleges that it was unintentional must prove that it was so.

7.11 A material or significant *alteration* to a cheque, unless made with the assent of all the parties liable on it, avoids the cheque except against:

(a) a party who made, authorised or assented to the alteration; and
(b) any person who endorses it after the alteration has been made: s 64.

An alteration of the date and of the sum payable are material alterations.

7.12 If, however, the alteration is not 'apparent' or obvious, and the cheque comes into the hands of a holder in due course, he can enforce it in its original form as if it had not been altered. Consider the following example:

---

- A draws a cheque for £500 on his bank and delivers it to
- B as payee, who alters the amount to £5,000 and endorses it for value to
- C, who endorses it to
- D for value.

(a) If the alteration is *apparent*, D is not the holder in due course but B, who made the alteration, and C who endorsed the cheque after it was made, are liable to D for £5,000. D has no rights against A.

(b) If the alteration is *not apparent* and D is a holder in due course, D has the same rights against B and C and can also claim £500 from A (drawer). D cannot, of course, recover more than £5,000 in total.

---

7.13 An *addition* is often a material alteration to which the above rules apply. But additions may be made without avoiding the cheque in the following cases.

(a) A drawer may issue a signed cheque (an 'inchoate instrument') with authority to the holder to complete it by inserting the amount, the payee's name etc. If it is then completed within a reasonable time and strictly in accordance with the authority given, it becomes enforceable in its completed form. If it comes to a holder in due course he can enforce it as it stands whether or not the additions were authorised.

(b) A cheque may be undated. If the missing date is necessary to fix the time for payment, a holder may insert the correct date. If the holder by mistake but in good faith inserts an incorrect date and the cheque comes into the hands of a holder in due course, he may claim payment in accordance with the date written on the cheque as if it were correct.

## 8. VALUE FOR A CHEQUE

8.1 Value for a cheque is essentially the same as consideration for an ordinary contract except that 'an antecedent debt or liability' (past consideration) is sufficient for a cheque: s 27. Most cheques and other bills are in fact issued to discharge existing debts.

8.2 The value given is usually money or other property. But it may take some other form.

*Case: Pollway v Abdullah 1974*
P, an auctioneer, sold property to D and accepted D's cheque in payment of a 10 per cent deposit. D later stopped the cheque and the owners of the property, for whom P was acting as agent, treated the contract as discharged by breach. P sued D (as drawer) on the cheque and D argued that no value had been given for it.

*Held:* in selling as agent for the owners, P warranted that he had authority to sell. This was sufficient 'value' by the normal rules applicable to consideration.

*Case: MacKenzie Mills v Buono 1986*
X, the payee of a cheque drawn by the defendant, B, endorsed it to the plaintiff, M, to cover continuing costs in litigation. At that time it was clear that further costs would be incurred in the future between M and X. B stopped the cheque, claiming he had drawn it in payment for goods which X had failed to deliver. M claimed against B.

*Held:* B had received value in the form of anticipated receipt of goods, and so M was a holder for value under s 27(2). In addition, because M had taken the cheque in payment of present and future debts, and had fulfilled other requirements of s 29, it was also a holder in due course. This decision gives a very wide interpretation to the idea of value.

8.3 As will be explained later, value need not be given by the holder. But where the value given is an antecedent (existing) debt it must be a debt owing *by the person who issues the cheque.*

*Case: Oliver v Davis 1949*
D owed £400 to O which he could not pay. D persuaded W to draw a cheque for this amount payable to O. The cheque was delivered to O. W later changed her mind and stopped the cheque. O sued W on the cheque.

*Held:* no value had been given for the cheque since W owed O nothing and 'antecedent debt' is limited to a debt of the person who issues the cheque. If there had been a bargain with W (in fact there was none) by which O accepted W's cheque in return for forbearing to press his claim against D, his forbearance would probably (an *obiter dictum*) have been sufficient value for the cheque.

8.4 *Oliver's* case above was decided on the basis that no value had been given to W. But where value is received it need not be provided by the holder.

*Case: Diamond v Graham 1968*
H, in obtaining a loan from D, issued a cheque to G in exchange for G's cheque payable to D. H's cheque was dishonoured and G stopped payment of his cheque to D. D sued G who argued that no value had been given by D for G's cheque.

*Held:* H's cheque, although it did not come from D, was value for G's cheque payable to D. (D himself had provided value by making his loan to H.)

## 9.  HOLDERS FOR VALUE AND IN DUE COURSE

9.1  A cheque for which no value has ever been given is a valid order to pay – the drawee is entitled to pay it and the holder to retain the money. But if the drawee refuses to pay, the holder has no rights on the cheque against anyone. The donor of a gift cheque may stop payment of his cheque and the donee has no claim, because he has never given value.

### Holder for value

9.2
> A *holder for value* is the holder of a cheque for which value has *at some time* been given – but not usually by him. For example, A issues a cheque to B in payment of A's debt to B; B gives and A receives value. B then endorses the cheque to C and delivers it to C as a present.
>
>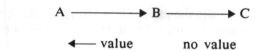
>
> A ─────────▶ B ─────────▶ C
>
> ◀─── value          no value
>
> C, who has given no value himself, is nonetheless a holder for value.

9.3  The original payee of a cheque (unless it is a gift) is no more than a holder for value.

9.4  The rights of a holder for value are limited.

(a)  His rights are against the latest party to the cheque who received value and all parties previous to that latest party whether or not they received value. (A holder in due course has rights against all previous parties – see paragraph 9.13.) For example:

A ─────────▶ B ─────────▶ C ─────────▶ D ─────────▶ E
                                                    Holder for
no value  ◀─── value  ◀─── value   no value     value

A issues a cheque to B as a gift; B and then C negotiates it for value, D gives the cheque to E as a gift. If the cheque is not paid, E can sue A, B or C but not D. B and C received value; A did not but he is liable because value was given *after* he issued his cheque. E has no rights against D who received no value from E; C is the latest party in the sequence to receive value.

(b)  His rights are no better than those of his immediate transferor. If, for example, a thief steals a bearer bill, for which value has been given, the thief is the holder (since the holder of a bearer bill is the person in possession of it). If he gives it to his wife she, as holder for value, has no better title than the thief – none at all.

### Holder in due course

9.5  A *holder in due course* is one:

(a)  who is a holder;
(b)  to whom the cheque has been negotiated; and
(c)  who satisfies six conditions prescribed by s 29.

9.6    *He must be the holder* – he must be in possession of a bearer cheque or an order cheque payable (by one or more valid endorsements) to him. If an apparent chain of endorsements from the payee to him is broken by forgery, he is not the holder.

9.7    The conditions of s 29 must be satisfied *at the time* when the cheque is negotiated (transferred) to him. Hence the original payee cannot be a holder in due course since there is no negotiation to him.

*Case: Jones v Waring & Gillow Ltd 1926*
B owed £5,000 to WG. By fraud B persuaded J to draw a cheque for £5,000 payable to WG, which B delivered to WG. J later sued to recover the money from WG on the ground that the cheque had been obtained by fraud. WG argued that they satisfied the conditions of s 29 and were a holder in due course entitled to the proceeds of the cheque.

*Held:* the working of s 29 precludes the payee from asserting that he was a holder in due course. The money had been paid under a mistake of fact and must be returned.

9.8    Two of the six conditions of s 29 relate to the condition of the cheque when negotiated:

> (a)    it must not then be overdue for payment; and
> (b)    it must be complete and regular on the face of it.

9.9    A cheque is not 'complete and regular' if it is incomplete, or has an alteration which is apparent, or even has an irregular endorsement.

*Case: Arab Bank Ltd v Ross 1952*
R issued two promissory notes (subject to the same rules on this point as a cheque) to 'FFN and Company'. The payee endorsed the notes to AB (the plaintiffs) by signing on the reverse 'FFN' (without 'and company'). AB claimed to be holder in due course.

*Held:* an endorsement which does not correspond exactly with the payee as named is irregular (see paragraph 4.8 above). It is an effective endorsement to transfer ownership but the cheque is no longer 'regular' so that a subsequent holder cannot be a holder in due course.

9.10   Following on from paragraph 9.8, the other four requirements of s 29 relate to the circumstances in which the holder acquires the cheque – he must do so:

> (c)    in good faith;
> (d)    for value;
> (e)    without notice of previous dishonour; and
> (f)    without notice of defect of title of the person who negotiates it to him.

9.11   Requirement (e) only arises if there is in fact previous dishonour or a defect of title of a previous party. The holder has then to show that when he took the cheque he had no notice (knowledge or strong grounds for suspicion) of the facts in question.

9.12 It is presumed that a holder is a holder in due course unless and until some irregularity is established in the history of the cheque. Only then must the holder show by positive proof that he gave value and took the cheque in good faith (and without notice): s 30.

9.13 A holder in due course holds the cheque free from any defect of title of previous parties (and any rights such as set-off which one may have against another) and he may enforce payment in full against all the previous parties: s 38(2). (Contrast the more limited rights of a holder for value as described in paragraph 9.4.)

9.14 A holder of any kind who derives his title through a holder in due course has the same rights against parties *before* the holder in due course as the latter had, unless the subsequent holder is a party to some fraud or illegality affecting it: s 29. For example, if a holder in due course gives the cheque to his wife, she is a mere holder for value but with the same rights as he had against all previous parties. If the holder in due course had acquired the cheque from a person who obtained it by fraud that would still be the position. But if, to vary the facts, the holder in due course negotiated the cheque back to the crook from whom he originally acquired it, the latter (as a party to the fraud) would not be protected by this rule.

## 10. LIABILITIES OF THE PARTIES TO A CHEQUE

10.1 By signing a cheque as drawer, or endorser, the signatory becomes a party to whom special liabilities and restrictions apply. Very broadly these are of two kinds.

(a) An obligation to pay the cheque is accepted: the drawer and any endorser is merely a guarantor who becomes liable only if another party with prior liability defaults.

(b) The signatory confirms a number of points which may affect his liability to a subsequent holder: he has the opportunity to dispute these matters before he signs. By signing he gives up any right to dispute them (if relevant facts come to light later) and guarantees that all the factors affecting subsequent rights on the cheque are in order.

10.2 There is a chain of responsibility: each signatory is liable to subsequent parties and each party has rights against any previous signatory.

### Liabilities of the drawer

10.3 By drawing and issuing the cheque the drawer:

(a) undertakes that it shall be paid at the due date, and that if it is dishonoured he will compensate the holder or any endorser who is compelled to pay, provided that the proper action is taken when it is dishonoured under s 49 (see paragraph 7.3). In the case of a cheque, the drawer guarantees that if his bank does not pay it, he will. But like any other party he is only liable if value has been given;

(b) may not deny to a holder in due course that the payee (i) exists and (ii) has capacity to endorse. He does not guarantee the genuineness of a payee's endorsement (only added later) but he cannot deny that the payee (specified by himself) was competent by genuine endorsement to negotiate the cheque to an endorsee: s 55(1).

**Liabilities of the endorser**

**10.4** By endorsing a cheque, the endorser:

    (a)  gives the same undertaking regarding payment etc as the drawer, but his liability is limited to the holder and any endorser *after* himself;

    (b)  may not deny to a holder in due course the genuineness and regularity of the drawer's signature and any endorsements *before* his own; and

    (c)  may not deny to his immediate or a subsequent endorsee that at the time of his own endorsement:

        (i)   the cheque was valid and subsisting; and
        (ii)  he had good title to it: s 55(2).

**10.5** The general effect of endorsement is thus to guarantee to subsequent parties that

    (a)  all previous signatures are genuine;
    (b)  the cheque is valid and will be paid; and
    (c)  the endorser will pay if parties previous to himself default.

It is this which protects the transferee who finds that he is not even a holder (and so not a holder in due course) because some endorsement on an order cheque is (unknown to him at the time) a forgery. He can recover damages for his loss from any endorser who signed *after* the forgery. For example:

$$A \longrightarrow B \longrightarrow C \quad \text{forged} \quad D \longrightarrow E \longrightarrow F$$
$$\text{endorsement}$$

(Drawer)     (Payee)

C remains the owner of the cheque and can compel F to hand it back to him. But F can claim compensation (because they guaranteed that C's apparent endorsement was genuine) from either D or E provided that he gives them due notice of dishonour. In practice, F would recover from E and E from D. The loss (arising from forged endorsement) always falls on the first endorser (D) after the forgery. D of course will have a claim against the forger but it is likely to be valueless.

**10.6** Endorsement of an order cheque therefore serves a double purpose - firstly, combined with delivery it transfers ownership and secondly, it serves as a guarantee. So it is possible to endorse a cheque merely to provide a guarantee to a holder in due course.

*Case: Rolfe Lubell v Keith 1979*
A company accepted a bill of exchange drawn on itself. A director and the secretary also signed their names on the back 'for and on behalf of the company'. The company defaulted.

*Held:* these signatures (although expressed in agency terms) must be treated as personal endorsements (they served no other purpose) and so the endorsers were liable as guarantors.

10.7 This decision is based on s 26(2) which provides that in determining whether a person has signed a cheque as principal, so as to assume personal liability, 'the construction most favourable to the validity of the instrument shall be adopted'. A cheque which is supported by a personal guarantee (even if valid without it) is a more effective instrument of credit.

10.8 It is also possible to endorse a cheque for the purpose of negotiation but without assuming liability on it by the use of a disclaimer such as 'sans recours' (which means 'without recourse to me': s 16). But even with that formula the endorser has a liability (independent of the cheque) as transferor equivalent to that of the transferor of a bearer cheque who does not usually endorse it at all.

**Liability of the transferor by delivery**

10.9 If the holder of a bearer cheque negotiates it by delivery without endorsement, he does not become a party and has no liability on the cheque itself: s 58. But he warrants (guarantees) to his immediate transferee (but not to any subsequent holder) that if the transferee is a holder for value:

(a)  the cheque is what it purports to be;
(b)  he has the right to transfer it; and
(c)  at the time of transfer he is unaware of any fact which renders it valueless.

10.10 For example, if a bearer cheque passes without endorsement through the hands of several holders and is then dishonoured, the ultimate holder can claim against his immediate transferor (but only on the grounds of invalidity in (a), (b) or (c) above) and he in turn against his transferor and so on. But the ultimate holder has no direct right of action against previous transferors further back along the sequence such as endorsement of an order cheque would give.

10.11 Even a transferor by delivery may endorse a bearer cheque by way of guarantee only. He is then liable down the chain to any subsequent holder.

## 11. CROSSINGS ON CHEQUES

11.1 There are four recognised types of crossing on cheques - general, special, not negotiable and a/c payee. The first three are recognised by statute, s 76, and the a/c payee crossing has been given statutory recognition by Cheques Act 1992, which inserts a new s 81A into the Act.

11.2 A *general* crossing is two transverse lines across the cheque (usually pre-printed on the cheques when issued by the bank to customers). The words 'and company' or an abbreviation ('A/Co') may be written between the lines but it is no longer usual to do so. *A general crossing instructs the paying bank to make payment only to another bank.* It is a considerable safeguard to the paying bank against liability if payment is obtained by a person not entitled to it.

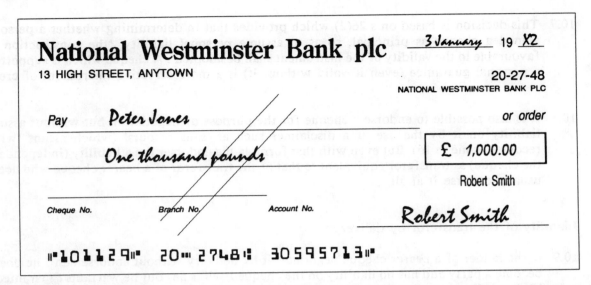

11.3 A *special crossing* is the name of the collecting bank (and often its branch address) written across the cheque. It is usual (though not strictly necessary) to have two transverse lines and to stamp the name of the bank between them.

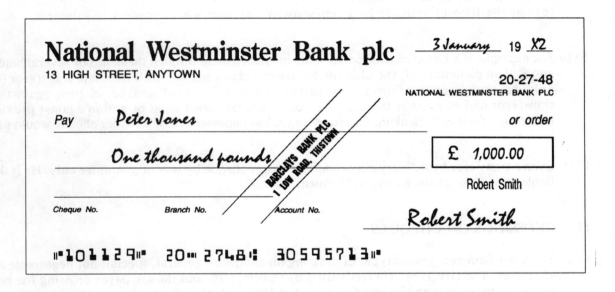

This is an instruction to the paying bank *to make payment only to the bank designated by the special crossing* (or to its London agent which must be another bank). The words of the special crossing are added by the collecting bank (for identification) before the cheque is put through the clearing between banks. It is a precaution against loss in the clearing system.

11.4 A general or a special crossing may be combined with either or both of the 'not negotiable' or 'a/c payee' crossings: s 76.

11.5 The practical effect of a general or special crossing is that the paying bank:

(a)   should only pay a generally crossed cheque to another bank (as agent for the holder);

(b) should only pay a specially crossed cheque to the designated collecting bank or to another bank which it specifies as its agent for collection.

If the paying bank ignores these obligations it is liable to the true owner of the cheque for any loss he may suffer: s 79. There is also a positive advantage to both bank and customer in paying a crossed cheque according to the crossing: s 80. Who is the true owner of a particular cheque is a matter usually for the court to decide in each case.

### 'Not negotiable' crossing

11.6 The words 'not negotiable' may be written (between the lines of the crossing) by the drawer or any subsequent holder. The effect is that any person into whose hands the cheque may come does not have (and cannot give to his transferee) any better title than that which the transferor to him had: s 81. It is primarily a protection against theft of *bearer cheques* which are transferable merely by delivery.

For example, A delivers a cheque payable to B in payment of A's debt to B. B endorses the cheque in blank, converting it to a bearer cheque. C steals the cheque from B and negotiates it to D who takes it in good faith, for value and qualifies in all other respects as a holder in due course. D has then acquired good title to the cheque though C as the thief had none (since it had not been transferred to him). But if A or B had crossed the cheque 'not negotiable' D could have no better title than C, who had none.

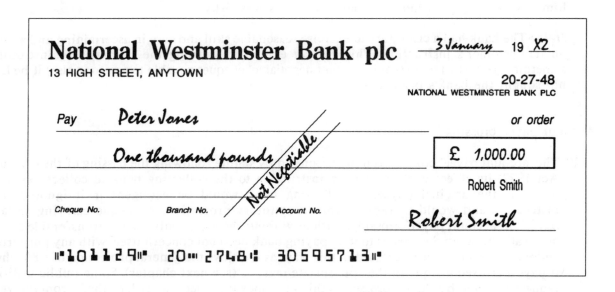

11.7 The not negotiable crossing is less significant on an *order cheque*. To vary the facts of the above example, suppose C steals B's cheque when it is unendorsed, forges the endorsement of B, and negotiates it to D. The forged endorsement has no legal effect: the cheque remains the property of B. D's remedy is a claim (probably worthless) against C. But if an order cheque is obtained by fraud, endorsed by the payee and negotiated for value to an honest endorsee the 'not negotiable' crossing would deny to the latter any better rights than the payee had. The following case is another example relating to an order cheque.

*Case: Wilson and Meeson v Pickering 1946*
W signed a cheque crossed 'not negotiable' and handed it to an employee to fill in the amount and the name of the payee. The clerk inserted an amount in excess of her authority and the name of P as payee and delivered the cheque to P in payment of a debt which she owed to him.

*Held:* the clerk had no title to the cheque and (by reason of the 'not negotiable' crossing) P could acquire no better title than she had. P's claim against W as drawer of the cheque failed.

11.8 The not negotiable crossing on a cheque does *not* prevent its transfer. It merely ensures that the transferee has no better rights than his transferor had. The transferee for value of a cheque issued for an illegal consideration and crossed 'not negotiable' can recover nothing on it since his transferor had no rights by reason of illegality: *Ladup Ltd v Shaikh and Ritz Casino Ltd 1982*.

11.9 A bank is not directly affected by the not negotiable crossing, which places no obligations on a paying or a collecting bank, but only affects the holder. The case below has an interesting bearing on the bank's duty to its customer with respect to cheques.

*Case: Redmond v Allied Irish Bank plc 1987*
The customer, R, paid in cheques for collection crossed 'Not negotiable a/c payee only'. R was not payee of the cheques. When the cheques were returned unpaid the bank debited his account with their amounts. R claimed for loss arising from this action since the bank had not warned him that dealing with 'not negotiable' cheques was risky.

*Held:* The bank had a clear duty to exercise reasonable skill and care in ascertaining and acting on its customer's instruction. This did *not* extend to warning the customer against doing something he wished to do (paying in 'not negotiable' cheques payable to someone else) if he had not sought the bank's prior advice.

**Account payee crossing**

11.10 The 'account payee' crossing is now recognised by statute following the passing of the Cheques Act 1992. Its effect is clear. It is an instruction to the collecting bank to collect payment only for the original payee. A collecting bank would be negligent if it ignored that instruction and would thereby forfeit its statutory protection. A cheque carrying an 'a/c payee' or 'account payee' crossing, with or without the word 'only', is not transferable and is only valid between the parties to it. A paying bank need not concern itself with any purported endorsement on a cheque crossed in this way, as it enjoys the general protection of s 80 when it pays a crossed cheque in the appropriate manner (see next chapter). Some public utilities request payment by cheque crossed in this way since it reduces the risk of theft from the very large number of cheques which they receive. They do not need transferable cheques but pay them in to their own bank accounts.

**National Westminster Bank plc** _3 January_ 19 _X2_

13 HIGH STREET, ANYTOWN

20-27-48
NATIONAL WESTMINSTER BANK PLC

Pay _Peter Jones_ or order

_One thousand pounds_ A/C Payee £ 1,000.00

Robert Smith

Cheque No.　　Branch No.　　Account No.

_Robert Smith_

⑈101129⑈ 20⑈2748⑈ 30595713⑈

## Altering crossings

11.11 Most printed cheque forms bear a pre-printed general crossing. The drawer may always cross a cheque by inserting a general crossing (if none is printed), or adding words to make it a special crossing, not negotiable or account payee crossing.

11.12 A holder may similarly insert a general crossing or change a general crossing to a special and/or 'not negotiable' one.

11.13 A bank to which a crossed cheque is delivered for collection may:

(a) specially cross it to another bank as its agent for collection although it bears a special crossing for payment to itself; or

(b) specially cross a cheque for payment to itself if it receives the cheque which is uncrossed or with a general crossing only: s 77.

11.14 Once the cheque bears a crossing of any type inserted by the drawer or any subsequent holder, the crossing becomes a 'material part' of the cheque: s 78. No one but the drawer may obliterate or delete any part of an existing crossing. If this is done then there has been a material alteration with the effects already described.

11.15 The drawer (but no one else) may alter a cheque which bears a pre-printed general crossing by writing between the lines 'Pay Cash' and adding his signature or initials. If a subsequent holder did this he would be altering the drawer's instructions for payment and this would be a material alteration: s 78.

11.16 A bank may pay a crossed cheque at the counter, thereby ignoring the instruction, in the following circumstances.

(a) If the drawer (or some representative well known to the bank such as the cashier of a company customer collecting wages each week) presents a crossed cheque for payment in cash, banks usually ignore the crossing on the grounds that there is no risk of the money passing to a person not entitled to it.

(b) The crossing may have been skilfully deleted (or the drawer's authority to delete it may have been skilfully forged). The fact that it is still a crossed cheque (since a forgery has no legal effect) is then not apparent and the paying bank escapes liability if it pays in good faith (without knowledge of the alteration) and without negligence (without carelessness in failing to detect it): s 79.

## 12. CONCLUSION

12.1 A cheque is a form of bill of exchange and so the law and rules of practice regarding cheques have built up over quite a long time. Although bills of exchange as such are not included in your syllabus, it will help you to know the statutory definition of one in the 1882 Act in order to combine it with that of a cheque contained in the Cheques Act 1957.

12.2 You must be sure to understand the advantages of negotiability as compared with transferability. The former allows full and legal title to be transferred 'free of equities' - the transferee *may* have better rights than the transferor had.

12.3 An order cheque can only be negotiated by delivery *and* endorsement. The rules on endorsement are therefore very important, as are signatures and the effect of forgeries.

12.4 You must understand the definitions and respective rights of a holder for value and a holder in due course. The former has rights only against the last previous party to him who received value (and all parties before that person), and he has no better rights than his immediate transferor. The holder in due course, on the other hand, holds the cheque free from any defect of title of previous parties and can enforce these rights against *any* of the previous parties.

12.5 The rules on cheque crossings and correct endorsement are very important in the context of your examination, and you should be sure to understand both the purpose and form of each.

---

## TEST YOUR KNOWLEDGE
*The numbers in brackets refer to paragraphs of this chapter*

1   What is the difference between assignability, negotiability and transferability? (1.1, 1.6, 1.13)

2   What is the statutory definition of a cheque? (2.1)

3   Explain the three vital elements of a cheque. (2.9, 2.15, 2.23)

4   Define a 'holder' of a cheque (2.22)

5   How is a cheque negotiated? What is the effect if a necessary endorsement of an order cheque is (i) forged (ii) omitted by the transferor in delivering the cheque for value? (3.4, 3.6, 3.5)

6   In what ways may a cheque be or become a bearer cheque? (3.8)

7   Describe and illustrate an endorsement which is (i) in blank, (ii) special, (iii) conditional, (iv) restrictive, (v) partial and (vi) irregular, and say what is the effect of each. (4.1, 4.6, 4.3, 4.5, 4.8)

8   What are the relevant rules on endorsement (i) by joint holders, (ii) by partners and (iii) by company officers? (4.10, 4.12)

9   What is the effect of a forged signature on a cheque? (5.3)

10   What is a minor's liability on a cheque? (6.1)

11   What are the effects of (i) cancellation (ii) alteration and (iii) additions on a cheque? (7.10, 7.11, 7.13)

12   Distinguish between the rights of a holder for value and a holder in due course. (9.2, 9.13)

13   State the respective liabilities of (i) a drawer (ii) an endorser and (iii) a transferor by delivery of a cheque. (10.3, 10.4, 10.9)

14   Describe the four legally recognised types of crossing on cheques. (11.2)

---

*Now try question 28 to 30 at the end of the text*

*Chapter 17*

# THE PROTECTION OF BANKS

---

**This chapter covers the following topics.**

1. The protection of banks
2. The paying bank's protection
3. The collecting bank's protection
4. House debits
5. Banker's drafts
6. Other bank payment orders
7. Cheque guarantee cards
8. Credit cards

---

## 1. THE PROTECTION OF BANKS

1.1 The huge number of cheque transactions handled by the banks on every working day makes it necessary to modify the basic rules of liability to give to the banks a reasonable degree of protection. Because the number of individual transactions is large and dispersed over thousands of bank branches in the UK, the banks must develop and apply standard working procedures (including the use of computers and other forms of mechanised accounting).

1.2 Those procedures, which are kept under review and improved as the need arises, are 'the ordinary course of business' for a bank. Cheques are dealt with in this ordinary course of business and it is hardly possible for bank staff to stop in order to examine, consider and make enquiries or reference to records in connection with each individual cheque. Up to a point the law recognises this fact and sets the standard of care which is required in relation to it.

1.3 The law does not however usually recognise the ordinary course of business as the *automatic* required standard (the rules on endorsements do however impose that standard). What is required (to avoid liability arising from negligence) is that the ordinary course of business shall be followed with some alertness and care to discern (and then investigate) what is unusual or even suspicious in the context of what a bank knows or ought to know of the attendant circumstances. The courts have never found it easy to set a standard of care. It has been said that each decision in this field of law depends on its particular facts. Hence a sound knowledge of case law is essential. Examination questions are often set on the facts of reported cases - the examiner is thus assured that he at least knows the answer to his own question!

1.4 The other key point to keep in view is that in deciding whether there has been negligence, much depends on the degree of knowledge about the customer and his affairs which the bank possesses. A bank which pays a crossed cheque can usually have no knowledge of the payee or other holder of the cheque. The collecting bank stands between the paying bank and the stranger who receives the payment. The paying bank is therefore not usually at fault. But the collecting bank, because it collects crossed cheques for its own customer, can and should know something about him - something which may call for enquiry.

1.5 In connection with open cheques the position is obviously different. If these are presented at the counter the paying bank is in direct contact with the recipient - who may nonetheless be a stranger.

## The bank's contractual liability

1.6 There are two quite different principles upon which a bank may incur liability on a cheque transaction. The bank upon which a cheque is drawn has obligations to its customer as drawer. That is generally a *contractual liability* (though 'Refer to Drawer' may be defamatory). That branch of the law of cheques has already been explained.

## The tort of conversion

1.7 The second principle of possible liability is 'conversion'. This common law tort is now defined by statute as a form of 'wrongful interference with goods' under the Torts (Interference with Goods) Act 1977.

Conversion, which is only one form of wrongful interference, is dealing with the property of another person in a manner which denies or is inconsistent with that person's ownership of and right to possess his property.

1.8 A bank which pays a cheque to or collects a cheque for a person other than the true owner is liable to him, usually for the value of the cheque. It is no defence that the bank was quite innocent and unaware of the fraud or of the true owner's claim. In tort, liability (in most cases) depends on the act and not on the state of mind.

1.9 It is also no defence that the bank has gained no benefit for itself from the transaction. The bank acts as agent for another person. But an agent who innocently commits a tort in acting for his principal is personally liable.

*True owner*

1.10 In giving banks protection against conversion in certain circumstances the 1882 and 1957 Acts refer to 'the true owner' (eg s 80 of the 1882 Act and s 4 of the 1957 Act).

1.11 True owner is not a defined term. Essentially it means:

(a) the drawer of a cheque up to the moment of issue; and
(b) the person who is the lawful owner of the cheque at a particular time after issue.

### Stolen cheques

1.12 In normal circumstances once a cheque has been issued the true owner is also the holder, he has possession (directly or through the agent such as his bank) and the cheque is payable to him (or to bearer): s 2. But theft of a cheque creates a different situation.

   (a) The *true owner* is still the owner but he is no longer the holder since he has lost possession. If he can trace the cheque he can recover possession from anyone except a holder in due course.

   (b) The *thief* has possession but he is not the holder of an order cheque, since it was not delivered to him. If it is a bearer cheque payable to the person in possession then he is the holder. If the thief is the holder of a bearer cheque it is not his property, but as holder he can transfer it. If on the other hand it is an order cheque, an endorsement forged by the thief has no legal effect (s 24) and mere delivery of an order cheque (with a forged endorsement) gives the transferee no title: s 31.

   (c) A *person who obtains* a stolen cheque innocently and for value has no title to it if it is an order cheque (bearing a forged endorsement). But if it is a bearer cheque he is likely to be not only the holder (by virtue of possession) but also the holder in due course: s 29. In that case only, he has better rights (unless the cheque is crossed 'not negotiable') than the previous owner. He may enforce his rights on the cheque against the drawer, his immediate transferor, and any endorser (if the drawee bank refuses to pay): s 38. If he is not the holder (because it is an order cheque not genuinely endorsed) he has rights of indemnity against any person who endorsed the cheque subsequent to the theft.

1.13 It is necessary to keep these principles in view in answering questions on rights and liabilities on a cheque. But where a true owner claims against a bank he bases his claim on innocent conversion since the bank is not a 'party' to the cheque – it is neither the drawer nor the endorser of the cheque.

1.14 In its defence the bank will rely on:

   (a) the statutory rules (explained below) which protect a paying or a collecting bank as the case may be; or possibly

   (b) contributory negligence on the part of the plaintiff: s 47 Banking Act 1979. This issue usually arises only when the drawer of a stolen cheque is suing a collecting bank and the bank can show that the fraud was facilitated by the drawer's carelessness in drawing his cheques.

## 2. THE PAYING BANK'S PROTECTION

2.1 When a cheque is presented the paying bank must first satisfy itself that it has the customer's authority to pay (and funds available). *The protection rules have no effect if the cheque is, for example, forged or altered so that it is not a genuine authority from the customer to pay at all.*

## Payment of crossed cheques

2.2   The bank must next consider the possibility of a claim by the true owner (if he is not the person claiming payment). If the cheque is crossed, the paying banker has a duty to pay according to the crossing, general or special, making payment to a collecting bank. Unless it does so it is liable to the true owner if the latter suffers loss: s 79.

A paying banker who pays a crossed cheque:

(a)   in accordance with the crossing; and
(b)   in good faith; and
(c)   without negligence

is in the same position as if he had made payment to the true owner (even if in fact he has not): s 80.

This is the basic safeguard of a paying bank.

2.3   When payment is made in accordance with the crossing, in good faith and without negligence of a crossed cheque which the drawer has delivered into the hands of the payee, *the drawer also* is in the same position as if payment had been made to the true owner, even if in fact it had not. If, for example, A draws a crossed cheque and delivers it to B in payment of a debt, and C steals it and obtains payment, B bears the loss and cannot demand payment a second time from A. But if the cheque were stolen from A by C before it came into the hands of B, then B's claim as creditor of A is unaffected and he may demand payment from A by other means: s 80.

2.4   The paying bank is *not* protected by s 80 if:

(a)   it acts in bad faith;

(b)   it ignores a crossing and does not make payment to another bank (unless there is no risk, as when the drawer presents his own cheque to pay cash at the counter);

(c)   it fails to detect some defect of endorsement (this might be negligence which deprives him of the protection of s 80); or

(d)   the holder of an open, uncrossed cheque (other than the drawer) presents it for payment in cash at the counter. An open cheque is outside the scope of protection under s 80, which is limited to *crossed* cheques.

## Payment of cheques with a forged or unauthorised endorsement

2.5   The principle which underlies the paying bank's risk of liability is that it has a duty to 'discharge' the cheque by 'payment in due course'.

Payment is made in due course if the paying bank (as is normally the case) pays *to the holder* in good faith and without notice (if it be so) that his title is defective: s 59.

2.6   The most obvious risk is that payment will be obtained by someone who is not the holder because, whether he is aware of the fact or not, there is a forged or unauthorised endorsement of an order cheque.

2.7   In normal circumstances the paying bank is absolved by s 80 from responsibility on paying a crossed cheque because it cannot know anything of the person claiming payment. The collecting bank stands between them. But if s 80 does not apply (say, because the cheque is not crossed) the paying bank can usually fall back on s 60 which provides that:

if payment is made:

(a)   in good faith and
(b)   in the ordinary course of business

the bank is deemed to have paid the cheque 'in due course' even if it bears a forged or unauthorised endorsement (so that in fact payment is made to someone not the holder). The bank is not required to show that any endorsement is genuine or authorised: s 60.

*Case: Thackwell v Barclays Bank plc 1984*
The plaintiff claimed recovery of £44,227, the value of a cheque on which his endorsement had been forged, from Barclays Bank, a branch of which had both paid and collected the cheque, on the grounds of negligence and conversion.

*Held:* the circumstances were so unusual that the bank should have made further enquiries and therefore it lost the protection given to the collecting bank (described later). Nevertheless, since the cheque formed part of a fraudulent transaction, there were no grounds for the claim since to allow the claim would contravene public policy by assisting indirectly in the commission of a crime.

2.8   Banks do not usually act in *bad faith*. For example, if the bank is informed that a cheque which is later presented for payment bears a forged endorsement or has been stolen (after being endorsed by the holder) it would refuse to pay. (But in case of doubt it would have to act quickly and prudently to avoid risk of wrongful refusal.) The bank would be acting in bad faith if, despite reliable information, it paid such a cheque.

2.9   The other condition required by s 60 is that payment shall be made *in the ordinary course of business*. That condition is breached in the following circumstances.

(a)   If payment is made out of banking hours. But some latitude is given for payment a minute or two after closing time.

*Case: Baines v National Provincial Bank Ltd 1927*
A person who held an open cheque drawn on the bank entered the banking hall before 3pm (which was closing time) and waited his turn. Payment to him was made at 3.05pm. The customer's countermand of authority to pay was received later. The customer objected that the bank had not paid the cheque *in the ordinary course of business* since payment was made after hours.

*Held:* the bank was justified in paying in the circumstances described. It would probably not be so if the person to whom payment is made is not already on the premises at closing time.

(b)   If a crossed cheque is paid contrary to the crossing. But banks will risk this if the person concerned is the drawer or is well-known.

(c) If an open cheque is presented for payment through the post by a stranger who asks that cash be sent to him by post. Such a mode of payment is unusual and therefore not 'in the ordinary course of business'. But the bank is protected if it remits cash *to the drawer* by post at his request.

(d) If an open cheque is paid at the counter without endorsement or without proper enquiry if the circumstances require it.

## Encashment of open cheques at the counter

2.10 If an open cheque is presented for payment at the counter the following general principles apply.

(a) If the cheque (including a crossed cheque payable to 'cash') is *presented by the drawer* or his representative well known to the bank it is sensible and normal practice (though strictly a breach of legal rules) to pay without formality.

(b) If the cheque (which should only be paid in this way if it is an *open* cheque) is *presented by a third party* and it is payable to him or to bearer, the bank should:

   (i) request that he endorse the cheque (this is explained below); and

   (ii) consider whether there is anything suspicious. If so, payment should be refused, though it need not be shown - if the bank is later challenged - that the bank acted without negligence. All that is required is that it should be payment made 'in the ordinary course of business', which is a less demanding standard.

   *Case: Auchteroni & Co v Midland Bank Ltd 1928*
   The plaintiffs drew a bill of exchange (not a cheque) payable to themselves and the drawee accepted the bill payable at the defendant bank. The drawers endorsed the bill and instructed their employee to deliver it to their own bank for collection and credit to their account. But the employee presented the bill direct to the defendant bank, obtained cash and absconded. The issue which arose was whether the bank had discharged the bill by 'by payment in due course'.

   *Held:* this was payment in due course and the bank was not liable. The court said that the result would have been different if the bill had been presented in quite abnormal circumstances, eg by a tramp, or an office boy or a postman (presumably because he would have intercepted it in the post and could not ordinarily obtain it honestly).

## Payment of unendorsed or irregularly endorsed cheques

2.11 S 60 protects a bank from liability in paying a cheque on which the endorsement is forged or unauthorised. Until 1957 a paying bank still had to inspect the back of every cheque as a matter of routine to see whether it was endorsed at all and if so whether the endorsement was 'regular' - whether it corresponded with the endorser's description as payee (or in a previous endorsement). From this inspection the bank might have to refer the cheque back to the customer for endorsement. It was considered that all this procedural action served no useful purpose and the Mocatta Committee recommended that the law be altered so that a paying bank would never be affected by defective endorsement of a cheque and need never inspect or query an endorsement (or the lack of it).

2.12 That result is achieved by the Cheques Act 1957 which provides that

a paying bank which pays

(a) in good faith and
(b) in the ordinary course of business

a cheque which is not endorsed or which is irregularly endorsed, shall be deemed to have paid in due course and shall not be liable by reason only of the absence or irregularity of an endorsement: s 1 Cheques Act 1957.

2.13 The combined effect of s 60 and s 1 of the 1957 Act is to exclude liability if the endorsement is forged, unauthorised, irregular or if there is no endorsement at all. Good faith and payment in the ordinary course of business are the qualifying conditions in these cases.

### The need for endorsement

2.14 It was still necessary however to advise paying (and also collecting) banks when they should ensure, in the ordinary course of business, that a cheque is endorsed. That guidance is given in the 1957 Memorandum issued by the Committee of London Clearing Banks. This requires a paying bank (or its agent bank at which the cheque is presented) to obtain an endorsement of a cheque if it is either:

(a) a *cheque marked 'R'* - where the drawer instructs that he requires a receipt for payment of the cheque; or

(b) an *open cheque presented at the counter* for payment in cash.

### Summary of the paying bank's protection

2.15 If a paying bank pays a cheque (bearing the genuine signature of its customer and in its original unaltered form) there is a risk that the payment may nonetheless be made to a person not entitled to it. In resisting any claim against it on this account the paying bank can rely on:

(a) *s 80* - if it is a *crossed* cheque paid:

(i) in accordance with the crossing;
(ii) in good faith; and
(iii) without negligence.

This puts the bank in the same legal position as if payment had been made to the true owner. Where, however, s 80 does not apply;

(b) *s 60/s 1 (1957 Act)* relieves the bank of any obligation to show that an endorsement was valid and the bank is deemed to have discharged the cheque by payment to the holder if it acted:

(i) in good faith and
(ii) in the ordinary course of business

despite any defect or lack of endorsement.

## 3.   THE COLLECTING BANK'S PROTECTION

3.1   When a customer delivers a cheque to his bank for collection and credit of the proceeds to his account, the normal result is that the bank deals with the cheque as the customer's agent.

### Collection of cheques for the customer

3.2   A collecting bank is not liable to the true owner of a cheque if:

   (a)   in good faith; and
   (b)   without negligence;
   (c)   (i)    it receives payment of the cheque for a customer; or
          (ii)   it receives payment for itself after previously crediting the cheque to his account: s 4 Cheques Act 1957.

The collecting bank is in these circumstances not liable to the true owner of the cheque if the bank's customer had no title or a defective title to the cheque.

3.3   Where there is negligence by a collecting bank, it usually arises in one of the following circumstances.

   (a)   Opening an account for a *previously unknown customer* without proper enquiry.

   (b)   Obtaining payment for a customer of a cheque drawn by his *employer* in favour of a third party or drawn by a third party in favour of the employer, and in either case endorsed over to the customer. The same principle applies to company and partnership cheques if the customer is a director or a partner as the case may be.

   (c)   Obtaining payment for a customer of a cheque for an *abnormally large amount* in relation to his circumstances.

In cases (b) or (c) - as with (a) - it is a defence that the bank made proper enquiries (which requires that credible and reliable information should be obtained).

3.4   At the time when the proceeds of the cheque are made available to the person who delivered it for collection there should be an existing relationship of customer and bank. A customer is any person who has an account (even a deposit account) into which a cheque is likely to be paid. As soon as he opens such an account he is a customer even if the first credit is the stolen cheque for which s 4 protection (of the bank) is required: *Commissioners of Taxation v English, Scottish and Australian Bank Ltd 1920*. A bank may be a customer of another bank if it has a drawing account - but the cheques are then described as banker's drafts.

3.5   In opening an account the bank should satisfy itself on three points.

   (a)   *Identity* - that the new customer has given his genuine and not an assumed name (often the name of the payee of a stolen cheque) (see *Marfani's* and *Lumsden's* cases).

(b) *Character* - that the new customer is vouched for by at least one, preferably two referees. If the referee given by the customer in opening the account is unknown to the bank, then the bank should ask for particulars of the referee's bank and contact the latter. Apart from the risk that a referee may be unsatisfactory, the customer (having assumed a false name himself) may name himself as his own referee (as in *Lumsden's* case).

(c) *Employment or occupation* - where the new customer is employed or, if self-employed, what is his business or source of income. There is more opportunity to steal a cheque (without immediate detection) at the place of work. Whenever a third party cheque is delivered for collection and credit to the account the bank should be able to recognise a cheque originating at his place of work.

We have seen these rules when we looked at opening an account in Chapter 10.

3.6 A collecting bank has been held to be negligent in either failing to make enquiries or in accepting inadequate answers in the following situations.

(a) A *director* paid in to his personal account cheques payable to his company but endorsed by him as 'sole director' of the company. The bank was unaware that the company had an account at another bank: *A L Underwood Ltd v Bank of Liverpool and Martins Ltd 1924*.

(b) A *partner* endorsed cheques payable to the firm and negotiated them to a third party whose bank collected them after obtaining an unlikely explanation: *Baker v Barclays Bank Ltd 1955*.

(c) An *official* to whom cheques were made payable in his official capacity paid them into his personal account: *Ross v London County Westminster and Parr's Bank 1919*. This principle was followed in a case where the cheques were payable to the customer by name 'for Marquess of Bute' and were then negligently paid into his personal account: *Bute v Barclays Bank Ltd 1954*.

(d) An *agent* or employee authorised to draw cheques on the account of the principal or employer *drew cheques payable to himself* and paid them into his private account: *Morison v London County and Westminster Bank Ltd 1914*.

(e) *Employees* stole cheques drawn by their employer payable to bearer and paid them into the account of the employee or his wife: *Savory's* case.

(f) *Company cheques:* a cheque payable to Company A was paid into the account of Company B and collected without enquiry: *London & Montrose Shipbuilding and Repairing Co Ltd v Barclays Bank Ltd 1926*. The proper course is for Company A as payee to endorse the cheque specially to Company B unless the bank has received instructions (in respect of companies in the same group) to collect and credit *all* cheques payable to different companies to a single account. This is not uncommon if a group of companies has a central financial system but it must be specified by the group.

(g) Cheques drawn payable to a *payee other than the customer* were paid in to the customer's account on his unverified statement that he was trading under a business name other than his own: *Baker v Barclays Bank Ltd 1955*.

(h) Cheques drawn payable to a payee other than the customer endorsed to him but crossed 'a/c payee': *House Property Co of London Ltd v London County and Westminster Bank Ltd 1915*.

(i) A company secretary opened an account under an assumed name and informed the bank that he was setting up in business as a freelance agent. He paid in cheques drawn by his employers in favour of third parties to a total of £4,855. The bank was held liable as it had been negligent in failing to query cheques for *larger amounts* than were consistent with the customer's own information of his business: *Nu-Stilo Footwear Ltd v Lloyds Bank Ltd 1956* (NB. in the 1950's a cheque for £550 (the first stolen cheque) was for a very substantial sum.)

3.7 On receiving a reply to its enquiries, the bank should consider whether further enquiry or verification is needed. If the information comes from an apparently reliable source, such as a solicitor who says that he is paying client's money into his client account *(Penmount Estates Ltd v National Provincial Bank Ltd 1945)*, it is not negligent for the bank to accept it. But if the customer's past transactions with the bank cast doubt on his reliability it may be negligent to accept his explanation without further enquiry: *Motor Traders Guarantee Corporation Ltd v Midland Bank Ltd 1937* (where it was also decided that breach of the bank's own rules is not conclusive evidence of negligence). The test is whether a prudent bank would (on the basis of previous knowledge and what it is now told) decide to pursue the enquiry further.

## Collection of cheques with defective endorsements

3.8 A collecting bank, like a paying bank, is not negligent because it fails to concern itself with the absence of endorsement or irregularity in an endorsement: s 4(3) Cheques Act 1957.

3.9 If it innocently collects a cheque bearing a forged or unauthorised endorsement it is only liable if it is negligent in doing so (as illustrated above). *Failure to recognise that an endorsement is a forgery is not negligent.* The endorser is a stranger, not a customer, and the bank has probably never seen his genuine signature.

*The need for endorsement*

3.10 The 1957 Memorandum also lays down guidelines for collecting banks in connection with endorsement of cheques delivered for collection. The following are the main points.

(a) *Cheques originally payable to a third party* should be endorsed by the payee (and any intermediate holder). But if the cheque is specially endorsed to the customer by the previous holder no further endorsement is required.

(b) *Cheques marked 'R'* (requiring a receipt) should be endorsed since the drawer has in effect required it.

(c) *Misdescription of payee.* If the payee's name is incorrectly spelt or if he is incorrectly designated on the cheque, endorsement by him is not required unless there are circumstances to suggest that the customer is not the person to whom payment is intended to be made.

(d) *Joint payees and joint accounts.* If a cheque is drawn payable to joint payees, such as trustees, executors or partners, it may be collected without endorsement for credit to an account of which *all* are joint account holders. But in any other case (such as a single trustee delivering for credit to his personal account a cheque payable to the trustees jointly) endorsement by all payees is required. The converse does not apply however (eg. if a cheque payable to one joint account holder is delivered for credit to the joint account his endorsement need not be obtained).

## Collecting bank as holder of the cheque

3.11 Although it has no interest in the cheque because it acts as a customer's agent, the collecting bank may be liable for conversion unless it is protected by s 4 Cheques Act 1957 – and to rely on that defence the bank must not have been negligent.

3.12 However, if the bank itself becomes the holder for value or holder in due course of the cheque (by giving value for it) that status will improve its position in two respects.

(a) If the drawer of the cheque stops payment the bank as *holder for value* may recover payment from him (or from an endorser).

(b) The bank may by negligence have forfeited the protection of s 4 Cheques Act 1957 against a claim by the true owner. But if the bank is a *holder in due course* it can resist a claim for damages by the true owner since the bank has superior title. Negligence in acquiring a bill does not prevent the holder from being a holder in due course. It is only necessary that he should have acquired it in good faith, that is honestly.

*Case: Lloyds Bank Ltd v Hornby 1933*
A new account was opened and the customer paid in a cheque for £250 against which he was allowed to draw before clearance and before any reference had been obtained. The drawer stopped payment of the cheque and resisted a claim by the bank as holder in due course on the ground that it had been negligent in opening the account.

*Held:* on the facts of the case there had been no negligence but even if there had been it would not have disentitled the bank from claiming as a holder in due course.

3.13 A number of factors may, however, operate to prevent the bank becoming a holder with those improved rights.

(a) If the customer delivers an order cheque for collection which bears a *forged endorsement* he is not the holder. The bank as transferee cannot be in any better position so it cannot become the holder.

(b) In the ordinary course, negotiation of an order cheque requires that it be *endorsed* by the holder (the customer) to the transferee (the bank): s 31. Otherwise the transferee merely has possession and is not the holder. The effect of s 1 Cheques Act 1957 is that a customer does not ordinarily endorse cheques on delivering them to the bank for collection (but we have seen that there are exceptions). The need for endorsement to constitute the bank a holder, *if* it also gives value (see below), is removed by s 2 of the 1957 Act.

(c) The bank can only be a holder in due course of a cheque delivered for collection if it gives *value*. What amounts to giving value is considered below.

(d) If the cheque is crossed *not negotiable* the bank, if it is the holder at all, has no better rights than the customer had as the previous holder. If of course the customer's title was not defective the crossing does not prejudice the bank's position.

*Case: Bank of New South Wales v Ross 1971*
The customer delivered the defendant's cheque for £10,000 to the customer's bank for collection in circumstances which constituted the bank as holder in due course. The defendant later instructed its bank to refuse payment as it had heard that the payee was insolvent. The cheque was crossed 'not negotiable'.

*Held:* there was no fraud or defect of title in the customer's acquisition of the cheque as payee. The bank's title as holder in due course was not prejudiced by the crossing as the transferor's title was valid.

3.14 As explained in paragraph 3.13, s 2 Cheques Act 1957 was enacted as a consequence of the removal (by s 1 Cheques Act 1957) of the need to endorse cheques handed to the bank for collection. The section reads:

'A banker who gives *value* for, or has a lien on, a cheque payable to order which the *holder* delivers to him for collection without endorsing it, has such (if any) rights as he would have had if, upon delivery, the holder had endorsed it in blank'.

The significance of the words in italics has already been explained. They are important limiting conditions.

3.15 The section only deals with the absence of an endorsement. It does not assist the bank if the customer endorses by an irregular endorsement. The effect of an irregular endorsement is that the bank may become the holder but is not the holder in due course (by reason of s 29).

*Giving value for the cheque*

3.16 A bank cannot rely on s 2 Cheques Act 1957 unless it gives value for the cheque or has a lien on it. It does not give value unless it both:

(a) agrees to do so and assumes a binding obligation; and

(b) actually does so.

3.17 There is *no binding obligation* in either of the following cases.

(a) If the bank (eg. by conditions printed on paying-in slips or cheque books) reserves the *right to refuse* payment of customer's cheques drawn against 'uncleared effects' (cheques delivered for collection but not yet paid) as in *Zang's* case below.

(b) If the bank without prior arrangement merely *allows* the customer to draw cheques (or credits his overdrawn account) before a cheque delivered for collection has been paid. This practice may (over a period) imply an agreement but it is difficult to prove.

3.18 There is *no actual value* given if the bank charges interest on the unreduced amount of an overdraft pending clearance of a cheque paid in. This is so even if the cheque paid in is immediately credited to the account (but without reducing the balance on which interest is calculated - *Zang's* case). There is also no value given if the cheque is merely credited to an overdrawn account.

3.19 A bank *does* give value (under s 2 Cheques Act 1957) in the following circumstances.

(a) If the bank pays cash (whether to a customer or a stranger) in exchange for a cheque drawn on another bank. By the payment the bank buys the cheque. But this principle does not apply when the bank cashes the cheque by prior arrangement with the drawee bank (an 'open credit') or on presentation of a cheque guarantee card. In these latter circumstances the bank which pays cash acts merely as the agent of the bank on which the cheque is drawn and it does not become the owner of the cheque. It can of course as agent recover from the other bank as its principal.

(b) If the bank receives a cheque on the basis (agreed with the customer) that the proceeds when received are to reduce his overdraft permanently. For example, the customer might obtain a bridging loan to buy a new house and later pay in the cheque received on the sale of his old house to repay the loan outright: *McLean v Clydesdale Banking Co 1883*.

(c) If the bank agrees with the customer that he may draw against uncleared cheques. If there is such agreement it may either be a continuing arrangement or related to particular cheques only.

*Case: Midland Bank Ltd v R V Harris Ltd 1963*
There was an express agreement that the customer might draw against two uncleared cheques drawn by the defendants and later stopped. The bank sued as holder in due course.

*Held:* the bank was entitled to recover on this basis from the defendants as drawers. NB. as already stated an *implied* agreement to permit drawings is a possibility but not easy to prove.

*Obtaining a lien on the cheque*

3.20 S 2 Cheques Act 1957 also applies when the bank has a lien on the cheque. The essential characteristic of a lien is that the bank has possession of the cheque and the customer is indebted to the bank. The lien is limited to the lesser of the amount owing and the cheque: s 27(3). In *Keever's* case (see Chapter 15) the bank had a lien on part of the cheque only. The lien extended to the entire value of the cheques in the case below.

*Case: Barclays Bank Ltd v Astley Industrial Trust Ltd 1970*
On 18 November 1964 M was overdrawn to the extent of £1,910 (the limit was £2,000) and two more cheques drawn by M for a total of £2,673 were presented. The bank agreed to honour these cheques on receiving an assurance from M that cheques for £2,850 drawn in its favour by AIT would be banked the next day. The AIT cheques were duly banked but they had been obtained from AIT by fraud. AIT stopped the cheques. The bank sued as holder in due course.

*Held:* (1) a bank which receives cheques for collection as agent of the customer may also rely on s 2 Cheques Act 1957 if the facts justify it;

(2) the bank had a lien on the cheques as security for reduction of the overdraft which then stood at £4,673.

3.21 In the *Keever* case there was a lien though probably no 'value given' since the cheque was delivered merely to reduce the debit balance and not as a permanent repayment. To that extent a lien can improve a collecting bank's position. But (as appears in *Zang's* case below) a bank must retain possession of the cheque in order to claim a lien over it. In particular if returned unpaid the cheque should not be sent back to the customer (if the bank intends to claim a lien).

3.22 The most important modern case on s 2 Cheques Act 1957 is set out below. The three members of the Court of Appeal reached the same conclusion but for different reasons. The House of Lords upheld the decision of the Court of Appeal but left open certain issues which it was unnecessary to decide. It is therefore a most difficult decision to interpret.

*Case: Westminster Bank Ltd v Zang 1966*

Z borrowed £1,000 from T, who provided the money from funds of a company of which T was managing director. To repay the loan, Z issued a cheque for £1,000 payable to 'T or order' which T delivered to the bank for collection and credit of the proceeds to the company bank account which was overdrawn. Z's bank dishonoured the cheque and returned it to T who began proceedings against Z as drawer. T abandoned his action and handed the cheque to the company's bank so that the bank as holder for value or holder in due course of the cheque might sue Z. The following issues were considered in the course of the bank's action against Z.

(1)   Had the bank received the cheque 'for collection' (as required by s 2) in view of the fact that T (the payee) had instructed the bank to collect for a third party (T's company)? Yes – 'collection' under s 2 need not be for the account of the holder.

(2)   Had the bank 'given value' (as required by s 2) in receiving the cheque to reduce the existing overdraft of the company? No, said the House of Lords, since the bank had charged interest on the unreduced overdraft and had reserved the right (by notice printed on its paying in slips) to refuse payment of cheques drawn against uncleared effects. There was no evidence of any contrary agreement to pay later cheques nor had any been presented and paid during the relevant period.

(3)   Had the bank a lien on Z's cheques (as an alternative to giving value)? No: if there was any lien the bank had lost it when it gave up possession of the returned cheque to T so that he could use it in his action against Z.

## The need for endorsement

3.23  The practical conclusion to be drawn from *Zang's* case is that unless the collecting bank pays over money against an uncleared cheque, or has a clear agreement that the customer is entitled to draw cheques against uncleared effects, it should require him (on delivering the cheque) to endorse it so that the bank can claim (without having to rely on s 2 Cheques Act 1957 ) that it is the holder of the cheque (as well as the agent for collection). If the bank is holder by virtue of an endorsement it can show that it is a holder for value or probably a holder in due course by reference to the reduction of an existing overdraft (an antecedent debt is value – s 27) or the customer's drawings.

## Cheques as receipts

3.24  An unendorsed cheque which appears to have been paid by the bank on which it is drawn is evidence of receipt of payment by the payee: s 3 Cheques Act 1957. This section (like s 2) was included in the 1957 Act as a consequence of the more extensive change (dispensing with the need of endorsement of cheques so far as concerns a bank) made by s 1. The unintended result of s 3 is that most trade creditors now stipulate that they will not issue a receipt as evidence of payment by cheque unless the payer asks for one. It is only a *cheque* (no other form of payment order) which is declared to be evidence of payment.

## 4.   HOUSE DEBITS

4.1   The legal position of a bank which is both paying and collecting bank in respect of the same cheque (a 'house debit') is illustrated by the case below.

*Case: Carpenters Company v The British Mutual Banking Company 1937*
A clerk employed by a City livery company stole cheques drawn by his employer on the defendant bank, forged the payees' endorsements and paid the cheques into his personal account with the same bank which had only one branch. The employer sued the bank for conversion.

*Held* (1) As paying bank the defendant bank should have discharged the bill by payment in due course *to the holder*. But as it had paid in good faith and in the ordinary course of business it was deemed to have done so: s 60.

(2) As collecting bank the bank failed to qualify for the protection of s 4 Cheques Act 1957 since it had been negligent in paying the cheque into the clerk's personal account without enquiry.

Note that in neither capacity was the bank liable for failing to detect a forged endorsement.

## 5. BANKER'S DRAFTS

5.1 A banker's draft is not a defined term but s 4(2)(d) of the 1957 Act refers to it as 'any draft payable on demand drawn by a banker *upon himself*, whether payable at the head office or some other office of his bank'.

5.2 It is not a cheque because bills of exchange, including cheques, are defined as orders 'addressed by one person to *another*': s 1 Cheques Act 1957. It should follow that if Bank A draws a cheque on Bank B (with which A has an account) it is a cheque in the proper sense. But it is normal practice to refer to such cheques as 'bankers' drafts' - presumably because (like bankers' drafts in the narrower sense) the holder can be assured of obtaining payment. In answering examination questions on 'bankers' drafts' you should include cheques drawn by one bank on another - since this is the examiner's intention.

5.3 The essential advantage of banker's drafts is that the bank as drawee may be relied upon to pay since (i) it has the financial resources and (ii) it will not accept an order from the customer to countermand payment merely because he no longer wishes or is no longer able to meet the expenditure (which he must reimburse to the bank).

5.4 A banker's draft must always be payable to order. This is because a bill drawn by a person on himself as drawee may be treated as a promissory note: s 5. A promissory note to bearer is equivalent to a banknote and only the Bank of England may lawfully issue banknotes in England.

5.5 There is of course a risk that a banker's draft may be obtained in the course of a fraudulent transaction or be stolen after issue or otherwise used in such a way that the bank, even though innocent, could be exposed to liability. The bank is however protected to the following extent.

(a) *Crossed cheque rules* (ss 76 - 81) also apply to payment of a crossed banker's draft paid in accordance with the crossing in good faith and without negligence: s 5 Cheques Act 1957.

(b) *Defective endorsement rules* apply with substantially the same effect as for payment of cheques:

(i) when a banker's draft is presented for payment bearing an endorsement and paid, the paying bank is not required to show that the endorsement is genuine or authorised;

(ii) if there is no endorsement (when required or the endorsement is irregular) payment in good faith and in the ordinary course of business discharges a banker's draft just like a cheque: s 1 Cheques Act 1957.

(c) *Protection of collecting banks* - the rules on cheques apply also to banker's drafts: s 4(2)(d) Cheques Act 1957.

*(Note:* when a 'banker's draft' is drawn by one bank on another it is a cheque to which normal provisions apply.)

## 6. OTHER BANK PAYMENT ORDERS

6.1 With the exception of s 60, the banker's safeguards in handling cheques are extended to cover 'a document issued by a customer of a banker which, though not a bill of exchange, is intended to enable a person to obtain payment from that banker of the sum mentioned in the document'.

This takes in (i) *conditional payment orders* and (ii) *orders to pay cash*, neither of which is a bill of exchange.

### Conditional payment orders

6.2 Where the problem arises from a forged or unauthorised endorsement of a conditional payment order, the paying bank is not protected since s 60 does not apply. In all other circumstances a bank has the same legal safeguards as apply to payment or collection of a cheque. The safeguards are as follows.

(a) *Paying bank* - the same rules apply if the order is crossed as apply to crossed cheques: s 5 Cheques Act 1957. Secondly the protection of s 1 Cheques Act 1957 applies if a necessary endorsement is absent or irregular. However a bank which makes payment (to a person not entitled) of an order bearing a forged or unauthorised endorsement is not protected by s 60 (though it may be protected by the rules on crossed cheques if the order is also crossed).

(b) *Collecting bank* - has the same protection as applies to the collection of cheques: s 4(2) Cheques Act.

6.3 A payment order may be conditional (and so fail to qualify as a cheque) if it calls for a receipt as a pre-condition of payment. There is however no denying the presence of a condition in the case of a 'traveller's cheque' (payment order not a cheque) which must be signed by the payee before the paying agent may pay it.

### Orders to pay cash

6.4 A more common example of a payment order to which the definition applies (with consequent protection for the bank) is a cheque form marked 'Pay cash' or some other impersonal purpose. This fails to comply with the statutory definition of a bill because it does not require payment 'to or to the order of a specified person or to bearer'.

*Case: Orbit Mining and Trading Co Ltd v Westminster Bank Ltd 1963*
A company customer had given to its bank a mandate to pay cheques signed by the two directors. As one director was often absent abroad he was in the habit of signing cheque forms in blank so that the other director could complete and issue them for company purposes in his absence. The other director inserted 'cash' between 'pay' and 'or order' on three of these cheques and delivered them to the Westminster Bank for collection and credit to his personal account. The collecting bank was unaware that its customer was a director of the company and did not recognise his signature as co-drawer owing to its illegibility. The company sued the bank as collecting bank for damages for conversion. The bank relied on s 4 Cheques Act 1957.

*Held:* the 'cheques' were not cheques in the proper sense but they were within the definition. The bank could therefore rely on the application of cheque rules to these orders for payment. The bank had not been negligent in failing to have up-to-date information of the customer's present business activity. The company's claim against the bank failed.

## 7. CHEQUE GUARANTEE CARDS

7.1 The drawee bank is never liable *on the cheque* to the holder. Liability on any bill is restricted to those who have signed it: s 23. The bank cannot sign (as acceptor) a bill payable on demand. The purpose of a cheque guarantee card is to create a collateral contract by which the bank (through the customer as its agent) undertakes to pay the holder of the cheque the lesser of its value or a fixed amount (mostly £50, though some banks now guarantee up to £100 or £200).

7.2 As a means of limiting fraudulent use of stolen cheque cards the following conditions apply.

(a) Only one cheque may be used in one transaction. This is to block the device used successfully in *Metropolitan Commissioners of Police v Charles 1976* where a large number of cheques (each for an amount within the limit) were issued to make up a large aggregate amount.

(b) The cheque card bears a specimen signature and the signature on the cheque must be written in the presence of the payee and must correspond – the payee should compare the two before accepting the cheque.

(c) The cheque card bears a serial number which the payee must write on the back of the cheque as evidence that it has been produced to him.

(d) The name, sort code number and account number on the card must agree with those on the cheque.

(e) The cheque must be issued and dated before the expiry date on the card.

(f) The card must not have been altered nor defaced.

7.3 The other risk is that the customer, while in possession of the card, will use it to obtain acceptance of cheques (which the bank must pay) for larger sums than his credit balance (and any agreed overdraft facility) at the bank. This can be a criminal offence - obtaining a pecuniary advantage by deception: Theft Act 1968 s 16(1) and *Charles* case above.

## 8.   CREDIT CARDS

8.1   The use of credit cards is now quite extensive, some people using them because of their convenience instead of cash or cheques and settling the whole of their credit card account on a monthly basis so as to avoid the payment of the company's interest charges. The two leading bank credit cards in the UK are Access and Visa or Barclaycard.

### The nature of a credit card transaction

8.2   The use of a credit card involves three parties and three transactions between them.

(a)   on producing his card to a supplier for goods and/or services, the card-holder can obtain what he requires without paying for it immediately;

(b)   the supplier recovers from the credit card company the price of the goods or services less a discount which is the credit card company's profit margin;

(c)   at monthly intervals the credit card company sends to the credit card holder a monthly statement. The card-holder may either settle interest-free within 28 days or he may pay interest on the balance owing after 28 days. He is required to pay a minimum of 5% or £5 whichever is the greater.

8.3   The exact legal nature of a transaction completed by credit card is that there are three contracts - one between cardholder and supplier, one between supplier and card company and the other between cardholder and card company. Payment by credit card is an unconditional payment, unlike payment by cheque where the drawer of the cheque is not discharged from his debt until the cheque has been honoured (it is a conditional payment). Hence as soon as a buyer completes and signs a valid credit card voucher which is accepted by the supplier, the former's obligations are complete.

*Case: Re Charge Card Services Ltd 1988*
Charge Card Services Ltd operated a chargecard scheme for garages. A buyer signed a voucher filled out by the supplier, who then claimed payment from CC. Since CC usually paid the supplier before being paid by the cardholder, it financed its operations by factoring debts. It went into liquidation, and the garages who were creditors sought a declaration that they could claim payment from the cardholders since their debts had not been discharged at the point of sale.

*Held:* the garages had no claim against the cardholder in the card company's insolvency - the former's obligations to the garages had been discharged.

### Credit cards and the Consumer Credit Act 1974

8.4   A credit limit is set for each card-holder, the limit usually being well below £15,000. Hence the card issued to an individual is subject to regulation by the Consumer Credit Act 1974 which we covered in Chapter 6.

8.5   It is an offence to issue a credit card to a person if he has not asked for it. Unless the credit to be given is limited to £50 maximum the request must be made in writing and signed by the person who makes it.

8.6 The debtor is liable for up to £50 for misuse of his credit card *before* he reports it stolen or lost. He is not liable at all after he has reported it lost or stolen nor if the creditor did not give him a contact name, number and address to which to send notice of loss or theft.

8.7 The effect of forgery in a credit card transaction is the same as for cheques - forgery is a nullity.

### The credit card agreement

8.8 The exact terms of the contract between the credit card holder and the issuer of the card are defined in the agreement signed by the holder which contains the card's 'conditions of use'. It is a standard form contract.

8.9 Examples of the conditions of use contained in credit agreements are as follows:

(a) the card is to remain the property of the issuing company at all times;
(b) the card holder is to notify the issuer promptly on loss or theft of the card;
(c) joint card holders are to have joint and several liability; and
(d) the issuer can appropriate payments on the account.

8.10 The issuing company, since it retains ownership of the card, is entitled to call for its return, usually when it is being used to run up debts beyond the credit limit. Misuse of a credit card is an offence under s 16 Theft Act 1968. This is because the user is making a false representation that he has the authority to make a contract which will be honoured by the issuer even though the latter has withdrawn its consent: *R v Lambie 1981.*

## 9. CONCLUSION

9.1 We have not concerned ourselves in this chapter with the mechanics of the clearing system. We are more concerned here with the legal protection given to banks in paying and collecting cheques. This protection is necessary because of the huge volume of cheque transactions handled by banks each day of each year.

## TEST YOUR KNOWLEDGE
*The numbers in brackets refer to paragraphs of this chapter*

1 What is meant by conversion? (1.7)

2 What is meant by the 'true owner' of a cheque? (1.10)

3 Is a person in possession of a stolen cheque the holder of it? (1.12)

4 What is the statutory protection against liability given to a paying bank if it pays a crossed cheque to a person not entitled? (2.2, 2.7)

5 What is meant by payment 'in the ordinary course of business'? (2.9)

6 When should a bank insist on endorsement of a cheque presented to it for payment? (2.14, 2.22)

7 What statutory protection is given to a collecting bank if it obtains payment for a person not entitled? (3.2)

8 Illustrate the duty to make enquiries of a collecting bank in opening an account and give illustrations of negligence in that connection. (3.3 - 3.6)

9 Is a collecting bank concerned with irregular endorsements of cheques? (3.8, 3.9)

10 What advantages accrue to a collecting bank in being the holder of a cheque delivered for collection and how do statutory rules affect the position? (3.12, 3.14)

11 In what circumstances is a collecting bank deemed to give value for a cheque? (3.16)

12 What is meant by a 'house debit' and what legal duties has a bank in dealing with it? (4.1)

13 State the rules which protect banks in connection with:

(a) banker's drafts; (5.5)
(b) conditional orders; (6.2); and
(c) orders to a bank to pay cash. (6.3)

14 Describe the conditions imposed by banks in issuing cheque guarantee cards and the legal consequences of their use. (7.1 - 7.3)

15 What contracts underlie a credit card transaction? (8.2, 8.3)

*Now try questions 31 to 35 at the end of the text*

*Chapter 18*

# ELECTRONIC BANKING

---

**This chapter covers the following topics.**

1. Electronic money transmission services
2. BACS
3. CHAPS
4. The legal aspects of BACS and CHAPS
5. Automated Teller Machines (ATMs)
6. EFTPOS
7. Other legal aspects of EFT

---

## 1. ELECTRONIC MONEY TRANSMISSION SERVICES

1.1 So far we have looked in great detail at the systems of money transfer based on cheques and other negotiable instruments. These are the most common forms of money transfer but developments in banking mean that we also need to examine electronic funds transfer systems.

1.2 Much of the law in this area is based on the Bills of Exchange Act 1882, the Cheques Act 1957 and the Consumer Credit Act 1974, and where appropriate the legal principles applied in the case of paper-based money transfer are expected to be applied to electronic transfers. However, because much of the technology is new, the law is still evolving in this area.

### Electronic payment systems

1.3 Electronic payment systems allow payment to be cleared directly to a customer's account without the need for any paper vouchers. There are two main types:

(a) BACS (Bankers Automated Clearing Services); and
(b) CHAPS (Clearing House Automated Payments System).

## 2. BACS

2.1 BACS automates the clearing of a huge number of standing orders and direct debits and handles the majority of wages and salary transfers.

(a) A bank or building society activates its standing orders and direct debits by sending to BACS a tape of the payments to be made. These are processed through a computerised system to the credit or debit of any customer of a bank or building society which has similar links with BACS.

## 18. ELECTRONIC BANKING

(b) Certain customers, typically large employers or major companies, may also submit direct debits or make automated fund settlement for wages etc through the BACS system for themselves, provided they are sponsored by a member bank or building society.

2.2 BACS is a self-balancing system, in that a set of transfers to the credit of large numbers of accounts is matched or balanced by debits to the appropriate accounts at the paying bank. Both credits and debits are 'settled' at the end of the three-day BACS clearing cycle.

2.3 BACS instructions can be sent by magnetic and cassette tape, floppy disks, or directly over telecommunication lines (BACSTEL). Transfer details received before 9 am on Day one are processed overnight. Transfers are sorted onto tapes for each payee bank and the tapes reach payee banks by 6 am on Day two. The payee banks credit their customers' accounts at 9.30 am on Day three.

## 3. CHAPS

3.1 Where the payer wishes payment to be made to the payee very quickly, use may be made of the CHAPS system. Both paying and collecting banks must be members of APACS (Association of Payment Clearing Services) and they are then known as 'settlement banks'. On payment of a fee, the funds may be transferred in a very short time by means of computer-generated entries with a credit to the payee and a corresponding debit on the customer's account at the paying bank. There is a minimum amount for CHAPS of £5,000.

3.2 Because of the fee and the high minimum level, CHAPS is mainly used by business customers as a same-day payment system. Payment is guaranteed by the paying bank once its payment message has been received and acknowledged by the receiving bank.

3.3 CHAPS can only be used for 'irrevocable guaranteed unconditional sterling payments for same day settlement'. Payment is made through an electronic 'gateway' (a terminal). There is no processing operation, unlike BACS. Payments made before 3 pm are settled later the same day.

## 4. THE LEGAL ASPECTS OF BACS AND CHAPS

### The mandate to pay

4.1 The paying bank receives a transfer mandate from its customer:

(a) when it receives a continuing standing order or direct debit instruction from the initiator, or when it agrees with the customer that, say, salary payments may be made via BACS *and* the time for payment arrives; or

(b) when it receives a payment instruction from the customer (CHAPS).

### Completion of payment

4.2 The initiation or notification of the transfer mandate does not, in itself, give rise to the transfer of funds (rather as a cheque form, whilst giving a mandate to pay, does not in itself effect a transfer until presented for payment). The question therefore arises as to when payment is *completed* in an electronic system. The general answer is that payment is completed when the paying bank irrevocably commits itself to pay, and the payer can no longer revoke payment. Payment is completed when the payee has a right of action against his *own* bank (the payee bank) and the payer's duties have been discharged.

(a)  For paper-based payment systems, this is when the amount of the payment has been included in the daily inter-bank settlement at the Bank of England: *Pollard v Bank of England 1871*.

(b)  When an electronic clearing system is used, payment is completed between the bank, and between drawer and payee, when the receiving bank accepts payment in the form tendered. At this stage the payee is said to have an accrued right of action against the payee bank, and hence none against the payer: *Mardorf Peach & Co Ltd v Attica Sea Carriers Corporation of Liberia 1977*. It is not necessary for the receipt to be credited to the payee's account in order for payment to be said to be complete.

4.3  In the CHAPS system, the issue of a Logical Acknowledgement (LAK) is *prima facie* evidence of completion of payment. It is not necessary that the payee's account be credited. This means that a CHAPS payment cannot be countermanded at all once made: *Delbrueck & Co v Manufacturers Hanovers Trust Co 1979* (a US case).

4.4  In the BACS system, the payer will be told that the payment is irreversible, as revocation creates administrative difficulties and amendment of the computer files is a cumbersome process. However, if revocation is required by the payer he can contact his bank (*not* BACS) and countermand payment. If the sponsoring bank accepts the countermand, BACS may stop payment up to two days into the clearing cycle. This arises because the payee bank does not actually receive *payment* but receives a payment instruction, which can be revoked if the payee bank has not acted on the instruction.

**Payment by mistake**

4.5  Even where an electronic credit transfer has been completed the amount may be recoverable if it was made in error or where it was unauthorised (because of forgery or an unauthorised signature). The two actions open are to recover money paid under a mistake of fact or to 'trace' the proceeds.

*Action for money paid under a mistake of fact*

4.6  Similar principles apply to payments effected by electronic means as to cheques. An action may be brought by the payer or the paying bank (whoever suffers the loss) against the payee or the receiving bank, as appropriate. However, if the receiving bank, acting in good faith, has allowed the payee to draw against the credit whilst unaware of the payer's or paying bank's rights, it is only liable to repay so much of the amount as can be met out of the payee's credit balance when the bank was notified of the claim: *Barclays Bank Ltd v W J Simms & Cookes Ltd 1979* (described earlier).

*Tracing payments made under a mistake of fact*

4.7  Whereas the remedy above is a personal one between, say, paying bank and receiving bank, tracing or following is a proprietary one which allows the person to 'trace' money which is still his own. It can be used as an alternative remedy. This remedy is based on the premise that the funds still belong in equity to the paying bank.

## 18. ELECTRONIC BANKING

### Liability for equipment failure

4.8 Both paying and receiving banks in an electronic payment system have the usual duties of care of any bank in carrying out the customer's mandates. Additional duties arise, however, due to the use of the electronic equipment, since in using this the banks are providing a service which they must carry out with skill and care: s 13 Supply of Goods and Services Act 1982.

(a) *Duty to ensure that the service undertaken is carried out efficiently* - the paying bank must ensure that funds are made available to the receiving bank, and the latter must ensure that it is in a position to receive the paying bank's message. With CHAPS payments there is a cut-off time for receiving payment instructions to be transmitted of 3 o'clock on a business day. Backlogs can occur and the paying bank should give the customer a disclaimer as to its liability for not making payment instructions where there are circumstances outside its control (eg freak weather).

(b) *Duty to ensure equipment is adequate and well-maintained* - the bank's has an absolute duty in respect of its own equipment, even if the fault actually rests with its independent contractors: *Greaves & Co (Contractors) Ltd v Baynham Meikle 1975*. It cannot be liable when it has no control over the equipment, such as British Telecom lines, the central CHAPs computer or the other settlement bank's equipment. However, if a paying bank sends a payment message to a receiving bank which is not acknowledged, it should be put on notice that transmission has failed and should take appropriate steps.

## 5. AUTOMATED TELLER MACHINES (ATMs)

5.1 Automated teller machines (also known as cash dispensers) are electronic funds transfer terminals capable of dispensing cash, handling deposits, transferring funds between accounts, paying bills and displaying balances.

5.2 An ATM can only be used after a plastic card is inserted and a personal identification number (PIN) is punched in by the customer. The PIN is central to the security of the system.

5.3 Cash cards are not regulated by the Consumer Credit Act 1974 as there is no provision of credit. Most ATM systems are 'on-line', which means that the customer's instruction to withdraw cash is debited to his account immediately. This means that the transaction is irrevocable and cannot be countermanded. Even in 'off-line' systems, the debit will be made within 24 hours: this is not likely to be regarded as a credit transaction either.

5.4 Where the customer's account is in overdraft the following rules apply:

(a) *agreed overdraft:* the debit caused by a cash card withdrawal may increase the customer's overdraft within the limits agreed by the bank. However, the overdraft agreement is separate from that relating to the cash card and it is possible therefore to say that it is not the cash card which is advancing credit;

(b) *unauthorised overdraft:* most machines will not allow a customer to overdraw to an unauthorised amount. Where a machine error does this, it can be argued that the payment is not a provision of credit with the creditor's agreement, and hence is not covered by s 14 CCA.

5.5 The position has become more complicated as banks have set up networks so that customers of one bank can use the ATMs of other banks and building societies to obtain cash. However, the third party bank acts as an express agent of the card issuer and so the transaction is not affected by the 1974 Act. Hence it may be concluded that cash cards do not give rise to a regulated agreement under the Consumer Credit Act 1974.

## Completion and countermand of payment

5.6 Payment of an ATM transaction is completed (that is, paid):

(a) when cash is dispensed to the customer (cash withdrawal);

(b) when the debit is passed to his account in other transactions. In most on-line machines this is instantaneous with the instruction, but with off-line machines it may be later.

## Fraud in the use of ATMs

5.7 The price of the convenience of ATMs is the increased risk they represent that fraudulent access will be gained to the customer's account. The principal safeguard against this is the PIN, but problems occur:

(a) when the customer carries the card and PIN together, and an unauthorised person obtains and uses them;

(b) when the card and PIN are intercepted in the post. Although these are now posted separately, it is not unknown for both items to be intercepted; or

(c) when an unauthorised person 'skims' the PIN off an off-line card (where it is magnetically encoded).

5.8 When a customer *consents* to the use of his cash card by another person, or is *negligent* in protecting the card and PIN, he will be liable to the bank which can debit his account.

5.9 If a customer queries a debit to his account made on the basis of an ATM transaction, the bank will first seek to demonstrate that the transaction is evidenced by the records produced by the ATM. If these records indicate that the customer's card was used, the customer will need to show that he and his card were somewhere else at the time or that he had lost the card or was not in possession of it at the time. The bank must maintain a tally-roll printout of amounts dispensed which is admissible as evidence under the Bankers Books Evidence Act 1879.

5.10 A customer is unlikely however to go through the above process by reference to the law, as the Code of Banking Practice offers a more favourable remedy in the event of a dispute, and the banks have agreed to be bound by the decisions of the Banking Ombudsman.

5.11 The Code of Banking Practice was examined in the chapter on bank accounts, but it is worth reporting here some of the key provisions from the sections on customers and their cards.

(a) 'Card issuers will issue cards to customers only when they have been requested in writing or to replace or renew cards that have already been issued. (15.1)

## 18. ELECTRONIC BANKING

(b) Card issuers will tell customers if a card issued by them has more than one function. Card issuers will comply with requests from customers not to issue Personal Identification Numbers (PINs) where customers do not wish to use the functions operated by a PIN.' (15.2)

(c) 'Card issuers will inform customers that they must tell their card issuers as soon as reasonably practicable after they find that:

(i) their card has been lost or stolen;
(ii) someone else knows their PIN;
(iii) their account includes an item which seems to be wrong. (17.1)

(d) Card issuers will tell customers, and will remind them at regular intervals on their statement or by other means, of the place and the telephone number where they can give the details of a lost or stolen card at any time of the day or night. Card issuers will arrange for that telephone number to be included in British Telecom Phone Books.' (17.2)

(e) 'Card issuers will bear the full losses incurred:

(i) in the event of misuse when the card has not been received by the customer;

(ii) for all transactions not authorised by the customer after the card issuer has been told that the card has been lost or stolen or that someone else knows or may know the PIN (subject to 18.4 below);

(iii) if faults have occurred in the machines, or other systems used, which cause customers to suffer direct loss unless the fault was obvious or advised by a message or notice on display. (18.1)

(f) Card issuers' liability will be limited to those amounts wrongly charged to customers' accounts and any interest on those amounts. (18.2)

(g) Customers' liability for transactions not authorised by them will be limited to a maximum of £50 in the event of misuse before the card issuer has been notified that a card has been lost or stolen or that someone else knows the PIN (subject to 18.4 below). (18.3)

(h) Customers will be held liable for all losses if they have acted fraudulently. They may be held liable for all losses if they have acted with gross negligence. (18.4)

(i) In cases of disputed transactions the burden of proving fraud or gross negligence or that a card has been received by a customer will lie with the card issuer. In such cases card issuers will expect customers to co-operate with them in their investigations.' (18.5)

5.12 This means that:

(a) if the customer has *authorised* a third party transaction, he will be liable for the full amount;

(b) if he has *not* authorised a third party transaction, his liability will be limited to £50, unless he has been grossly negligent or fraudulent;

(c) if he has been grossly negligent or fraudulent, he will be liable without limit; and

(d) cardholder liability will be limited to £50 in all other cases.

**Equipment failure and ATMs**

5.13 The bank provides a service when it permits customers to use an ATM to make cash withdrawals. It is therefore bound by s 13 Supply of Goods and Services Act 1982 to act with care and skill. This means it should:

(a) design and programme the ATM system so as to ensure its compliance with customers' instructions (and thus fulfilment of the mandate);

(b) design the ATM system so that the bank has timely and accurate information with which to debit the customers' accounts; and

(c) maintain all ATM equipment in good working order, as far as is reasonable.

5.14 The most frequent problem is that the machine dispenses a different amount to what was requested but debits the account with what was requested. The principle remains however that *a bank cannot debit its customer's account unless it has authorised instructions to do so:*

(a) if it dispenses *more* than requested then the customer holds the excess on trust for the bank, and the bank can sue for return of a payment made under a mistake of fact;

(b) if it dispenses *less* than requested then it must adjust the customer's account to reflect what was dispensed.

5.15 The bank's duty to maintain machines does not extend to ensuring they are all full and in working order all the time, through they must be repaired within a reasonable time if their use is widely advertised by the bank.

*Limitation of liability*

5.16 The way in which banks have attempted to deal with the problem of equipment failure and error is to include an exclusion clause in the customer agreement by which the bank is authorised to debit the account with *all* amounts processed by the computer, even where these are due to computer error, theft or misuse of the card and PIN. Such a clause is one which is examinable in the light of the Unfair Contract Terms Act 1977, which requires that any such exclusion should satisfy a test of *reasonableness* (which it is up to the bank to prove). No case on this point has yet reached court, although it is a real worry to customers and a constant cause of complaint to the Banking Ombudsman.

5.17 The Jack Committee recommended that banks should be made liable for losses arising out of any type of equipment failure and this is likely to be one of the key changes effected by Government legislation following the White Paper. In addition, banks will be liable for a failure to complete an ATM transaction once a card has been accepted by the machine. The Code of Banking Practice addresses this issue in Section 18.1(c) (refer paragraph 5.11 above).

## 6.  EFTPOS

6.1  Electronic Funds Transfer at the Point of Sale (EFTPOS) is a consumer payment system which allows a bank customer to pay for goods and services by conveying details of the transactions to the payer's and the payee's banks without using paper vouchers at all - it is made electronically.

6.2  An EFTPOS system can accept credit cards or debit cards. It involves:

(a)  a terminal in the retailer's or other person's outlet;

(b)  a message transmission facility linking the terminal to the banks' computers; and

(c)  a magnetic stripe on the plastic card which allows the system to be activated.

### Debit cards

6.3  Debit cards are a recent innovation, designed for customers who like paying by plastic card but who do not want credit. The customer signs a voucher at the point of sale, which is then processed through the manual credit card system (eg Barclays Connect card is a Visa card). Alternatively, by using the PIN it can be processed through an EFTPOS system.

(a)  The legal implications of a debit card using the manual voucher system are the same as for the credit card system.

(b)  A debit card used to obtain cash is covered by the same rules as a cash card system.

(c)  A debit card used in the EFTPOS system is discussed below.

### *Debit cards and EFTPOS*

6.4  There is no legislation as yet on EFTPOS so its legal status is likely to depend on the law as set down in *Re Charge Card Services 1988* with some added complications. There are five contractual relationships:

(a)  between cardholder and retailer (purchase of goods);

(b)  between cardholder and card issuer (debiting of payment);

(c)  between retailer and 'retailer-acquirer' which operates the debit card scheme (supply of terminal and 'floor-limit' authorisation procedures);

(d)  between retailer-acquirer and card issuer (agreement on operating scheme); and

(e)  between retailer-acquirer and retailer's bank (crediting of payment).

6.5  Although the line of cases up until 1988 stated that a person is not discharged from his liability to pay until his conditional payment (payment other than in cash) is actually paid, the *Charge Card* case provides that, once the person has handed over his payment card and the retailer has allowed him to take the goods, the customer's liability is extinguished: it is an unconditional payment. This extends to debit cards by virtue of the fact that, as part of the debit card and EFTPOS systems, the card issuer makes an unequivocal agreement to transfer funds to the retailer's bank. Hence contract (a) in 6.4 above is discharged immediately.

6.6 Under the second contract in 6.4 above, the card issuer agrees with the cardholder that it will pay the retailer when the cardholder initiates the transaction using his debit card, and that it will debit its cardholder's account accordingly.

6.7 The third contract is entered into when the retailer agrees with the retailer-acquirer that he will accept the EFTPOS equipment and that the retailer-acquirer will sponsor him to join the system. This results in the fourth agreement between the retailer-acquirer and the card issuer. Finally the fifth agreement is between the retailer-acquirer and the retailer's bank, which credits the retailer's account on receiving EFTPOS instructions although these will only be effectively 'cleared' when they are collected.

6.8 The keys steps of a typical payment by debit card at the retailer's terminal are as follows:

(a) cardholder's card swiped through terminal;

(b) data captured: sort code, account number, expiry date, card number;

(c) amount of purchase keyed in;

(d) data, together with retailer's identification, coded and transmitted to central electronic funds transfer switch, run by Nexus;

(e) central switch forwards electronic message to cardholder's bank computer system for authorisation;

(f) bank decodes message, checks account balance and returns coded approval (or decline), logging item against cardholder's account;

(g) central switch forwards message to retailer's terminal;

(h) cardholder and cashier advised of approval and advice slip printed for signature;

(i) customer signs advice slip as identification and transaction completed;

(j) settlement occurs two or three days later when the respective banks' accounts with the Bank of England are debited and credited.

6.9 Under the contract between the retailer and the retailer-acquirer, the latter sets a 'floor limit' (say, £100) for transactions over which the former must obtain authorisation. If he neglects to do so the retailer-acquirer is entitled to refuse to credit the retailer's bank, and the retailer is prevented from pursuing the cardholder for payment because the use of the debit card constitutes unconditional payment: *Re Charge Card Services 1988*.

### Fraud, mistake and equipment malfunction

6.10 The problem associated with BACS, CHAPS and ATMs are also likely to apply to EFTPOS transactions using credit and debit cards - namely fraud, mistake and malfunction. Because of the numbers of contracts involved liability should be allocated by agreement between cardholder, card issuer, retailer, retailer's bank and retailer-acquirer - depending on the cause of the problem.

## 18. ELECTRONIC BANKING

*Fraud*

6.11 If the fraud is perpetrated by a retailer's employee (by using a cardholder's card and PIN) then the loss will fall on the retailer.

If an unauthorised third party uses the card and PIN in an outlet, the innocent cardholder's liability will be limited to £50 (following the Code of Banking Practice).

*Mistake*

6.12 An EFTPOS transaction in an on-line system is completed once the card issuer approves and authorises it (usually at the point of sale, by means of an 'ACCEPTED' sign on the retailer's machine). It cannot then be countermanded.

6.13 However many EFTPOS systems are off-line, so that debits are not made to the account until two or three days after the transaction. In theory therefore a cardholder may countermand payment at any time before the debit reaches his account. This presents the card issuer with a problem – it will want to charge the value of the transaction back to the retailer, who in turn will seek payment from the cardholder or return of the goods. But the cardholder's contract with the retailer is discharged when he tenders the payment card.

*Malfunction*

6.14 If the EFTPOS system breaks down, liability is allocated according to fault (but if the Jack Committee recommendations are given the force of law, no liability will be allocated to the cardholder).

**Consumer Credit Act 1974 and debit cards**

6.15 Debit cards fall under the definition of credit tokens in s 14 of the Act, so again they cannot be sent unsolicited: s 51 1974 Act. However, under of s 89 Banking Act 1987 debit card agreements are *not* treated as regulated agreements and there is thus no connected lender liability.

## 7. OTHER LEGAL ASPECTS OF EFT

7.1 The lack of a legal framework for non-paper payment systems was one of the main forces behind the Jack Committee and the ensuing White Paper. Some of these aspects are as follows:

(a) *Multifunction cards* - plastic cards are now issued which are at once credit cards, cash cards, debit cards and cheque guarantee cards. At present the customer cannot choose which functions he wants. The White Paper proposes:

(i) to require banks to 'block off' unauthorised functions if requested to do so; and
(ii) to make banks liable if they fail to do this.

(b) *Customer confidentiality*. Because an EFTPOS transaction is validated or rejected straightaway, it is possible that the customer's confidentiality can be breached by giving a reason for non-authorisation. In addition, information on the customer, because it is electronically held, can be disseminated easily. Banks must be careful, therefore, to breach neither confidentiality nor the Data Protection Act 1984.

(c) *Proof of transaction* - in an EFT transaction there may be a lack of proof that the transaction either took place or was authorised, because the PIN replaces the signature. At present this problem is not resolved, although the following recommendations are likely to be effected:

(i) expressly limiting the customer's liability for unauthorised debits to £50 (as the Consumer Credit Act 1974 probably already does); and

(ii) requiring banks to have a duty to provide receipts - the Criminal Evidence Act 1984 s 69 provides that a document produced by a computer will be admissible as evidence if it is shown that the statement is reasonably accurate and that the computer was working properly at the relevant time.

## 8. CONCLUSION

8.1 To some extent the law has not caught up with recent developments in modern banking - which is one of the reasons why reform of banking services law is necessary. However, some of the principles which we saw at work in paper-based payment systems apply also to other paper-based transmission services (such as standing orders) as well as to electronic payment systems.

---

**TEST YOUR KNOWLEDGE**
*The numbers in brackets refer to paragraphs of this chapter*

1   Describe:

(a)   BACS; and
(b)   CHAPS. (2.1, 3.1)

2   What remedies are there for payment by mistake? (4.6, 4.7)

3   What are a bank's duties regarding its electronic payment system equipment? (4.8)

4   Until what point may a customer countermand:

(a)   an ATM transaction (5.3); and
(b)   a debit card transaction? (6.12)

5   What legal principles apply to a debit card when used to make payment in an EFTPOS system? (6.4)

6   How does the Consumer Credit Act 1974 affect debit cards? (6.13)

---

*Now try question 36 at the end of the text*

## APPENDIX 1: THE CODE OF BANKING PRACTICE

### Preface

This Code sets out the standards of good banking practice to be observed by banks, building societies and card issuers when dealing with personal customers in the United Kingdom. Any of those institutions may observe higher standards if they wish.

The Code is effective from 16 March 1992 and will be reviewed from time to time. This will be at least once every two years.

### Code of banking practice

*Introduction*

1.1   The Code has been prepared by the British Bankers' Association (BBA), the Building Societies Association (BSA), and the Association for Payment Clearing Services (APACS).

1.2   The Code is written to promote good banking practice. Specific services may have their own terms and conditions which will comply with the principles contained in the Code.

1.3   The Code is in two parts.

*Part A - Customers, their banks and building societies* - is addressed to banks and building societies who adopt the Code and offer personal customers ('customers' for short throughout the Code) banking services such as current accounts, deposit and other savings accounts, overdrafts and loans, and various services delivered by the use of plastic cards.

*Part B - Customers and their cards* - is addressed to banks, building societies and others who adopt the Code and provide financial services by means of plastic cards. All such providers are called card users in Part B of the Code and in this introduction.

1.4   The governing principles of the Code are:

(a)   to set out the standards of good banking practice which banks, building societies and card issuers will follow in their dealings with their customers;

(b)   that banks, building societies and card issuers will act fairly and reasonably in all their dealings with their customers;

(c)   that banks, building societies and card issuers will help customers to understand how their accounts operate and will seek to give them a good understanding of banking services;

(d)   to maintain confidence in the security and integrity of banking and card payment systems. Banks, building societies and card issuers recognise that their systems and technology need to be reliable to protect their customers and themselves.

1.5   The Code requires banks, building societies and card issuers to provide certain information to customers. This will usually be at the time when an account is opened. Information will also be available to customers from branches, if any, of the bank, building society or card issuer. Banks, building societies and card issuers will provide additional information and guidance about specific services at any time on request.

# APPENDIX 1: THE CODE OF BANKING PRACTICE

## Part A - Customers, their banks and building societies

### Opening an account

2.1 Banks and building societies will satisfy themselves about the identity of a person seeking to open an account to assist in protecting their customers, members of the public and themselves against fraud and other misuse of the banking system.

2.2 Banks and building societies will provide to prospective customers details of the identification needed.

### Terms and conditions

3.1 Written terms and conditions of a banking service will be expressed in plain language and will provide a fair and balanced view of the relationship between the customer and bank or building society.

3.2 Banks and building societies will tell customers how any variation of the terms and conditions will be notified. Banks and building societies will give customers reasonable notice before any variation takes effect.

3.3 Banks and building societies should issue to their customers, if there are sufficient changes in a 12 month period to warrant it, a single document to provide a consolidation of the variations made to their terms and conditions over that period.

3.4 Banks and building societies will provide new customers with a written summary or explanation of the key features of the more common services that they provide.

3.5 Banks and building societies will not close customers' accounts without first giving reasonable notice.

### Charges and interest

4.1 Banks and building societies will provide customers with details of the basis of charges, if any, payable in connection with the operation of their accounts. These will be in the form of published tariffs covering basic account services which will

- be given or sent to customers:

    (a) when accounts are opened;
    (b) at any time on request;
    (c) before changes are made.

- and be available in branches.

4.2 Charges for services outside the tariff will be advised on request or at the time the service is offered.

4.3 Charges on charges. Banks and building societies will disregard the charges to be applied to customers' accounts for any charging period if those charges were incurred solely as a result of the application of charges for the previous charging period. The foregoing shall not apply when customers have effectively been notified in advance of the charges and given a reasonable opportunity to fund their accounts.

4.4 Banks and building societies will tell customers the interest rates applicable to their accounts, the basis on which interest is calculated and when it will be charged to their accounts. These will include the rates applicable when accounts are overdrawn without prior agreement or exceed the agreed borrowing limit. Banks and building societies will explain also the basis on which they may vary interest rates.

4.5 When banks and building societies change interest rates with immediate effect they will publicise those changes by notices in their branches, if any, or in the press, or both.

*Handling customers' complaints*

5.1 Each bank and building society will have its own internal procedures for the proper handling of customers' complaints.

5.2 Banks and building societies will tell their customers that they have a complaints procedure. Customers who wish to make a complaint will be told how to do so and what further steps are available if they believe that the complaint has not been dealt with satisfactorily either at branch or more senior level within the bank or building society.

5.3 Banks and building societies subscribing to the Code should belong to one or other of the Banking and Building Societies Ombudsman Schemes or the Finance Houses Conciliation and Arbitration Scheme. Banks and building societies will provide details of the applicable scheme to customers using such methods as leaflets, notices in branches or in appropriate literature.

*Confidentiality of customer information*

6.1 Banks and building societies will observe a strict duty of confidentiality about their customers' (and former customers') personal financial affairs and will not disclose details of customers' accounts or their names and addresses to any third party, including other companies in the same group, other than in the four exceptional cases permitted by the law, namely:

  i)   where a bank or building society is legally compelled to do so;
  ii)  where there is a duty to the public to disclose;
  iii) where the interests of a bank or building society require disclosure;
  iv)  where disclosure is made at the request, or with the consent, of the customer.

6.2 Banks and building societies will not use exception (iii) above to justify the disclosure for marketing purposes of details of customers' accounts or their names and addresses to any third party, including other companies within the same group.

6.3 Banks and building societies will at all times comply with the Data Protection Act when obtaining and processing customers' data.

Banks and building societies will explain to their customers that customers have the right of access, under the Data Protection Act 1984, to their personal records held on computer files.

*Bankers' references*

7.1 Banks and building societies will on request:

a)  advise customers whether they provider bankers' references or bankers' opinions in their reply to status enquiries made about their customers;

b)  explain how the system of bankers' references works.

*Marketing of services*

8.1 Banks and building societies will not pass customers' names and addresses to other companies in the same group, in the absence of express consent.

8.2 Banks and building societies will give new customers at the time they open their accounts the opportunity to give instructions that they do not wish to receive marketing material.

8.3 Banks and building societies will remind customers from time to time, and at least once every three years, of their right to give instructions at any time that they do not wish to receive marketing material.

8.4 Banks and building societies will not use direct mail indiscriminately and in particular will exercise restraint and be selective.

(a)  where customers are minors; and
(b)  when marketing loans and overdrafts.

*Marketing and provision of credit*

9.1 Banks and building societies in their advertising and promotional material will tell customers and potential customers that all lending will be subject to appraisal of their financial standing by the banks and building societies concerned.

9.2 Banks and building societies will act responsibly and prudently in marketing. All advertising will comply with the British Code of Advertising Practice, the British Code of Sales Promotion Practice, and other relevant Codes of Practice of similar standing.

In particular banks and building societies will ensure that all advertising and promotional literature is fair and reasonable, does not contain misleading information and complies with all relevant legislation.

## APPENDIX 1: THE CODE OF BANKING PRACTICE

9.3 In considering whether or not to lend, banks and building societies will take account of information which may include:

- prior knowledge of their customers' financial affairs gained from past dealings;
- information obtained from Credit Reference Agencies;
- information supplied by applicant;
- credit-scoring;
- age of applicants; and
- applicants' ability to repay, with the aim of avoiding over-commitment by an applicant.

9.4 Banks and building societies will give due consideration to cases of hardship. They will encourage customers who are in financial difficulty to let them know as soon as possible.

### Availability of funds

10.1 Banks and building societies will provide customers with details of how their accounts operate, including information about:

- how and when they may stop a cheque or countermand other types of payments;
- when funds can be withdrawn after a cheque or other payment has been credited to the account;
- out of date cheques.

### Foreign exchange services

11.1 Banks and building societies will provide customers with details of the exchange rate and the commission charges which will apply or, when this is not possible at the time, the basis on which they will be calculated.

11.2 Banks and building societies will provide customers with a fair indication of when money sent abroad on their instructions should normally arrive at its destination.

### Guarantees and other types of third party security

12.1 Banks and building societies will advise private individuals proposing to give them a guarantee or other security for another person's liabilities that:

i) by giving the guarantee or third party security he or she might become liable instead of or as well as that other person;

ii) he or she should seek independent legal advice before entering into the guarantee or third party security.

Guarantees and other third party security forms will contain a clear and prominent notice to the above effect.

# APPENDIX 1: THE CODE OF BANKING PRACTICE

## Part B – Customers and their cards

### *Opening an account*

13.1 Card issuers will satisfy themselves about the identity of a person seeking to open an account or to obtain a card to assist in protecting their customers, members of the public and themselves against fraud and other misuse of the banking and card processing systems.

13.2 Card issuers will provide to prospective customers details of the identification needed.

### *Terms and conditions*

14.1 The written terms and conditions of a card service will be expressed in plain language and will provide a fair and balanced view of the relationship between the customer and the card issuer.

14.2 Card issuers will tell customers how any variation of the terms and conditions will be notified. Card issuers will give customers reasonable notice before any variation takes effect.

14.3 Card issuers should issue to their customers, if there are sufficient changes in a 12 month period to warrant it, a single document providing a consolidation of the variations made to their terms and conditions over that period.

14.4 Card issuers will publish changes to their interest rates in their branches or their stores or in the press or in the statement of account sent to card holders, or by all those methods when such changes are made with immediate effect.

14.5 Card issuers will tell customers the time it normally takes for a transaction to appear on their account and how frequently they can expect a statement.

### *Issue of cards*

15.1 Card issuers will issue cards to customers only when they have been requested in writing or to replace or renew cards that have already been issued.

15.2 Card issuers will tell customers if a card issued by them has more than one function. Card issuers will comply with requests from customers not to issue Personal Identification Numbers (PINs) where customers do not wish to use the functions operated by a PIN.

### *Security of cards*

16.1 Card issuers will issue PINs separately from cards and will advise the PIN only to the customer.

16.2 Card issuers will tell customers of their responsibility to take care of their cards and PINs in order to prevent fraud. Card issuers will emphasise to customers that:

(a) they should not allow anyone else to use their card and PIN;

(b) they should take all reasonable steps to keep the card safe and the PIN secret at all times;

(c) they should never write the PIN on the card or on anything usually kept with it;

(d) they should never write the PIN down without making a reasonable attempt to disguise it.

*Lost cards*

17.1 Card issuers will inform customers that they must tell their card issuers as soon as reasonably practicable after they find that:

(a) their card has been lost or stolen;
(b) someone else knows their PIN;
(c) their account includes an item which seems to be wrong.

17.2 Card issuers will tell customers, and will remind them at regular intervals on their statement or by other means, of the place and the telephone number where they can give the details of a lost or stolen card at any time of the day or night. Card issuers will arrange for that telephone number to be included in British Telecom Phone Books.

17.3 Card issuers will act on telephone notification but may ask customers also to confirm in writing any details given by telephone.

17.4 Card issuers, on request, will inform customers whether they accept notification of loss or theft of a card from card notification organisations.

17.5 Card issuers on being advised of a loss, theft or possible misuse of a card or that the PIN has become known to someone else will take action to prevent further use of the card.

*Liability for loss*

18.1 Card issuers will bear the full losses incurred:

(a) in the event of misuse when the card has not been received by the customer;

(b) for all transactions not authorised by the customer after the card issuer has been told that the card has been lost or stolen or that someone else knows or may know the PIN (subject to 18.4 below);

(c) if faults have occurred in the machines, or other systems used, which cause customers to suffer direct loss unless the fault was obvious or advised by a message or notice on display.

18.2 Card issuers' liability will be limited to those amounts wrongly charged to customers' accounts and any interest on those amounts.

18.3 Customers' liability for transactions not authorised by them will be limited to a maximum of £50 in the event of misuse before the card issuer has been notified that a card has been lost or stolen or that someone else knows the PIN (subject to 18.4 below).

18.4 Customers will be held liable for all losses if they have acted fraudulently. They may be held liable for all losses if they have acted with gross negligence.

18.5 In cases of disputed transactions the burden of proving fraud or gross negligence or that a card has been received by a customer will lie with the card issuer. In such cases card issuers will expect customers to co-operate with them in their investigations.

## Records

19.1 Card issuers will provide customers with a written record on their statement of account of all payments and withdrawals made. In addition, in many cases customers will be provided with an immediate written record.

## Handling customers' complaints

20.1 Each card issuer will have its own internal procedures for the proper handling of customers' complaints.

20.2 Card issuers will tell their customers that they have a complaints procedure. Customers who wish to make a complaint will be told how to do so and what further steps are available to them if they believe that the complaint has not been dealt with satisfactorily by the card issuer.

20.3 Card issuers subscribing to the Code should belong to one or other of the Banking and Building Societies Ombudsman Schemes, the Finance Houses Conciliation and Arbitration Scheme, the Consumer Credit Trade Association Arbitration Scheme or the Retail Credit Group Mediation and Arbitration Scheme. Card issuers will provide details of the applicable scheme to customers using such methods as leaflets or notices or in appropriate literature.

## APPENDIX 2: SECTION A EXAMINATION QUESTIONS

### SOURCES OF LAW AND RESOLVING CONFLICT

A1  Name *one* equitable remedy.                                    S91, A88

A2  Which of the following is an equitable remedy?

    A    Foreclosure of a mortgage
    B    An injunction
    C    An award of damages
    D    A banker's lien                              A89

A3  What is the origin of the common law?                          S89

A4  Equity is said to act *in personam*. Give an example where this principle is relevant to banking.
                                                             S89

A5  One person may be liable in tort for the action of another. What is the name of this type of liability?                                                A91

A6  The rules of modern equity have their origin in the decisions of the

    A    Court of Common Pleas
    B    Court of Chancery
    C    Ecclesiastical courts
    D    Admiralty Court                              A88

A7  Explain, using one example, equity's relationship with common law. (50 words max) S88

A8  Name *two* of the three literary sources of law in England.    S92

A9  What is delegated legislation?                          S91, S90, S88

A10 Distinguish between consolidating and codifying Acts of Parliament. (50 words max) S88

A11 The Companies Act 1985 was enacted primarily:

    A    as a consolidating statute
    B    as a codifying statute
    C    as an enabling Act
    D    to implement an EEC directive                A87

A12 The concept of negotiability has its origin in

    A    mercantile custom
    B    equity
    C    statute
    D    common law                                   S91, S88

A13 What do you understand by the 'law merchant'?            A90, A88

A14 The concept of 'negotiability' has its origins in

    A    common law
    B    mercantile custom
    C    the principles of law developed in the Court of Chancery
    D    the Bills of Exchange Act 1882        S90

A15 Which of the following best defines the term *ratio decidendi?*

    A    The evidence brought before the court on which it makes its decision
    B    The court's judgement in the dispute
    C    The rules of law on which the court makes its decision
    D    The reasons for the court's decision        A90

A16 What is binding precedent?        S92

A17 Which English courts' decisions are 'binding precedents'?        S90

A18 What is meant by the term *ratio decidendi* in the context of case law?        A89

A19 What is meant by *obiter dicta* (things said by the way) in case law?        S89

A20 Explain what is meant by 'distinguishing' in the context of case law.        A88

A21 The decisions of which of the following courts must be followed by all of the others?

    A    House of Lords
    B    Judicial Committee of the Privy Council
    C    Court of Appeal (Civil Division)
    D    Court of Appeal (Criminal Division)        S88

A22 The decisions of which of the following bodies are of only persuasive authority in later cases?

    A    House of Lords
    B    Judicial Committee of the Privy Council
    C    Court of Appeal (Civil Division)
    D    Court of Appeal (Criminal Division)        A87

A23 Regulations and orders made by government ministers under powers delegated to them under Acts of Parliament are known as

    A    statutory instruments
    B    secondary legislation
    C    directives
    D    *obiter dicta*        A91

A24 What is the *literal* rule of statutory interpretation?        S91

A25 What is the 'mischief' rule?        S90

A26 When is the *golden rule* used in the interpretation of statutes?        A89

A27 Which is the principal rule applied by the courts when the meaning of legislation is disputed?

    A    The golden rule
    B    The *eiusdem generis* rule
    C    The literal rule
    D    The mischief rule        A88

A28 The 'golden rule' of statutory interpretation is said to be used where the courts

    A    apply the natural meaning of the words in the statute
    B    consider documents other than the statute itself to determine what was the intention of Parliament
    C    avoid an interpretation which would lead to an absurd result
    D    choose not to apply the natural meaning of the words in order better to implement Parliament's intention        S88

A29 In which division of the High Court would an action involving a breach of trust be heard?    A90

A30 In what *two* ways is the jurisdiction of a county court limited?    S90

A31 Which of the following bodies is the *lowest* in the hierarchy of those dealing with criminal cases?

    A    County court
    B    Administrative tribunal
    C    Magistrates' court
    D    Crown court        S90

A32 In which of the following courts would a bank bring an action to recover an overdrawn balance of £10,000?

    A    Magistrates' court
    B    County court
    C    Crown Court
    D    High Court        A89

A33 What are the *two* identifying characteristics of 'inferior courts'?    S89

A34 Which of the following courts has exclusive original jurisdiction to try indictable offences?

    A    Magistrates' court
    B    Crown Court
    C    Queens Bench Division of the High Court
    D    Court of Appeal (Criminal Division)        S89

A35 In which division of the High Court are actions based on contract law heard?    A88

A36 Which is the final Appeal Court in England for both civil and criminal cases?    S92

A37 If a bank wished to appeal against a first instance decision against it in an English court, which of the following courts could ultimately hear the appeal?

    A   The High Court
    B   The Crown Court
    C   The House of Lords
    D   The Judicial Committee of the Privy Council         A88

A38 The House of Lords is the highest appeal court for all civil cases brought in the UK. True or false?         S88

A39 The Crown Court has criminal jurisdiction only. True or false?         S88

A40 Which of the following courts has exclusively civil or exclusively criminal jurisdiction?

    A   House of Lords
    B   High Court
    C   County court
    D   Magistrates' court         A87

A41 Which famous case/rule deals with the customer's and bank's rights of appropriation of payments?         S92

A42 What is the maximum amount covered by the Consumer Credit Act 1974 and to which types of customers does it relate?         S92

A43 Which Act covers the use of information on individuals stored on computer?         S92

A44 State one advantage of referring commercial disputes to arbitration.         A89

A45 How did the office of the Bank Ombudsman come to be set up?

    A   By the Banking Act 1979
    B   By the Banking Act 1987
    C   By the Financial Services Act 1986
    D   By the banks without legislation         A90

A46 Give an example of a disputed issue between a bank and its customer over which the Bank Ombudsman has *no* jurisdiction.         A88

## BASIC CONTRACT LAW

B1 What type of contract need not be supported by consideration?         A91

B2 If an offer states that acceptance should be by post, when is that offer complete?         S91, S90

B3 If a contractual offer can be accepted by post, the acceptance is effective when

    A   the offeror acts upon it
    B   it comes to the offeror's attention
    C   it is delivered
    D   it is posted         A90, A87

B4   'Consideration must be sufficient but need not be adequate'. What does this statement mean?   A89

B5   In contract law, in what way are cheques an exception to the requirement for consideration?   A88

B6   Under the Bills of Exchange Act, s 27, 'an antecedent debt or liability is valuable consideration'. This is a statutory exception to one common rule of contract law. Which one?
S92

B7   In which of the following situations does the rule that 'past consideration is no consideration' *not* apply?

   A   In an action against the bank by the payee of a 'stopped' cheque
   B   In an action against the drawer by the payee of a 'stopped' cheque
   C   When a 'guarantee' is taken to secure a loan to a minor
   D   When a mortgage is taken to secure unauthorised borrowing   A87

B8   An enforceable regulated agreement under the Consumer Credit Act 1974

   A   can be made verbally
   B   can be made verbally provided there is a sufficient written memorandum of the agreement
   C   must be made in writing
   D   must be written and in the form of a deed   A90, A88

B9   Which of the following types of contract is required to be evidenced in writing under the Statute of Frauds 1677?

   A   Legal mortgage contracts
   B   Credit card contracts
   C   Contracts for the sale of furniture
   D   Contracts of guarantee   A90

B10  Which of the following contracts must by law be in writing?

   A   A guarantee
   B   A legal mortgage
   C   An agreement covered by the Consumer Credit Act 1974
   D   An agreement to open and operate a joint account   S89

B11  State *one* way in which the Minors' Contracts Act 1987 altered the law.   A90

B12  What *two* types of contract are binding whilst a minor?   S90

B13  Briefly outline a situation where a contract would be voidable at the option of one of the parties to it.   A89

B14  A private limited company's legal capacity to enter into a particular contract is determined by its

   A   certificate of incorporation
   B   trading certificate
   C   memorandum of association
   D   articles of association   A87

B15  What is the meaning of the phrase *non est factum*?   A91

B16 Since 1987 minors, on reaching the age of majority, can accept responsibility for liabilities previously incurred. Which Act covers this?　　　　　　　　　　　　　　S92

B17 If one party to a contract misrepresents the facts to the other, that other party is always able

A　to claim damages
B　to seek amendment and specific performance of the contract
C　to rescind the contract
D　to repudiate the contract　　　　　　　　　　　　　　　　　　S91

B18 What remedy is available for all types of misrepresentation in the law of contract?　A90

B19 If one party to a contract misrepresented the facts to the other, that other party is always able

A　to rescind the contract
B　to repudiate the contract
C　to claim damages
D　to seek amendment and specific performance of the contract　　　　S89

B20 What does the doctrine of 'estoppel' mean?　　　　　　　　　　　　S92

B21 In which of the following relationships is undue influence presumed to exist in contract law?

A　Employer and employee
B　Banker and customer
C　Parent and child
D　Husband and wife　　　　　　　　　　　　　　　　　　　　S91

B22 In which of the following situations could the contract be void?

A　Shahid guarantees his wife's business borrowing after she has exerted pressure on him to do so
B　Sam buys a car from Banger Motors after the salesperson mistakenly told Sam that the recorded mileage was genuine
C　Charles orders radios from Ho, a manufacturer based in Hong Kong, but when they are delivered Charles and Ho find that they misunderstood each other as to the specifications
D　Assia, a minor, obtains a loan from the Midtown Bank　　　　　　A89

B23 If a customer is dissatisfied with the terms of a contract, under which Act may he seek to redress the position/test the reasonableness of the terms?　　　　　　　S92

B24 If one party to a contract breaks a 'condition' of the contract, what remedies are available to the innocent party?　　　　　　　　　　　　　　　　　　　　S89

## THE BANK'S CONTRACTS

C1 *Ladbroke v Todd 1914* established that

A　a person becomes a customer of a bank when the bank accepts money from that person and agrees to open an account in that person's name
B　a course of dealings is necessary to establish a person as a customer of the bank

C   a bank can owe legal duties to a person before that person becomes a customer

D   a person becomes a customer of the bank on using any of the bank's facilities or services

S89

C2  State *one* exception to the bank's duty of secrecy to its customers.       S91

C3  A written countermand of a cheque is effective

A   at the start of the next business day
B   when it comes to the bank's attention
C   when it is posted
D   when it is delivered to the bank.       S91

C4  State the rule in *Clayton's* case.       A90

C5  *Tournier's* case gives four exceptions to the bank's duty of secrecy in respect of the affairs of its customers. State any two of these exceptions.       A91

C6  What is the name of the case which states the rule for the appropriation of payments on a current account when neither the customer nor the bank has done so?       S90

C7  In the context of the banker-customer contract, what is the importance of the decision in *Curtice v London City & Midland Bank Ltd 1908?*       A89

C8  Cite the case which is authority for the rule that customers owe no duty to their bank to check their bank statements and inform the bank of any inaccuracies in them.       A89

C9  *Devaynes v Noble (1816)* ('*Clayton's* case') established legal principles in relation to

A   set-off
B   limitations on the time within which an action for the recovery of a debt may be taken
C   the appropriation of payments
D   the circumstances under which banks may dishonour cheques       A91

C10 How does the 'rule in *Turquand's* case' protect third parties dealing with a company? S92

C11 In the context of the banker-customer contract, what is the importance of the decision in *Tournier v National Provincial and Union Bank of England 1924?*       S89

C12 State the underlying legal reasons for the decision in *London Joint Stock Bank v Macmillan and Arthur 1918* (max 50 words)       S88

C13 Give *one* example of a situation in which a bank may act as the agent of its customer. S91

C14 Which of the following relationships is the essence of most banker-customer contracts?

A   Agent-principal
B   Bailee-bailor
C   Debtor-creditor
D   Creditor-debtor       A87

C15 The actual decision in *Hedley Byrne & Co v Heller and Partners Ltd 1963* established that

A    a special relationship exists between a bank and its customer

B    a bank has implied permission to reply to status references on its customers unless specifically instructed not to do so

C    when providing a reference, a bank can avoid possible liability for negligence by including a suitable disclaimer in the reference

D    the Unfair Contract Terms Act may prevent a bank from relying on any disclaimer it has included in a reference.    S90

C16 *Lloyd's Bank Ltd v Bundy (1975)* established that

A    banks have an obligation to obtain a legal witness to a female's signature to a guarantee form

B    a joint guarantee must be signed by all guarantors

C    a guarantor is not bound if he does not understand the nature of the document he is signing

D    banks owe a strict duty of care to customers who customarily rely on their advice    A91

C17 When a new customer opens an account, a bank's prime purpose in taking references is to

A    obtain protection under the Cheques Act 1957

B    check the address of the customer

C    check that the customer is creditworthy

D    discover whether the customer has bank accounts elsewhere    A91

C18 What is the minimum debt upon which a bankruptcy petition may be based?    A91

C19 Define a debenture.    A91

C20 What is a bailee?    S91

C21 Give an example of a standard form contract used by banks.    S89

C22 What is the name of the personal representative(s) who wind(s) up the estate of a person who dies intestate?    A91

C23 Give *one* reason why joint accountholders are required to assume joint and several liability for their account.    S91

C24 A partner in a non-trading partnership does *not* have implied authority

A    to buy and sell goods in the course of the firm's business

B    to give receipts for payment of debts due to the firm

C    to draw cheques on the partnership account

D    to borrow money on behalf of the partnership    S90

C25 In order to avoid claims of undue influence, or misrepresentation, or *non est factum*, what should banks offer potential security givers?    S92

C26 In the event of the death of a customer, at what point is the bank's authority to pay cheques terminated?    S92

C27 What is a power of attorney?    S92

## APPENDIX 2: SECTION A EXAMINATION QUESTIONS

C28 Ordinary members of a non-trading partnership incur:

    A    unlimited liability for all debts of the firm
    B    limited liability for all debts of the firm
    C    liability only for debts on contracts they personally authorised
    D    liability as laid down in the articles of partnership        A87

C29 In a non-trading partnership, each partner has implied authority to

    A    borrow money in the firm's name
    B    draw cheques on the firm's account
    C    sign a bill of exchange on the firm's behalf
    D    give security on behalf of the firm        A91

C30 A contract of loan made to a minor is

    A    valid
    B    unenforceable
    C    voidable
    D    void        A91

C31 A garnishee order requires the bank to pay

    A    a specified sum to a third party
    B    all the monies on the account to a third party
    C    a specified sum to the court
    D    all the monies on the account to the court        A91

C32 A personal representative appointed in a will is known as

    A    an executor
    B    an attorney
    C    a notary
    D    an administrator        A90

C33 Following the Companies Act 1989, the problem of *ultra vires* trading by newly incorporated companies is capable of being totally overcome. Why?    S92

C34 You are advised that a partner in a firm whose account works to credit retires. What steps should the bank take?    S92

C35 Give a situation in which a bank would be liable for breach of trust in relation to the operation of a trust account.    A90

C36 If the bank delivers a safe custody item against a forged authority and to the wrong person, what tort has the bank committed?    A91

## APPENDIX 2: SECTION A EXAMINATION QUESTIONS

### PROPERTY AND SECURITY

**D1** Explain the difference between 'real' and 'personal' property.     S90

**D2** Distinguish between an estate in land and an interest in land. (max 50 words)     S88

**D3** What are the *four* types of registered title?     S92

**D4** Which of the following is *not* an essential characteristic of a leasehold estate?

    A    It must always be created and transferred by deed
    B    It gives the right to exclusive possession
    C    It is for a definite period
    D    It creates the relationship of landlord and tenant     A87

**D5** The right of the owner of Mabridge farm to cross a field in Robchester farm is

    A    a right of entry
    B    a restrictive covenant
    C    a profit à prendre
    D    an easement     S91, S89, S88

**D6** What is a *puisne* mortgage?     A90

**D7** Title to unregistered land is proved by

    A    searching the Land Charges Registry
    B    a collection of deeds and documents
    C    a land certificate
    D    the Land Register     A90

**D8** How is title to registered land proved in law?

    A    By searching the Land Charges Registry
    B    By examining a collection of deeds and documents
    C    By examining a land certificate
    D    By searching the Land Register     S90, A87

**D9** In land law, what is meant by an *overriding interest?*     A89

**D10** An overriding interest

    A    must be registered at the Land Charges Registry
    B    can be registered at the Land Charges Registry
    C    must be registered when there is a single registered proprietor
    D    cannot be registered     S89

**D11** When a bank lends money on mortgage, the bank is the mortgagee. True or false?     S88

D12 Which of the following statements is true about a mortgage?

    A    The mortgagee retains possession of the mortgaged property
    B    The mortgagor retains possession of the mortgaged property
    C    The lender acquires the right to retain the mortgaged property until the mortgage debt is repaid
    D    It must be created by deed        A87

D13 Which of the following is an equitable remedy?

    A    An action for damages
    B    The exercise of a banker's lien
    C    An action to enforce an undertaking, given in a memorandum of deposit, to execute a legal mortgage
    D    Foreclosure on a mortgage        A87

D14 How is an equitable mortgage of registered land protected?        A88

D15 Why is the decision in *Williams & Glyn's Bank Ltd v Boland and another 1980* so important to the lending banker?        S89

D16 *Williams & Glyn's Bank Ltd v Boland 1980* established that:

    A    a legal mortgagee is under a duty to take reasonable care to obtain the true value for property if he exercises his right of sale
    B    a legal mortgagee must act in good faith in making arrangements for the sale of property held as security
    C    a legal mortgage gives a bank an overriding interest in the property mortgaged
    D    a legal mortgagee may be prevented from exercising his power of sale if a third party is in actual occupation of the property mortgaged        A87

D17 Explain how a bank's ability to recover moneys owed under a legal mortgage differs from that under an equitable mortgage. (max 50 words)        S88

D18 Which of the following remedies is available to *both* legal and equitable mortgagees of land without recourse to the court?

    A    An action for the debt
    B    Sale of the property
    C    Appointment of a receiver
    D    Foreclosure        A87

D19 The following remedies can be available to a bank holding a charge over land

    (i)    an action for the debt
    (ii)    sale of the property
    (iii)    foreclosure
    (iv)    taking possession of the property.

When a bank holds an equitable charge by deed, which of the following represents the extent of its remedies?

A    (i)
B    (i) and (ii)
C    (i) and (iii)
D    (i) and (iv)                                                                                          A88

D20  What is a lien?                                                                                S91, A88

D21  A lien is best defined as

A    a conveyance of an interest in property as security for the payment of a debt
B    a deposit of goods, or documents of title to them, with a lender as security for a debt
C    a right to retain another's property until that person has paid a debt
D    an agreement giving a lender specified rights over property used to secure borrowing
                                                                                                              A90

D22  A pledge is

A    a right to retain another's property until that person has paid a debt
B    a conveyance of an interest in property as security for the payment of a debt
C    an agreement giving a lender specific rights over property used to secure borrowing
D    a deposit of goods, or documents of title to them, with a lender as security for a debt
                                                                                                      S91, A88
D23  Define a guarantee                                                                       A91

D24  At common law, which of the following statements concerning the nature of a guarantee is *incorrect?*

A    An enforceable debt must always exist between the creditor and the debtor
B    The guarantor incurs primary liability
C    The guarantor has no direct interest in the contract between the creditor and the debtor
D    A guarantee must be evidenced by a written note or memorandum to be enforceable A89

D25  A guarantor incurs primary liability for a debt. True or false?                 S88

D26  What *minimum* action is required to create an equitable mortgage over stocks and shares in favour of a bank?

A    Their deposit as security with the bank
B    Their deposit with the bank supported by a memorandum of deposit
C    Their deposit with the bank supported by a 'blank transfer form'
D    Their deposit with the bank supported by a memorandum of deposit and a blank transfer form                                                                                                        S90

D27  When a bank takes a life policy as security, what is the correct term for the legal process by which the bank acquires rights to the policy?                                              S89

D28  How is title in a life policy transferred to a bank as security?                    S92

D29 A legal mortgage of a life policy can be effected by:

    A    taking a deposit of the policy
    B    taking a deposit of the policy supported by a memorandum of deposit
    C    exercising a lien over a policy already held in safe custody
    D    an assignment of the policy                    A87

D30 A *puisne* mortgage is

    A    a legal mortgage over unregistered land without deposit of the deeds
    B    a legal mortgage over registered land without deposit of the Land Certificate
    C    an equitable mortgage over unregistered land without deposit of the deeds
    D    an equitable mortgage over registered land without deposit of the Land Certificate A91

D31 What is a floating charge?                                 A90

D32 What is a debenture?                                  A89

D33 A charge taken from a company to secure an issue of debentures must be registered with the Registrar of Companies within

    A    7 days
    B    14 days
    C    21 days
    D    28 days                             S89

D34 A charge is best defined as

    A    a conveyance of an interest in property as security for the payment of a debt
    B    a deposit of goods, or documents of title to them, with a lender as security for a debt
    C    a right to retain another's property until that person has paid a debt
    D    an agreement gives a lender specified rights over property used to secure borrowing S88

## CHEQUES AND OTHER MEANS OF PAYMENT

E1 If a bank wrongfully dishonours a cheque and returns it marked 'refer to drawer', it could be sued for:

    A    slander
    B    libel
    C    slander and libel
    D    slander or libel                            S91

E2 If, after a cheque has been paid, it is discovered that the customer's signature is forged, a bank

    A    can only debit the account if the customer was aware that his or her signature was being forged
    B    can only debit the account if the cheque has been properly endorsed
    C    can debit the account provided that it acts in good faith
    D    can only debit the account if the customer's actions enabled his or her signature to be forged       S91

351

E3  To be effective a countermand of a cheque must meet several criteria. State *two* of these criteria.                                                                                                    S90

E4  A cheque can be countermanded by the

    A  drawer
    B  drawee
    C  acceptor
    D  payee                                                                                          A88

E5  How long after its issue do banks normally consider that a cheque has become 'stale'? A91

E6  Which of the following statements is untrue?

    A  The drawer of a cheque never accepts it
    B  All order cheques must be endorsed before they can be paid into the account of someone other than the payee
    C  An endorsement on a bearer cheque can be ignored
    D  A cheque may be countermanded by telephone                                                    A87

E7  State *one* way in which negotiation differs from assignment.                                     A90

E8  A draws an order cheque on Blank Bank in favour of B. B negotiates the cheque to C. How many parties are there to the cheque?                                                                   S90, S89

E9  By which section of which statute is a cheque defined?                                             A89

E10 Define a cheque.                                                                                   S88

E11 Explain the difference, aside from payment, between an order cheque and a bearer cheque.  A90

E12 A draws a cheque on X bank in favour of B who negotiates it to C in payment for services provided to her by C. C's bank tries to collect the cheque but finds that A has 'stopped' it. Against whom can C enforce payment of the cheque?

    A  The drawer
    B  The drawer and the endorser
    C  The drawer and X bank
    D  The drawer, endorser and X bank                                                                S90

E13 At law, which of the following statements is true?

    A  A bank is liable to the holder in due course of a cheque
    B  A forged endorsement on a bearer cheque does not prevent a transferee from becoming its holder in due course
    C  All order cheques must be endorsed before a bank will collect them
    D  A cheque can be countermanded by telephone                                                    A90

E14 A draws an order cheque on B (a bank) made payable to C. D steals the cheque from C, forges C's endorsement on it and transfers the cheque to E who takes it in good faith and for value. E gives the cheque to F as a present. Against whom can F enforce the cheque: A, B, C, D or E?  A89

E15 At law, which of the following statements is true?

    A    A bank is liable to the holder in due course of a cheque
    B    A forged endorsement on a bearer cheque does not prevent a transferee from becoming its holder in due course
    C    All order cheques must be endorsed before a bank will collect them
    D    A cheque can be countermanded by telephone        S88

E16 What is 'a holder for value'?        S91

E17 Distinguish between a 'holder for value' and a 'holder in due course'.        A88

E18 Smith draws a cheque in favour of Brown for goods supplied to him by Brown. Brown negotiates the cheque to Jones as a gift. In this situation, which of the following statements is *not* correct?

    A    Brown can enforce the cheque against Smith
    B    Jones can enforce the cheque against Smith
    C    Jones can enforce the cheque against Brown
    D    Both Brown and Jones can enforce the cheque against Smith        S88

E19 What is the significance of the words 'account payee' on a cheque?        S91, A88

E20 Which of the following statements is true?

    A    Only cheques can be crossed
    B    Banks never accept bills of exchange
    C    A £50 note is a negotiable instrument but a pound coin is not
    D    An instrument made out to 'wages' is within the legal definition of a cheque    A90

E21 What is the effect of the words *not negotiable* used in conjunction with a crossing on a cheque?
        S92, A89

E22 A cheque payable H Sanderson is endorsed by her 'pay S Green only'. This endorsement is

    A    blank
    B    general
    C    special
    D    restrictive        A91

E23 In relation to cheques and other bills of exchange, which of the following statements is true?

    A    A bill of exchange cannot be drawn on a banker
    B    The drawee of a cheque never becomes liable to the payee
    C    The phrase 'not negotiable' only has significance in relation to cheques
    D    The rules relating to negotiation do not apply to cheques    A89

E24 Which of the following does *not* form part of a crossing on a cheque?

    A    Two transverse parallel lines
    B    The name of a particular bank
    C    The words 'not negotiable'
    D    The words 'account payee'        A89

E25 Including the words 'not negotiable' in a crossing on a cheque prevents ownership of the cheque from being transferred. True or false? S88

E26 A bank must make enquiries before collecting a cheque for someone other than the named payee in cases where the cheque is crossed:

A  'not negotiable'
B  'account payee'
C  neither of the above
D  both of the above A87

E27 Which of the following statements is true?

A  Only cheques can be crossed
B  Banks never accept bills of exchange
C  A £5 note is negotiable but a pound coin is not
D  A cheque crossed 'not negotiable' may not be transferred A87

E28 If a customer's signature on a cheque is forged, a bank:

A  can debit the account provided it acts in good faith
B  can only debit the account if the cheque is properly endorsed
C  can only debit the account if the customer's actions enabled his or her signature to be forged
D  can only debit the account if the customer was aware that his or her signature was being forged A87

E29 A bank would definitely be *unable* to rely on s 60 Bills of Exchange Act 1882 where it pays a cheque

A  a few minutes after its advertised close of business
B  negligently
C  which lacks an endorsement where one is necessary
D  which is uncrossed S90

E30 *Baines* v *National Provincial Bank Ltd 1927* established that

A  a customer owes a duty to his bank to draw cheques with reasonable care
B  a bank is allowed a reasonable period of time to complete its business after its advertised closing time
C  an acceptor of a bill of exchange is not under a duty to take precautions against the bill's subsequent alteration
D  a bank can owe a special duty of care to a customer who has come to rely upon the bank for advice A89

E31 When collecting cheques, in order to gain the protection of Section 4 of the Cheques Act 1957 a bank must

A  act in the ordinary course of business
B  act without negligence
C  give value
D  have credited the cheque to the payee's account A91

E32 S 60 of the Bills of Exchange Act 1882 protects the payment of a bill of exchange subject to certain conditions. Which of the following is *not* a required condition?

A   The bill must be drawn on a banker
B   Payment must be made in good faith
C   Payment must be made without negligence
D   Payment must be made in the ordinary course of business                    A87

E33 Give an example of a bank becoming a holder in due course of a cheque which it receives for collection.                                                        S91, S89

E34 Give *one* example of a situation in which a bank could be considered negligent under the Cheques Act 1957                                                           S90

E35 The most important statutory protection of a collecting bank is found in

A   s 60 Bills of Exchange Act 1882
B   s 80 Bills of Exchange Act 1882
C   s 1 Cheques Act 1957
D   s 4 Cheques Act 1957                                                        S89

E36 Which of the following instruments always entitles the collecting banker to protection under the Cheques Act 1957 against a claim in conversion?

A   Bills of exchange
B   Promissory notes
C   Bankers' drafts
D   Postal orders                                                              A88

## APPENDIX 2: SECTION A EXAMINATION SOLUTIONS

### SOURCES OF LAW AND RESOLVING CONFLICT

A1  Equitable remedies: decree of specific performance, injunction, rectification, rescission or *quantum meruit*.

A2  B

A3  The common law originated in the bringing together of local customs by commissioners sent by the King on 'circuits' around the country to hear criminal and civil cases.

A4  An equitable mortgagee has no rights against the mortgaged property as such (eg to sell it) so any action must be brought personally against the mortgagor.

A5  Vicarious liability. This usually arises in the employer/employee relationship, where an employer may be vicariously liable for the actions of an employee working in the course of his or her employment.

A6  B

A7  Equity is said to provide a 'gloss' on the common law; it can provide a fairer, or simply a different, remedy or judgement. For example, common law can only order damages for breach of contract; equity can order an injunction, a decree of specific performance, rectification, rescission or *quantum meruit*.

A8  Statute books (containing Acts of Parliament), law reports and (occasionally) text books.

A9  Delegated legislation comprises detailed bye-laws and statutory instruments which are made by persons (such as ministers) who are specified in particular statutes as being qualified to make them.

A10 A consolidating act of Parliament brings together statutory rules contained in a number of previous Acts into one consolidated statute. A codifying statute makes statutory rules where previously only case law dictated the situation.

A11 A

A12 A

A13 The law merchant is a body of law which was built up in medieval times on the customs and practices of merchants throughout the world. It principally covers trade and was absorbed into common law in the seventeenth century.

A14 B

A15 D

A16 Decisions of the higher courts which have not been overruled by legislation or by subsequent decisions. Judges in later cases are bound to follow these decisions.

A17. Binding precedents are made as follows:

| Court decision | Binding on |
|---|---|
| House of Lords | All courts (usually including itself) |
| Court of Appeal | Itself and all lower courts |
| Divisional Court of High Court | Other Divisional Courts, all lower courts |
| High Court (single judge) | Lower courts (*not* itself) |

A18 *Ratio decidendi* means 'the reasons for deciding'. They are stated by the judge who has made a binding precedent in a case.

A19 *Obiter dicta* (things said 'by the way') are those parts of a court's written judgement which do not represent the actual reasons for deciding the particular case but reflect, say, what would have been the decision if some fact had been different.

A20 'Distinguishing' in the context of case law means that a court reaches a different decision on a case which appears to be similar to a previous one because it 'distinguishes' the facts presented in the two cases: that is, it finds that the facts differ in a material way and so it need not be bound by the precedent set by the previous case.

A21 A

A22 B

A23 A

A24 The literal rule of statutory interpretation states that words in a statute should be given their ordinary grammatical sense consistently throughout the statute.

A25 The mischief rule states that, where a statute is ambiguous, it will be given a meaning which best gives effect to remedying the mischief which the statute set out to remedy.

A26 The *golden rule* of statutory interpretation is used in order to avoid a manifest absurdity or contradiction contained in a statute.

A27 C

A28 C

A29 Trust cases are heard in the Chancery division.

A30 The jurisdiction of county courts are restricted financially (up to £50,000 under normal circumstances) and geographically (can only hear civil cases arising in their local area).

A31 C

A32 B (jurisdiction of county court was raised in 1991).

A33 Lower courts (that is, magistrates', county and Crown Courts) have limited jurisdiction financially and geographically; they are also subject to the supervision of the Divisional Court of the High Court which may order them to do, or to refrain from doing, certain things.

A34 B

A35 Queens Bench Division (QBD)

# APPENDIX 2: SECTION A EXAMINATION SOLUTIONS

A36 The House of Lords

A37 C

A38 False (it can be heard in the European Court)

A39 False (it has limited civil jurisdiction, for example for betting, gaming and licensing)

A40 C

A41 *Devaynes v Noble 1816* (*Clayton's* case)

A42 £15,000. Personal customers

A43 The Data Protection Act 1984

A44 Choose one advantage of arbitration from: relative quickness; relative cheapness; greater privacy; better expertise in person hearing case; rules of evidence different; procedure simplified and more informal at the convenience of the parties.

A45 D

A46 The Bank Ombudsman has no jurisdiction over cases involving company customers, over cases involving more than £100,000, over cases which have not been seen through the individual banks' complaints procedures, over cases which are the subject of legal proceedings and over cases disputing the bank's commercial judgement.

## BASIC CONTRACT LAW

B1  A contract made under seal

B2  When the acceptance is posted, which may be some time before it is received

B3  D

B4  Consideration (the mutual promises exchanged by parties to a contract) must be capable in law of being treated as consideration (sufficiency) and must be of some value, although this need not be of the same or similar value as that received in return (adequacy)

B5  Bills of exchange (including cheques) may be supported by an existing debt as consideration, even though strictly speaking this is *past:* s 27 Bills of Exchange Act 1882

B6  Consideration must not be past

B7  B

B8  C

B9  D

B10 C

B11 The Minors' Contracts Act 1987:

    (a)   removed the provision that minors' contracts would be void if not valid or voidable; most types of contract – including loans – are simply unenforceable and may be ratified;

    (b)   provided that an adult's guarantee of a minor's unenforceable loan would be valid;

    (c)   altered the rules on restitution of assets

B12 Contracts for necessaries (as defined in s 3 Sale of Goods Act 1979) and contracts of service

B13 A contract may be voidable at one person's option:

    (a)   where one party is a minor and the contract is one concerning land, the purchase of shares in a company, a partnership agreement or a marriage settlement (only the minor may rescind it);

    (b)   where there has been misrepresentation, duress or undue influence

B14 C

B15 'Not my deed'

B16 The Minors' Contracts Act 1987

B17 C

B18 Rescission

B19 A

B20 If P leads X to believe that A is P's agent, and X deals with A on that basis, P is bound by the contract with X which A has made on his behalf. P is 'estopped' from denying A's agency.

B21 C

B22 C

B23 Unfair Contracts Terms Act 1977

B24 Damages and/or repudiation

## THE BANK'S CONTRACTS

C1 A

C2 The *Tournier* exceptions to the bank's duty of secrecy apply where:

    (a)   the bank is required by law to disclose customer details;
    (b)   there is a public duty to disclose;
    (c)   the bank's interest requires disclosure; or
    (d)   the customer has given consent.

C3  B

C4  The rule in *Clayton's* case is that:

(a)  where a current account continues or goes into credit, the first payments into the account are reduced by the first payments out; and

(b)  where a current account continues or goes into debit, the first payments out of the account are reduced by the first payments in.

C5  Where the bank is required by law to disclose, where there is a public duty, where disclosure is in the public interest or where the customer has given consent.

C6  *Clayton's* case

C7  A customer's countermand of payment of a cheque is effective only when it comes to the actual notice of the branch of the bank on which it is drawn

C8  *Tai Hing Cotton Mill Ltd v Liu Chong Hing Bank Ltd 1986*

C9  C

C10  *Turquand's* case gave rise to the 'indoor management' rule. An outsider may assume that a company has complied with its own internal procedures for authorising the actions of directors.

C11  *Tournier's* case sets out the exceptions to the rule that a bank owes a duty of confidentiality to its customer

C12  In *London Joint Stock Bank v Macmillan and Arthur 1918* a bank was allowed to debit a customer's account with the amount of a forged cheque because the customer had not exercised care in drawing cheques and so facilitated the forgery

C13  The bank acts as its customer's agent when, for instance:

(a)  it collects cheques on the customer's behalf;
(b)  it offers investment advice; or
(c)  it undertakes the buying and selling of a customer's shares.

C14  C

C15  C

C16  D

C17  A

C18  £750

C19  A document issued by a company which acknowledges a debt due to the debenture holder

C20  A bailee is a person to whom another person (the bailor) has delivered property in order that the former shall safeguard it and redeliver it to the bailor or his authorised representative on request

C21 A legal or equitable mortgage form

C22 An administrator or administratrix

C23 So that the bank can seek payment from either or both joint account-holders separately. Liability to pay is not terminated by death.

C24 D

C25 Independent financial advice

C26 On reliable notice of death

C27 A deed giving a person (the donee or attorney) power to act on behalf of the donor

C28 A

C29 B

C30 B

C31 C

C32 A

C33 S 35 Companies Act 1985 now states that the validity of an act done by a company cannot be challenged on the grounds of lack of capacity irrespective of anything contained in the company's articles

C34 Obtain new mandates from remaining partners. Obtain new security forms. Consider whether account should be broken; as a minimum obtain confirmation as to cheques drawn by retiring partner

C35 Where it allowed a trustee to use trust funds to pay personal debts or to offer trust property as security for a personal loan

C36 Conversion

## PROPERTY AND SECURITY

D1 Real property is land held under perpetual (freehold) title; personal property is all other types of property

D2 An estate in land is a right of ownership which entitles the owner to occupy or possess the land. An interest in land is a right given to a non-owner which does not entail possession but is valid against everyone

D3 Absolute title, possessory title, qualified title and good leasehold title

D4 A

D5 D

D6 A *puisne* mortgage is a legal mortgage of unregistered land which is not protected by deposit of title deeds, usually because it is a second or subsequent mortgage

D7 B

D8 C

D9 An overriding interest is an interest in registered land which is not registered yet still binds the land's purchaser. Overriding interests include short leases and easements such as rights of way

D10 D

D11 True

D12 B

D13 C

D14 An equitable mortgage of registered land is protected by registration at the Land Registry

D15 The *Boland* case established that a person acquires an overriding interest in property by contributing to its cost, and his or her occupation of the property operates as constructive notice of that interest

D16 D

D17 Under a legal mortgage, the bank can recover money by an action for debt, sale of the property, appointment of a receiver, foreclosure or taking possession of it. A bank with an equitable mortgage can only bring an action for the debt (unless the mortgage is created by deed, in which case it can sell the property)

D18 A

D19 B

D20 A lien is a right to retain property belonging to another person until the debt due from the owner of the property to the holder of the lien is paid

D21 C

D22 D

D23 A guarantee is defined by s 4 Statute of Frauds Act 1677 as 'a promise to answer for the debt, default or miscarriage of another' if that person fails to meet his obligations

D24 B

D25 False

D26 A

D27 Assignment

D28 By assignment

D29 D

D30 A

D31 A floating charge is a charge on a company's present and future assets which change from time to time. Until the holder of the charge enforces it the company may carry on business and deal with the assets charged

D32 A debenture is a document which states the terms on which a company has borrowed money

D33 C

D34 D

## CHEQUES AND OTHER MEANS OF PAYMENT

E1 B

E2 D

E3 An effective countermand of a cheque must be made by the drawer in writing; it must be clear and accurate and must be communicated to the branch of the bank on which the cheque was drawn.

E4 A

E5 Six months

E6 D

E7 | *Negotiation* | *Assignment* |
|---|---|
| Effected by transfer, plus endorsement in some cases | Must be in written form |
| No notice to debtor necessary | Written notice must be given to person who is to pay |
| Transferee takes title free of defects (if a holder in due course) | Transferee takes title subject to equities |

E8 Two - A and B (because they signed the cheque)

E9 S 73 Bills of Exchange Act 1882

E10 A cheque is a bill of exchange drawn on a banker payable on demand: s 73 Bills of Exchange Act 1882

E11 An order cheque must be endorsed for it to be negotiated; a bearer cheque is negotiated simply by delivery

E12 B

E13 B

E14 D

E15 B

E16 A holder for value is the holder of a cheque for which value has at some time been given, but not necessarily by him

E17 A holder for value of a cheque is a person in possession of a cheque for which value has at some stage been given; a holder in due course is a person in possession of a cheque which has been negotiated to him and who satisfies certain conditions (he must have given value and acted in good faith)

E18 C

E19 An account payee crossing on a cheque means that the paying bank should pay only to another bank for the account of the named payee the cheque is not transferable.

E20 A

E21 A 'not negotiable' crossing on a cheque means that a transferee cannot acquire better rights to it than his immediate transferor

E22 D

E23 C

E24 None of them; following the Cheques Act 1992, the 'account payee' crossing is recognised by statute

E25 False

E26 B. However, following the Cheques Act 1992 a cheque crossed in this way is not transferable and so should not be collected for a third party.

E27 A

E28 D

E29 C

E30 B

E31 B

E32 C

E33 A collecting bank may find itself as holder in due course of a cheque if:

(a) it is paid in to reduce an existing overdraft with the bank;
(b) it gives value for the cheque by cashing it at the counter;
(c) it allows the customer to draw against the funds before they are cleared; or
(d) it has a lien on the cheque

E34 One example from:

(a) opening an account for a previously unknown customer without proper enquiry;
(b) allowing an employee to obtain cash against a cheque drawn by or made payable to his employer;
(c) obtaining payment for a customer of a cheque of an unusually large amount in relation to his known circumstances.

E35 D

E36 C

# ILLUSTRATIVE QUESTIONS
# AND
# SUGGESTED SOLUTIONS

## ILLUSTRATIVE QUESTIONS

### 1  LEGAL RULES

Outline the sources from which a judge may draw the legal rules to apply in deciding a case.

### 2  STATUTORY INTERPRETATION                                          11/87

Respond in a suitable manner to the following note.

Memo to: A student                                          From: Manager

I should like a memorandum from you giving me your opinion on the problems below. As you have studied the Insolvency Act 1986, I have given the text of relevant sections with each problem. I hope it helps you.

Please let me have any views expressed by your teachers as to how this act is likely to be interpreted by the courts.

(a)  Are the following transactions with a customer in the process of being wound up void under s 127?

  (i)   paying a company cheque to one of its suppliers when the company's account is in credit?

  (ii)  paying a company cheque to one of its suppliers when the company's account is overdrawn?

  (iii) crediting a cheque payable to the company to its overdrawn account?

  S 127 states 'In winding up by the court, any disposition of the company's property ... made after the commencement of the winding up is, unless the court otherwise orders, void.'

(b)  A few months before a company customer of ours went into insolvent liquidation I sent a letter insisting that it pay off its overdraft. It did so. Do you think the court will regard this payment as a preference under s 239 and therefore set it aside. It is s 239(5) that I'm not sure about.

  Excerpts from the relevant section are:

  'a company gives a preference to a person if ... the company does anything ... which has the effect of putting that person into a position which in the event of the company going into insolvent liquidation, will be better than the position he would have been in if that thing had not been done.' s 239(4)

  If a preference is proved the court can 'make such order as it thinks fit for restoring the position to what it would have been if the company had not given the preference'. s 239(3)

  Thus the court can order repayment of money paid to a creditor to reduce its debt but 'the court shall not make an order ... unless the company ... was influenced by a desire to produce in relation to that person the effects mentioned in subsection 4'. s 239(5)

369

## 3   LEGISLATION                                                     5/87

By reference to four examples explain how recent or planned legislation has affected or could affect banking operations.


## 4   COURTS AND TRIBUNALS

Explain which court or tribunal would settle the following matters. Indicate in each case any provisions which exist for appeal.

(a)   A claim for damages of £10,000 for negligence.
(b)   A claim for compensation for unfair dismissal.
(c)   An action to recover a debt of £100.


## 5   ADMINISTRATIVE TRIBUNALS

In recent years many disputes have been settled through administrative tribunals instead of through the courts.

(a)   Explain what is meant by an administrative tribunal.
(b)   Why are such tribunals established?
(c)   What controls exist over their work and decisions?


## 6   DISPUTES                                                        11/87

(a)   Disputes between parties to a contract can be settled either by a 'judicial process' or by a 'quasi-judicial process'. Explain what these terms mean and describe the nature of each process. Give the advantages and disadvantages.

(b)   Briefly describe the role of the Bank Ombudsman.


## 7   OFFER AND ACCEPTANCE

A contract comes into being when an offer is accepted. Discuss:

(a)   the forms that an acceptance may take;

(b)   when an acceptance may be effective without actual communication to the person making the offer.


## 8   A MINOR

Consider the enforceability of the following agreements entered into by E, aged 17:

(a)   he books a holiday with a travel agent, paying £20 down and promising to pay £5 per month for six months. After paying £30 in all, E has his holiday and thereafter refuses to pay any more;

(b)   he buys 50 shares from a limited company promoted by his friend;

(c) he borrows £100 from F, pretending that he is 19 years of age, and spend £50 on a record player, £20 on shirts and the remaining £30 on paying his fees at a college where he is studying accountancy.

## 9  DURESS AND UNDUE INFLUENCE

Distinguish between duress and undue influence and explain their effect upon the validity of a contract.

## 10  EXCLUSION CLAUSES

(a) Explain what is meant by a 'standard form' contract.
(b) How does the law curtail the severity of exclusion of liability clauses in contracts?

## 11  REMEDIES FOR BREACH

What is the nature of the equitable remedies which may be awarded when a contract is breached?

## 12  DEPOSIT

Last month a customer arranged to deposit jewellery (said to be a legacy from an aunt who has died), at his bank. Today's post has brought two letters to the bank. One letter from the customer states that he will be calling on the following day to withdraw the jewellery. The other letter from a person unknown to the bank states that the writer believes that jewellery obtained from him by fraud may be in the possession of the bank and should be retained while he takes legal action to establish his title to it. The jewellery deposited with the bank corresponds with the description given in the letter. The bank manager wonders whether he can extricate himself from this difficult situation by putting the matter in the hands of the police. Advise him.

## 13  CONFIDENTIALITY                                                        11/87

Memo to: A Student                                                    From: A Manager

*Re: Confidentiality of customer information*

Recently I have seen several articles in the press alleging that it is far too easy for an unauthorised person to obtain details of other people's bank accounts. I am concerned that our staff should be fully familiar with their duties in this respect and I have often found that it helps them to do their jobs properly if they know why they have to follow certain rules.

I would therefore like you to prepare an explanatory note for circulation in the branch setting out just what the rules are about disclosure of information on customers' accounts. Please make sure that you give some guidance on circumstances in which we can give out information. It would also be useful to cover the dangers of breaking the rules. Apart from making the customer angry, what risks would be run?

*Required:* A suitable note in response to your manager's memorandum.

## 14   BANKS AND CONTRACT                                                5/87

To: A Student                                                From: Bank Manager

*Re: Bank accounts and the law of contract*

The third year pupils at our local comprehensive have been doing a business studies project about 'Everyday Commercial Law' and the headmistress has asked for a representative of the bank to go along and talk about how the law of contract affects the operation of a bank account. I have agreed and put forward your name. I would like you to prepare a few notes on the legal nature of the contract between banker and customer and the types of contract it can incorporate. Remember that the way you set out your answer should be appropriate for the purpose of the notes.


## 15   CUSTOMERS

Explain how you would deal with the following situations, giving your reasons in each case.

(a)   Miss Virginia Jones calls to open an account with you and tells you that her father has banked with you for many years and would be happy to provide her with a reference. You know Mr Jones to be a satisfactory customer who maintains a large credit balance. Miss Jones then tells you she has some bills to pay and asks for a cheque book immediately. She pays in a cheque for £50 payable to her which she explains is for an article she has written for a woman's journal. You give her the cheque book.

The reference is taken up with Mr Jones who replies that he has disowned his daughter, that she is thoroughly dishonest and that the bank would be well advised to have nothing to do with her.

(b)   Mr Albert Peters has an account with you that has been conducted in an unsatisfactory manner. He has frequently countermanded payment of his cheques when there have been insufficient funds to meet them. A 'stop' has recently been overlooked and the cheque returned 'refer to drawer'. Your customer claims that this has seriously damaged his credit.


## 16   JANICE AND JANE                                                  11/87

Last year your branch opened an account for Janice Brown, an eighteen year old student nurse, to which her pay is credited. It was the first time she had had a bank account. Recently this accounted was over-credited in error with an amount of £20 which had been paid in by another customer - Jane Brown - for her account.

On receiving her bank statement Janice Brown realised she had more money in the account then she had expected, but she felt that the bank's records were probably more reliable than her own. In view of this 'windfall' she treated herself to a new pair of shoes.

*Required*

Prepare a brief report for your manager on the bank's position setting out what actions you think the bank should take. In particular you should explain with reasons whether it can recover the money from Janice and what liabilities (if any) it has to Jane.

## 17  JOHN JACKSON                                                                5/87

Your customer John Jackson has recently repaid a bank loan which was secured by charges over his house and some share certificates. These charges have now been released and the branch securities clerk has written to Mr Jackson offering to hold the items in safe custody and asking whether he has any other valuables he would like to keep in the bank's vaults.

Mr Jackson is a careful (and inquisitive) man and has written back asking for an explanation of the legal aspects of the service. He must have been reading a legal textbook because he has asked specifically for information on the following points.

(a)   What are bailors and bailees and who would be which?

(b)   What is the difference between the terms 'paid bailee' and 'gratuitous bailee'

(c)   Does the bank have any rights over the items deposited in safe custody and will they act as security for loans?

*Required*

Prepare a general reply on the rights and duties of the parties to a safe custody contract, making sure you cover the points raised, as well as anything else you think he ought to know.

## 18  JOINT ACCOUNT

Twelve months ago you opened a joint deposit account for Patricia Bradley and Peter Smith. The bank's usual form of mandate was signed incorporating joint and several liability and instructions that withdrawals should only be allowed against the signatures of both parties. The account was opened with a transfer from Patricia Bradley's current account which was already maintained at your branch, and subsequently the only transactions have been credits in the form of cash received over the counter.

Miss Bradley explained when the joint account was opened that Mr Smith was her fiance and that the deposit account was a 'savings' account to assist them to set up home when they married. You took not further reference on Mr Smith at that time.

Miss Bradley has now called to see you and says that her engagement was broken off three months ago, that Peter Smith has now married somebody else, and she has lost contact with him. She says that all the funds in the joint account have been provided by herself and she asks you to transfer the balance of £1,050 to her current account to enable her to issue a cheque to a travel agent, as she is taking a long holiday abroad to recover from her experience.

(a)   How do you deal with her request? Give reasons for your answer.

(b)   Would your approach be different if, when the account was opened, you had omitted to take a mandate?

(c)   Would your approach be different if all the entries in the deposit account had been by way of internal transfer from Miss Bradley's current account?

## 19 JOINT AND SEVERAL

11/87

Memo to: A Student

From: A Manager

We recently sent applications and mandate forms to Mr and Mrs Smith and I have had a letter from Mrs Smith wanting to know the meaning and effect of the following sentence in the mandate:

'We agree that we shall be liable to you jointly and severally for all amounts due to you now or in the future on the account(s).'

Please let me have a draft reply.

## 20 CORPORATE CUSTOMER

Describe, with brief comments, the contents of a company's memorandum of association.

## 21 LAND

What legal estates and interests in land are capable of being created in accordance with the provisions of the Law of Property Act 1925?

## 22 DEEDS

A valued customer, Thomas Brown, called to tell you that he has to pay the Inland Revenue £7,000 in respect of his profits and asks if you will agree to allow him an overdraft of that sum for twelve months. You agree to his request provided that suitable security is available until any borrowing is repaid. He mentions that you are holding the deeds of his property in the country, valued at £20,000, and these should prove sufficient for your needs. He refers to the fact that you are pressing his son about his overdraft of £1,000 and that the deeds will also secure this borrowing up to a limit of £1,500. He does not wish to sign a legal charge, or any other document.

What is the bank's position if you agree to these arrangements and difficulties arise later on either account?

## 23 LEASE

Your customer, Isaac Walton, intends to buy a village store. He has just retired from his company and received a £4,000 gratuity which he will use in the transaction. The leasehold premises and goodwill are valued at £5,000 and the stock at £1,200. He asks you for a loan of £2,500 against a charge over the leasehold deeds. The lease is for twenty-one years, of which eight have gone by.

(a) Discuss the acceptability of the lease as security.

(b) Set out the procedure for completing the bank's charge by way of legal mortgage over the security.

## 24 MORTGAGE PROCEDURE

To:     A student                                 From:   Manager
*Re:*      *Mortgage procedures: unregistered land*

It is clear that many of our customers are uncertain about what a mortgage really is and equally some of the staff are not good at explaining either this or the steps to be followed in taking the security.

I want you to write a few suitable paragraphs for an information sheet explaining the nature and purpose of a mortgage, outlining how we take a mortgage of unregistered land (you could include a flow-chart if you have time) and our rights if repayment is not made.

## 25 GUARANTEE AND INDEMNITY

Explain the difference between a guarantee and an indemnity.

## 26 UNDUE INFLUENCE                                          5/87

To:     A student                                 From:     Manager
*Re:*      *Attached letter*

---

Wilmton Widgets Ltd,
Wilmton Park,
Cheshire.

The Manager,
Training Bank,
High Street,
Wilmton,
Cheshire                                                   1st May 19X9

Dear Sir,

As you know, my business has experienced some cashflow problems in the last couple of years, partly through over-trading and partly through bad administration. I think the tide has now turned and I would like to buy some new flange turning machines. I would like to make an appointment to discuss a £20,000 loan for this purpose.

I doubt whether there is adequate equity in my home to secure this but my mother is prepared to charge her house as security. She, as you will surely know, has been a customer of yours for about 35 years. In fact, since my father died 7 years ago she has been regularly popping into the bank to ask advice on a whole range of topics.

I hope to hear from you in the near future.

Yours sincerely,

Joe Smith

Wilmton Widgets Ltd: J. Smith, Director  N. Smith, Secretary

---

I have considered the proposition and I think it is viable. I am going to arrange an appointment. However, I am a little worried about the mother charging her home as security.

I would like you to make some clear, structured notes for me on our legal position on this specific point. Let me have your notes backed up by an explanation of the principles involved and references to one or two relevant decisions.

## 27  LIFE POLICY                                                              11/87

To:     A student                                              From:     Manager

Our old friend Mrs Angelides telephoned me today asking for another loan to renovate yet another one of her houses. As usual the proposition is OK but this time she wants to use a life policy for a considerable sum as security. She said that 'a friend said all I need to do is give it to you'. Although she has an excellent business instinct and is a valued customer we shall want a legal mortgage over the house, as well as a charge over the life policy.

She is coming to see you tomorrow. She does not understand legal or banking jargon, so you will have to use simple words in what you say.

*Required*

Prepare notes for your interview with Mrs Angelides covering:

How a charge is taken over a life policy; why you need a legal charge over the house; the difference between a legal and equitable mortgage.

## 28  LOST IN THE POST

(a)  Sam has received a statement of account from Quicksupplies Ltd in respect of goods to the value of £50 which the company supplied to him last month. Sam proposes to send a cheque to the company by post in payment of this account.

Explain how the cheque should be completed by Sam, bearing in mind that the cheque may be lost or stolen in the post.

(b)  If the cheque were to be lost on the post, what action should Sam take?

## 29  CROSSINGS                                                              11/87

While on counter duty the following cheques are presented for the credit of the named accounts. Giving reasons in each case, state whether or not you would accept the cheque for the credit of the stated account.

NB. All signatures are correct.

# ILLUSTRATIVE QUESTIONS

(a)  For the credit of B. Taylor's account

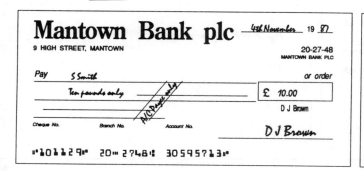

Reverse of cheque

(b)  For the credit of C. Jones's account

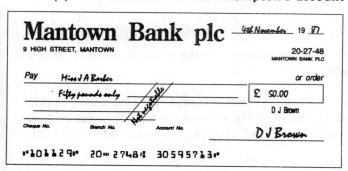

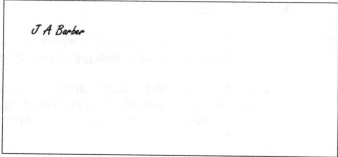

Reverse of cheque

(c)  For the credit of L. Thompson's account

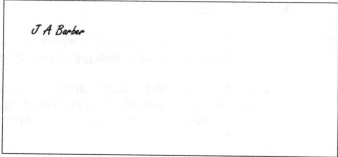

Reverse of cheque

(d)  For the credit of Mr D. Simpson's account

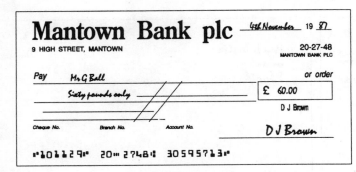
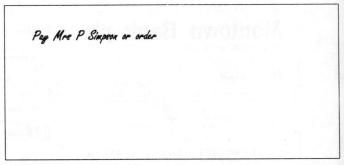

Reverse of cheque

(e)  For the credit of Mr James Dean's account

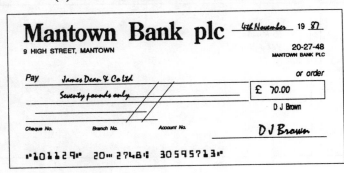

Reverse of cheque

**30  FORGERY**                                                                 5/87

(a)  With the aid of diagrams where appropriate, state and explain the types of crossings that a cheque can bear and the effect of each.

(b)  Your customer, Jones, draws a cheque for £100, payable to Green. He uses a correctable ball-point pen to make out the cheque. Green skilfully alters it on receipt to read £400. He then negotiates the cheque to Brown in settlement of a debt and in due course your bank pays the cheque.

When Jones discovers what has happened he demands that you credit his account with the amount of the payment. Discuss whether or not his demand would be upheld at law. (You are not required to discuss Brown's position.)

## 31    CLOSE OF BUSINESS

Mr Walsh, whose account is overdrawn, calls on a Friday to see your manager to discuss the future operation of his account. This interview takes longer than expected and it ends thirty minutes after closing time. As he is being shown out of the bank, Mr Walsh remembers that he wanted to pay in a crossed cheque for £1,530 in his favour, drawn by another customer of your branch, Mr Martin. As cashier you are asked to accept the credit slip and cheque and Mr Walsh then asks if the cheque is paid, and is told that it is.

After he has left, however, it is discovered that the final entries in the branch books for that day have been put through on the computer and no further entries are possible. It is therefore decided to hold over the credit slip and cheque until the following business day, which is a Monday.

During the weekend, Mr Martin is killed in a road accident and you read of this in the morning newspaper before you arrive at the branch on Monday morning.

What is the bank's position and what action should be taken? Give reasons for your answer.

## 32    STOP

(a)    Your local publican Mr Andrew Dunn maintains a very good account with you. He pays in mainly cash but occasionally also a cheque which he has cashed for a customer. This morning in the post is a cheque in his favour for £10 which has been returned unpaid by the paying bank marked 'refer to drawer'. A little later this bank telephones to say that the cheque will be paid as cash has been received and asked you not to inform your customer that the cheque has been returned.

How would you deal with that request? Give reasons for your answer.

(b)    A customer, Mr Spark, telephones and asks to 'stop' a cheque for £65 he has drawn in favour of a local firm for a television he has bought. He mentions that it does not work properly and that he will be taking the matter up with the vendor. His instructions are noted and he is asked to confirm them by post. He does not do this but calls at the branch a few days later to hand in his written confirmation. You then find that the cheque in question was paid the day following the receipt of the instructions.

What are the bank's rights in this situation?

## 33    CHEQUES

(a)    Two weeks ago Mr A Payne instructed you to stop payment of his cheque for £500 in favour of B Swift and you subsequently returned it with the answer 'orders not to pay'.

Mr Payne tells you that he has received a letter from a firm of solicitors saying that their client, Mr B Quick, is a holder in due course and they seek reimbursement on his behalf. Mr Payne says that he does not understand what the solicitor's letter means.

What would you reply to him?

(b) In this morning's post is a letter from one of your customers, Mr A Smith:

---

Dear Sir,

I was unable to call at the bank yesterday and I gave my wife a cheque for £20, payable to cash but your cashier refused to cash it. She tells me that the cashier said he could only cash cheques for the account holder and that, as far as he know, she could easily have stolen the cheque. My present balance is £500 credit and in view of your cashier's attitude I am transferring my account to another bank.

Yours faithfully,

A Smith

---

Your records show that Mr Smith uses only crossed cheques and has banked with you for 20 years; the present balance of the account is credit £500.

What would you say to the cashier?

## 34 NEGOTIABILITY
5/87

To:     A student                    From:     Branch manager

*Re:*   Mrs Jane Smith

Last week Mrs Smith asked us to 'stop' payment of a cheque for £150 which she had issued on the first of the month to Joe Jones. She had bought a reconditioned refrigerator from Mr Jones who runs an electrical business but after it was delivered she found it did not work. The cheque was presented to us on the 4th and we duly sent it back as requested. It was an open cheque which did not have any crossing on it except for the stamp of the presenting banker.

We have now received the attached letter from a Mr Runne who claims to be entitled to the money.

---

5th of the month

Dear Sir,

On the 2nd of this month Joe Jones gave me a cheque for £150 in settlement for a debt he owed me for some work I had done to his shop. The cheque was made out in his favour by your customer, Jane Smith, so I got him to sign it on the back and I paid it into my account straight away. On the 5th my bank phoned me to advise that your customer had stopped the cheque and you had returned it. I don't think she has any right to do this and I want my money. Please let me know when you will let me have it!

Arthur Runne

---

I have already written to Mr Runne to tell him we cannot do anything without our customer's instructions and that he will have to refer to her. I would like you to prepare a note on the legal position for me before I speak to Mrs Smith. Could Mr Runne have a right to the funds and could he enforce payment of the cheque? What actions could Mrs Smith take to prevent any similar claims arising about future cheques.

## 35 JUDICIAL DECISIONS                                               5/87

By reference to four examples, explain how judicial decisions have affected or could affect banking operations.

## 36 ATM

Whit Drawl inserted his cash card in Techni Bank's Cash Dispensing Machine (ATM), entered his personal number (PIN) and pressed the keys to request £50. Whit made no mistakes but, due to an internal mechanical error, the ATM dispensed only £40. The ATM's internal tally roll recorded £50 as having been dispensed to Whit, and his account with Techni Bank was debited with £50.

(a)   What are Techni Bank's legal obligations to Whit Drawl in respect of its ATMs?

(b)   To what extent can Techni Bank Ltd, by express agreement, limit or exclude its liability to Whit Drawl for breach of those obligations (for instance, by a clause, in its Cardholder Terms and Conditions, relating to use of its cash cards)?

## 1 LEGAL RULES

In presenting his case to the court a barrister specifies the rules of statute or case law on which he relies. He usually reads the section of an Act of Parliament or a passage from a judgement in an earlier case if he relies on it as part of his argument. He also develops his points by legal argument. The judge listens to both sides and then explains (in a judgement) the reasons for his conclusions.

If the dispute before the court depends on a statute (or delegated legislation made under powers given by an Act of Parliament), the judge has to consider in the light of the arguments and any previous decisions (precedents) put to him by counsel what those statutory words mean.

A statute usually contains an interpretation section which sets out what certain defined expressions used in the statute are intended to mean. For example, the Companies Act 1985 s 741 states that 'directors' includes any person occupying the position of director, by whatever name called. There is also a general Interpretation Act 1978 which provides, for example, that a singular word (such as 'person') also includes its plural (persons). Private Acts in particular contain preamble sections which set out the Act's overall objects.

There are a number of general principles on interpretation of statutes which the court may have to apply. The most basic and important of these rules is that usually any word should be given its literal meaning as found in a dictionary, in preference to a less obvious meaning (but an interpretation section of the statute can override that). There are subsidiary rules of interpretation such as the golden rule (make sense of it if possible), the contextual rule, the mischief rule and the *eiusdem generis* rule.

If the point at issue is related to delegated legislation the court may be asked to decide whether the 'statutory instrument' is invalid because it has been made in excess of (*ultra vires*) the delegated power to make it.

The counsel, in presenting their case to the court, are likely to cite 'precedents', which are earlier decisions on the same issue given in a previous case. The judge will decide whether these are genuine precedents to which he should turn for guidance.

When an earlier case is cited as a precedent it is necessary to extract from it the reason given for the decision in that case (called the *ratio decidendi*). Only that reason can be a precedent. The court will also consider whether the facts of the earlier case are so like those of the present case as to make the earlier decision a relevant precedent.

The court will also consider whether a relevant precedent is binding or only persuasive. A decision of a superior court such as the House of Lords or the Court of Appeal is binding on a High Court judge. The Court of Appeal is also bound by earlier decisions of that court. If it is not a binding precedent the court will give it due attention as a persuasive precedent but need not follow it. It sometimes happens that decisions of foreign, such as Commonwealth or US courts are persuasive only. Finally, if there is a ruling of the European Court on the point at issue, an English court would usually follow it.

# SUGGESTED SOLUTIONS

## 2   STATUTORY INTERPRETATION

*Tutorial note*. Whilst at first sight this question looks daunting (only one candidate attempted it!), what the examiner is looking for is very simple. All he wants is for the student to put into plain words the meaning of the various sections of the Insolvency Act 1986, a very recent piece of legislation, and then answer the questions he has posed.

(a)   The act states that after winding-up has commenced all transactions are void unless the court states otherwise. Therefore the answer to (i), (ii) and (iii) would be that, unless the court stated otherwise, the transactions would be void and the bank would have to give the monies back to the company's liquidator. When winding-up has commenced the company's accounts should be frozen irrespective of whether they are in credit or overdrawn. The credit balance vests in the liquidator and he will authorise any release of these funds, usually to himself, the credit being placed to his liquidation account for distribution to the creditors in due course. The debit balance will either be repaid during the liquidation from the realisation of any company security held by the bank or from third party security. Any increase in the debt after the commencement of winding-up cannot be claimed as part of the debt other than interest and charges. The credit received for the company should have been placed in a separate account as the monies are due to the liquidator.

As the transactions are void unless the court deems otherwise the bank will have to suffer the loss in (i) and (ii), debit the company account in (iii) and try to rely on any security held.

(b)   Under s 239(4) the bank has been preferred as the company, by previously paying its overdraft, has placed the bank in a better position than if the overdraft was still outstanding at the time of the company's insolvent liquidation. It is up to the liquidator to prove this preference and then take the matter before the court. The court can then order that the bank give the money back to the liquidator, restoring the company's current account to its previous state, which was on overdraft: s 239(3).

Finally this is further qualified by s 239(5) which states that the court will not so order the bank if the company reduced/repaid its debt to the bank with no intention of putting the bank in a better position. Therefore, the liquidator may be able to recover from the bank as the bank had put 'pressure to repay' on the company by writing to them in the terms described in the question. The liquidator would have to show that the pressure of the manager's insistence was such that the company was motivated to put the bank in a better position.

## 3   LEGISLATION

*Tutorial note*. This question was set to test whether the student could relate knowledge to banking - allowing him to choose the particular piece of knowledge. With the wealth of recent legislation it is easy to pick four examples. The student could choose from the following.

Cheques Act 1957 (Is 1957 recent? The examiner stated that he accepted any genuine offerings of legislation.)
Consumer Credit Act 1974
Sex Discrimination Act 1975
Unfair Contract Terms Act 1977
Supply of Goods and Services Act 1982
Data Protection Act 1984
Companies Acts 1985 and 1989
Insolvency Act 1986
Drug Trafficking Offences Act 1986
Financial Services Act 1986
Banking Act 1987
Prevention of Terrorism Act 1989
Cheques Act 1992

Having selected four examples, all that was necessary was to discuss their affect on banking operations. It would have been easy to pick, say, three major pieces of consumer legislation, such as the Consumer Credit Act 1974, the Unfair Contract Terms Act 1977 and the Supply of Goods and Services Act 1982, and discuss how the government's intervention in the provision of services to the consumer had affected banking. The regulation of credit up to £15,000 and the provision of regulated agreements (CCA 1974), combined with the restrictions on liability for breach of contract and negligence, disclaimers, their relevance to status enquiries (UCTA 1977) and the implications of any supplier of services carrying out his duties with skill and care and within a reasonable time scale (Supply of Goods and Services Act 1982), could all have been covered.

All that was then required was to identify a further example of legislation to discuss. One of the most keenly debated acts recently has been the Insolvency Act 1986 and its effect on the banker-customer contract. This act relates to the insolvency of either individuals or companies. Its importance surrounds the need for the bank to be aware of its contents when conducting accounts for or lending to individuals or companies alike. Its main objectives are to establish straightforward and effective procedures for companies or individuals who recognise they have financial difficulties at an early stage and for them to act in the interest of their creditors.

## 4 COURTS AND TRIBUNALS

(a) An action for negligence is a civil proceeding based on the law of tort. The financial limit of county court jurisdiction in tort is, usually, £25,000 increasing to £50,000 if a case is more suitable for the county court than the High Court. Hence the action would be heard in the county court.

From the county court either party may appeal either to the Chancery Division of the High Court or to the Court of Appeal (Civil Division). From the Court of Appeal there is a further right of appeal (but only with leave of the Court of Appeal or the House of Lords) to the Judicial Committee of the House of Lords. If the case depends on the existing precedent of the Court of Appeal a litigant may obtain leave to appeal direct from the High Court to the House of Lords (the 'leapfrog' procedure) as the Court of Appeal must follow its own precedents. The House of Lords can overrule such precedents.

(b) This is a criminal prosecution which would usually take place in a magistrates' court. From that court the accused, if convicted, may appeal to the Crown Court. If, however, objection is made to the magistrates' decision (to convict or acquit) on a point of law, either party can ask the magistrate to state his findings in a written case stated and appeal to a Divisional Court of the Queen's Bench Division to decide whether the point of law was correctly decided.

If the offence were very serious the prosecution could invite the magistrates to consider its case at committal proceedings with a view to a trial of the case before the Crown Court.

(c) This is a *civil* action for debt. The county court of the district in which the debtor resides or carries on business has jurisdiction to hear the case. From a county court there is a right of appeal to the Court of Appeal (Civil Division) and thence to the House of Lords.

As the debt is less than £1,000 the county court district judge could hear the case as an arbitrator sitting in a 'small claims' court. As a general rule, no costs are recoverable except the cost of issuing the summons (this rule is an inducement against using legal advocates in such cases).

## 5   ADMINISTRATIVE TRIBUNALS

(a) Administrative tribunals serve mainly to decide disputes between private persons and public officials or local authorities over decisions taken by the latter in administering the law. There are also tribunals which exist to decide disputes between private persons arising out of legal codes, such as the employment protection law. Administrative tribunals differ from ordinary courts in the narrow and specialised range of their activity which is related to detailed rules and particular claims rather than broad questions of law. Their procedure is informal.

The Lands Tribunal deals with disputes over the value of land eg for compulsory purchase. Rent tribunals fix fair rents for certain tenanted dwellings. Industrial tribunals are very busy these days in hearing complaints of unfair dismissal, claims for redundancy pay etc from employees.

(b) The reason for establishing these tribunals is that they can deal quickly and informally with claims which require a knowledge of law and practice, sometimes very complicated, in a particular area. The members of the tribunal rely to some extent on their general knowledge of past practice in the relevant matters. For example, an industrial tribunal which hears a complaint by an employee that he was unfairly selected for dismissal as redundant will know what is general industrial practice in redundancy situations. It does not need to hear as much evidence as a court might require in reaching its decision.

Since there is a general informality in hearings before tribunals, the claimant is more willing to state his case in person or to bring a friend to do it for him. Employers sometimes retain lawyers to present their case but an employee will usually ask his trade union to represent him (unless he appears in person).

(c) The absence of legal procedures in tribunal hearings may result in errors, especially on legal points. In some cases there is an established appeal procedure. From an industrial tribunal, for example, there is an appeal to the Employment Appeal Tribunal (which is equivalent to the High Court), with the possibility of further appeal to the higher appeal courts.

The Queen's Bench Division of the High Court can be asked to review the proceedings of a tribunal (and possibly to quash the decision) by application for a prerogative order of *certiorari*.

There is also a standing Council on Tribunals with the task of keeping the general working of tribunals under review.

## 6 DISPUTES

> *Tutorial note.* This question is trying to draw out from the student the principal features of the judicial and quasi-judicial process.

(a) The judicial process consists of an independent adjudicator or judge, making a reasoned decision according to consistent rules of law on the basis of evidence available from both parties and offered to the court. Each party, usually through their solicitors, puts forward factual or legal arguments.

This process assumes that there is an applicable legal rule which will resolve the conflict and it is the judge's role to examine all statutes and case law to discover the rule. The judge therefore normally follows a past precedent.

The advantages are that:

(i) the process is independent, the judge having no preconceived ideas about the conflict;

(ii) the conflict is clear;

(iii) there is equal opportunity for both sides to put their case by presentation of the best evidence available;

(iv) irrelevant evidence and information can be excluded; and

(v) the decision is made by the application of known rules, eg statutes and case law.

The disadvantages are:

(i) the judicial process is adversarial;

(ii) the cost of court time, solicitors etc is expensive;

(iii) it is a very formal and technical process.

The quasi-judicial process is similar to the judicial process. Each involves establishing facts and applying rules of law. However, the quasi-judicial process has less strict rules of evidence and procedure. It is also generally cheaper, less formal and tends to produce quicker decisions than the judicial process.

(b) The question asks the student to describe briefly the role of the Bank Ombudsman and it may be appropriate to tabulate the information.

(i) personal customers' complaints are investigated after bank's own procedure is exhausted

(ii) company customers are excluded

(iii) the bank's judgement or policy decisions cannot be referred

(iv) claim must be for less than £100,000

    (v)    office is funded by major banks

    (vi)   Ombudsman can order bank to rectify a mistake and banks are bound to abide by his decision

    (vii)  customers, if still unhappy, may take the matter to court.

## 7   OFFER AND ACCEPTANCE

(a)   The minimum requirement of acceptance is that the offeree shall by some act indicate that he accepts the offer. There is no acceptance by mere passive inaction: *Felthouse v Bindley 1863*.

The act of acceptance may be but need not be expressed in words, spoken or written. Mere conduct which indicates agreement to the offer suffices: *Brogden v Metropolitan Railway Co 1877*.

If, however, the offeror stipulates that he requires acceptance of a particular kind eg by letter and the offeree does not accept in that way but in some other way, it is necessary to decide whether the prescribed method of acceptance was the only effective type. The offeror may say that no alternative of acceptance suffices; if he does so, that is the result. If he merely indicates how he prefers the acceptance to be made, eg by registered letter, an acceptance by some other means such as an unregistered letter which is actually received is sufficient. In these circumstances the offeror has suffered no detriment by the use of a different method. If however he had requested acceptance in writing so as to have a record, verbal acceptance would probably not suffice.

(b)   It is usually necessary that the offeree should communicate his acceptance to the offeror and the acceptance takes effect when the offeror receives it. The offeror may, however, by his offer indicate that an act of acceptance shall be effective without communication to him: *Carlill v Carbolic Smokeball Co 1893*.

By requesting a reply by letter or even by sending his offer by letter the offeror may by implication constitute the post office as his agent to receive the acceptance by letter on his behalf. If the offeree posts a letter, properly stamped and addressed to the offeror, his acceptance is complete as soon as it is posted even if it is delayed or lost in the post: *Household Fire Insurance Co Ltd v Grant 1879*.

But if the terms of the offer or the nature of the transaction suggest that the offeror did not intend acceptance by letter, the courts will readily conclude that there was no acceptance until the letter reached the offeror: *Holwell Securities Ltd v Hughes 1974*.

The postal acceptance rule applies only to contracts by letter. It does not affect an offer and acceptance by telex. In that case acceptance is effective when it reaches the telex terminal of the offeror: *Entores Ltd v Miles Far East Corporation 1955*.

## 8   A MINOR

In all the problems given E is a minor, being under the age of 18 years.

(a)   If the travel agent can show that the holiday was 'necessary' to E, having regard to his condition in life and actual requirements at the time of booking and taking the holiday E must pay a reasonable sum for it. 'Necessaries' are not confined to goods but may include services; a holiday could qualify as a necessary but the travel agent may have difficulty in showing that it was. If he cannot do so his claim will fail.

Even if the travel agent fails to show that the holiday was a necessary it would not be open to E to claim back to the £30 which he has paid since he has had the benefit of the holiday.

(b) A contract to buy shares in a company is voidable by a minor during his minority or within a reasonable time after attaining his majority. Thus if E has only paid part of the nominal value of the shares he could avoid the contract so that he will not be liable for any future calls on the shares. It will not be possible for E, however, to recover the money he has paid because he has received some consideration, being the allotment of the shares: *Steinberg v Scala (Leeds) Limited*.

(c) A contract for the repayment of money lent is unenforceable under the Minors' Contracts Act 1987, and this is so even though the infant has falsely represented himself to be of full age: *Leslie v Sheill 1914*. If, however, the lender can show that the money borrowed by infant has been spent on necessaries, he has the same right of recovering the money he has lost as the tradesman would have had if he had not been paid.

In the problem it is likely that F could show that the £20 spent on shirts and £30 on instruction in accountancy are necessaries and so he would be able to recover this part of the sum borrowed by E, provided that these were reasonable prices.

# 9 DURESS AND UNDUE INFLUENCE

The effect of both duress and undue influence is that a person is so dominated by another that he enters into a contract (or makes a gift) not by genuine consent to the transaction but because his will is overborne. A contract made under duress or undue influence is voidable if the weaker party avoids it within a reasonable time of escaping from the domination of the other.

Duress is a common law concept of actual or threatened violence or imprisonment of the party to the contract or a close relative. It has been extended in equity to general threats of criminal prosecution and the like: *Williams v Bayley 1866*.

Undue influence is domination of the mind by use of the authority or influence of one party over another. It may exist because the relationship between the parties enables one to dominate the other. Doctor and patient, solicitor and client, parent and child, religious adviser and disciple are relationships in which undue influence is readily presumed to have affected the willingness of the weaker party to enter into the contract.

Undue influence may also be deduced from the course of dealing and circumstances of the parties if the result was to the manifest disadvantage of the weaker party: *Lloyds Bank Ltd v Bundy 1975* and *National Westminster Bank v Morgan 1985*.

The presumption of undue influence may be rebutted by showing that the weaker party had independent advice from a professional adviser in possession of the full facts. It will not be rebutted if the plaintiff was offered, but refused, independent legal advice: *Goldsworth v Brickell 1987*.

# 10 EXCLUSION CLAUSES

(a) A 'standard form' contract is one, usually a printed document, which is drawn up for general use of a particular trader or group of traders.

In many trades or business activities, such as the chartering of ships or policies of insurance, a trade association may have produced a standard form of contract for the general use of its members. The Law Society, for example, issues standard conditions of contract for use by solicitors in preparing contracts for the sale of land. An individual member of the trade or professional association makes use of the standard form, sometimes with variations to suit the circumstances of the case, mainly as a matter of convenience. The standard form, based on shared experience, usually deals clearly and explicitly - and also with balance and fairness - with the problems which may arise. The other party is equally familiar with the standard form and will agree to use it as the basis of the contract.

The other type of standard form contract is drawn up by the legal advisers to a substantial business for use in that firm's dealings with customers or suppliers. Its main purpose is to secure for the firm as many safeguards and advantages as the other party will agree to. In particular it often restricts or excludes liability for breach of contract.

(b)  The courts have always been concerned to restrain the abuse of standard forms of the second type described above. An exclusion clause may fail if it is not proposed before the contract is made or if the other party did not have a reasonable opportunity of becoming aware of it and deciding whether he would agree to it. Even if the standard form is accepted as part of the contract any ambiguity in it will be interpreted to limit the advantage gained by the party who proposed it; he may in this way be deprived of the safeguard which he expected to obtain.

The Unfair Contract Terms Act 1977 is the most important of a group of statutes which override any clauses of a contract which conflict with the principles of the statute. For example a consumer cannot be deprived of the benefit of the statutory conditions and warranties which are implied terms of a contract under which he buys goods for his own use from a trader: Sale of Goods Act 1979 ss 12 - 15 and the 1977 Act above. In other cases the 1977 Act applies a test of reasonableness - a clause which seeks to restrict or exclude liability is void unless the person who introduced it (as part of his standard terms) can justify it as reasonable.

# 11  REMEDIES FOR BREACH

The usual remedy for breach of contract is damages, an award of money intended to restore the party who has suffered loss to the same position he would have been in if the contract had been performed. It is a common law remedy available as of right but it is not always appropriate; in some cases, a money award is not sufficient to compensate the injured party. At this stage, equity steps in and there are a number of alternative remedies available at the discretion of the court.

## Quantum meruit

*Quantum meruit* is a restitutory financial award which may be given as an alternative to damages. It is designed to put the injured party in the position in which he would have been had the contract never been made. It is usually awarded where one party performs all or part of his obligations and the other party then repudiates the contract: *De Bernardy v Harding 1853*. Similarly there may be a *quantum meruit* award where one party pays over money and the contract is subsequently declared void, or the other party is in breach. It is intended as restitution rather than compensation.

### Decree for specific performance

A decree for specific performance requires the defendant to perform his side of the bargain instead of buying himself out of his obligations by the payment of damages. It will only be ordered in cases where damages are not an adequate remedy eg where goods to be supplied are unique. For this reason, contracts for the sale of land are often enforced by a decree for specific performance.

The order will only be made where the contract can be performed quickly and simply. Contracts which are to be performed over a period of time, or which are personal and require obligations which the court could not ensure were performed, are unlikely to be enforced in this way.

### Injunction

An injunction is a court order prohibiting some action in accordance with a negative clause in a contract. It is available in cases where specific performance is not, for example in a contract for personal services: *Warner Bros v Nelson 1937*. Provided the clause is negative in effect, it can be enforced in this way, even if it is not so expressed.

Because the plaintiff may not be ultimately successful in his case, he must give an undertaking to pay damages to the defendant if the case fails. This is because injunctions are often granted pending the hearing of the case, and this can cause unfair prejudice to an innocent defendant.

### Rescission

In some cases it is possible to rescind the contract. This means that the contract is cancelled or rejected and the parties are returned to their pre-contract conditions, as if it had never been entered into. For this order to be made the following conditions must be met:

(a)   it must still be possible for each party to return to their pre-contract conditions;

(b)   there must be no interceding innocent third party (for example someone who buys a car which has been obtained by misrepresentation);

(c)   the right to rescind must be exercised within a reasonable time of it arising - otherwise the equitable doctrine of 'laches' prevents rescission; and

(d)   the contract must neither have been expressly nor implicitly affirmed by the plaintiff.

## 12   DEPOSIT

The bank accepted the jewellery as bailee for the customer. In principle, the bank must return a customer's property to him on demand. A refusal to do so would be conversion (an action inconsistent with the owner's rights), for which the bank would be liable to pay damages.

However, if the other person who lays claim to the jewellery proves to have a better claim to it than the depositor, the bank might be liable in conversion to that claimant (after receiving his letter) if it delivers the jewellery to the customer. The bank must obviously satisfy itself that the claimant's assertion has some basis of fact and that he does intend to pursue his claim by action in the courts if necessary. If the customer (to whom these developments must be disclosed) claims against the bank, the bank should ask the court to join the other claimant in the proceedings between the customer and the bank so that the dispute over ownership can be resolved. The bank would then deliver the jewellery to the person entitled to it.

BANKING CERTIFICATE—FINAL SECTION

# BANKING: THE LEGAL ENVIRONMENT

## 13 May 1994

1. Read the instructions on the cover of the answer book.
2. This examination is in THREE sections.

   **Answer ALL parts of Section A.**

   **Answer FOUR other questions, at least ONE from Section B and at least TWO from Section C.**
3. The number in brackets after each question, or part of a question, shows the marks allotted.
4. Answers in listed note form are acceptable where appropriate, provided they are presented clearly and logically, and the points made are adequately developed.
5. Candidates are reminded that orderly presentation and clear handwriting are essential in their answers.
6. **No books, papers, calculators or any other aids except writing materials may be used in this examination.**
7. Time allowed: **three hours.**

**THIS QUESTION PAPER CONSISTS OF A TOTAL OF EIGHT QUESTIONS.**

**[P.T.O.**

# SECTION A

*Answer **ALL** parts of question 1. Each part carries one mark.
Do not start a fresh page for each part. Give **brief** answers only (a
few sentences at most; some parts may only require a few words).*

**1.1** If one party to a contract involving the sale of land fails to perform their obligations what can the other contracting party ask the court to order?

**1.2** What is an injunction?

**1.3** In the case of a married woman opening a sole account, which Act prevents the bank from asking for details of her husband's occupation?

**1.4** What is an unenforceable contract?

**1.5** Give **one** example of a standard form contract used in a bank.

**1.6** Which Act would be used to test the 'reasonableness' of the clauses in a bank contract?

**1.7** What principle was established by the case of *Kleinwort Benson Ltd* v *Malaysian Mining Corporation* (1989)?

**1.8** What is the literal translation of *non est factum*?

**1.9** In the leading case *United Dominions Trust* v *Kirkwood* (1966) the Court of Appeal identified three activities as definitive characteristics of a bank. State **one**.

**1.10** Which Court of Appeal case laid down the principal terms implied in the banker/customer relationship?

**1.11** Which division of the High Court exercises statutory jurisdiction in insolvency matters, tax cases and planning matters?

**1.12** Which English case set out the principle that a bank has a duty to keep an accurate record of transactions on a customer's account?

**1.13** What is a power of attorney?

The bank should certainly not disclose the matter to the police. To do so would be a breach of its duty to keep in confidence what it knows about the affairs of a customer. At this stage the bank is only aware of a dispute between two persons over the ownership of property. None of the exceptions (established in *Tournier v National Provincial Bank 1924*) could possibly apply.

## 13 CONFIDENTIALITY

> *Tutorial note.* The examiner did not want the student to write all he knew about the law on this topic. He was looking for a balanced answer including the legal framework and practical advice on how to avoid disclosure. This answer could be in tabulated or note form.

(a) The banker/customer relationship carries an implied duty of secrecy that customers' affairs will not be disclosed to third parties.

(b) However, there are four circumstances (the *Tournier* exceptions) in which that implied duty does not apply:

    (i) under compulsion of law such as the Drug Trafficking Offences Act 1986;

    (ii) public duty, for example trading with the enemy in times of war;

    (iii) in the bank's interest - such as calling on a guarantor for less than the full amount of the guarantee; and

    (iv) with implied or express consent of the customer - for example, status enquiries.

(c) To protect themselves, most banks require written confirmation of any specific consent to disclosure. An example is where a customer asks the bank to advise his auditors of the balance on his accounts on a certain day.

(d) Special care must be taken to identify the customer when there is a telephone request for information. In many banks internal regulations prevent any responses to such requests.

(e) Disclosure which does not fall under (a)-(d) above leaves the bank open to an action for damages for breach of contract and possibly for defamation if incorrect details are given. It may also lead to bad publicity and poor customer relations.

## 14 BANKS AND CONTRACT

> *Tutorial note.* The examiner was looking for brief *notes* setting out an explanation of the complex nature of the contract between banker and customer related to the general rules of contract.

(a) Contractual agreement since the potential customer makes an offer to the bank by completing an account opening form

(b) Bank then accepts offer by agreeing to open account (or rejects the application)

(c) If references are required then the acceptance is dependant on satisfactory references being obtained

(d) When the account is opened and funds are paid in the banker-customer contract begins - it is not a detailed contract but has implied terms

(e)  Any express terms will be contained in any mandates signed, such as a cheque card mandate, joint account mandate etc

(f)  Business accounts when opened involve rather more specific terms and mandates are taken to deal with the opening and operation of account

(g)  Rule in *Clayton's* case. This rule states that in a current account, payments in are appropriated to the debit items in date order unless the customer or bank has taken steps to appropriate particular credits

(h)  Agency – banker acts as customer's agent, particularly in collecting cheques paid in by the customer for the credit of his account

(i)  Bailment – banker acts as bailee for customer (bailor) in safe custody facilities. Under such an arrangement the bailee has a duty of care and acquires a right to be paid

(j)  The bank as bailee may be liable in tort for loss or damage to property. It is unlikely that bank will be liable for tort of negligence, although there is a possibility of conversion – giving property to the wrong person

(k)  Certain legal rights and duties of the bank arising from the banking contract

    (i)  **Rights:**

        (1)  to make a reasonable charge for services rendered;
        (2)  to be indemnified by the customer for any liabilities incurred;
        (3)  to exercise a lien over its customers' securities in its possession which were not handed in for a specific purpose; and
        (4)  to use its customers' money eg making loans etc.

    (ii)  **Duties:**

        (1)  to abide by any express mandate given by the customer;
        (2)  to honour its customers' cheques;
        (3)  not to disclose information about the customers' affairs except in certain limited circumstances;
        (4)  to render a statement of account(s);
        (5)  to collect cheques and other banking instruments; and
        (6)  to exercise proper skill and care.

## 15  CUSTOMERS

(a)  Before opening an account for a stranger a bank should obtain at least one reference. This serves to establish the customer's good character and may be useful as an aid to establishing his identity. If Mr Jones had introduced his daughter to the bank the introduction would have served as a reference.

As it is, however, the bank has made two mistakes. Firstly, it has accepted Miss Jones' statement of her identity without taking any steps to verify it – as it should: *Lumsden & Co v London Trustee Savings Bank 1971*. Fortunately, this mistake has had no adverse consequences, ie she is the person she said she was. Secondly, the bank has allowed Miss Jones to open an account by accepting the cheque for collection and issuing the cheque book, instead of insisting politely that 'formalities' such as a reference from her father or some other referee must first be obtained. As it is, the reference is most unsatisfactory.

As a result of the mistakes, the bank would be found negligent if the £50 cheque has been collected in circumstances which entitled some third party to sue for conversion. As, however, the cheque was payable to Miss Jones there does not appear to be any risk on this count – unless she had stolen the cheque from another person of the same name. The protection given by Cheques Act 1957 s.4 to a collecting bank is lost if the bank is negligent in, among other possibilities, opening the account without proper enquiries: *Ladbroke v Todd 1914.*

In view of the forthright statement by Mr Jones, the bank should inform Miss Jones that it has been unable to complete the formalities satisfactorily. It would be much too risky to retain a customer on whom this information had been obtained even if it were somewhat exaggerated by parental indignation.

Miss Jones should be informed that the account has been closed and that the cheque book should be returned. It may be difficult to get it back but without a cheque card she will have only limited opportunities of getting a cheque accepted. Moreover, after being told that the account is closed she might commit a criminal offence if she obtained cash or goods by the issue of a cheque which she knew would be dishonoured: Theft Act 1968.

The £50 credit should be held in a suspense account for repayment to Miss Jones either in cash or by cheque crossed 'A/C payee not negotiable' to prevent its transfer in what might be a fraudulent transaction.

(b)  The customer's past conduct provided sufficient grounds for closing the account after giving reasonable notice. Apparently the bank, which does not have to justify such a decision, has deferred taking that action.

The immediate problem is that by returning the cheque marked 'refer to drawer' the bank has used an inappropriate formula which could be defamatory: *Jayson v Midland Bank Limited 1967.* The cheque should have been marked 'payment countermanded by drawer' to describe the true position.

Mr Peters must however establish that the innuendo of 'refer to drawer' was damaging to his credit. In view of his previous conduct in issuing cheques and then countermanding them, his credit cannot be good in the circle in which he has financial dealings.

He cannot logically sue the bank for breach of contract in dishonouring the cheque since he himself had countermanded it. His complaint is essentially damage to his reputation by the explanation given for complying with his instructions.

## 16  JANICE AND JANE

> *Tutorial note.* The examiner was looking for a well structured memorandum containing information and advice on which the manager can act.

Janice Brown's account has been credited with monies that should have gone to the account of Jane Brown. Upon receiving her statement Janice realises she has more money than she thought and consequently acts upon the information. The bank owes a duty to its customer to keep accurate records of the transactions which pass through its accounts. A customer has no duty to check bank statements: *Tai Hing case*. This customer checked her bank statement but was still unaware that it was inaccurate.

The bank does not have an automatic right to recover the monies credited to Janice's account. It may claim repayment from her and to defeat such a claim she must fulfil three conditions which were laid down in the case of *United Overseas Bank v Jivani 1976*:

(a) The state of the account must have been misrepresented to the customer by the bank.

(b) The customer must have been misled by the information.

(c) As a result, the customer must have altered her position accordingly, so that it would be unfair to require her to pay the monies back.

Whilst the customer satisfies points 1 and 2, 3 is harder to determine. She has had the benefit of a new pair of shoes. Would it be unfair to ask her to pay the monies back? Obviously the bank will have to make a policy decision as to whether they are going to ask Janice to repay. Perhaps, in view of the amount involved and the prospect of losing a customer, the bank will leave matters as they are.

However, in respect of Jane's account, they must immediately credit her with the money and refund any charges. There could be a potential problem if it has returned items unpaid due to lack of funds in the intervening period. If this is the case the bank would be open to an action for wrongful dishonour (breach of contract) and for defamation (a tort). In the latter case Jane would be unlikely to receive much compensation unless she is a trader whose credit has been damaged.

## 17   JOHN JACKSON

> *Tutorial note.* The examiner was looking for a letter answer to the questions raised by the customer. He did not wish the answer to include a general discussion of how safe custody is arranged or the specific facilities that may be available. A good answer would include the following points.

A contract of bailment arises when the bailor, John Jackson, deposits with the bank (the bailee) the deeds to his property and share certificates. The deeds are deposited, even though if John Jackson takes up the offer they are not actually moved physically, for a specific purpose on the terms that they will ultimately be redelivered to the bailor or otherwise dealt with according to his instructions. The bailee has possession of the property but ownership remains with the bailor. Under such a contract the bank as bailee owes a duty of care and acquires a right to be paid if a fee is to be charged. It has no lien over the property since it was handed to the bank for a particular purpose - safe custody.

There are legal distinctions between paid bailee and gratuitous bailee (unpaid). Both may be liable in tort for loss or damage to the property placed with them by the bailor. But a paid bailee owes an additional contractual duty to the bailor and must take care of the bailor's property to the highest professional standards. Banks prefer to consider themselves as gratuitous bailees. However they do normally charge a nominal fee for the safe custody service, and it would be up to a court to decide the extent to which the bank should take care of the bailor's property.

In view of the fact that the items will be in the bank's safe it is unlikely that the bank will be liable for the tort of negligence in the event of any misfortune befalling them. It is more likely to incur liability in respect of the tort of conversion, if it gives them out to someone other than the true owner.

Property that comes into the bank's hands for safe custody purpose (a specific purpose) cannot become the subject of a banker's lien, as it did not come into the bank's hands in the normal course of business. Therefore the safe custody items would not act as security.

## 18 JOINT ACCOUNT

(a) The legal position is quite clear and must be explained in the course of dealing with Miss Bradley. She and her fiance, in signing the mandate, instructed the bank that withdrawals should be authorised by both parties. The signature of only one is not enough. If the bank acted on Miss Bradley's request, Mr Smith would be entitled to recover damages from the bank which is not relieved of its liability because Miss Bradley provided the money in the account. Her story may, after all, be only half the truth and Mr Smith may have some claim to it.

The bank might, in dealing with Miss Bradley's request, suggest to her that she can, if Mr Smith is an honourable man, apply to him directly or through an intermediary for written authority for Mr Smith to the bank for the repayment of the entire balance to Miss Bradley.

Miss Bradley's immediate need is for £1,050 with which to pay for her holiday. She is an established customer; her story tallies with the facts known to the bank; she may be regarded as creditworthy for an advance of say £1,000 pending the resolution of her problem over the joint account.

(b) The legal position is the same even if no mandate was obtained. The effect of opening an account in joint names is that the bank requires authority from both account holders for any withdrawal of money.

(c) Again, the source from which the money reached the account makes no difference to the fact that the bank must, in the absence of instructions to the contrary, treat the money when in the account as subject to joint control.

## 19 JOINT AND SEVERAL

*Tutorial note.* The examiner was looking for a reply in the form of a draft letter explaining the term 'joint and several' and its effects.

The sentence in the mandate on joint and several liability ensures that the bank has a right of action against the debtors severally (individually) and successively until the whole debt is recovered, as well as an action against both together (jointly). This give the bank greater flexibility.

In addition it gives the right of set-off between private accounts in credit and an overdrawn joint account when the mandate for the joint account is terminated or when otherwise agreed. The joint account mandate is determined on death, bankruptcy or mental incapacity of one of the partners.

If a joint account-holder is made bankrupt then the joint and several liability clause enables the bank to claim for money owing on the joint account against the estate of the bankrupt joint account holder while retaining its rights against the solvent party.

If the customers did not sign the mandate and a joint account was opened then the parties would only have joint liability. This means that the bank or any other creditor has only one right of action. This could be exercised by suing one of the debtors, a combination of them or all of them. However, once judgement is obtained this prevents any further action against the remaining debtors, even if the judgement remains unsatisfied. In addition to this there are numerous other disadvantages associated with joint liability.

## 20  CORPORATE CUSTOMER

The memorandum of association of a private company limited by shares must contain a minimum of five substantive clauses. These are as follows.

(a) *The name of the company.* There are a number of regulations which apply to the choice of name. It cannot be the same as (or too similar to) the name of another company; it cannot be (in the Registrar's opinion) offensive or constitute a criminal offence; and it must not suggest an unjustified connection with the government or a local authority, or be in some other way misleading. For example, words such as 'International' will only be sanctioned by the Registrar if the size of the company justifies it.

The name must end with the words 'Limited' (or 'Ltd') if the company is a private limited company, or 'public limited company' (or 'plc') if the company is public. Welsh companies may use Welsh equivalents. A very small number of limited companies are exempt from the requirement to include the word 'limited', and unlimited companies may, of course, always omit it.

(b) *The situation of its registered office.* In the case of a company registered at Cardiff, this will be England and Wales; in the case of a company registered in Edinburgh, this will be Scotland.

(c) *The objects of the company.* This will comprise a list (often complex and lengthy) of the company's possible business activities, along with a description of the company's powers and often an 'independent objects' declaration. As a result of the Companies Act 1989, it is possible to register a very simple 'general commercial company' objects clause which should solve many of the problems which used to be associated with the doctrine of *ultra vires.*

(d) *The statement of the limitation of members' liability.* If the company is not limited by shares, it may be limited by guarantee. In this situation, the extent of each member's guarantee must be noted. A further possibility is that the company is unlimited; in this case the liability of members is not limited in any way, so this clause of the memorandum is not necessary.

(e) *The authorised share capital.* This is a statement of the maximum amount of share capital that the company may issue, divided into shares of specified values. Companies limited by guarantee which have a share capital can no longer be formed.

The memorandum of a public company includes a sixth clause (placed second in order) stating that the company is public.

# SUGGESTED SOLUTIONS

## 21  LAND

Before 1926 there were several different classes of interest over land, each carrying its own rights and duties. The Law of Property Act 1925 simplified this situation considerably by recognising only two types of legal estate and five types of legal interest. An estate in land gives the owner a right to possess the land - the right of occupation. An interest gives a right over land to the non-owner. It does not give a right of possession but it is a valid right against other persons.

There are two legal estates in land; these are freehold ownership and leasehold ownership. A freeholder has the fee simple absolute in possession, and so may transfer ownership at death at his own will; there are no overriding conditions to his ownership and he has an immediate right of occupation. A leasehold is a term of years; it can however be of any duration (eg 999 years), provided it is defined or terminable. The essential difference is that a lease comes to an end, whereas a freehold goes on forever. The immediate holder of that freehold may transfer it, or die, but the right of ownership continues. Leaseholds are carved out of the freehold and will be absorbed by it when the lease ends (a landlord's or freeholder's rights are *in reversion* because possession reverts to the freeholder when the lease expires). The lease may be transferred, in which case the new holder will have privity of lease with the freeholder; he will be a party to the lease agreement although he did not take part in its creation.

The 1925 Act also created five legal interests in land. An *easement* is a right or privilege enjoyed by one person over the land of another. It is a restriction of the landowner's rights to use his land. The right may be, for example, to light (perhaps preventing the development of the land) or it may be to remove the produce of the land (grazing or shooting rights); this latter type of right is called *profit a prendre*.

The second type of legal interest is the *legal charge*, and may be given by a mortgagor to a mortgagee as security for a loan of money. If the landowner mortgagor defaults on the loan then the mortgagee has the right to take various steps to reclaim his money, the most direct being the sale of the land and satisfaction of the debt from the proceeds. The landowner is entitled to receive any excess payment received.

The other legal interests are a *rentcharge*, a *charge imposed on land by law* and *a right of entry*. A rentcharge is a right, not arising from a lease, to receive rents from the landowner. This type of interest is gradually being abolished by the Rentcharges Act 1977. A right of entry is a right to reclaim possession given to a lessor or to a person entitled to a rentcharge in the event of default.

## 22  DEEDS

In respect of his own borrowing, Brown is proposing as security an equitable mortgage by deposit of title deeds. The bank already holds the deeds for safekeeping. Hence there will be no deposit at the time when the mortgage is created nor any written agreement to show that the existing deposit has changed its character.

It is essentially a question of evidence. All which need be shown, if the matter is ever disputed, is that at this point Brown expressed an intention to create an equitable mortgage by deposit.

As a minimum precaution the bank should make a note of the interview and what was said and preserve the note in its file on Brown's affairs. If he becomes bankrupt or dies his trustee or executor would probably accept such evidence without question. Unless it will irritate Brown, the bank might write him a letter to confirm that it holds the deeds under an equitable mortgage. The letter would not bind Brown but if he does not dispute it at the time of receipt it will be useful confirmation.

The other difficulty over the equitable mortgage as security for Brown's overdraft is that if he defaults the bank has no power to realise its security by sale of the property. It would have to apply to the court for an order for sale. This difficulty is avoided under the procedure by which the bank obtains a memorandum of deposit by deed, authorising it to sell the land as the customer's agent. Following the Law of Property (Miscellaneous Provision) Act 1989 the bank's equitable mortgage will *only* be actionable if it is made in writing and signed by both Mr Brown and the bank. The bank should therefore insist that a memorandum be signed.

In respect of his son's overdraft, Brown is offering to act as guarantor with the equitable mortgage as support for the guarantee. Here there is a real problem because a guarantee is unenforceable unless it is given in writing or there is written evidence of it signed by the guarantor or his agent. The verbal offer is ineffective and the proposed security unenforceable.

Brown has volunteered the guarantee. It does not appear from the question that the bank took the initiative in asking for it. However, it does appear that Brown is expecting the bank to cease from pressing the son to reduce his overdraft now that Brown has, in his view given a guarantee.

The bank should explain its difficulty to Brown and propose to him that he sign the bank's standard form of guarantee limited to £1,500 in respect of his son's overdraft.

## 23  LEASE

(a)  The bank should at the outset consider carefully whether a lease of a small shop is acceptable security. Walton attributes a value of £5,000 to the premises and the goodwill. If he fails in his venture and becomes insolvent there may at that stage be little remaining goodwill.

The unexpired period of the lease is comparatively short - 13 years - though Walton may be eligible to apply to the court for a new lease, at full economic rent, when the present lease expires. It may be that at the present stage his landlord would be prepared to extend the lease or grant a new lease of longer duration.

The lease itself should be carefully examined and a bank official or possibly a professional valuer should inspect the premises. The general state of repair and the condition of the structure must be considered. In the course of inspection the bank can probably form an impression whether this is a successful or a run-down business.

(b)  If the bank decides that the premises are a sufficient security for a loan of £2,500 it must investigate the title. The original lease and all subsequent assignments should be produced by the present owner to provide a complete chain of title. A report on title should be obtained from a solicitor, possibly the solicitor acting for Walton as purchaser. The fact that Mr Walton has 'deeds' and not a land certificate indicates that the land is unregistered; a search must be made by the solicitor at the Land Charges Registry and at the local land charges registries maintained by district and county councils. The insurance cover should also be investigated and in due course the bank should give notice of its interest to the insurers and require to see receipts for premium payments.

The lease may provide that the landlord's consent is to be obtained for a mortgage of the lease. It will almost certainly require his consent for the assignment by the present tenant to Walton. The bank should ensure that any necessary consents are obtained. The lease may require that notice of a mortgage shall be given to the landlord if it is not necessary to apply for his consent.

The mortgage is to be by legal charge. The bank will require that its standard form of charge shall be used and it must ensure that it is signed on the bank's behalf. It would be useful to add to the form an extra clause by which Walton charges the goodwill of the business as well as the lease to the bank. In this way if the bank has to enforce its security it can offer the shop and the existing business to a purchaser. This could increase the value of the security substantially.

When the transaction has been completed, the bank should retain the charge, the lease and the assignments, consents, searches etc and the insurance policy in safekeeping until the mortgage is discharged. As it is a charge protected by possession of deeds it does not require registration at the Land Charges Registry. Notice should be given to the insurers.

## 24 MORTGAGE PROCEDURE

> *Tutorial note.* The examiner actually stated in the question his requirements and this question could have been answered partly in note form.

A mortgage is the creation or transfer of an interest in property as security for the payment of a debt or the discharge of some other obligation. The parties to the mortgage are the mortgagor (the customer or borrower) and the mortgagee (the bank or lender). A mortgage may be either legal or equitable. A legal mortgage creates rights against the property itself and therefore places the lender in a stronger position whilst an equitable mortgage creates only personal rights against the mortgagor. A mortgage can sometimes be referred to as a legal charge.

*Procedure in taking a legal mortgage over unregistered land*

(a) Investigate customer's title to the land. Title to unregistered land comprises a set of deeds and documents and this investigation, if the bank is taking a first charge, should be carried out by a solicitor.

(b) Search at (i) Land Charges Register (ii) the Local Land Charges Register and (iii) the Companies Registry (if prospective mortgagor is a company).

(c) Value the property.

(d) Ensure that the property has insurance cover and have the bank's interest noted on the policy.

(e) The customer must now execute the appropriate bank's form of mortgage as a deed; to be actionable it must also be signed by the bank. The title deeds if available will then be deposited with the bank.

(f) If it is to be a second charge then notice of the bank's charge must be given on the Land Charges Register.

*The bank's remedies*

A legal mortgagee has five remedies available. It may:

(a)  take legal action personally against the borrower for repayment of the debt;

(b)  exercise the power to sell the property;

(c)  appoint a receiver - usually this takes place where it is either impractical to sell the property (there are sitting tenants) or where the property market is depressed;

(d)  foreclose - this is rarely used as the property becomes the mortgagee's absolutely;

(e)  obtain possession of the property.

## 25  GUARANTEE AND INDEMNITY

The distinction between a guarantee and an indemnity is that a guarantor gives a collateral or supplementary undertaking that the debtor will pay his debt and if he fails to do so the guarantor will pay it. By contrast under a contract of indemnity the person who indemnifies undertakes that the creditor shall not suffer loss from the transaction between creditor and debtor. The indemnity constitutes a primary liability to the creditor.

It is not always easy to decide from the words used whether a commitment is a guarantee or an indemnity. However, an undertaking that if work is done the person who does it shall be paid is not dependent on there being a liability of someone else to pay even though that is the intention. Accordingly, it is an indemnity not a guarantee: *Mountstephen v Lakeman 1871.*

If the contract between creditor and debtor is void, say because the latter is an enemy alien a guarantee of the contract has no effect since the guarantor undertakes that the debtor will discharge his liability and there is none. An indemnity however covers such a case since it applies if the creditor suffers loss - as he does if a debt is irrecoverable. For this reason bank forms of guarantee include a clause giving an indemnity in addition.

A second practical consequence of the distinction is that a guarantee is not enforceable unless made in writing or supported by written evidence: Statute of Frauds 1677. An indemnity may be enforced on oral evidence only.

## 26  UNDUE INFLUENCE

> *Tutorial note.* The question gives undue influence as the main area for consideration although the examiner did not actually advise the student of this but set out a situation which had been previously seen in case-law.

Undue influence can take many forms and enables the person giving the security to avoid his liabilities. The effect of undue influence is to prevent the person influenced from making a free and independent judgement. In the relationship cited in the question, parent and child, a position of dominance is presumed to exist of the mother over the son, although this may be rebutted. The dominant party, be it either parent or child, victimises the weaker so that a contract entered into by the weaker is clearly to the advantage of the dominant party and to the 'manifest' disadvantage of the weaker party. If this is proved, the weaker party can set aside the contract for undue influence. This was the decision in *National Westminster Bank v Morgan 1985*.

The bank may in certain circumstances be held to be in domination over a particular customer. Where this is so and the customer offers the bank security, especially for the obligations of another party, the bank owes a very strict duty of care to the customer: *Lloyds Bank Ltd v Bundy 1975*.

The bank should always ensure that people giving third party security receive independent legal advice before signing the documents; but even if this is refused, undue influence may still be found: *Goldsworthy v Brickell 1987*.

A free will clause is usually contained in all security documents which states that the guarantor understands the nature of the document and the liability he will incur. This clause is usually completed by the guarantor's solicitor.

## 27  LIFE POLICY

> *Tutorial note.* The examiner was once again looking for the answer to be in note form covering the three topics indicated.

*Basic steps for taking a charge over a life policy:*

(a)  Obtain policy and ensure terms and benefits are correct and that assured is correctly identified.

(b)  Ensure the policy can be assigned to the bank.

(c)  Obtain an up-to-date surrender value.

(d)  Ask customer to complete the bank's form of charge.

(e)  Give notice to the assurance company of the bank's charge. This notice vests legal title to the policy with the bank.

(f)  Life assurance company should return copy of notice with details of any prior charges.

(g)  Place policy, charge form and copy notice in the bank's safe.

*Legal mortgage over house*

The bank wishes to take a legal mortgage over the property because a legal mortgagee acquires rights against the property itself, in addition to the personal action available against the mortgagor for the principal and interest due. An equitable mortgage gives no rights against the property, only personal rights against the borrower; these are principally the right to share in the proceeds of sale if the property were to be sold and the right to seek the court's assistance in enforcing this right. The main practical distinction now between a legal and equitable mortgage is the remedies available.

*Difference between legal and equitable mortgage*

A legal mortgage is usually created by a charge by deed expressed to be by way of legal mortgage. An equitable mortgage can be created in two ways by:

(a) deposit of the title deeds or land certificate, provided the deposit is intended to be used as security (not for safe custody); and

(b) taking an equitable charge, usually created by written memorandum (memorandum of deposit) in which the borrower states that his property shall be security for the money advanced. An equitable charge does not convey a legal interest in property to the mortgagee, so the mortgage cannot be enforced without the court's consent. If an equitable mortgagee wished to sell the property he could not do so without the court's permission, but a legal mortgagee could. The bank's standard memorandum of deposit includes an undertaking to execute a legal mortgage when the bank requests the mortgagor to do so.

## 28   LOST IN THE POST

(a) Sam should draw the cheque payable to Quicksupplies Ltd so that it is an order cheque which may not be paid to anyone else except by order (endorsement) by Quicksupplies Ltd.

Sam will use a printed cheque form supplied by the bank and normally bearing a pre-printed general crossing which is two parallel lines across the cheque from top to bottom. If there were no such crossing on the blank cheque form Sam should add it. This ensures that payment of the cheque cannot be made by presenting it at the counter at Sam's bank. Instead Quicksupplies Ltd, or any subsequent holder, would have to deliver the cheque to their bank, where they were known as existing customers with a bank account. That bank (the collecting bank) would then present the cheque to Sam's bank (the paying bank) through the bank clearing system.

Sam's bank has no means of knowing whether the money paid to the collecting bank is credited to the account of the person entitled to it. But the collecting bank should be able to ensure that this result is achieved since it collected payment for its own customer.

As an additional precaution Sam might write the words 'Not negotiable' or ' A/C Payee' or both between the lines of the crossing. 'Not negotiable' means that any holder of the cheque after Quicksupplies Ltd has no better title than the transferor to him. By this means a person who innocently acquires a stolen cheque is denied any title to it. 'A/C Payee' is a direction to the collecting bank to obtain payment only for the original payee. The cheque is non-transferable, and this crossing is supported by the Cheques Act 1992.

(b) Sam should inform his bank that the cheque has been lost and instruct the bank to refuse payment if the cheque is later presented to it. The bank will require a countermand in writing, which identifies the cheque correctly, including its serial number. Sam should then issue a replacement cheque in favour of Quicksupplies Ltd.

## SUGGESTED SOLUTIONS

## 29   CROSSINGS

> *Tutorial note.* In this question the examiner was testing both the work experience and the legal knowledge of the student. Each answer must not only be correct but must also give the right reasons for arriving at the answer to ensure that full marks are obtained.

(a)   An 'account payee' crossing is a direction to the collecting bank as to how the cheque should be dealt with after it receives it. The crossing has been given statutory backing by the Cheques Act 1992, and is a direction to the collecting bank that collection of the cheque should only be for the person named as payee. Therefore the cheque payable to S. Smith 'account payee only' which has been endorsed to B. Taylor, who wishes to pay it into his account, should not be accepted by the collecting bank. The paying bank will not, under the Cheques Act 1992, be held as negligent under s 80 Bills of Exchange Act 1882 by virtue of any failure to observe this endorsement.

(b)   'And Company' is a general crossing and rarely seen today. A general crossing instructs the paying bank to make payment to another bank. Therefore, as the cheque has been endorsed in blank by the payee, so making it a bearer cheque, the bank can accept it for the credit of C. Jones's account. If the bank had any doubt regarding the endorsement being genuinely that of the payee then it could refuse to accept it.

(c)   A 'not negotiable' crossing means that any person into whose hands the cheque comes does not have any better title than that of the immediate transferor. This is primarily a protection against theft of cheques. The crossing does not affect the cheque's transferability. Therefore the endorsement in blank by the payee is acceptable and the cheque can be transferred to L Thompson. However, L Thompson will only have as good a title to the cheque as the person who transferred it to him. The bank would accept the cheque on the basis that its customer was considered respectable and trustworthy, and it received a satisfactory explanation of the transaction. If the cheque was stolen in the past then the true owner could demand the money back from L Thompson at a later date as he would have no better title than the thief. The bank could be liable for conversion, although it will have a right of indemnity against its customer for any loss incurred.

(d)   The two transverse parallel lines ensure that the cheque is paid into a bank account. However, as the endorsement on the cheque has not been signed, it is not effective and requires the payee's – G Bell's – signature before it can be acted upon. Also, the endorsement is in favour of Mrs P. Simpson or order and it is Mr D. Simpson who is trying to pay the cheque into his account. The bank should refuse to accept the cheque and ask Mr Simpson to obtain a correct, signed endorsement. This would mean the addition of Mr Bell's signature and then that of Mrs Simpson.

(e)   A company cheque must be credited to the company's own bank account. The bank would be held negligent if it accepted a cheque payable to the company for the collection of an account of one of the directors and so would lose the protection of s 2 of the Cheques Act 1957. The bank may, if it accepts the cheque, be converting the money, ie depriving the true owner of it. Enquiry into the circumstances surrounding the cheque are essential and only in very rare cases where the company and directors are highly regarded by the bank might the bank accept the cheque and the risk of a conversion claim in the future.

## 30  FORGERY

> *Tutorial note.* This was a straightforward question relating to crossings and the bank and customer's duty in respect of cheques.

(a)  *Crossings*

A general crossing consists of two transverse parallel lines across the face of a cheque with or without the words 'and Co', 'not negotiable' or 'a/c payee' between the lines. A crossing ensures that a cheque has to be paid into a bank account and cannot be cashed over the counter.

'Not negotiable' added to a crossing deprives the cheque of its negotiability. This means that anyone taking the cheque does not receive and cannot give better title than the person transferring it. This crossing also deprives the cheque of its transferability following the passing of the Cheques Act 1992. 'Account payee' has statutory significance and is a direction to the collecting bank to ensure the monies go to the payee's account; the cheque crossed in this way is not transferable.

*Special crossings*

A special crossing consists of the name of a particular bank and/or branch to which payment must be made. The words 'not negotiable' and 'account payee' can be added.

| Barclays Bank plc | National Westminster Bank plc - A/C payee | Lloyds Bank plc not negotiable | The Royal Bank of Scotland plc Anytown branch |
|---|---|---|---|

(b)  A bank is liable in damages to its customer if it wrongfully debits the customer's account with a cheque which has been materially altered without the customer's consent. In this case the cheque had been altered from £100 to £400. However, the customer owes a duty to draw cheques with reasonable care to avoid fraudulent alteration and it would appear in this case that the customer has broken this duty by using a correctable ball-point pen.

In this case it would appear that the bank may debit his account as the non-apparent alteration facilitated the fraud by his own negligence. In the case of *London Joint Stock Bank v Macmillan and Arthur 1918*, a cheque was signed payable to the payee or bearer, made out by a clerk for £2. The amount payable was shown in figures only and the clerk fraudulently altered the figure to read £120, wrote the amount on the cheque and obtained the money. Because of the firm's negligence the bank was able to debit the account with the amount of the cheque.

## 31  CLOSE OF BUSINESS

Notice of the death of a customer (Martin) revokes the authority of his bank to pay a cheque drawn on his account: Bills of Exchange Act 1882 s 75. However, it does not invalidate authority under which a cheque was paid before the bank had notice of the death.

On Monday morning the bank must decide whether it considers that Martin's cheque had been paid on Friday while he was alive. If it was not paid it cannot be paid on Monday nor debited to his account.

Walsh, on Friday afternoon, was told that the cheque had been paid in to his account. As the drawer's account is at the same branch the payment is entirely a domestic matter within the control of the branch.

There are of course two factors which may suggest that the bank should not consider that it had made the payment on Friday. First, the cheque was only delivered to the bank 30 minutes after closing time. However, there is authority (*Baines v National Provincial Bank Limited 1927*) for holding that payment may be effected within a short period of time after closing if the person who presents it is on the bank's premises at closing time. Thirty minutes, in this case, is appreciably more than the five minutes late in *Baines* case but the principle is the same.

The second difficulty is that, although both accounts are at the same branch, the transaction was not put through the central computerised record on Friday. This, however, is a matter of recording, or not recording, at another place what had been done at the bank. The record is subsidiary and in the circumstances could properly be adjusted to record what was done late on Friday afternoon before the bank closed.

If it were decided that the payment was not made on Friday, as suggested above, the bank might try to argue that in crediting Walsh's account, which was overdrawn, it became a holder for value under s 2 Cheques Act 1957.

## 32  STOP

(a)  There is no difficulty in complying with the request to return the cheque so that it may be paid.

The paying banker is trying to protect his customer's reputation by arranging that notice of dishonour of the cheque, when it was first presented, shall not be given to Dunn, the customer of the collecting bank.

The collecting bank should consider whether, if it agrees to this request, it prejudices the interest of its own customer, Dunn. If he is told that the cheque was dishonoured he may decline to take any further risks and refuse to cash any more cheques for the person concerned.

If, however, he is led to believe that the first cheque for £10 was paid on first presentation he is likely, in ignorance of the true facts, to expose himself to further risk of loss by cashing other cheques for the same person.

To protect its own customer the bank should disclose to him what has happened.

(b) The question does not say whether Spark gave the required particulars of the cheque which he wished to stop, that is the date, amount and name of payee, and – most important of all – the number of the cheque. It is assumed that in the telephone conversation he did give correct and complete details.

He should have delivered written confirmation more promptly than he actually did. But in the meantime the bank should have acted on his verbal instructions by returning the cheque, marked 'payment countermanded by telephone and postponed pending confirmation'.

The bank has failed to comply with the customer's instructions and has made an unauthorised payment which it may not debit to his account.

However, it is likely that Spark is liable to pay the supplier of the television the agreed price. He may have intended to withhold payment to induce prompt attention by the supplier to his complaint. If the defect is made good he has merely paid the price, by the unauthorised act of the bank, before he intended to pay it. He has – on this basis – suffered no loss and cannot recover substantial damages from the bank.

He can compel the bank to cancel the debit to his account but the bank is by subrogation entitled to enforce the supplier's rights against Spark for the price of the television. Alternatively, if Spark has the right to repudiate the contract for the purchase of the television (this depends on legal points arising from the Sale of Goods Act 1979) the bank can demand that the television be handed over so that the bank may return it to the supplier in exchange for a refund of the price.

## 33 CHEQUES

(a) The claim has been made against the customer, not the bank, which has no liability to the holder of a cheque (unless the customer used his cheque guarantee card) and has a definite obligation to comply with the customer's countermand. However, the banker should be able to explain to a customer the limits imposed on his right of countermand arising from the rights obtained against him by a holder of his cheque, especially if the latter is a holder in due course.

The bank should explain to Mr Payne that any person who became a holder in due course of his cheque can claim its value from him as drawer if the drawee bank refuses payment - as in the present case it was bound to do. A cheque is a negotiable instrument and so the transferee, as holder in due course, has rights of recourse against all previous parties, including the drawer.

Since the claim is made on behalf of a client who is described as a holder in due course, the answer should set out the conditions (s 29 1882 Act) which determine who is a holder in due course. The customer should be advised that he may dispute the assertion that Quick is a holder in due course but it will be presumed in Quick's favour that he is a holder in due course unless fraud or illegality is shown to have occurred in connection with the issue or negotiation of the cheque: s 30.

The bank might also explain to Mr Payne that he could possibly avoid a repetition of this situation by crossing his cheque 'not negotiable'. It depends on the reasons for stopping the cheque whether this crossing would help him to resist the claim.

(b)   One must here distinguish between the legal position and the sensible course of action. A banker should always have a clear grasp of the relevant law but he may have to retreat from a strict legal stand if the risk is small and a concession is necessary to preserve customer goodwill.

The answer should make the point that s 79 of the 1882 Act imposes on a bank a duty to pay a crossed cheque only to another bank under the sanction of liability to the true owner for any loss resulting from the bank's failure to do so. A cheque form payable to 'cash' is not a cheque but nothing turns on that point here.

On the other hand the banks for their own convenience issue to customers books of cheques bearing a pre-printed general crossing (unless the customer insists on having open cheques). The banks also permit customers in person or through their agents known to the bank to use a crossed cheque form to obtain cash. It was reasonable for Smith to suppose that his wife would be permitted to obtain payment of his cheque payable to 'cash'.

The cashier appears to have been extremely tactless in explaining to Mrs Smith that in his eyes she might be a thief. She was presumably unknown to him. But he could have attempted to resolve the difficulty by asking her to produce evidence of identity, or by referring to a more senior bank official to whom Mrs Smith may have been known, or by telephoning Mr Smith.

(The full question requires an answer to Mr Smith's letter which should be apologetic, give an explanation and perhaps invite Mr Smith to call to see the manager and talk the matter over - in the hope of persuading him not to transfer his account.)

## 34   NEGOTIABILITY

> *Tutorial note.* This question relates to negotiability and the examiner was looking for students to explain the effects, actions and conditions of negotiability to obtain good title.

A cheque is a negotiable instrument and therefore title passes by delivery or endorsement and delivery. Any person taking transfer of the cheque in good faith and for face value is unaffected by any defects in the title of prior parties as well as any personal defences such as counterclaims. A bona fide transferee for value shall acquire a perfect title. The holder can sue in his own name and does not need to give notice to prior parties to establish title.

Mrs Smith paid for the refrigerator by uncrossed cheque. The item did not work, so she stopped the cheque thinking that this would ensure that Mr Jones put the article right. If he did not she would not have lost any money. However, Mr Jones had negotiated the cheque to Mr Runne in payment of an existing trade debt. This means that title to the cheque had passed to Mr Runne as holder in due course, provided he fulfilled s 29, and he can enforce the cheque against Mrs Smith even though she has stopped the cheque. It is irrelevant to Mr Runne's claim that she stopped the cheque.

If the cheque had been crossed 'not negotiable' in the first place this would have stopped the situation arising because Mr Runne would then take the cheque subject to any defect in Mr Jones's title or subject to any counterclaim that Mrs Smith had against him in respect of the refrigerator which was not working. The crossing would deprive the cheque not of its transferability but of its negotiability, which in this case would be beneficial to the customer.

## 35  JUDICIAL DECISIONS

> *Tutorial note.* The examiner was looking for four examples of case law which have affected or could affect banking. With the wealth of cases included in this course this question should not have proved difficult.

The following cases are used by way of example:

*Williams & Glyn's Bank v Boland 1980.* Mr and Mrs B occupied a house which was registered land and which was registered solely in the name of Mr B. The latter mortgaged the house to the bank without his wife's knowledge. The bank tried to enforce the mortgage. It was held that, despite the fact that Mrs B had not protected her minor interest in the house by lodging a caution at the Land Registry, her actual occupation was constructive notice of her overriding interest under s 70(1)(g) LRA 1925. The bank could not enforce the mortgage. Ever since, banks have been careful to check on persons in occupation of land offered as security; where an equitable interest exists this must be postponed or mortgaged along with the land.

*Lloyds Bank v Bundy 1975.* An elderly farmer with little business sense twice mortgaged his only asset (his house) to the bank to secure his son's company's overdraft. The bank knew that the son's company was in financial difficulties but did not explain this to his father. The son's company soon became insolvent and the bank sought possession of the house. The action failed because the relationship between customer and banker is one of trust and confidence, and the bank had breached that duty. To avoid any claims of undue influence banks now ask any person giving security, especially if he is a third party, to obtain independent legal advice. Even if he refuses, undue influence will still be found if there is manifest disadvantage: *Goldsworth v Brickell 1987.*

*Tai Hing Cotton Mill Ltd v Liu Chong Hing Bank Ltd 1986* – An audit of the company's books showed that over a considerable period of time one of the company employees had been forging signatures on cheques. As soon as this was discovered the bank was informed and the company claimed a refund for the cheques debited to the account. The Privy Council held that banks which had paid out on forged cheques could not debit the customer's account since the only duties owed by the customer were to exercise reasonable care and to notify the bank of any forgery of which he became aware. The customer has no duty to check his bank statements for an unauthorised debit item. This case has effectively put the whole banker/customer relationship back to that of the 1920's, to long-standing cases such as *Joachimson v Swiss Bank Corporation 1921.* The duty of care expected from the banker's customer has again altered dramatically.

## 36  ATM

(a)  Techni Bank provides a service when it permits customers to use an ATM to make cash withdrawals. It is therefore bound by s 13 Supply of Goods and Services Act 1982 to act with care and skill. This means it should:

(i)  design and programme the ATM system so as to ensure its compliance with customers' instructions (and thus fulfilment of the mandate). The bank must comply not only with the original mandate completed by Whit Drawl when he opened his account, but also with subsequent documents which form part of a continuing mandate, including cheques, standing orders and ATM instructions. The bank must honour the customer's mandate: *Joachimson v Swiss Bank Corporation 1921.* If a valid card and PIN number are used by the customer and the amount requested for withdrawal is within limits available to him, the bank must ensure that the ATM will dispense cash in accordance with this request.

The most frequent problem is that the machine dispenses a different amount to what was requested but debits the account with what was requested. The principle remains however that *a bank cannot debit its customer's account unless it has authorised instructions to do so:*

(1) if it dispenses *more* than requested then the customer holds the excess on trust for the bank, and the bank can sue for return of a payment made under a mistake of fact;

(2) if it dispenses *less* than requested then it must adjust the customer's account to reflect what was dispensed. In this case Whit Drawl has an action against the bank for breach of contract.

(ii) design the ATM system so that the bank has timely and accurate information with which to debit the customers' accounts.

Most ATM systems are on-line, so accounts are debited almost instantaneously. A problem arises relating to the evidence available when a withdrawal is disputed. The bank must maintain a tally-roll printout of amounts dispensed which is admissible as evidence under the Bankers Books Evidence Act 1879. The burden of proof is heavily on the customer if he seeks to dispute this evidence, although courts in the US have expressed preference for human evidence over computer evidence. The bank has an absolute obligation to record transactions accurately in its own and its customers' accounts and statements. Whit Drawl is therefore entitled to have his account amended to show the true position.

(iii) maintain all ATM equipment in good working order, as far as is reasonable.

The bank's duty to maintain machines does not extend to ensuring they are all full and in working order all the time, though they must be repaired within a reasonable time if their use is widely advertised by the bank.

If Whit Drawl's shortfall arises because the ATM is empty, the bank will escape liability provided that it has taken reasonable steps to provide regular and effective maintenance.

(iv) warn the customer of the dangers of revealing his PIN to *any* third party, or of handing his card to any third party: *Ognibene v Citibank 1981.*

(b) The first point of reference in assessing whether Technibank can limit or exclude its liability to Whit Drawl for breach of its legal obligations in respect of its ATMs is the absolute duty, described above, to honour its customers' mandates: *Joachimson v Swiss Bank Corporation 1921.* The bank must comply with Whit Drawl's lawful withdrawal instructions.

The second point of reference is the formal contract between banker and customer. Whit Drawl may have been asked to sign or accept terms and conditions which purported to exclude or limit the bank's liability in this situation. Any clause of this nature is subject to the reasonableness test of the Unfair Contract Terms Act 1977. The courts, in assessing what is reasonable, will consider the respective bargaining power and resources of the two parties. In this case, one party to the contract is a consumer and the other party is acting in the course of business. In such a case the latter party cannot exclude or restrict performance of his contractual obligations or exclude or limit his liability for breach of those obligations, unless in any such case it is reasonable to do so (s 3). The test of reasonableness will be made having regard to the circumstances which were or ought reasonably to have been known to the parties when the contract was made (s 11).

# INDEX OF CASES

A L Underwood Ltd v Bank of Liverpool and Martins Ltd 1924 — 188, 308
Abbey National Building Society v Cann 1990 — 226
Adams v Lindsell 1818 — 55
Agip (Africa) Ltd v Jackson and Others 1991 — 139
Allcard v Skinner 1887 — 95, 111
Alliance Bank Limited v Kearsley 1871 — 171
Alliance Bank v Broom 1864 — 59
American Express Banking Corporation v Hurley 1986 — 265
Applegate v Moss 1970 — 111
Arab Bank Ltd v Ross 1952 — 290
Arrale v Costain Engineering 1976 — 59
Associated Japanese Bank (International) v Credit du Nord 1988 — 241
Atlantic Baron, The 1979 — 92
Atlas Express Ltd v Kafco (Exporters and Distributors) Ltd 1989 — 92
Attorney-General's reference (No 1), Re 1988 — 18
Auchteroni & Co v Midland Bank Ltd 1928 — 305
Avon Finance Co Ltd v Bridger 1985 — 248

Bahbra v United Bank 1990 — 86
Baines v National Provincial Bank Ltd 1927 — 304
Baker v Barclays Bank Ltd 1955 — 308
Balfour v Balfour 1919 — 66
Bank of Credit and Commerce International v Aboody 1988 — 95
Bank of England v Vagliano 1891 — 279
Bank of New South Wales v Ross 1971 — 310
Barclays Bank Limited v W J Simms Son and Cooke (Southern) Limited 1979 — 131
Barclays Bank Ltd v Astley Industrial Trust Ltd 1970 — 312
Barclays Bank Ltd v Quistclose Investments Ltd 1968 — 138
Barclays Bank Ltd v W J Simms Son and Cooke (Southern) Ltd 1979 — 125
Barclays Bank plc v Khaira 1991 — 139
Barclays Bank plc v O'Brien 1991 — 245
Bavins & Sims v London & SW Bank 1900 — 274
Beswick v Beswick 1968 — 10
Bettini v Gye 1876 — 70
Bigg v Boyd Gibbons 1971 — 50
Bisset v Wilkinson 1927 — 87
Bondina Ltd v Rollaway Shower Blinds Ltd 1986 — 153, 190
Bradford Banking Co Limited v Henry Briggs Son & Co Limited 1886 — 252
Branca v Cobarro 1947 — 54
Brandao v Barnett 1846 — 239
Brewer v Westminster Bank Limited — 167
Brightlife, Re 1987 — 258, 259
Brinkibon v Stahag Stahl 1982 — 56
Bristol & West Building Society v Henning 1985 — 225
British & North European Bank v Zalstein 1927 — 155
Brogden v Metropolitan Railway Co 1877 — 53
Brown v Westminster Bank Ltd 1964 — 124
Buckingham & Co v London and Midland Bank Limited 1895 — 159
Bute v Barclays Bank Ltd 1954 — 308
Byrne v Van Tienhoven 1880 — 52

Caparo Industries plc v Dickman and Others 1990 — 140
Carlill v Carbolic Smokeball Co 1893 — 51
Carpenters Company v The British Mutual Banking Company 1937 — 314
Casey's Patents, Stewart v Casey 1892 — 58
Caunce v Caunce 1969 — 225
Cehave v Bremer, The Hansa Nord 1975 — 70
Central London Property Trust v High Trees House 1947 — 62
Chaplin v Leslie Frewin (Publishers) Ltd 1966 — 78
Chappell & Co v Nestle Co 1959 — 59
Charge Card Services, Re 1988 — 327, 328
Chatterton v London & County Bank 1890 — 154
City of London Building Society v Flegg 1987 — 227
Clarke v Dickson 1858 — 91
Clayton's case (see Devaynes v Noble 1816)
Clutton v Attenborough 1897 — 279
Combe v Combe 1951 — 63
Commissioners of Taxation v English, Scottish and Australian Bank Ltd 1920 — 307
Cooper v National Provincial Bank Ltd 1945 — 245
Cornish v Midland Bank plc 1985 — 139, 244
Cowern v Nield 1912 — 78
Cuckmere Brick Co Ltd v Mutual Finance Ltd 1971 — 233
Cumming v Ince 1847 — 92
Curtice v London City and Midland Bank Ltd 1908 — 125
Curtis v Chemical Cleaning Co 1951 — 119

D and C Builders v Rees 1966 — 63
Delbrueck & Co v Manufacturers Hanovers Trust Co 1979 — 322
Derry v Peek 1889 — 89
Devaynes v Noble 1816 — 120, 167, 215, 250
Diamond v Graham 1968 — 288
Dickinson v Dodds 1876 — 52
Donoghue v Stevenson 1932 — 10
Doyle v White City Stadium 1935 — 78
Dudley and District Benefit Building Society v Emerson 1949 — 233
Dunlop v New Garage & Motor Co 1915 — 109
Dunlop v Selfridge 1915 — 64
Durham Fancy Goods Ltd v Michael Jackson (Fancy Goods) Ltd 1968 — 190, 283

Eaglehill v J Needham Builders 1973 — 286
Earl of Oxford's Case — 6
Edward Nelson & Co Ltd v Faber & Co 1903 — 259
Edwards v Skyways 1964 — 67
Entores v Miles Far Eastern Corporation 1955 — 55
Equity and Law Home Loans Ltd v Prestidge 1991 — 226
Esso Petroleum Co Ltd v Mardon 1976 — 90
Evans v Cross 1938 — 18

F and H Entertainments v Leisure Enterprises 1976 — 90
Factortame Ltd v Secretary of State for Transport (No 2) 1991 — 20
Felthouse v Bindley 1862 — 53
First National Securities Ltd v Hegarty 1984 — 223
Fisher v Bell 1961 — 50

Foakes v Beer 1884                                                          62
Foley v Hill 1848                                              121, 132, 138
Ford Motor Co (England) Ltd v Armstrong 1915                               109
Forman v Bank of England 1902                                             122
Foster v Mackinnon 1869                                                    85


Gallie v Lee 1971                                                          85
Gardiner v Sevenoaks RDC 1950                                             17
George Mitchell v Finney Lock Seeds 1983                                  99
German Date Coffee Co, Re 1882                                           184
Gibbons v Westminster Bank Limited 1939                              122, 156
Glasbrook Bros v Glamorgan CC 1925                                        60
Goldsworthy v Brickell 1987                                               94
Gould v Gould 1969                                                        67
Great Western Railway Co v London and County Banking Co Ltd 1901         117
Greaves & Co (Contractors) Ltd v Baynham Meikle 1975                     323
Greenwood v Martins Bank Ltd 1933                                        130
Griffiths v Dalton 1940                                                  277
Guardians of St John's Hampstead v Barclays Bank Limited 1923           146
Gunthing v Lynn 1831                                                      50


Hamilton v Watson 1845                                                   246
Harding v London Joint Stock Bank Limited 1914                          149
Harrold v Plenty 1901                                                   251
Hartley v Ponsonby 1857                                                  60
Harvey v Facey 1893                                                      50
Hedley Byrne & Co Ltd v Heller & Partners Ltd 1963                   14, 140
Hely-Hutchinson v Brayhead 1968                                         188
Hillas v Arcos 1932                                                      69
Hodgson v Marks 1971                                                93, 206
Holwell Securities v Hughes 1974                                         56
Horsfall v Thomas 1862                                                   86
House Property Co of London Ltd v London County and Westminster Bank 1915   308
Household Fire and Carriage Accident Insurance Co v Grant 1879           56
Howard v Patent Ivory Manufacturing Co 1888                             188
Hutton v Warren 1836                                                     21
Hyde v Wrench 1840                                                       53


Inche Noriah v Shaik Allie bin Omar 1929                                94
Interfoto Picture Library Ltd v Stiletto Visual Programmes Ltd 1988     109


Jackson v White and Midland Bank Limited 1967                          168
James Graham & Co (Timber) Ltd v Southgate-Sands 1985                  243
Jarvis v Swan Tours 1973                                                108
Jayson v Midland Bank 1968                                              123
Joachimson v Swiss Bank Corporation 1921                               118
Jones v Waring & Gillow Ltd 1926                                        290

Keever, Re 1966                                                          239, 312
Kelner v Baxter 1866                                                          181
Kemp v Baerselman 1906                                                        65
Kings North Trust Ltd v Bell 1985                                            248
Kings North Trust v Tizard 1986                                             225
Kleinwort Benson Ltd v Malaysian Mining Corporation Bhd 1989                  68
Kreditbank Cassel GmbH v Schenkers Ltd 1927                               188, 284


L'Estrange v Graucob 1934                                                     119
Ladbroke v Todd 1914                                                117, 146, 150
Ladup Ltd v Shaikh and Ritz Casino Ltd 1982                                  296
Langtry v Union Bank of London 1896                                          137
Lazenby Garages v Wright 1976                                                108
Les Affreteurs v Walford 1919                                                 72
Leslie v Sheill 1914                                                      80, 166
Liggett (Liverpool) Ltd v Barclays Bank Ltd 1928                            122
Liverpool City Council v Irwin 1977                                          72
Lloyds Bank Limited v Brooks 1950                                           155
Lloyds Bank Ltd v Bundy 1975                                         24, 94, 139
Lloyds Bank Ltd v Hornby 1933                                                310
Lloyds Bank Ltd v Rossett 1990                                              226
Lloyds Bank Ltd v Savory & Co 1933                                           13
Lloyds Bank plc v Waterhouse 1990                                        84, 244
London & Montrose Shipbuilding and Repairing Co Ltd v Barclays Bank        308
London Assurance v Mansel 1879                                                88
London Joint Stock Bank Ltd v Macmillan & Arthur 1918                       130
Lumsden & Co v London Trustee Savings Bank 1971                          147, 307


Macaura v Northern Assurance Co 1925                                        178
MacKenzie Mills v Buono 1986                                                288
Mackenzie v Royal Bank of Canada 1934                                       245
Mardorf Peach & Co Ltd v Attica Sea Carriers Corporation of Liberia         322
Marfani & Co v Midland Bank Limited 1967                                147, 307
McArdle, Re 1951                                                             58
McCarthy and Stone Ltd v Julian S Hodge Ltd 1971                            202
Mercantile Credit Co Limited v Garrod 1962                                  170
Mercantile Union Guarantee Corporation v Ball 1937                           77
Merritt v Merritt 1970                                                       67
Metropolitan Commissioners of Police v Charles 1976                        316
Midland Bank Ltd v R V Harris Ltd 1963                                      312
Midland Bank plc v Perry 1987                                               244
Miller v Jackson 1977                                                         7
Moorcock, The 1889                                                           72
Morison v Kemp 1912                                                         284
Morison v London County and Westminster Bank Ltd 1914                       308
Motor Traders Guarantee Corporation Ltd v Midland Bank Ltd 1937            309

# INDEX OF CASES

| | |
|---|---|
| Nash v Inman 1908 | 77 |
| Nathan v Ogdens Ltd 1905 | 274 |
| National Provincial Bank of England Ltd v Brackenbury 1906 | 243 |
| National Provincial Bank of England Ltd v Glanusk 1913 | 246, 247 |
| National Westminster Bank Ltd v Barclays Bank International Ltd 1974 | 131 |
| National Westminster Bank plc v Morgan 1985 | 94, 95, 226 |
| Neale v Merrett 1930 | 54 |
| Nicolene v Simmonds 1953 | 69 |
| Nu-Stilo Footwear Ltd v Lloyds Bank Ltd 1956 | 309 |
| | |
| O'Hara v Allied Irish Banks 1985 | 244 |
| Oliver v Davis 1949 | 288 |
| Orbit Mining & Trading Co Limited v Westminster Bank Limited 1963 | 149, 316 |
| Oscar Chess v Williams 1959 | 71 |
| | |
| Payzu v Saunders 1919 | 108 |
| Penmount Estates Ltd v National Provincial Bank Ltd 1945 | 309 |
| Phillips Products v Hyland 1984 | 100 |
| Pilmore v Hood 1873 | 89 |
| Pinnel's Case 1602 | 62, 63 |
| Pollard v Bank of England 1871 | 322 |
| Pollway v Abdullah 1974 | 288 |
| Poussard v Spiers 1876 | 70, 106 |
| Powell v Lee 1908 | 56 |
| Prosperity Limited v Lloyds Bank Limited 1923 | 159 |
| | |
| R v Kylsant 1931 | 87 |
| R v Lambie 1981 | 318 |
| Ramsgate Victoria Hotel Co v Montefiore 1866 | 52 |
| Redgrave v Hurd 1881 | 88 |
| Redmond v Allied Irish Bank plc 1987 | 296 |
| Rolfe Lubell v Keith 1979 | 292 |
| Rondel v Worsley 1969 | 9 |
| Rose and Frank v J R Crompton & Bros 1923 | 66 |
| Ross v London County Westminster and Parr's Bank 1919 | 308 |
| Routledge v Grant 1828 | 52 |
| Royal Bank of Scotland v Greenshields 1914 | 246 |
| Royal British Bank v Turquand 1856 | 187 |
| Royscot Trust Ltd v Rogerson & Others 1991 | 90 |
| | |
| Salomon v Salomon Ltd 1897 | 177 |
| Saunders v Anglia Building Society 1971 (see Gallie v Lee) | |
| Savory & Co v Lloyds Bank Ltd 1932 | 148, 308 |
| Scammell v Ouston 1941 | 69 |
| Shadwell v Shadwell 1860 | 60, 61 |
| Sheffield Corporation v Barclay 1905 | 251 |
| Sigsworth, Re 1935 | 17 |
| Smith v Eric Bush 1989 | 100 |
| Smith v Land and House Property Corporation 1884 | 87 |
| SS Ardennes 1951 | 71 |
| Standard Chartered Bank Ltd v Walker 1982 | 265 |

Steinberg v Scala (Leeds) 1923   79
Stevenson v McLean 1880   54
Stewart Gill Ltd v Horatio Meyer & Co Ltd 1992   118
Stilk v Myrick 1809   60
Stoke-on-Trent CC v B & Q plc 1991   20

Tai Hing Cotton Mill Ltd v Liu Chong Hing Bank Ltd and others 1986   129, 154
Thackwell v Barclays Bank plc 1984   304
Thames Guaranty Ltd v Campbell 1984   224
Tournier v National Provincial (and Union Bank of England) 1924   126
Turquand's case   284
Tweddle v Atkinson 1861   63

United Dominions Trust Ltd v Kirkwood 1966   115, 116
United Overseas Bank v Jivani 1976   129, 155
Universal Permanent Building Society v Cooke 1951   233

Van Duyn v Home Office 1974   19
Vauxhall Estates v Liverpool Corporation 1932   12
Vinden v Hughes 1905   279

Walker v Boyle 1981   100
Wallis & Simmonds (Builders) Ltd, Re 1974   262
Warner Bros v Nelson 1937   110
Westminster Bank Ltd v Cond 1940   246
Westminster Bank Ltd v Hilton 1926   125
Westminster Bank Ltd v Zang 1966   240, 313
White v Bluett 1853   59
White v City of London Brewery Co 1889   232
Williams and Glyn's Bank Ltd v Barnes 1980   131
Williams and Glyn's Bank Ltd v Boland 1980   24, 225
Williams and Glyn's Bank Ltd v Brown 1980   225
Williams v Bayley 1866   94
Williams v Roffey Bros & Nicholls (Contractors) Ltd 1990   61
Wilson and Meeson v Pickering 1946   296
Wilson v Midland Bank Limited 1961   158
Winkworth v Edward Baron Development Co Ltd 1986   226
With v O'Flanagan 1936   88
Woodroffes (Musical Instruments) Ltd, Re 1986   258
Woodstead Finance Ltd v Petrou 1986   95

Yates Building Co v R J Pulleyn & Sons (York) 1975   55
Yorkshire Woolcombers Association 1903   258
Young v Bristol Aeroplane Co 1944   9
Young v Grote 1827   130

**A**bsolute title, 207
Abstract of title, 204
Acceptance of an offer, 53
Account payee crossing, 296
Actions
- for the price, 107
- in personam, 5
- in rem, 5
Administrative tribunals, 24, 36
Administrators, 173
Agency, 152, 283
- apparent authority, 189
- banks, 301
- customers, 152
Alteration
- of cheques, 290
- of crossings, 297
Arbitration, 37
- clauses, 38
Articles of association, 178, 183
Assignment, 65, 256, 269
- of a lease, 205
Automated teller machines (ATMs), 323

**B**ACS, 320
Bailment, 136
Bank
- as mortgagee, 139, 212
- definition of, 115
- duties, 121ff
- rights, 131f
Bank payment orders, 315
Banker's drafts, 307, 314
Banker's lien, 239
Banker's references, 140
Banker-customer contract, 115ff
Banking Act 1979, 15
Banking Act 1987, 15
Banking hours, 304
Banking Ombudsman, 24, 39ff, 162, 326
Bills of Exchange Act 1882, 13, 58, 269ff
Breach of contract, 14, 27, 106

**C**anvassing consumer credit, 102f
Capacity to contract, 49, 76ff, 165
Case law, 4, 7ff
Case stated appeals, 30
Certificate of incorporation, 181
Chancery Division, 33
CHAPS, 321
Charge certificate, 219
Charges, 258
- register, 205

Cheques, 13, 269ff
- delivery, 278
- discharge, 286
- dishonour, 285
- encashment, 305
- endorsement, 270ff
- guarantee cards, 316
- issue, 278
- negotiation, 278
- stolen, 302
- unpaid, 122
Cheques Act 1957, 13, 269ff
Cheques Act 1992, 15, 162
Civil law, 3, 24
Class C land charges, 202
Class D land charges, 202
Clearing system, 294
Closing an account, 158
Co-ownership of property, 197
Code of Banking Practice, 41, 101, 118, 127f,
    162, 324
Collecting bank
- as holder of a cheque, 310
- protection of, 307ff
Combination, 132
Commercial Court, 32
Commission on Banking Services, Law and Practice,
    159
Common law, 4ff
Companies Act 1985, 14, 80
Companies Act 1989, 14, 81
Companies Court, 33
Companies
- borrowing powers, 186
- cheques, 189
- directors, 186
Company Securities (Insider Dealing) Act 1985, 18
Conditions of a contract, 69
Confidentiality, 160
Conflict resolving, 23ff
Connected lender liability, 329
Consent in a contract, 48
Consideration
- in contract, 48, 57
- past, 58
Constructive notice, 188
Consumer Credit Act 1974, 13ff, 39, 47, 66, 72,
    101ff, 317, 329
Content of a contract, 48
Contract law, 26, 30, 47ff
- and banking, 115ff
Contract terms, 71, 118
Contracts
- by deed, 73
- in writing, 70, 73

Contractual capacity, 76ff
Contributory negligence, 161, 302
Conversion, 137, 301
Conveyance, 204
Countermand of payment, 123
County courts, 9, 30, 38
Court of Appeal, 8, 9, 33
Court of Protection, 82
Court process, 24
Credit reference agencies, 128
Criminal law, 3, 24, 27
Crossings on cheques, 293
Crown Court, 9, 29, 31
Crystallisation of floating charge, 258
Custom, 4, 20
Customer
  - definition of, 116
  - duties of, 129ff
Customer's employment, 148

**D**amages for breach of contract, 107
Data Protection Act 1984, 14, 330
Debentures, 257, 263
Debit cards, 327
Deed, contract by, 57, 203
Deed of Postponement, 225
Delegated legislation, 15ff
Disclaimer of liability, 14, 98, 141
Drug Trafficking Offences Act 1986, 14
Duress, 48, 96
Duty of confidentiality, 246
Duties
  - of bank, 121ff
  - of customer, 129ff

**E**asement, 200
EC law, 4, 19ff, 33
EFTPOS, 327
Electronic banking, 320ff
Electronic money transmission services, 320
Employment Appeal Tribunal, 33
Endorsement, 270, 274, 280
  - irregular, 281
  - need for, 306ff
Enduring Powers of Attorney Act 1985, 82, 152
English law, 3ff
Equipment failure, electronic banking, 323
Equitable interests, land, 200
Equitable mortgage, 216, 234
Equitable rights, land, 197
Equity, 4ff
Equity of redemption, 6, 200, 212
European Court of Human Rights, 35

European Court of Justice, 34
Exclusion clauses, 14, 68, 98, 101, 326
Executors, 173

**F**amily Division, 33
Fictitious payee, 279
Financial Services Act 1986, 14, 17
Forgery, 278, 283, 290, 292
Form of the contract, 48, 73
Fraud, 160
Fraudulent misrepresentation, 89
Free banking, 61
Freehold ownership, 198

**G**arnishee orders, 159
General crossing, 293
Good leasehold title, 207
Guarantees, 240

**H**igh Court, 8f, 27ff
Holder
  - for value, 289
  - in due course, 278, 289
House of Commons, 12
House of Lords, 8ff, 34

**I**nchoate instrument, 277
Indemnity, 241
Indoor management rule, 187
Inheritance tax, 202
Injunctions, 107, 110, 159
Innocent misrepresentation, 90
Insanity, 81
Insolvency Act 1986, 14, 15
Intention to create legal relations, 48, 66
Interpretation Act 1978, 17
Investment advice, 136
Invitation to treat, 49, 50

**J**ack Committee, 159, 326, 329
Joint accounts, 166
Joint and several guarantees, 242
Joint and several liability, 167, 243
Joint ownership, 223
Judicature Acts 1873-75, 6, 27
Judicial precedent, 4ff
Judicial process, 24ff
Jury, 30

**L**aches, doctrine of, 96, 111
Land, 30, 195ff
  - as security, 211ff
  - estates, 198ff
  - interests, 200ff
  - rights, 196ff
Land certificate, 205
Land charges registry, 201
Law of Property (Miscellaneous Provisions) Act
  1989, 73
Law reports, 7
Leasehold ownership, 198
Legal aid, 42
Legal estates in land, 198ff
Legal interests in land, 200ff
Legal mortgage, 202, 214, 231
Legality of a contract, 49
Legislation, 4, 11ff
Licensing system, 102
Lien, 138, 238
Life assurance policies, 253ff
Limitation Act 1980, 58, 110

**M**agistrates' courts, 9, 27ff
Manifest disadvantage, 94
Matrimonial homes, 203, 223
Memorandum of association, 183
Memorandum of deposit, 216
Mental incapacity, 81
Mercantile custom, 21
Merchant law, 4, 21
Minor interests, 205f
Minors, 6, 102, 165, 285
Minors' Contracts Act 1987, 76, 79
Misrepresentation, 48, 86ff, 244
Misrepresentation Act 1967, 89
Mistake, 48, 84
Mortgage
  - discharge of, 230
  - law, 30, 211ff
  - of registered land, 219, 229
  - of shares, 250
  - of unregistered land, 218, 227
Mortgagor, 139, 212

**N**ecessaries, 82
Negative pledge clause, 260
Negligence, 14, 27, 98
  - by collecting bank, 307
Negligent misrepresentation, 89
Negligent misstatement, 141
Negotiability, 270ff
Negotiable instruments, 269ff

*Non est factum*, 84, 96
Not negotiable crossing, 295
Notice of dishonour, 285
Notices of deposit, 207

**O**biter dicta, 8
Objects clause, 183
Offer and acceptance, 48ff
Old Bailey, 29
Open cheques, 305
Overdraft lending, 102
Overriding interests, 206ff, 220ff

**P**arliament, 3, 11, 15
  - procedure, 12
  - sovereignty, 11
Part payment of a debt, 61
Past consideration, 58
Pay cash, 275, 297, 315
Paying bank's protection, 302
Payment by mistake, 131, 322
Phantom withdrawals, 41
Pledge, 240
Possessory lien, 238
Possessory title, 207
Post-dated cheques, 277
Precedent, 7ff
Preferential debts, 259
Prevention of Terrorism Act 1989, 14, 126
Priority notice, 228
Priority of charges, 259
Privy Council, 10, 34
Promissory estoppel, 62
Property register, 205
Protection
  - collecting bank, 307ff
  - paying bank, 302ff
Public companies, 178
Puisne mortgage, 202, 219

**Q**ualified title, 207
*Quantum meruit*, 107
Quasi-judicial process, 24, 35ff
Queen's Bench Division (QBD), 32

**R** (receipting), 306
*Ratio decidendi*, 8
Reform of banking services law, 159
Registered companies, 176
Registered land, 205, 231
Registered office, 183
Registrable interests, 201ff

Registration of charges, 202, 261
Regulated agreements, 73, 101
Representations, 71, 87, 244
Repudiation of contract, 106
Rescission of contract, 96
Restrictive Practices Court, 33
Rights of occupiers, 203, 223
Rights of the bank, 131f
Romalpa clause, 259

Sale of Goods Act 1979, 48, 77
Second mortgages, 221, 226
Securities and Investment Board (SIB), 14, 40
Sequestration, 159
Set-off, 132
Settlement banks, 321
Sex Discrimination Act 1975, 13
Signatures on cheques, 282ff
Small Claims Court, 30, 38
Sources of law, 4ff
Special relationship (banker/customer), 139
Stale cheques, 276, 277
Standard form contracts, 38, 47, 104, 318
Status opinions, 128
Statute law, 11ff
Statute of Frauds Act 1677, 241
Statutory instruments, 15, 19
Statutory interpretation, 16
Stocks and shares, 249
Stolen cheques, 302
Strict liability, 25
Subrogation, 122, 130
Supply of Goods and Services Act 1982, 14, 103ff,
    135, 323ff

**T**AURUS, 250
Terms of a contract, 70, 118
Terrorism, 14
Title, proof of, 204
Title deeds, 201ff
Tort, 26, 30, 90
Tracing, 322
Transferability, 272
    - by delivery, 270, 282, 293
Travellers' cheques, 315
True owner, 295, 301
Truncated cheques, 161
Trusts, 30
    - for sale, 203
Trustee accounts, 174

**U**berrima fides, 245
Ultra vires, 16, 80f, 184, 213, 285
Undue influence, 48, 93ff, 139, 226, 247
Unenforceable contracts, 49
Unfair Contract Terms Act 1977, 14, 47, 98, 105,
    118ff, 326
Unregistered land, 201, 230

**V**alue, concept of, 276, 287
Value for a cheque, 311
Veil of incorporation, 177
Vicarious liability, 25

**W**arranties, 69
White Paper, 161, 326, 329
White credit information, 128, 232

## FURTHER READING

For further question practice on English law, you may wish to test your grasp of the subject by tackling short questions in multiple choice format. BPP publish the Password series of books, each of which incorporates over 300 multiple choice questions with solutions, comments and marking guides. The Password title which is particularly relevant to this paper is *Business Law*. This is priced at £6.95 and contains about 300 questions.

To order your Password book, ring our credit card hotline on 081-740 6808. Alternatively, send this page to our Freepost address or fax it to us on 081-740 1184.

**To: BPP Publishing Ltd, FREEPOST, London W12 8BR**     **Tel: 081-740 6808**
                                                          **Fax: 081-740 1184**

Forenames (Mr / Ms): _____

Surname: _____

Address: _____

_____

Post code: _____

**Please send me the following books:**            *Quantity*    *Price*    *Total*
Password *Business Law*                              .......      £6.95      .........

**Please include postage:**
**UK:** £1.50 for first plus £0.50 for each extra book                               .........
**Overseas:** £3.00 for first plus £1.50 for each extra book                         .........
                                                                                     _____
                                                                                     ══════

I enclose a cheque for £_____ or charge to Access/Visa

Card number  | | | | | | | | | | | | | | | | |

Expiry date _____ Signature _____

---

On the reverse of this page there is a Review Form, which you can send in to us (at the Freepost address above) with comments and suggestions on the Text you have just finished. Your feedback really does make a difference: it helps us to make the next edition that bit better.

# CIB - BANKING: THE LEGAL ENVIRONMENT (10/92)

**Name:** _____

**How have you used this Text?**

Home study (book only) ☐

With 'correspondence' package ☐

On a course: college _____ ☐

Other _____ ☐

**How did you obtain this Text?**

From us by mail order ☐

From us by phone ☐

From a bookshop ☐

From your college ☐

**Where did you hear about BPP Texts?**

At bookshop ☐

Recommended by lecturer ☐

Recommended by friend ☐

Mailshot from BPP ☐

Advertisement in _____ ☐

Other _____ ☐

**Your comments and suggestions would be appreciated on the following areas.**

*Syllabus coverage*

*Illustrative questions*

*Errors (please specify. and refer to a page number)*

*Presentation*

*Other*